W9-AAT-754

BY THE SAME AUTHOR

The Struggle for Syria

Red Flag, Black Flag (with Maureen McConville)

The Hilton Assignment (with Maureen McConville)

Philby: The Long Road to Moscow (with Maureen McConville)

The Shaping of an Arab Statesman: Abd al-Hamid Sharaf and the Modern Arab World (ed.)

Asad of Syria: The Struggle for the Middle East

ABU NIDAL:

A GUN FOR HIRE

ABU NIDAL:

A GUN FOR HIRE

Patrick Seale

RANDOM HOUSE
NEW YORK

Copyright © 1992 by Patrick Seale

All rights reserved under
International and Pan-American Copyright Conventions.
Published in the United States by Random House, Inc., New York,
and simultaneously in Canada by
Random House of Canada Limited, Toronto.

Library of Congress Cataloging-in-Publication Data
Seale, Patrick.
Abu Nidal: a gun for hire/Patrick Seale.—1st ed.
p. cm.
Includes index.
ISBN 0-679-40066-4
1. Terrorism. 2. Abu Nidal. 3. Terrorists—Biography.
4. Palestinian Arabs—Biography. 5. Terrorism in mass media.
I. Title.
HV6431.S4 1992
303.6'24'092—dc20
[B] 91-36450

Manufactured in the United States of America
24689753
First Edition

Set in Times Roman

Book design by Oksana Kushnir

For Farah
in the hope that she will be freed from fear

ACKNOWLEDGMENTS

Readers of this book will recognize the debt I owe to a large number of Palestinian, Arab, Western, and Israeli informants. Some of these sources I acknowledge in the text, but many more have asked me to respect their confidence by withholding their names. I wish to thank them all nonetheless for the generosity with which they shared their knowledge.

London, October 1991

CONTENTS

ABU NIDAL:
A GUN FOR HIRE

chapter

1

THE STORY OF JORDE

More than twenty years have passed since Colonel Muammar al-Qaddafi seized power in Libya and yet his capital city, Tripoli, retains the lazy feel of a provincial backwater taking a long siesta. There are no crowds or traffic jams there, no urgent pulse of a metropolis. It is a place one can drift out of easily. Heading away from the thin sprawl along the coast, and with the Mediterranean at one's back, one drives through low-built, shuttered suburbs that soon give way to straggling villages and then to a vast dun-colored horizon. A lot can be hidden away in this empty landscape of scrub and dune. Far to the southwest is the rough and desolate al-Hamra steppe hugging the Tunisian frontier; deeper still into the desert to the southeast are the formidable Soda Mountains. Somewhere between the steppe and the mountains, some 170 kilometers down the highway from Tripoli, the capricious master of Libya has provided the terrorist Abu Nidal with his principal base camp.

THE DESERT CAMP

A barbed-wire fence runs along the road for a couple of miles. The entrance is a pole between two posts, guarded by a lonely young fellow, his head swathed in the checkered Palestinian kaffiyeh.

Beyond, partly sheltered by some low hills, widely scattered clusters of low buildings can be seen, a line or two of tents, a radio antenna, and perhaps a water tanker trucking in supplies from the nearest water hole for this parched spot. At first glance, it seems to be a camp for foreign construction workers engaged in building yet another of the colonel's projects, and indeed it was just that until Abu Nidal took it over and set about expanding it in 1987.

Spread over some six square kilometers of sand and gravel, the camp is vast and comprises a number of distinct, and mutually wary, subdivisions: four or five smaller camps, each in its own barbed-wire enclosure. There is a "village" of bungalows for married cadres and their families, from which nonresidents are strictly barred; the administrative offices, billets, lecture rooms, canteen, and training grounds of the main fighting force; a tented camp, set well apart, where small groups of men, their faces covered with the traditional Arab headscarves, are groomed for clandestine missions; a well-guarded research center known as Station 11, protected by a couple of anti-aircraft missile batteries; and a prison and interrogation bloc, with an underground row of cells, called Station 16, which no one mentions without a shudder and from which Arabic love songs can be heard blaring at night to drown out, I was told, the screams of men being tortured within. Forever on the alert against hostile penetration, shot through with fear and suspicion, the camp is not a happy place, as the fortunate few who have defected from it can testify.

For the most part, the camp is a training establishment for units of Abu Nidal's People's Army, a more-or-less overt militia much like the forces of other Palestinian factions. But the real core of the camp, where men are prepared for foreign operations, is as covert as any in the intelligence world. The ordinary fighting men serve only as protective cover and camouflage for the secret inner workings.

Eccentrically, Abu Nidal has named his Libyan camp after Naji al-Ali, an irreverent Arab cartoonist who was gunned down in a London street on July 22, 1987, outside the offices of *al-Qabas,* the Arabic daily he worked for. Some say Yasser Arafat ordered the killing, because the cartoonist made a habit of exposing the follies and foibles of the PLO chairman, and that the operation was planned and directed by Abd al-Rahman Mustafa, a major in Arafat's personal security guard, Force 17. This is unproven, because the gunman was never caught. Others say it was a Mossad job to smear Arafat as a killer and the PLO as a murderous organization. Investigating the murder, British police found a cache of rifles, grenades, and Semtex explosives, allegedly belonging to Mustafa, in the apartment of another Palestinian, Isma'il Sawwan, a self-confessed Mossad penetration agent, whose Mossad connection was revealed in a British court a year after the murder. Sawwan was sentenced to eleven years in prison, and two Israeli diplomats were expelled from Britain for being his controllers. They were the first Israeli diplomats ever to be expelled from Britain.

Most likely, Abu Nidal chose Naji al-Ali as the name for his Libyan camp because he hates Arafat as much as Israel does, holding him responsible not just for a cartoonist's death but for the persistent "betrayal" of the Palestinian cause, which, according to Abu Nidal, is the annihilation of the state of Israel. He seeks to instill hatred for the PLO leader into every man who passes through his hands. For close on twenty years, Arafat's PLO has been caught between two fires—heavy broadsides from Israel and murderous sniping from Abu Nidal.

Abu Nidal does not live at the camp himself, preferring not without reason a three-villa complex set in the large garden of a Tripoli suburb, which is his headquarters and principal residence. But every month or so, driving his own car and casually dressed in shirt and slacks, he puts in an appearance unannounced, and invariably upsets the camp, from the commander to the new recruits, who tremble in his presence. A pale-skinned, balding, pot-bellied man, with a long thin nose above a gray mustache, he comes without fanfare, making an entry that is restrained and almost shy. Usually, he is accompanied by Amjad Ata, a tall, dark man of about forty, who is his confidant and whose official title in the organization is second secretary of the Central Committee. Ata is, if anything, more terrifying to the camp inmates than Abu Nidal. It is said that every time he comes, a "traitor" is taken away for execution or is sent to face the horrors of Section 16. Most Middle Eastern "strongmen" like to surround themselves, for safety's sake, with members of their own family, and Abu Nidal is no exception: Amjad Ata is the husband of one of his many nieces.

Colonel Qaddafi, Abu Nidal's current patron, has been generous. In addition to the camp and the headquarters complex in

Tripoli, he has given Abu Nidal a score of houses in the city for use by his principal aides, houses belonging to opponents of Qaddafi's regime who have been jailed, exiled, or liquidated—"stray dogs," as the Libyan leader likes to call them; also, a three-story building on Umar al-Mukhtar Street, in central Tripoli, used as a safe house by the Special Missions Committee; a well-appointed villa near the airport, where agents rest and are briefed between assignments; and a farm some seventeen kilometers outside the city, where fruit and vegetables are grown for the men in the camp. Abu Nidal, the son of a Jaffa orange grower, loves to see things grow, takes great pride in his well-ordered farm and sees to it that its choicest fruits reach his own table.

THE MEN

Since the camp opened in 1987, most of its inmates have been Palestinian youths, with a sprinkling of other Arabs, recruited in Lebanon from among the lost souls of that tormented country and flown out to Libya from the Damascus airport in batches of a hundred or so on Libyan military transports. These men are the human debris of the Middle East's two main breeding grounds of rage and alienation: the Palestinian refugee camps and the towns of Lebanon since the civil war. For them, the one way to survive in the last two decades of upheavals, the one way to feel that their lives had some meaning, was to join one of the militias that sprang up to fill the vacuum in Lebanon when the state collapsed in 1975.

Hard as it is to believe, Abu Nidal managed to appeal to some of the best of them. He was on the lookout for lively students, preferably very young ones, who were eager to get ahead and who also wanted to strike a blow for the Palestinian cause. He promised to help with their education—the classic escape route from the dead-end refugee camps; to set them on the road to a career; to help their families. And he paid good money. He also provided them with the thrill of belonging to a militant secret organization. Scorning the feebleness and compromises of the PLO, he preached that Palestine could be wrested back from the Israelis by armed struggle. It was impressed on his recruits that in joining the organization, they were fulfilling their duty not just to Palestine but to the whole Arab nation. Other organizations were treacherous, corrupt, compromising; their own was inspired by the noblest Arab virtues. It was the last standard-bearer of the true cause.

Recruitment was highly selective, because it had to be. Abu Nidal wanted to make sure that his members were untainted by contact with any other political organization or secret service. They were made to sign warrants agreeing to be put to death if any intelligence connection in their backgrounds were later to be discovered. This was not mere paranoia: It was widely suspected that the Mossad, as well as a number of Western intelligence agencies, recruited Palestinians in Europe and the occupied territories and, after suitable training, sent them back to the refugee camps and dangerous back streets of Beirut in order to penetrate Palestinian guerrilla movements. Who was a patriot and who a traitor? No one could be certain. Spy mania was a disease the whole Palestinian movement suffered from, and none more so than the ultrasuspicious, ultrasectarian Abu Nidal.

On joining, each new recruit was given a thick pad of paper on which to write the story of his life. Everything had to be put down—family, relatives, contacts, friends, lovers, schools, jobs, social situation, every single detail from birth to the moment of recruitment. This first document in the recruit's personal file was the touchstone against which later information would be tested as it came to light. Woe betide the man who strayed from the truth! Early on, when still on probation, the new member would be inducted into a two-man cell with his recruiter, told to mount guard at the organization's offices, to distribute its magazine, *Filastin al-Thawra* (*Palestine the Revolution*), to take part in marches and demonstrations. He might be given some small intelligence task to perform, such as keeping a particular person under surveillance or reporting on the activities in his locality of such enemy organizations as Arafat's Fatah or such rivals as George Habash's Popular Front, or the two Shi'ite factions, Amal and its more extreme sister, Hizballah. In order to be worthy of membership, the recruit's life would have to be reformed and purified: Alcohol, cigarettes, drugs, women—all had to be given up; no loose chatter or unnecessary questions would be tolerated; he was never to ask the real name of anyone in the organization or ever divulge his own; only code names were to be used; anything untoward, however trivial, had to be reported to his immediate superior, and at sessions of self-criticism in front of his colleagues, he had to confess publicly his own lapses and faults and recommend his own punishments.

Throughout his training, he was drilled and drilled again in the organization's ten fundamental principles until they became second nature, molding his every thought and action: commitment; discipline; democratic centralism; obedience to the chain of command; initiative and action; criticism and self-criticism; security and confidentiality; planning and implementation; assessment of experience gained; thrift. Each one of these was the subject of lengthy lectures by senior cadres.

When these and other lessons had sunk in and unsuitable candidates were weeded out, the chosen man would be told that he was being sent to another country for a six-month course that would mark him out for greater things. With a group of other young men, five or six to a battered Mercedes, he would be driven deep into South Lebanon, to a village above the port of Sidon, in hill country controlled by the Druze leader Walid Jumblat. There, billeted in houses scarred by shell fire and abandoned by their inhabitants, he would be issued a uniform, a track suit, and a weapon, and given some weeks of basic military training in the form of drill, physical exercise, and much prowling around the countryside by night to avoid being spotted by Israeli reconnaissance aircraft.

Some weeks later, he and the group he was with would be taken by coach to the Damascus airport. One such recruit I interviewed in the summer of 1990 recalled what happened next:

> We were given new code names for the journey and told to memorize them. But after hours of waiting in the airport lounge, several men forgot their new names and did not respond when they were called. They had to be called several times! The Syrian security men were very amused, but our commander was furious.
>
> Eventually we boarded a Libyan military aircraft and took off. We didn't know where we were going. There were rumors that it was Cuba or North Korea. Most of us were dizzy from the noise and air pressure. But three hours later we landed at Tripoli, in Libya.
>
> Then, after another long wait, we were driven into the desert in a fleet of Toyota buses. It was already dark

when we arrived at the camp. Our original code names were called out and we were individually searched before being let in.

Their ordeal had begun.

JORDE'S TESTIMONY

(What follows is based on one man's account of his experiences in Abu Nidal's organization, related to me in the summer of 1990.)

He was a short, stocky man in his late twenties, with a bull neck, close-cropped hair, and the round thighs and springy walk of an athlete or male dancer. His code name, he told me, was Hussein Jorde Abdallah, and for a Palestinian his background was unusual. His grandfather was a Kabyle from Algeria, one of several thousand Berbers who immigrated to Palestine from North Africa at the turn of the century. His father was born in Palestine, but when the Israelis took over in 1948, he fled with his family to Lebanon, ending up in Burj al-Shamali, a tented camp near Tyre, one of several erected by the United Nations Relief and Works Agency (UNRWA) in the immediate aftermath of the Palestine war. It was there that Jorde was born in 1961. But life for Palestinians in Lebanon was not easy. Sometime in the early seventies, once Algeria had settled down to its independence, Jorde's father decided to take his family back to their place of origin in Kabylia, the fiercely independent hill country just east of Algiers. And it was there that Jorde grew up, speaking Arabic, one or two Berber dialects, and a smattering of French. He was a restless, resourceful boy who scrounged for food, became a skilled shoplifter, and, after finishing school, joined Algeria's vast army of the unemployed. The family's main asset was Jorde's younger brother, Abdallah, who had gone to the Gulf in search of work and found a job with Kuwait Airlines.

When his father, the family breadwinner, died in 1986, Jorde was expected to provide for his mother and his two younger sisters. But he could hardly face the prospect and decided to escape. With money begged from Abdallah in Kuwait, he bought an air ticket to Barcelona and boarded an Iberia flight, with no visa for Spain and no passport save for a Lebanese laissez-passer, such as is issued to Palestinians. On arrival he had a stroke of luck. A domestic flight had landed at about the same time as his own and its passengers were filing into the arrivals hall a few feet away from those on his international flight. There was only a narrow passage between the two lines. When his fellow travelers, all of them Algerians, rushed for the immigration desk, Jorde quietly joined the other line and entered Spain unchallenged.

Jorde spent three months in Barcelona, living in cheap hotels and at night hanging about discos frequented by Arabs. He robbed those less sharp-witted than himself, stole food from supermarkets, and made friends with petty criminals, until one night he was picked up by the Spanish police in Plaza Catalonia and, after interrogation, deported to Lebanon.

In Beirut, he met a girl and started going out with her. She confided that she worked for a secret outfit that she called the Council, but she warned him not to get involved. He was intrigued. He coaxed the facts out of her. Its full name was Fatah: the Revolutionary Council, and it was run by Abu Nidal. Jorde was broke and seeking fame: With its aura of clandestinity and power, the Council seemed right for him. He heard it had an office in the Mar Elias refugee camp, and he knocked on the door and asked to volunteer.

A young man behind a desk looked him over and listened to his story. What could he do? What skills did he have? Why had he come? Jorde told him about his knowledge of languages. He said he was ready to work for a meal a day and somewhere to sleep.

"What do you think of Arafat?" the young man asked.

"Hopeless!" Jorde replied. He had an inkling this was their line. "He wants to liberate Palestine by making speeches. What was taken by force can only be recovered by force!"

Within days Jorde had signed on, been given a code name and a mattress on the first floor of the building, and written a twenty-seven-page life story in which, to make himself sound important, he told a lot of fibs. He wrote that he had murdered a Jew in Spain, that he had played football for a famous team in Algeria, that he had worked as an interpreter in a travel agency in Pamplona. He listed a score of Spanish women he claimed to have made love to. It was pure fiction.

Jorde was not well suited for the Council. He was a braggart and a compulsive talker; he did not take kindly to discipline; he showed undue curiosity in an organization where information was restricted to those with the need to know; he tried to make friends with colleagues, although friendships were discouraged as a matter of policy; he loved to show off his languages and was hopeless at self-criticism. In such a paranoid outfit, where everyone was constantly spying on everyone else and forever writing up reports, he was certain to get into trouble. But he showed a talent for martial arts and got to the top of the class. He was also good at drill and at physical exercises, and once he had been transferred down to Sidon, he was put in charge of a squad. However, the fact that he shaved every day aroused suspicion. Where had he learned such fastidious habits? Fearing that he had been planted on them, his superiors asked him once again to write his life story. He labored away, but this time around he could no longer remember the names of the girls he previously claimed to have known or the fictitious addresses he had given them.

Nevertheless, since nothing serious was found against him, he was soon flown to Libya with a batch of other recruits and bused to the desert camp. It was 1987. Billets and wash houses were still being built—by the men—and in the meantime the accommodation was in tents. The routine was punishing. Roused at dawn, the men were sent out to jog for an hour, returning to a light breakfast and a long, hard shift of building work from 7:30 A.M. to 1 P.M. This was followed by a break for a spartan lunch and a short rest until 3 P.M., before the start of another shift of work until six o'clock. They then were allowed to wash and change for the evening's program of lectures and political films. Jorde discovered to his agony that if one was five minutes late for meals, one would not be allowed into the canteen at all. If one didn't get up on time in the morning, one's mattress would be turned over or one would be doused by a pail of cold water. If one put down tools to take a breather, reproaches and abuse came raining down. One needed permission to go to the lavatory, and one had to be very ill indeed, practically spitting blood, before the camp doctor allowed any sick leave. Complaints were utterly forbidden, on pain of being hauled away to Station 16, from which men emerged scarcely able to walk. Jorde tried to sneak away in mid-morning for a shave and a rest, but he was soon found out and threatened with a thrashing.

When they had been at the camp for about a month, Jorde's section was told that it would shortly be receiving a visit from a "comrade" to whom every man could open his heart. "Speak freely and answer any question he puts to you," their commander instructed.

"What alerted me to Abu Nidal's arrival," Jorde said, "was a driver springing to attention and saluting. I saw a man dressed in civilian clothes and accompanied by three senior camp officials in uniform. I looked at him closely. He wasn't very tall. He had a bald head with a fringe of gray hair, blue-green eyes, and a plump face. I said to myself, This must be the big chief.

"When we assembled in the sports center, he began by telling us that our six-month course was just the first step in our career with the organization. Each of us would in time get the job of his choice, the one best suited to his talents. Then, very quietly, he started to draw us out, asking us about our background, interests, and ambitions. Each man in turn had to step forward, give his code name, and tell him his problem.

"When it was my turn, I stood up and said my name, Hussein Jorde Abdallah.

" 'Where do you come from?'

" 'North Africa.'

" 'Are you a Palestinian?'

" 'Yes.'

" 'Were you born in Algeria?'

" 'No. In a refugee camp in Tyre.'

" 'But Jorde is not an Arab name.'

" 'I am not an Arab!'

"At this, everyone stared at me in surprise. My group leader tried to say it was just my code name, but Abu Nidal waved to him to keep silent.

" 'Are you a Spaniard?'

" 'No, I'm a Kabyle.' And I explained my family's travels from North Africa to Palestine and then back again, via Lebanon, to the Berber capital of Tizi-Ouzo, in Algeria. Jorde, I said, was a Catalan version of Jorge or George: It was a name I had borrowed from a Spanish acquaintance. I told him about the languages I spoke. He asked the camp commander, Husam Yusif, to make a note of what I was saying."

This exchange with Abu Nidal made Jorde a marked man, for in drawing the leadership's attention to his potential, he was also sharpening its suspicions about him. He was asked to report the next day to the camp commander.

"Do any members of your family work for an intelligence or a security organization?" he was asked.

"No." He had an aunt and uncle living in Kuwait; two uncles

in America, one in Michigan and the other in Ohio, but he knew very little about them. Another aunt, his father's sister, whom he had not seen for twenty years, lived in Benghazi. It was the usual pattern of Palestinian dispersal.

"What about you? Have you ever worked in intelligence?"

"No."

"Are you quite sure?"

"Yes, I am."

"This is a matter of life and death. Don't forget that in Beirut you signed a statement saying you would accept death if you were found to have an intelligence connection. Write your life story for us again, but this time put down every single detail about yourself and about all your relatives—their names, addresses, and everything else about them."

This was the third time Jorde had been set this task. Confined to his tent with pens and a notepad, he spent the best part of two weeks writing and growing increasingly resentful and anxious. He was worried that his earlier lies would now be exposed. He stopped eating and cried a good deal. The camp commander, Husam Yusif, came to see him.

"What's the matter with you? What's wrong?"

"I want to get out of here! I can't stand it anymore."

The next morning Husam Yusif and a strongly built man called Baha, who was said to be the Palestinian karate champion, frog-marched him to the back door of the kitchen bloc and ordered him into a dark closet, cluttered with mops and dirty rags, situated just behind the kitchen's huge gas burners, whose roar could be heard through the wall.

"We haven't brought you here to imprison you but to stop you from doing anything foolish," Husam said. "Sami will want to see you when he gets back from Tripoli in a couple of days." Sami was the man in charge of Section 16, the prison and interrogation bloc.

Dirty and unshaven, Jorde was brought before Sami two days later.

"Where is your life story?"

Jorde told him he had hidden it under the mattress in his billet.

"Have you told us the whole truth?"

"Yes."

"Before we resort to other measures, let me make one thing absolutely clear. You are still our comrade! If you are in any sort of trouble, you must tell us about it. If you are in danger, so are we all. No one can fool us. God judges in heaven, we judge here on earth. Several of our comrades turned out to be agents of other intelligence services. When we caught them, they told us they had been blackmailed into it. We were able to help them. We can do the same for you. I am going to give you another week to write your life story. Forget about the earlier drafts. Just tell us whom you work for!"

"But I don't work for anyone!"

"Yes you do! We can prove it. But I want you to admit it yourself. Tell us the whole truth. Don't force us to use other methods."

So Jorde started scribbling again. He confessed that he had not played football in Algeria nor worked as an interpreter in Spain. The travel agency in Pamplona did not exist. The twenty-five girls he said he had slept with were all invented. But he really had entered Spain without a visa by jumping a queue at the Barcelona airport.

By this time he had been confined for ten days in the closet. His beard had grown. His body itched all over. When the burners were lit in the kitchen, the temperature soared. He stripped down to his underpants. One day, still scantily dressed, he was taken outside, and, wedged in the backseat of a Toyota between Sami and another man, he was driven out of the camp into the open desert. His first thought was that they were going to kill him. Behind a dune, they came on a single tent pitched directly on the sand. It was empty. There was no ground sheet or bed, nothing except for some iron pegs in the ground, to which they now tied him. There they left him for a couple of days, visiting him once a day with some bread and a cup of water.

"Have you decided to tell us the truth?"

"I've already told you the truth," he groaned.

"Listen," Sami said. "Beating is not allowed in our organization except by decision of the Central Committee. But if you don't talk, the Central Committee will have no alternative . . ."

Jorde remained silent. He was filthy and starving. He stank. He began to hope that a scorpion bite would finish him off.

The following day Sami, Baha, and three other men came to the tent. One was carrying a rope, another a length of rubber hose, the third an oxygen cylinder, a bottle of disinfectant, and some rags.

Baha came up to him. "Stand up!" he roared. "Are you going

to tell us the truth?" But before Jorde could utter a word, he was struck across the face. He fell down, only to be hauled to his feet again. "Stand to attention! Don't raise your hands! Give me the hose!" And they all set to, punching and beating him.

One of his tormentors was a young thug called Mas'ud, who had been in the physical-exercise squad that Jorde had led. Jorde had pushed him hard to run and jump, and Mas'ud had hated him for it. Now he got his own back. They tied Jorde down, propped his legs up on a stone, and attacked the soles of his feet. Screaming and weeping, his mouth full of sand, he begged them to spare him.

"Stop! Stop! I'll tell you the truth. It's Algeria. I work for Algerian intelligence. They sent me here. They made me do it. I was scared for my family. Stop!"

"OK," said Sami. "That's it. Don't be afraid. We'll look after your family." They sat him down and untied his bonds.

"Is that it?" asked Jorde through his tears. "All finished?"

"Yes, that's it. We'll have a chat together over dinner. Now you are safe. You are once again our comrade. But you will have to tell us everything!" Jorde could not stand up. They carried him to Sami's tent a little way off, gave him some tea, and treated his wounds.

This is what he told them: When he was living in Algeria with his family, he used to buy small quantities of hashish from his neighbor, a petty smuggler. This man told him that they had to watch out for a certain Captain Kamal of military intelligence, whose job it was to chase the drug dealers. Jorde learned to recognize the captain's car. One day Captain Kamal visited Jorde's family at home, and soon afterward he called Jorde to his office and offered him a job as an informer. He wanted to know about smugglers, then he asked Jorde to keep an eye on student agitators in the town, and finally, when Abu Nidal opened an office in Algiers, which it was feared might be used to plan attacks on visiting Palestinians, Jorde was sent to Spain and from there to Beirut to penetrate the organization.

This was Jorde's hastily concocted story. There were elements of truth in it. Captain Kamal was a real person. But the rest was invention. Under questioning, it did not stand up. He got confused and contradicted himself. Sami was unimpressed. Later that night, Jorde was taken back to the tent and the beatings resumed. Desperate to save himself, he racked his brains for a more plausible story.

He said he worked in Bilbao for the Basque nationalist movement ETA; he was a member of its military wing. It was ETA that had sent him to Beirut to join Abu Nidal, ETA that had made a soldier out of him! He had never been to Pamplona or slept with Spanish girls; that part was a lie. He was sorry, very sorry. He had only wanted to make himself interesting. The beatings went on at intervals throughout the night.

In the following days, they stopped asking him for the truth and concentrated only on breaking him. It was extremely hot inside the tent. Sami cut his water ration to three small mouthfuls a day. He was so thirsty he could hardly speak. They gave him a tin in which to do his business. Flies gathered on his back and on the filth around him. Blood dried on his wounds. His body was all pain. They forced a potato into his mouth, blindfolded him, and turned Mas'ud loose on him. To escape the blows, he feigned madness, throwing himself on the ground in spasms.

"What do you think?" he heard Sami say to Baha. "Shall we get him a doctor?" He was carried to the surgery, tied to a bed, and given an injection. He was aware that Sami and Baha came to see him several times during the night. Half-asleep, he answered their questions, and they realized he had been faking.

"Have you ever had a wire inserted in your penis?" Sami asked. "Have you been trussed up like a chicken and forced to sit on a broken bottle? We will cut out your tongue. What you've written is all untrue. Every word of it. Who recruited you? Who sent you to us? Tell us about the Syrians! Tell us about the Jordanians!"

"Have pity! Oh God, have pity! I swear I told you the whole truth in the kitchen. The more you beat me, the more I'll lie."

Mahmud, a tall, gray-haired man from the Central Committee, came to look him over. "Take him to Station 16," he said.

There, in a tiny concrete underground cell, they made him stand to attention all night facing the wall, and the next night and the whole of the next two weeks. Jorde learned to sleep standing up. In the morning the guards would crowd in and each one would slap him across the face a hundred times. He had to count the slaps silently and, when it was time, utter only the words "One hundred!" If he fell to the ground or let out so much as a moan, they would start again. His face swelled up like a football and an ugly liquid flowed from his ears. Once every two or three days he was allowed to go out to the lavatory. The stench in the cell was terrible. From time to time Sami would arrive and play a tape of Umm Kalthoum, the undisputed queen of Arabic song, whereupon the guards would rush in, throw Jorde to the ground, put a brick under his feet, bind his legs, and thrash his soles until he fainted.

A bucket of cold water would bring him half-alive again. "Where did you learn yoga? Who taught you to sleep standing up? Speak, you dog! Who but a soldier would shave every day? You're an agent. Confess it!"

"I'm not an agent! I am a poor son of the camps! Please believe me."

Jorde spent two months in prison, being beaten every day. One night, when he was still in his underground cell, a wedding was celebrated in the camp. A comrade was marrying a female member, and all the guards went to enjoy the festivities except for Mas'ud, who stayed behind.

"Tonight," he said, "I'm going to finish you off!" He unfurled a length of wire, threw a switch in the corridor, and dangled a bright electric bulb into Jorde's cell through the tiny skylight above the door. "Hold it!" he shouted. "Hold it in your hand! If you drop it, I'll break your bones." Jorde obeyed. After a few minutes, smoke rose from his fearfully blistered palm. Swooning with pain, he was saved by the guards returning from the party.

For the tenth time, Sami gave him a pad and a pen and told him to write his life story. The prescribed routine was for him to write during the day, sitting on the concrete step in his cell, and then stand to attention throughout the night.

One evening, after reading what he had written, a grim-faced Sami came down to the cellblock. "Tonight," he whispered, "you are going to die! You had better say your prayers." They brought him water for his ablutions and stood watching as he prostrated himself. Then they dressed him in military uniform, wrapped a scarf around his head, and took him out beyond the prison compound to where a deep hole, evidently part of the sewage system, had been dug. A ladder led down to the noisome depths. Below him was another hole, shaped like a grave.

"Lie down!" Sami ordered as he drew his Browning and cocked it. "Do you have anything to tell us? This is your last chance."

"I am innocent!" Jorde cried in a storm of tears. "I have told you the truth." And as the filthy water lapped about him, he closed his eyes in a last prayer.

"All right! Get him out," Sami ordered. Shivering and demented, racked by sobs, Jorde was carried back to prison, given fresh clothes, and put in a clean cell. It was warm and dark. He curled up on a blanket on the floor and fell asleep.

Sami woke him up the next morning.

"Congratulations!" he said. "You've passed!" He reached into his pocket and gave Jorde a handful of sweets. "I believe you are innocent! Have a wash and a shave and some breakfast. We'll talk later. We have to behave like this to protect ourselves. There are a lot of enemies outside . . ."

JORDE'S TRAINING

For a few weeks Jorde lived in an agreeable limbo. He was excused from work, training, and guard duty. His personal belongings were returned to him. He shared a tent in the prison compound with one of his former torturers and was given magazines to read and plenty of food. His cravings for cakes, fruits, fresh air, and frequent showers were indulged. He could sleep as long as he liked. He was free to move about the camp but was not allowed to contact anyone. His sores healed, hair grew on his shaved head, his injured feet recovered well enough for him to put on a pair of sneakers. He began to regain strength as well as something of his former cockiness.

Escape was very much on his mind. After the floggings and the mock execution, his one thought was to get away. One afternoon a bulldozer scooped out a hole at the foot of the hill behind Station 16. Jorde was curious to know what was going on, but Amjad Ata, the second secretary of the Central Committee, ordered the compound cleared for the rest of the day. A couple of hours later, when they were allowed back, Jorde noticed that the hole had been filled in. He was convinced bodies had been buried there. Loose talk was strictly forbidden and, in any event, each man lived in fear of being reported. Nevertheless, rumors of executions spread around the camp. A little while later, Jorde learned that the driver of the bulldozer had committed suicide. He wondered whether he would ever manage to get out of there alive.

Enjoying greater leisure as well as a certain immunity because of what he had gone through, he was able to observe more closely the workings of Station 16 and to gauge the general mood of the camp. He heard that a man had hit another for staying under the

We are planning to send you abroad, where your life will be totally under our control. You must report back in every detail. If we say, 'Drink alcohol,' do so. If we say, 'Get married,' find a woman and marry her. If we say, 'Don't have children,' you must obey. If we say, 'Go and kill King Hussein,' you must be ready to sacrifice yourself!"

Jorde said he was ready for anything.

"Let me give you an example of a possible mission," Ali continued. "We might say, 'Go to the Argentine consulate in Brussels and apply for a visa. Some fifty kilometers outside Buenos Aires is a region called La Plata, where there are several poor villages. Go to a village, find a destitute old woman, and give her two or three hundred dollars. Tell her you are her long-lost son now working in Europe. She will take you to the town hall and get you documents proving you are her son. Enlist in the army for your national service. When it is over, apply for a visa to Israel. Buy an air ticket to Tel Aviv. Then await our instructions!' "

Ali arranged for Jorde to have his photograph taken and the following day gave him a well-used North Yemeni passport, with various stamps and visas in it, in the name of Muhammad Ahmad al-Salihi, domiciled in Abu Dhabi, occupation petroleum engineer. He was told to memorize the passport details and think himself into his new identity. He was supplied with a suitcase full of clothes, a Samsonite briefcase, and $5,000 in one-hundred-dollar bills. Jorde had never seen so much money before and wondered whether the bills were forged.

"Spend it wisely," Ali cautioned. "Don't forget that one of our ten principles is thrift. We are a small organization with small resources. The money we have belongs to our martyrs and must be looked after carefully."

For an hour he rehearsed with Jorde an itinerary that was to take him to Athens, Rome, Zurich, and Paris, to Niamey, capital of the African republic of Niger, and then back to Paris and Tripoli. At each stop there were people to meet, passwords to exchange, warning signals to observe. If a tall black man with a silver-capped front tooth at his hotel in Niamey carried his cigarette lighter in his left hand, he was on no account to approach him; if the lighter was in his right hand, contact could safely be made. Jorde could not take notes but had to satisfy Ali that he had committed every last detail to memory.

"All right!" Ali said at last. "Tomorrow we will take a trip together. Go through your things carefully and eliminate anything that might connect you with Libya."

Dreaming of Africa, Jorde met Ali the next morning at Tripoli airport and was tested on his itinerary. Ali asked for his passport and, slipping a piece of paper into it, gave it to the officer at passport control. Jorde noticed that his passport was not stamped. In fact there were no Libyan stamps in it at all. Instead, there was an exit stamp from Cairo dated that day. They boarded an aircraft and, a short while later, landed not at Athens, as he had expected, but at Valletta in Malta.

"This is where we go our separate ways," Ali said. "Ask for a three-day transit visa. Say you are going on to Athens. Before collecting your luggage, go to the lavatory and get rid of your Libyan ticket. Change a hundred dollars into local currency. Don't talk to taxi drivers: They are all intelligence agents. Find a modest hotel and meet me at 8 P.M. in the cafeteria of the Holiday Inn."

But Jorde was stopped at the barrier. The woman immigration officer flicked through his passport and shook her head at his request for a transit visa. Glancing over his shoulder, he saw Ali watching him. Then he saw Ali talking to another official, who looked like an Arab. The man walked over and had a word with the immigration officer, who then stamped his passport and let him through. "Thank you very much," Jorde said in Arabic. "Don't say a word," the man replied.

In Valletta, Jorde found a cheap hotel by the sea and met Ali as arranged. They dined and spent the evening exploring the town, with Ali continuing to coach his pupil in intelligence techniques: Were they being followed? How could they be sure? Was the street "clean?" Where was a good place to rendezvous? Were there several exits in case of emergency? Who was the main enemy—Israel or Arafat? The lessons continued over breakfast the next morning.

Then they went to a small supermarket, where Ali bought several cartons of soap powder and two dozen films. He gave Jorde half the load to carry in his suitcase and arranged to meet him at the airport in the afternoon. There he bought two tickets for Libya and asked Jorde to hand over his remaining cash. It was only then that Jorde realized the trip had been a mere trial run, a sort of test, and that his hopes of flying deep into Africa had to be deferred. On landing in Tripoli, Ali was warmly welcomed by a Libyan official, who took their passports and, again without having them stamped, escorted them out of the airport by a back door. Ali said he had paid the man $300 to take them through, but Jorde suspected he wasn't telling the truth. Back in the flat on Umar al-Mukhtar Street, Ali asked Jorde for the films and soap powder he had carried in for him.

The training continued. A week or two later they found themselves in Belgrade, with Jorde traveling on a Mauretanian passport, once again with no Libyan exit stamp. This time he traveled on his own, with $5,000 in his pocket, flying first to Frankfurt, where he burned his Libyan ticket and flushed it down the lavatory, and then on to Belgrade. Ali walked him around the city, which, he told him, was the administrative center for Abu Nidal's European operations. He showed him airline offices and Western embassies, friendly cafés where meetings could safely be arranged, and hotels where he was on no account to show his face.

The working methods of the organization were becoming clearer to Jorde. Ali explained that considerable resources were devoted to the gathering of intelligence. Before a target could be selected or an attack carried out, data on everyone and everything concerned had to be collected. This was the routine side of the organization's work and the main activity of its agents in the field. There was a strong emphasis on photography, sketch making, and report writing. A second priority was transferring weapons to foreign countries, or obtaining them there, and then hiding them for future use. A third was acquiring genuine passports, which were always more highly prized than the forgeries produced by the organization's Technical Committee. And finally there was training: Abu Nidal believed in moving his cadres from one training course to another, constantly upgrading their abilities and testing their courage.

It was in Belgrade that Ali set Jorde his last training exercise before he became operational. The task was to get a visa for Belgium, fly to Brussels, and make friends there who would welcome him back and help him get subsequent reentry visas: in other words, establish a working relationship in Belgium to justify returning there. Jorde hit on the idea of posing as a used-car dealer who was looking for vehicles in good condition to export to North Africa.

As instructed by Ali, he traveled club class to Brussels on Swiss Air, booked into a small hotel, and hired a taxi driver—a man of

Greek origin, called Victor Roumis—to take him around the various garages on the outskirts of the city that dealt in secondhand cars. He paid him $220 for two and a half days' work, and together they made lists of vehicles, checked prices, bargained, made many contacts, and collected numerous business cards. Jorde's story was that he was working with two partners in Belgrade and was prospecting the market. After consulting his partners, he would return to place firm orders in a week or two. Would the dealers vouch for him to help him get a reentry visa? Several said they would. Roumis, his newfound friend, took him home for a meal prepared by his Greek wife, who turned out to be an ardent Jehovah's Witness. After supper, the three of them watched a religious video!

Back in Belgrade, Jorde wrote a detailed report for Ali, complete with names, addresses, descriptions, and topographical details. It had been his first assignment entirely on his own, and Ali was pleased with him. What Jorde did not tell him was that in Brussels he had thought of escaping. But he did not have much money, and he knew he could not get very far on a Mauretanian passport. In any event, while he was swanning around Europe at someone else's expense, the need to escape seemed less pressing.

FIRST OPERATIONS

Once Jorde's preliminary training was complete, Ali handed him over to a thin, dark man in his mid-thirties called Hisham Harb, a senior cadre in the Special Missions Committee who was said to have a special talent for directing foreign operations and assassinations.

Sitting in cafés, talking and getting to know each other, they spent a week in Belgrade together. Jorde told Harb about the torture he had suffered in the camp, the memory of which gave him nightmares. He was still troubled by a buzzing in his ears. Why had they done it? What was the point? He was not overjoyed to hear Harb respond that Jorde had been beaten not so much because of suspected treason but because he had complained a great deal! It was a form of training and Jorde should not feel bitter. Others had suffered even more. He was now a trusted cadre and would have occasion to prove himself.

Harb unveiled to Jorde some of the secrets of the outfit he had joined. He explained the history and structure of the organization, the function of its various directorates and committees and, at the center of the whole system, the elite Intelligence Directorate, of which he was now a member. He claimed it was the only effective instrument in the Palestinian struggle, the only truly disciplined force, the only one that made the world tremble! Other Palestinian factions were made up of clowns and charlatans, concerned only to protect their privileges and ready to sell out the cause at the first opportunity.

"Could you kill a man if we asked you to?" he inquired.

Jorde said he would obey whatever orders he received.

Harb gave him an expensive Nikon camera with a zoom lens and taught him how to work it. "You're a talented man," he said. "We're going to use you for ten years. After that, you'll be free to go your own way."

The first assignments were relatively easy. Jorde found himself "borrowing" airline timetables (for which the organization had an insatiable appetite) from travel agencies; photographing Israeli and American embassies, consulates, and airline offices in several European cities; prowling past these potential targets in taxis to observe their defenses; and above all, stealing or buying passports. In Paris, he managed to acquire no fewer than four—two French, one American, and one Algerian. He discovered that crowded discos were a good hunting ground, because tourists tended to take off their jackets when dancing and leave them unattended. On Boulevard Barbes, north of the Gare du Nord, he met old Algerian acquaintances who, after discreet negotiations, helped him buy, for a thousand francs, an Italian pistol, which he photographed carefully (to prove that he had gotten it) and buried in a public park. By Christmas 1987, he was running out of money, so he sent a coded message to Tripoli to announce his return and flew back from Zurich by Swiss Air.

He was met by the same official who, when he was traveling with Ali, had escorted them through the airport. "Have you anything to declare?" the man asked. "Don't worry! You can tell me. We work for the same outfit."

After some hesitation, Jorde produced the stolen passports. The man took them away but returned with them a little while later and waved Jorde through. Outside the airport, a car took him to the flat on Umar al-Mukhtar Street, where Hisham Harb was waiting to debrief him. Jorde gave him the films, sketch maps, and passports, but when he told Harb he had shown the passports to their colleague at the airport, Harb flew into a rage. "You fool!" he roared. "You stupid fool! You deserve a good beating! You've wasted your whole trip." In disgrace, Jorde was sent back to the camp to cool his heels for several months.

His first task was to write a report of self-criticism and, as was the organization's custom, to suggest his own punishment. He made it exceptionally harsh: one month's work on a construction site; an extra four hours of guard duty each night for ten days; two hours of physical exercise each morning instead of one, which would mean rising at 4 A.M.; and writing two articles for the organization's in-house magazine, *al-Tariq* (*The Path*), one on selfishness and the other on bad temper. Perhaps it was this spirit of abject contrition that caused Hisham Harb to waive the sanctions and to send Jorde instead on a weapons course, where he perfected his knowledge of the Browning, Scorpion, M16, Kalashnikov, and also of an American-built RPG.

Jorde was not sure whether it was a promotion or a punishment when, a short while later, Harb issued him a Tunisian passport in the name of Sha'ban Abd al-Majid Belqassim and sent him to photograph and report on Jewish synagogues in Istanbul. Harb warned him it would be dangerous because the Turkish police, as well as vigilantes in the Jewish community, were on their guard following a murderous attack two years earlier on the Neve Shalom Synagogue, Istanbul's largest. In that attack, on September 6, 1986, two members of the organization, posing as photographers, had entered the synagogue, locked the door from the inside with an iron bar, and opened fire on the congregation with submachine guns before blowing themselves up. Twenty-one Jewish worshipers had died and another four were wounded. Shimon Peres, Israel's prime minister at the time, had vowed to "cut off the arms of the murderers, murderers not seen since the days of the Nazis." Now the organization wanted to know how this and other synagogues were defended. Were there any special checks on people going in? Any searches? Any sign of armed guards? They wanted Jorde to visit the Jewish cemetery where the victims were buried, take photographs of their graves, and make sketch maps of their location. Harb, who advised Jorde to pose as a Tunisian Jew, taught him half a dozen words of Hebrew and gave him a skullcap and some brief instruction in how to behave at prayer.

Within three weeks, Jorde was back in Tripoli with a full report and a restored reputation for courage and resourcefulness. On a tourist bus, he had met and befriended a woman guide who happened to be a Jew and who had been very helpful to the pious young Tunisian during his stay. Nevertheless, Hisham Harb insisted that Jorde append to his report a page of self-criticism for having spent a good deal of the organization's money in a very short time.

THE SAUDI TARGET

In September 1988, Jorde was prepared for a mission that Hisham Harb told him was of the utmost importance—a year-long stay in Thailand, during which he was instructed to learn the language, marry a Thai woman (preferably one working in a hospital, pharmacy, airline, or bank), start the formalities for acquiring citizenship if that was possible, and establish an arms cache within easy reach of Bangkok. The main object of his attention was to be the Saudi presence in Bangkok: Saudi businessmen, the Saudia airline, and in particular the diplomatic staff of the Saudi embassy, about whom he was instructed to compile a detailed report and photographic record. It was plain to Jorde that Abu Nidal was planning to mount an attack, very probably an assassination, against a Saudi target in Thailand.

For very many years Abu Nidal, the apostle of Palestinian violence, had been at daggers drawn with the Saudi royal family, the Arab world's foremost champions of stability and conservatism. Indeed, Abu Nidal's first operation, even before his split from Fatah, had been an assault on the Saudi embassy in Paris, in September 1973, in which two Saudi diplomats had been taken hostage. No doubt he would have pressed his attack on Saudi interests over the years had his various state sponsors—Iraq in the 1970s and Syria in the early 1980s—not forbidden it. However, from 1985 onward, when Libya became his main patron, such a prohibition was lifted and Abu Nidal started issuing threats against the Saudis, who, in his paranoid way, he believed were the source of all the plots against him.

The Saudis were sufficiently alarmed to seek a channel of communication with him, which, after some discreet soundings, Algerian intelligence agreed to provide. Abu Nidal did not aspire to a political relationship with Riyadh—their differences were too ludicrously great for that to be discussible—but he did expect the Saudis to buy him off. His view was that since they contributed vast sums to the PLO, he too should have his share. Accordingly, Algerian intelligence arranged for Abu Nidal to visit the Saudi kingdom in 1987, and the blackmailer returned from there with a "first payment" of $3 million in cash.

However, he made one mistake, which was to torpedo the budding relationship: He accepted a Saudi offer of a private plane to take him back to Algiers, believing that such red-carpet treatment would boost his stock with the Algerians. But ever wary of plots against him and perhaps fearing an in-flight mishap, he requested that a Saudi prince accompany him on the flight. Defectors from Abu Nidal's organization told me that a prominent young prince, a veteran of top-secret missions, agreed to do so. However, the Americans are thought to have heard of his trip and put pressure on Riyadh to end the relationship. Be that as it may, no more payments were forthcoming. Abu Nidal's rage knew no bounds. As he saw it, the Saudis had struck a deal with him and had then failed to honor it.

Bent on revenge, he attacked "soft" Saudi targets. On October 25, 1988, Abdallah Ghani Badawi, second secretary at the Saudi embassy in Ankara, was gunned down. Two months later, on December 27, it was the turn of Hasan al-Amri, Saudi vice-consul in Karachi. Western Europe, where effective counterterrorist measures had been introduced, was becoming a dangerous place for terrorists, driving Abu Nidal to look for less well policed countries. Hence the choice of Thailand for a third attack. And this was Jorde's mission.

Jorde knew he would not be on his own. He would have shadowy partners in Thailand, although he could only guess at their identity and location. According to the organization's well-tried procedures, an attack required the coordination of several elements:

There was first a long-term "resident" responsible for establishing the arms cache and supplying the necessary background intelligence about the target. This was the role for which he was being groomed.

Second, a "supervisor" would fly in at the appropriate moment, examine the target in greater detail, make a feasibility study, and, after close consultation with the command back at base, call in a third component.

This was the hit team, usually consisting of three members and a leader, whose job it was to decide on the nuts and bolts of the operation: Where exactly was the target to be attacked? In his office, at home, or in the street? How should the team be deployed? Who would fire the lethal shot, and who would provide covering fire? What was the best getaway route? Each team member would travel on his own and make contact with the supervisor, who would assign him a place of residence. The team members did not know the resident or where the arms were hidden. Each member of the team would know the others only by their code names and would not know under what names they were traveling.

Fourth, and finally, there was the "intermediary," usually a high-ranking cadre, whose sole task was to collect the weapons from the resident and deliver them to the supervisor. Sometimes the intermediary would not even meet the resident but would merely collect the weapons from a prearranged drop. The minute the hand-over was accomplished, the intermediary would leave the country, so as to protect the arms cache and its custodian. The supervisor would not know the resident: His sole contact was with the intermediary. If the operation failed and the team was arrested, the police would be unable to trace the resident or the weapons. If the operation succeeded and the team got away, the supervisor would return the weapons to another prearranged drop, whence they would be collected by the resident and hidden for future use.

As he was being briefed for his assignment, Jorde's hopes of escape revived. He was certain he would be given a decent passport and a large sum of money to establish himself in Thailand. His tentative plan was to abscond with the cash and disappear underground, probably in Spain, where he hoped to resume his former life of petty and relatively carefree criminality.

Jorde spent much of October 1988 learning about Southeast Asia, and Thailand in particular. He pored over books, briefing papers, and maps. He was instructed to send his preliminary findings about the Saudi embassy personnel by coded letter, written in invisible ink and addressed to a certain Sulayman Taha, P.O. Box 83476, Tripoli, Libya. He was to sign his letters Sami Taha. He was given careful training in where to meet and how to identify the couriers who were to bring him money, weapons, and instructions.

When he was ready to go, Hisham Harb gave him a North Yemeni passport in the name of Hadi Abdallah al-Dawudi, a mere $5,000 in cash, and a one-way ticket on Libyan Airways to Vienna—on all counts a great disappointment! Hisham instructed him not to spend more than fifteen dollars a day on a hotel in Bangkok and twenty dollars a day on living expenses. Once again, his dreams of making a well-financed escape evaporated.

At the end of October 1988 he flew to Vienna and, on arrival, burned his ticket as instructed. The stamp in his passport indicated that he had flown in from Amman. He then traveled on to Belgrade, via Zagreb, and applied for a visa at the Thai embassy. He was asked to produce a return ticket—which cost him $1,700—and was given a tourist visa.

Jorde took the long flight to Bangkok, spent a few nights in a cheap hotel, and then, mindful of the need to economize, moved to a rented room. Within days he signed on for Thai classes, at a language school called the American University Alumni, under the name Marco al-Dawudi. He said he ran a video shop in Milan where he lived with his divorced Italian mother. Soon he was sending back to Tripoli voluminous reports and film of the Saudi embassy staff, whom he spent his afternoons following assiduously to their places of residence.

But his funds began to run low. With mounting concern, he sent repeated coded messages to Tripoli, by letter and then by telegram, asking for help and instructions. Day after day he waited patiently at the agreed places of rendezvous, an American ice-cream parlor and a self-service restaurant, called City Food, in the Ambassador Hotel, but no courier showed up. He resorted to what he knew best, picking pockets, befriending people in bars and taking their money, talking his way into the favor of Thai businessmen, who helped him out and paid for his meals. Charming and plausible, a born raconteur, he was able to scrape by on his wits. He met some criminals who were willing to sell him weapons, but he had no money to clinch the deals. Tripoli remained silent.

Had he fallen from grace? Did they suspect him of double-dealing? Had he been sent out as a decoy while the real action was elsewhere? Was there something wrong with his communications? Were they being intercepted? Jorde sank deeper into fear and anxiety. One night he got involved in a brawl and was stabbed in the chest with a broken bottle. His Thai friends rescued him, took him for treatment to the Deja General Hospital on Sriayuthaya Road, and paid the bill.

Then, on January 4, 1989, Salah al-Maliki, third secretary at the Saudi embassy in Bangkok, one of the men he had tracked and carefully photographed, was gunned down by unknown assailants. The Islamic Jihad, a Beirut-based fundamentalist group, claimed responsibility, and most foreign observers attributed the murder to terrorists loyal to Iran. But Jorde knew better.

In the wake of the Bangkok murder, he was arrested in a general sweep of Arabs. He was interrogated by the police and his room was searched, but no evidence against him was found and he was released forty-eight hours later. He was told, however, that he would have to leave Thailand once his visa expired on March 8. As so often in his life when he found himself in difficulty, Jorde appealed to his brother, Abdallah, for help. Through the Kuwait Airlines office, he sent him a message telling him of his whereabouts. His dutiful brother, who had not seen him in five years, came to Bangkok and gave him a present of $900, enough to get Jorde out to Rome on March 8—and then to lose himself somewhere in Europe.

He had no wish whatsoever to return to Tripoli and the uncertain fate of an Abu Nidal agent. He needed shelter. He feared the organization would track him down if he were to show his face at one of his usual haunts in Belgrade, Brussels, or Barcelona. Having worked for Abu Nidal, he was now something of a pariah in the whole Palestinian underground. The complicated, faction-ridden world of Palestinian politics was out-of-bounds. No one would trust him or give him safe haven. Nor could he sell his knowledge of the organization to a Western intelligence service without becoming a marked man for life, a target for revenge attack. So Jorde chose simply to disappear.

But why had the organization dropped him? The puzzle continued to rankle until Jorde eventually learned that in the months he had been away, Abu Nidal's previously tightly run organization had been ravaged by volcanic internal eruptions, for reasons that will be clear later. More than ever convinced that he was surrounded by spies and traitors, Abu Nidal had ordered the execution of dozens of men. Among the victims were Jorde's controller and the camp commander, Husam Yusif, accused of plotting to raise a mutiny and assassinate his leader. As men struggled to save their skins, Jorde had simply been forgotten.

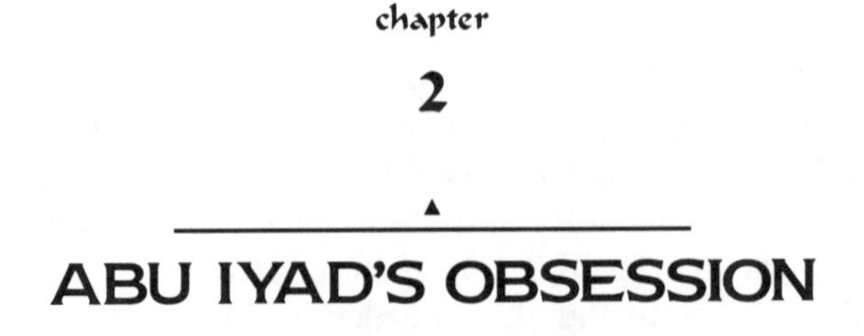

chapter

2

ABU IYAD'S OBSESSION

The UN ultimatum to Saddam Hussein expired at midnight on January 15, 1991, and within hours Desert Storm was to devastate Iraq with the ferocity of an act of nature. On the night before the deadline, at 7 P.M. on January 14, a deeply preoccupied Abu Iyad, chief of PLO intelligence, called for his bulletproof Mercedes and asked to be driven from his office in downtown Tunis to the house of Fatah's security chief, Hayil Abd al-Hamid (known as Abu al-Hol), who a day earlier had returned from Baghdad with Yasser Arafat.

The PLO was frantically trying to head off the war in the Gulf that Abu Iyad knew was imminent. All that day Arafat had held anxious consultations in Tunis with French, Italian, and Algerian envoys, and he was now already on his way back to Baghdad to beg Saddam Hussein to announce that he was ready to pull out of Kuwait. The PLO leaders had supported Saddam, but they knew that a war would destroy them all. To Arafat's horror, the Iraqi dictator was adamant. Pride or fatalism stupefied him in those last critical hours. In defiance of the vast armies ranged against him, he appeared to believe that the allies would not dare attack him and that even if they did, his forces could hold them off. Sick with worry, Abu Iyad wanted a firsthand report from Abu al-Hol about Saddam's alarmingly unrealistic mood. He also wanted to review the PLO's plans in the event of war.

Abu al-Hol's villa was in the outlying leafy suburb of Carthage, about half an hour's drive from Abu Iyad's office. Accompanied by a senior intelligence aide, Fakhri al-Umari, Abu Iyad was ushered indoors by Ahmad Sa'id, who that night was in charge of Abu al-Hol's personal security. Ten other guards were on duty: one at the front of the house, another at the back entrance, the others huddled together in a small room by the garden gate around a miniature television set that Abu Iyad's driver, Mahmud Mir'i, had brought out from the Mercedes he drove. It was a cold, rainy night. Inside the villa and in the guardroom everyone talked about the crisis in the Gulf. Abu Iyad and Abu al-Hol knew Saddam was gambling dangerously with their destinies, but the men in the guardroom were excited: An Arab champion had defied Israel and the West.

THE KILLING OF ABU IYAD

Security around the house was slack, as was usual in PLO domestic arrangements. Kalashnikovs had been left in cars outside or stacked in a corner cupboard. Abu Iyad's chief bodyguard, Fu'ad al-Najjar, had not arrived with his master but came an hour or so later, as he had gone to settle some problem with his landlord. Then he drove off again to see a man about a BMW he had his eye on and once more left to fetch a take-out dinner for the other guards.

One of these guards, an agitated young man called Hamza Abu Zaid, sauntered out of the guardroom and started to pick a quarrel with Ali Qasim, the man posted at the front door of the villa. The two of them made so much noise that Ahmad Sa'id called out to them to shut up. On the pretext of wanting to take a tissue from a box inside the car, Hamza threw open the door of Abu Iyad's Mercedes. Ali Qasim tried to stop him. Hamza then bet him that the bullets from his Kalashnikov could penetrate the car's armor plating, and Ali Qasim dared him to try. They were soon jostling and butting each other and had to be separated. Hamza then claimed the light bulb over the front door of the house was flickering and wanted Ali Qasim to ring the bell to get someone to change it, but Ali Qasim pushed him away.

A moment later, when Ali Qasim had moved off, Hamza went to the front door and rang the bell himself. A maid opened and he went in. It was about 10:45 P.M. Ali Qasim expected Abu al-Hol to come out and scold Hamza for disturbing him, but instead he heard shots inside the building. He shouted for help. Looking for their weapons, the guards came scrambling out and dispersed to their stations, thinking the attack had come from outside. It took them a few moments to realize that the shooting was coming from inside the house.

Asleep in her bedroom, Abu al-Hol's wife was suddenly roused by a deafening burst of gunfire from the living room below. Hamza had shot Abu Iyad in the head and gunned down Fakhri al-Umari, who had tried to hide behind a sofa. She heard Hamza scream again and again: "Let Atif Abu Bakr help you now!" Then she heard her husband cry, "What have you done, Hamza? What have you done?" And then another burst of gunfire and another. Abu al-Hol had tried to reach the door but had been shot in the legs. He grappled with Hamza, who then shot him in the stomach at close range.

Abu al-Hol's wife ran to the adjoining room, where her seventeen-year-old daughter cowered in bed. She took her in her arms as she heard a man racing up the stairs. Hamza broke in, closed the door, and locked it. "The Israelis are here," he shouted. "They've shot Abu al-Hol."

Abu Jihad, the PLO's military chief, had been killed three years earlier by Israeli commandos, and the women must have believed Hamza.

Abu al-Hol's wife screamed, "Is he alive? Let me go to him."

"He's wounded. Don't ask me more than that."

The two women sat together on the floor in a corner, the daughter crying and her mother trying to comfort her, while Hamza roamed silently about the room, picking up small objects from the girl's dressing table, examining them and putting them down, and peering out of the window. There were sudden flashes of lightning and the sound of rainwater pouring down from the eaves. It was very dark outside.

"Is this your bed?" he suddenly asked the girl. When she did not answer, he bellowed out: "Is this your bed?" Her mother nudged her pleadingly to say yes.

"Why don't I have a bed like this or a desk or a room?" he shouted angrily. "Is it because I'm not the son of a Palestinian fat cat?" He poured out his bile against the PLO and its leaders: agents, traitors, lackeys, a cesspool of corruption. Abu al-Hol's wife heard him curse Atif Abu Bakr, a leading defector from Abu Nidal's organization, and vow to kill him. Then he took an envelope out of his pocket and reached in it for a tablet, which he swallowed. Then another and another over the five hours that he held them hostage.

They heard cars drive up to the house and much running back and forth. The Tunisian police had arrived. Abu Iyad and Umari were already dead. Abu al-Hol, who had lost much blood, died in the hospital on the operating table a little while later.

Upstairs, the telephone rang again and again. Finally, Hamza answered it. He seemed very calm, Abu al-Hol's wife remembered later, and utterly convinced he had done the right thing. She heard him say: "I've killed Abu Iyad and I'm holding Abu al-Hol's family hostage. I won't release them until you bring me Atif Abu Bakr." He added grimly: "I have a message for him."

The Tunisian police brought up floodlights and a loudspeaker. "Hamza!" they called to him, flooding the windows with light. "Hamza! Let the women go free. We want nothing else from you." This message was repeated every half hour, after which a deadly silence would fall. Hamza took more pills from his envelope.

In the early hours of the morning, the police called up to say that they wanted to negotiate with him. What did he want? A plane to fly him out, he told them. They said they had to get permission from a higher authority. When they returned, they said they needed some identification from him. When he proposed throwing his identity card out of the window, they said the rain would ruin it. But a dialogue had started and they soon talked him into coming downstairs and passing the card to them through the front door, which he opened a fraction. Abu al-Hol's wife then heard him close the door and come back up the stairs dragging his feet. Then she heard his Kalashnikov clattering to the ground. Running out onto the landing, she saw him slumped unconscious on the stairs. She later discovered that he had been knocked out by gas, which the police had sprayed into the hall from the outside. She ran down the stairs past him, opened the door, and let the police in.

BIOGRAPHY OF A KILLER

Hamza Abu Zaid was just another young Palestinian with a troubled past, another Jorde. As recorded in a PLO file, his "permanent address" was:

> Mustafa Salim's shop,
> Behind the girls' school,
> Wahdat refugee camp,
> Jordan

He was born in the Wahdat camp in 1963 and spent his first nineteen years there. His family had fled from Palestine in 1948, leaving their home village of Safiriya, near Jaffa, ahead of the conquering Israeli armies.

From two internal PLO memoranda given me by Abu Iyad's intelligence colleagues I was able to trace Hamza's feckless, itinerant life in the ten years before he killed Abu Iyad and his two colleagues in Tunis. It reveals as much about the workings of the PLO as it does about Hamza himself.

> In July 1982, he crossed illegally from Jordan into Syria in order to enroll with Fatah, but the Syrians arrested him at the border. Finding nothing against him, they turned him over to Fatah, which put him on its payroll and posted him to the Salah al-Din camp, near Damascus.
>
> In October 1982, he was sent to Yugoslavia on a ten-week course in weapons handling and security duties, returning to Damascus in December.
>
> In February 1983, he was posted to Pakistan as a security guard in the office of the PLO representative.
>
> In September 1984, he spent a two-week vacation at PLO headquarters in Tunis.
>
> In October 1984, he was transferred to Bulgaria as a security guard in the office of the PLO representative. But he proved rowdy and undisciplined and in November he was sent back to Tunis, where Fatah sentenced him to a month's detention.
>
> In 1985, he was sent to Cyprus as a security guard in the PLO office. Some Palestinian intelligence sources, sensitive, or

perhaps oversensitive, to the risk of Israeli penetration, believe that it was here that an agent of the Mossad, Israel's foreign-intelligence service, disguised as a member of Abu Nidal's organization, approached him to persuade him to defect secretly to the organization. However, by the end of that same year, he was back in detention in Tunis for bad behavior.

On his release in early 1986, he was given a job as a security guard at PLO headquarters at Hammam al-Shatt, outside Tunis. But once again he proved quarrelsome and unreliable. It was decided to send him to Lebanon, but as no transport was immediately available, Abu al-Hol, head of Fatah security, took the extraordinary decision of appointing him as a bodyguard at his own home.

Three months later, Hamza ran away to Iraq with another security guard and managed to get himself taken on by the PLO representative in Baghdad. But the latter fell out with the Iraqi authorities. His office was closed in 1986, and his staff dispersed. Hamza and others soon found themselves in Hungary.

At this point in Hamza's career, the PLO lost track of him. They know that he spent some eighteen months, from mid-1986 to early 1988, bumming around Eastern Europe—in Budapest, Warsaw (where he spent twenty-one days in jail for petty theft), Prague, and Belgrade. It is in Belgrade, where Abu Nidal had a considerable base, rather than in Cyprus in 1985, that he was most probably recruited as a potential penetration agent by Abu Nidal's organization.

In July 1988, Hamza turned up in the Philippines. Traveling under a false name, he contacted the head of the Palestinian Students' Union in Manila. Hamza told him he had worked his way on a Greek ship and was trying to immigrate to Australia. He wanted an introduction to the PLO office. But his story failed to stand up. Suspecting that he worked for a hostile outfit, local PLO officials kept him away.

In Manila he moved in with some Palestinian students, borrowing small sums from them to keep alive. One of the boys had a pistol and another an M16 rifle, which he had bought locally from a Filipino. One day, hearing a rumor that General Ariel Sharon, to them the devil incarnate, was due in town, they determined to assassinate him and set up a watch for this purpose at the Israeli embassy. One of them saw an embassy car with someone in the back who looked like Sharon, so they rented a car of their own, loaded their weapons, and spent a day and night driving between the Israeli embassy, the principal hotels, and the foreign ministry looking for Sharon—needless to say, in vain.

In February 1989, Hamza left the Philippines very depressed, according to his roommates. There is no record of where he went next, until he surfaced in Libya in the spring of 1990, when he called several times at the PLO office in Tripoli asking to be taken back by Abu al-Hol.

In May 1990, Abu al-Hol went to Libya to attend a memorial service for Abu Jihad, the PLO military supremo killed in Tunis by Israeli commandos in April 1988. Hamza managed to see Abu al-Hol. Throwing himself at his feet, weeping, and lamenting his pathetic situation, he pleaded to be taken back. Abu al-Hol took pity on him and returned him to Tunis, where he put him to work again as a bodyguard at his house. At no time was Hamza properly interrogated about his activities during the years he had dropped out of sight.

In October 1990, on the pretext of wanting to see a long-lost sister, Hamza got leave from Abu al-Hol to go to Libya for two weeks. It was then, he later told his interrogators, that a man called Ghalib in Abu Nidal's organization gave him the mission to kill Abu Iyad. He said that he did not at first want to do it, but he was told that Abu Iyad was the source of all corruption in the Palestinian movement, the traitor who had used the defector Atif Abu Bakr to split the organization. Abu Iyad had to die for the Palestinian revolution to live. As for Abu Bakr, about whom we shall hear much more later on, he was a major defector from Abu Nidal's ranks and an important source for this book.

After the murders at Abu al-Hol's villa on the night of January 14, 1991, Hamza Abu Zaid was arrested by the Tunisians and taken away for interrogation. PLO officers were not allowed to take part in the questioning, nor were they given a transcript of what Hamza said. The Tunisian authorities feared the killings might be the prelude to an Israeli raid or might trigger popular disturbances, as the Tunisians were overwhelmingly on Iraq's side in the Gulf crisis.

They had had a taste of Israeli aggression in October 1985, when Israeli aircraft invaded their airspace and bombed Arafat's Tunis headquarters, and again in April 1988, when an Israeli seaborne team murdered Abu Jihad at his house. They were now anxious to play down the affair as much as possible.

But Arafat would have none of this. He took the matter up with Tunisia's president, Ben Ali, who, in February 1991, handed Hamza over to the PLO for trial. The deal was that he would be removed from the country, sparing Tunisia a controversial trial in a Tunisian court. A PLO doctor who examined Hamza pronounced him a drug addict and gave him five times the normal dose of sedatives before he was flown by private plane to San'a, capital of Yemen, where he was interrogated and tried by the PLO and sentenced to death. The idea was that the wives of Abu Iyad and Abu al-Hol should witness the execution. But Colonel Qaddafi and Abu Nidal are said to have put pressure on Yemen's president, Ali Abdallah Salih, not to allow a public execution.

In June 1991, Hamza was found dead in his cell. The PLO let it be known that he had committed suicide.

ABU IYAD'S CONFESSION

In the early summer of 1990, nine months before his murder, Abu Iyad sent word to me in London. If I happened to be coming to Tunis, he would like to see me. I was intrigued. What could he want? I had not yet made any holiday plans, so on impulse, I decided to take my wife and children to a hotel I knew outside Tunis. Its chalets, smothered in bougainvillea, were set in green lawns that stretched down to the Mediterranean. Whatever Abu Iyad had to tell me, I determined that it would not be a wasted trip.

I know the Middle East pretty well. I grew up there and, as an author and foreign correspondent (mainly for the London *Observer*), I have traveled in the region and written about it for thirty years, my main contribution to the subject being two books on Syria, *The Struggle for Syria,* first published in 1965, and, more recently, a biography of the Syrian leader Hafez al-Assad, which aroused a good deal of controversy. The Syrians banned the book—in fact (although I like to think it was avidly read), it was not allowed on public sale in any Arab country; the Israelis, too, thought I had been harsh on them; Americans objected to my criticism of U.S. Middle East policy; Lebanese Christians thought I had sold them out to the Syrians; Arafat and other Palestinians felt that in describing their tussles with Assad, I had not done justice to their cause; and the thought crossed my mind that this might be what Abu Iyad wanted to have out with me.

When researching my Assad biography in Damascus, I met and married the daughter of a retired Syrian diplomat, his country's ambassador to Washington for many years. Despite this Arab connection, I trust most readers consider me an independent observer with no ax to grind, no allegiance to one side rather than another, no hidden agenda save to pursue that elusive—and, in the Middle East, ever-fleeting—quarry, historical truth.

Abu Iyad I had met a number of times, but without really getting to know him. Involved with intelligence for much of his career, he was a shadowy figure and a good deal less accessible than other Palestinian leaders. I knew him, of course, as one of Fatah's *chefs historiques,* one of the four men who had founded the mainstream Palestinian resistance movement in 1959, the other three being Arafat; Muhammad Yusif Najjar, killed by the Israelis at his home in central Beirut in 1973; and Khalil al-Wazir (better known as Abu Jihad), the PLO's military supremo, the one killed by the Israelis at his home in Tunis in 1988—two commando operations in which Israel's current chief of staff, Ehud Barak, was intimately involved.

I had had my first long talk with Abu Iyad in Algiers in 1983, at a session of the Palestine National Council that I covered for *The Observer,* and was struck then by his realism, by the way his conversation came in rapid bursts of astonishing candor, by the absence of posturing. He seemed more worldly-wise and better informed than the other Palestinian leaders, perhaps the result of his extensive dealings over the years with intelligence agencies in many different countries on both sides of the Iron Curtain. Unlike some of the others, who affected a rough guerrilla appearance, he was immaculately turned out in a neatly pressed safari suit, such as African politicians wear, and smelled faintly of eau de cologne.

Held every few years, these meetings of the PNC, the Palestinians' "parliament-in-exile," were good occasions for observing Palestinian leaders doing their turn in the conference hall, for seeing Arafat's gift for political theater, and for informal meetings with the bosses of the various factions in the lobbies and corridors.

I will always remember the remarkable sight of George Habash at the rostrum. The extremist leader of the Popular Front for the Liberation of Palestine thundered away, with blazing eyes, against a negotiated settlement with Israel. He had had a stroke and could not raise his arm to turn the pages of his prepared speech. The mere effort to speak and to stand upright brought sweat pouring down his face. At his side his disciple, Bassam Abu Sharif, himself scarred and partially blinded by an Israeli letter bomb, mopped his master's brow with a large white handkerchief and turned the pages for him, as one might for a musician. Some while later, Bassam Abu Sharif gave up Habash's extreme rejectionism to become the most ardent dove in Arafat's moderate camp, the frontrunner of the process that led the PLO formally to renounce terrorism and recognize Israel at the 1988 session of the Palestine National Council.

At the Algiers conference I also met Nayif Hawatmeh, leader of the Democratic Front for the Liberation of Palestine, his permanently tortured expression seeming to suggest his efforts to squeeze the contradictions of Palestinian politics into the strict confines of his Marxist dialectic, and Ahmad Jibril, leader of the PFLP-General Command, a burly figure in a shiny black leather jacket, surrounded by a phalanx of crew-cut acolytes, who preached armed struggle and still more armed struggle. As a simple soldier, he held the windy theoreticians of the Palestinian movement in the greatest contempt. Sitting by himself in a discreet corner, overflowing out of his armchair in all directions, I found Abu Dawud, a giant of a man with a lopsided jaw where a bullet had got him. He was one of Fatah's most notorious guerrilla commanders and a wanted man—wanted, that is, by the Israelis. It was rumored that he had had a hand in the attack on the Israeli athletes at the Munich Olympics in 1972. In conversation he was mild, self-deprecating, exuding a sort of despair that his obvious energies could not be better directed.

Abu Iyad impressed me more than these others. Calm, softspoken, and very steady, he was the sort of man to whom authority came naturally. As we talked, runners came up to whisper something in his ear or give him bits of paper, which he glanced at before tucking them away in his pocket. Although Yasser Arafat, the PLO chairman and head of Fatah, was "Mr. Palestine," the public symbol of Palestinian aspirations, his closest colleagues, Abu Iyad, the intelligence chief, and the military chief, Abu Jihad, ran their own autonomous outfits with their own loyalists, much as barons might do under a medieval king. Abu Jihad, boss of the PLO's military wing, was rumpled and unimpressive to look at, with nothing soldierly in his bearing, but he was considered the best manager in the Palestinian movement, with a special grip over West Bank affairs (which is, no doubt, why the Israelis killed him). Abu Iyad, in contrast, had a sharp political brain and a fluent, seductive manner: He was the fixer, the man for confidential foreign missions, the keeper of PLO secrets. He was remarkable on several counts. Known as a committed nationalist on the left of Fatah, he was also one of the very first to recommend, in an interview with *Le Monde* back in 1972, a negotiated settlement with Israel based on a two-state solution, one in which a Palestinian statelet would live alongside and in harmony with its powerful Israeli neighbor—a compromise that most Palestinians were at that time not yet ready to accept.

Abu Iyad's mother was Jewish,* and he had grown up chattering in Hebrew to Jewish boys of his own age as they played together on the beach at Tel Aviv.

This was the man I went to see in Tunis in the early summer of 1990. A Tunisian policeman stood in a sentry box outside the garden gate, while just inside the gate was a gaggle of half a dozen gun-toting Palestinian guards, including one ugly, loose-mouthed fellow as large as a sumo wrestler. I took the path across the garden, bright with geraniums, rang the front doorbell, and was ushered in by a woman secretary (who, I noticed, doubled as a telephonist: She had a seat by a switchboard in a corner of the hall) into an almost feminine drawing room, crowded with sofas and gilt armchairs and little tables on top of which sat vases of flowers. A moment later Abu Iyad hurried in and affably embraced me in the Arab manner, giving me his clean-shaven cheek.

For a while we chatted about my biography of Assad. As I expected, there were things about it he didn't like. He thought I had seen events too much from Syria's standpoint. If ever I were to publish a new edition, there were some factual corrections he would

*In the mid-1970s Eric Rouleau, *Le Monde*'s outstanding Middle East expert (now French ambassador to Turkey), helped Abu Iyad write an autobiography, which appeared in 1978 under the French title *Abou Iyad, palestinien sans patrie.* In it Abu Iyad referred elliptically to his mother when he wrote that "my grandfather, a man of religion in Gaza, had brought up his children in a spirit of tolerance. One of his sons had married a Jewish woman." Abu Iyad was describing his own father.

like me to make. But it was soon clear that he had something else on his mind. He wanted to talk about terrorism—and in particular about Abu Nidal.

The Western world, he said with a frown, was not yet persuaded that the PLO was the indispensable partner for Middle East peace. It had underestimated the importance of the historic resolutions passed by the Palestine National Council in November 1988 that, for the first time, never so much as mentioned "armed struggle" and spelled out with absolute clarity the PLO's readiness to negotiate a peaceful settlement with Israel.

But how to get the West to see this? To his mind, the great obstacle was terrorism, an issue with which Israelis confronted every mention of peaceful compromise. If there was one man responsible for blackening the reputation of all Palestinian factions, it was, Abu Iyad believed, the archterrorist Abu Nidal.

The Israelis, Abu Iyad continued, were masters at penetration and deception. He had been sparring with the Mossad for a quarter of a century, and since the early 1980s, he had begun to suspect that the Israelis had infiltrated Abu Nidal's organization and were making use of him. "Every Palestinian who works in intelligence," he told me, "is convinced that Israel has a big hand in Abu Nidal's affairs." His suspicions had now hardened into a conviction: Abu Nidal was not just an extreme rejectionist who sold his services to Arab regimes. Israel had gained control of him. That was the key to his persistent sabotage of Palestinian interests.

In Abu Iyad's mind there was no great mystery about it: Israel wanted to destroy the PLO and prevent negotiations that might lead to a peaceful solution involving an autonomous Palestinian state on the West Bank. Any genuine negotiations would necessarily involve the surrender of territory, which is why Israel had gone to such lengths to persuade the world that the Palestinians were terrorists with whom no deal could be contemplated. Abu Nidal, he believed, was Israel's prime instrument for this purpose, central to its strategy. Until Abu Nidal was exposed and defeated, he said, the PLO's credibility would continue to be questioned and the peace process could get nowhere.

Leaning forward and talking very fast as was his habit, he told me that there was no other plausible explanation for the evidence that had accumulated over the years. Abu Nidal had killed th
PLO's most accomplished diplomats: Hammami, in L

Qalaq, in Paris; Yassin, in Kuwait; he had slaughtered hundreds of Palestinian fighters; he had debased the Palestinian national struggle with his senseless and savage terrorism and succeeded in alienating the Palestinians' best friends. He had made the word *Palestinian* synonymous with *terrorist.* He was either deranged or he was a traitor, and Abu Iyad did not think he was deranged. Abu Nidal, he told me, was the greatest enemy of the Palestinian people.

"He is a man wholly without principle!" he exploded angrily. "He would ally himself with the devil in order to stay alive and drink a bottle of whiskey every night!

"Try to see Abu Nidal," he urged me. "Go to Libya. Ask him to explain himself, and then make up your own mind."

He then made an extraordinary admission: "I feel very guilty that I was responsible for not facing up sooner to the threat from Abu Nidal. I should have killed him fifteen years ago. I confess this now. I wanted to believe that he was a patriot who had strayed from the path and that I could win him back. For far too long I was reluctant to accept that he was a traitor."

Abu Iyad's diatribe rather took my breath away. Abu Nidal an Israeli agent? The extravagance of the charge made me think that I had stumbled on yet another Palestinian feud. It is characteristic of the hothouse of Palestinian politics, and, I suppose, of revolutionary politics generally, that every man's hand is raised against his brother. One has to spend only a little time with the guerrilla factions to be amazed at the wild stories they tell about one another. I had recently spent ten hours talking to Ahmad Jibril at his military camp outside Damascus, trying to probe into his possible connection with the bombing of Pan Am 103 over Lockerbie, Scotland, only to find that it was almost impossible to get him off the subject of his bitter enemy Yasser Arafat. At great length, and with complicated excursions into Arafat's obscure genealogy, he had tried to persuade me that the PLO chairman was a Jew of Moroccan origin. Heaving himself out of his chair, Jibril threw his arms in the air and exclaimed: "The leader of the Palestine revolution, and we don't even know who he is!"

Was Abu Iyad playing the same game? I had heard rumors that when Abu Nidal was a young man in Fatah, Abu Iyad had been his friend and protector. Clearly, love had now turned to hate. This would explain Abu Iyad's injured tone. But his allegations were a different matter. It was of course well known that Israel's

Mossad, like other intelligence agencies, tried to penetrate terrorist groups, but to suggest that Abu Nidal had been "turned" and his organization taken over seemed to me a very tall story indeed.

I tried to question Abu Iyad. Where was the evidence? Disarmingly, he said it wasn't foolproof. When you didn't have your own country and couldn't control airports, ports, borders, hotels, and taxi drivers, gathering the evidence was difficult. Effective counterespionage depended on 100 percent control of the environment—something that the PLO had never managed to achieve. In Iraq and Syria, he said, the PLO could not monitor Abu Nidal's movements properly, and in Libya it was still more difficult. Even in Lebanon and Tunisia, which he claimed were both swarming with Israeli agents, the PLO had never been allowed the facilities it needed. He added, "We know for certain that Mossad came here to Tunis when we did in 1982, with its own safe houses, weapons, and communications."

Abu Iyad was no half-baked Palestinian youngster talking to me but the PLO's veteran intelligence chief. Skeptical as I was, I took careful notes. "Why don't you write something about it?" he said. Would he tell me what he knew? Would he open his archives? Would he help me find defectors from Abu Nidal's organization who were said to be hiding in Tunis and elsewhere under PLO protection? Two men, in particular, I was anxious to interview because they had broken with Abu Nidal in a blaze of publicity in November 1989 and then gone to ground. One was Atif Abu Bakr, whose name Hamza kept shouting the night he killed Abu Iyad. Bakr had been the head of Abu Nidal's Political Directorate and was well known in Palestinian circles as a thinker, diplomat, and poet; the other was a very different character: Abd al-Rahman Isa had been Abu Nidal's hatchet man and chief of intelligence for twenty years. If anyone knew Abu Nidal's secrets, these two men did. I asked Abu Iyad if he could arrange for me to see them. Anytime I wanted, he replied.

I returned to London to think hard about what I was getting myself into. I didn't buy Abu Iyad's story. I thought it was preposterous. But I was tempted to know him better, learn how his mind worked, see the complicated world of the Palestinians from the inside. Obviously, he wanted to use me to expose Abu Nidal, a man he now hated. The same would be true for the defectors. Obviously, information they gave me would be slanted. After quarrels and splits, revolutionaries notoriously hurl anathemas and invent stories. But I felt I was an old enough hand in Arab politics to pick my way through the maze. Could I see enough people to enable me to check and countercheck my material? Would I be able to test what I learned with intelligence specialists outside the Palestinian movement? In any event, the subject was important enough that whatever happened, I felt I had to get to the bottom of Abu Iyad's allegations if I could. I certainly didn't know what to expect. I had no idea where the trail would lead me, but I felt that if nothing else came of it, I would have the chance to learn something about one of the great mysteries of Arab politics: Who was Abu Nidal, and what was he all about? I let Abu Iyad know that I would return to Tunis later that summer.

Before leaving London, I did some preliminary research. Checking for references to Abu Nidal in a couple of data banks, I turned up grisly accounts of his attacks on synagogues in Istanbul and elsewhere and on El Al ticket counters at the Rome and Vienna airports, hardly the work of an Israeli agent. However, I remembered that Abu Iyad had made much of Abu Nidal's killing of prominent Palestinians. He had used a phrase that stuck in my head: "We were often not sure whether Mossad or Abu Nidal was the killer. I admit it confused us." What could he have meant?

Ransacking my files, I made a list of Palestinians who had been attacked or killed either by Israel or Abu Nidal, a list based on public sources available to anyone, except in one or two cases in which I had special knowledge. Although Abu Nidal surfaced for the first time in 1974, I chose 1971–72 as my starting point because this was when the Black September terrorist movement emerged after the Palestinians' bloody showdown with Jordan's King Hussein in 1970. The Palestinians had then fought a running battle with the Mossad across Europe—the so-called War of the Spooks—and Abu Iyad had been up to his neck in it. Israel's embassies, envoys, airlines, and overseas companies had all become vulnerable to attack. Determined to defeat the terrorists, Golda Meir, Israel's prime minister at the time, had instructed her intelligence chiefs to go out and kill. I pinned the list on my wall and started to think about it. This is how it read:

May 8, 1972—Four Black September hijackers seize a Sabena jet on a flight from Vienna to Tel Aviv and, on landing at Lod, threaten to blow up the plane unless Israel releases one hundred Palestinian prisoners. Paratroopers disguised as mechanics storm the aircraft, killing two gunmen and releasing ninety passengers.

May 31, 1972—In retaliation, three Japanese terrorists, allies of George Habash's PFLP, launch an indiscriminate gun and grenade attack at Lod Airport in Israel, killing twenty-four people.

July 9, 1972—Israel hits back with a car bomb in Beirut, which kills the PFLP spokesman Ghassan Kanafani and his seventeen-year-old niece.

July 11, 1972—To avenge Kanafani, a terrorist throws a grenade at Tel Aviv's bus terminal, wounding eleven people.

July 19, 1972—An Israeli letter bomb injures Dr. Anis al-Sayigh, director of the Beirut Center for Palestinian Affairs.

July 25, 1972—Another Israeli letter bomb delivered to a PFLP address in Beirut maims Bassam Abu Sharif, chief assistant to George Habash.

August 5, 1972—Black September terrorists, led by Ali Hasan Salameh, bomb an American-owned oil storage tank at Trieste, Italy.

September 5, 1972—Eight Palestinian terrorists break into the quarters of the Israeli team at the Munich Olympic village, killing two Israelis and taking nine others hostage. They name their operation Ikrit and Biram, after two Arab villages in northern Galilee razed by Israel, and demand the release of 250 Palestinians and Lebanese abducted in Lebanon by Israeli forces. In a gun battle with West German police, nine Israeli athletes and five Palestinians are killed.

September 11, 1972—Zadok Ophir, a Mossad clerk at the Israeli embassy in Brussels, is shot and badly wounded by a Palestinian.

September 19, 1972—Dr. Ami Shachori, agricultural attaché at the Israeli embassy in London, is killed by an Arab letter bomb.

October 17, 1972—Wa'il Zu'aiter, Fatah's representative in Rome, is killed by Israeli agents.

December 8, 1972—Mahmud al-Hamshari, PLO representative in Paris, is badly wounded by an Israeli bomb. He dies a month later.

December 28, 1972—Black September gunmen seize the Israeli embassy in Bangkok and take six Israeli hostages. They demand the release of thirty-six Palestinian prisoners held in Israel. The hostages are eventually released unharmed.

January 24, 1973—Hussein Abu al-Khair, Fatah representative in Cyprus, is killed by an Israeli bomb at a Nicosia hotel.

January 26, 1973—Baruch Cohen, a Mossad agent directing operations against Palestinians in Europe, is killed in Madrid by a Fatah agent.

February 22, 1973—Israeli fighters shoot down a Libyan Airlines Boeing that had strayed ninety kilometers off course over Sinai, killing 104 passengers and crew.

March 6, 1973—Black September gunmen raid the Saudi embassy in Khartoum during a diplomatic reception and demand the release of the Palestinian guerrilla commander Abu Dawud, then in jail in Jordan. They murder the American ambassador, Cleo Noel, the departing American chargé d'affaires, George Moore, and a Belgian diplomat, Guy Eid.

March 12, 1973—Simha Gilzer, a Mossad agent, is killed in a Nicosia hotel by Palestinian gunmen.

April 4, 1973—Dr. Basil al-Qubaisi, a prominent PFLP official, is killed by Israeli agents in Paris.

April 10, 1973—An Israeli assassination squad kills three prominent Fatah leaders—Muhammad Yusif Najjar, Kamal Udwan, and Kamal Nasser—in their homes in central Beirut, which is a devastating blow to the Palestinians and brings down the Lebanese government.

April 27, 1973—An Israeli employee of El Al is killed in Rome by a Palestinian gunman.

June 27, 1973—Muhammad Boudia, an Algerian member of Fatah, is killed in Paris by an Israeli bomb.

July 2, 1973—Col. Yosef Alon, an Israeli defense attaché, is shot outside his home in Washington.

July 21, 1973—Israeli agents looking for Ali Hasan Salameh, a Black September commander, kill a Moroccan waiter by mistake in the Norwegian town of Lillehammer. Six Israeli agents are captured and put on trial, exposing Israel's counterterrorist network in Europe.

October 1974—Abu Nidal agents try to kill Mahmud Abbas (Abu Mazin), a close colleague of Yasser Arafat.

January 3, 1977—Mahmud Salih, a PLO representative in Paris and manager of an Arabic bookshop, is killed by Israeli agents.

January 4, 1978—Sa'id Hammami, PLO representative in London and a well-known dove, is killed by an Abu Nidal gunman.

June 15, 1978—Ali Yassin, PLO representative in Kuwait, is killed by an Abu Nidal gunman.

August 3, 1978—Izz al-Din Qalaq, PLO representative in Paris and, like Hammami, a prominent dove, is killed by an Abu Nidal gunman.

August 5, 1978—Yusif Abu Hantash, PLO representative in Pakistan, escapes an assassination attempt by Abu Nidal gunmen. Four other people are killed.

January 22, 1979—Ali Hassan Salameh, head of Arafat's security unit, Force 17, is killed by an Israeli car bomb in Beirut.

April 22, 1980—Abu Iyad (or, to give him his real name, Salah Khalaf) escapes an assassination attempt in Belgrade by Abu Nidal agents. They attack a car in which they think he is traveling.

June 1, 1981—Na'im Khudr, PLO representative in Brussels and another well-known dove, is killed by an Abu Nidal gunman.

July 27, 1981—Abu Dawud (or, by his real name, Muhammad Awda), the Fatah guerrilla commander, narrowly survives an attack on his life in Warsaw by an Abu Nidal gunman.

October 8, 1981—Abu Tariq (or, by his real name, Sulaiman al-Shurafa), Fatah representative in Libya, escapes an attack on his life in Malta by an Abu Nidal gunman, who kills another man by mistake.

October 9, 1981—Majid Abu Sharar, a prominent Fatah leader, is killed by an Israeli bomb in Rome.

April 10, 1983—Dr. Isam Sartawi, a close associate of Arafat and the most prominent dove in the Palestinian movement, is killed by an Abu Nidal gunman in Lisbon, Portugal.

April 16, 1988—Abu Jihad (or, by his real name, Khalil al-Wazir), the PLO's military supremo, is killed at his home in Tunis by a seaborne Israeli assassination squad.

I looked at the list long and hard. It fell into two halves, with an obvious break after 1973. Up to 1973, Israel had been killing Palestinian terrorists and guerrilla leaders. After 1977 Abu Nidal began killing Palestinian moderates—"doves" who wanted to negotiate with Israel, not to bomb it out of existence. My list wasn't all that neat, but there seemed to be a general pattern. Was there some sort of link between the two halves of the list? And why the gap in the mid-1970s?

I didn't have to look far into the historical record. While the War of the Spooks was raging in the early 1970s, Egypt's President Sadat was pleading with the Americans to bring Israel to the negotiating table. But Henry Kissinger, then secretary of state, ignored him. By 1973 Arafat was trying to disassociate himself and the PLO from terror and counterterror. He was largely successful, though there were groups within the PLO, like that of Abu'l Abbas for example, that he could not control. Nevertheless, Arafat, who had lost some of his best men, was now ready to steer his fractious movement away from violence and toward a negotiated peace. Immediately after the Israeli fiasco at Lillehammer, Arafat sent four messages to Kissinger, between July and October 1973, calling for a dialogue with the United States. But Kissinger sent General Vernon Walters, then deputy director of the CIA, to tell an Arafat aide in Morocco that "the United States has no proposals to make."

In October 1973, Egypt and Syria went to war to break the stalemate, recover part, at least, of the occupied territories, and force Israel to negotiate. Much as Desert Storm did in 1991, the October War revived hopes of a general Arab-Israeli settlement brokered by the United States, with Kissinger then in charge of American diplomacy. Again Arafat appealed to Kissinger to let him join the process, and Sadat urged Kissinger to meet the PLO chairman. But Kissinger shied brusquely away. For him, as for many Israelis, the PLO was not the advocate of a legitimate national claim but a "terrorist group," "unacceptable as a negotiating partner." A PLO-run state, Kissinger believed, was bound, with Soviet help, to develop into a radical fortress like Libya or South Yemen, from which operations against Israel would inevitably be mounted.

Accordingly, Kissinger dropped the West Bank from his agenda and agreed with Israel to exclude the PLO from any post-war settlement. As his "step-by-step" diplomacy unfolded, it gradually became clear that his prime aim—and that of Israel as well—was to take Egypt, the most powerful of the Arab states, out of the Arab lineup and push the Palestine question over the horizon. Kissinger agreed with Israel that the Palestinians were a security problem to be dealt with by tough physical means rather than a political problem to be solved by negotiation and compromise.

After that, much that Arafat did was irrelevant. In October 1974, he persuaded Arab leaders to recognize the PLO as "the sole legitimate representative of the Palestinian people." In November 1974, he told the United Nations, "I have come bearing an olive branch and a freedom fighter's gun. Do not let the olive branch fall from my hand," signaling his readiness to negotiate with Israel. He coaxed his followers into accepting the notion of a mini-state alongside Israel rather than the maximalist demand of destroying Israel entirely. But Israel and Kissinger said no.

In 1975, the Lebanese civil war broke out, fueled by the Palestinians' frustrated hopes for peace and the fears of the Christians that if the Palestinians were not to get a state of their own, Lebanon would never be rid of them. The war sucked in several outside parties, notably Syria, and distracted the region for the next couple of years.

Then in May 1977, Menachem Begin, the former Irgun terrorist and zealous champion of a "greater Israel," came to power. It had been his lifelong ambition to absorb the West Bank into the state of Israel by establishing Jewish settlers on West Bank territory and crushing Palestinian nationalism. For Begin, Arafat was obviously a major problem. The PLO leader wanted to negotiate. But for Israel negotiation could mean losing the West Bank. Thus, Israeli strategy aimed to destroy the PLO by all possible means—by promoting a worldwide political and diplomatic campaign to isolate and undermine it, by demonizing it as a "terrorist organization," by stifling any dialogue the PLO might try to conduct with the West and particularly with the United States.

In January 1978, some months after Begin took office, the list I made showed that Abu Nidal began killing prominent PLO moderates—precisely the men who were trying to influence Western opinion by preaching negotiation and reconciliation with Israel.

More than any previous Israeli leader, Begin was determined to cast Arafat and his colleagues as terrorists with whom it was impossible to talk, a view that fitted the Reagan administration's obsession with "international terrorism." Not surprisingly, terrorism preoccupied the Reagan administration from the start, in 1981. The long incarceration of Americans in the American embassy in Tehran had done much to destroy Jimmy Carter and ensure Reagan's election. Reagan, his secretary of state Alexander Haig, and CIA director William Casey all gave credence to the comic-strip reports by the American journalist Claire Sterling in her book *The Terror Network* (1981) of tens of thousands of terrorists, sponsored directly or indirectly by Moscow, being trained in guerrilla camps across the world as "elite battalions in a worldwide army of Communist Combat." The Cubans, she wrote, had a big hand in it, but so did the Palestinians—the "second great magnetic pole for apprentice terrorists." Intelligence professionals knew that Sterling was talking nonsense, but Begin was happy to encourage the White House and the State Department to see terrorism as the main scourge of the modern world and Syria, Libya, and the PLO as its practitioners.

Reflecting on all this, I wondered whether this was what Abu Iyad had in mind. He had told me that Abu Nidal's murdering Palestinian moderates was connected with Begin's determination never to negotiate with Palestinians for fear of losing the West Bank. For Begin, the moderates, who wanted to negotiate, were the real danger and had to be eliminated. If the Israelis had in fact infiltrated Abu Nidal's organization, perhaps some spymaster in Jerusalem had said, "We've got someone who can do the job for us." There was very little evidence to go on, but I was beginning to grasp Abu Iyad's logic or, at any rate, the stimulus to his paranoia.

There was, of course, a perfectly sensible alternative explanation. Abu Nidal might simply be what he said he was, an out-and-out rejectionist who considered Arafat a traitor for even contemplating a settlement with Israel and who was prepared to murder any doves, like Hammami in London, who dared to speak out in favor of peace. In the shadowy world of killers and secret agents, who knew what to believe?

At about this time I was visited in London by a former general in Aman, Israel's military intelligence service, who was doing research on a quite different topic. After our talk I asked him point-blank whether Israel penetrated and manipulated Palestinian groups. He looked at me carefully. "Penetration, yes," he said, "but manipulation, no." He paused, then added with a little smile, "No one would admit to that."

IN PURSUIT OF ABU NIDAL

I returned to Tunis a number of times that summer and autumn, and Abu Iyad was as good as his word. In great secrecy, he arranged for me to interview Atif Abu Bakr, the most prominent defector from Abu Nidal's organization. Abu Bakr was then in hiding, fearing Abu Nidal's revenge. He proved an invaluable source. Before joining Abu Nidal in 1985, Abu Bakr had represented the PLO in Belgrade (1974–76), Prague (1976–83), and Budapest (1983–84). He was highly articulate, one of the cleverest men I had met in the Palestinian movement. Abu Bakr in turn introduced me to members of his Emergency Leadership—an anti–Abu Nidal splinter group—including its military commander, "Basil," who had worked with Abu Nidal since the 1970s. From there, one source led to another.

I tried to persuade another prominent defector, Abd al-Rahman Isa, Abu Nidal's former intelligence chief, to cooperate and telephoned him in Algiers, hoping to visit him there. But he said that he would only talk in exchange for a very large sum of money. When I reported this to Abu Iyad, he laughed and gave me the unedited tapes of a long conversation he had had with Isa, over several hours, after he broke with Abu Nidal in 1989. Isa had not been aware of the hidden microphones and did not know his "debriefing" was being recorded. So, although I never interviewed Isa myself, I had access to the account of his career he had given to Abu Iyad.

Abu Iyad also put me in touch with several of his intelligence officers and with his archivist, a plump man with an encyclopedic memory and a sallow complexion the color of his buff files. Outside Abu Iyad's intelligence orbit, I was of course able to talk at length with a great many other Palestinians who had once had dealings with Abu Nidal or who knew about him indirectly. The most valuable of these was the guerrilla commander Abu Dawud, whose career had meshed with Abu Nidal's over the years.

Jorde, I met in a seaside town on the Mediterranean. After his adventures in Thailand, he had wandered about southern Europe for a few months, getting by as best he could. He was tempted, he told me, to slip back into a life of petty crime, but his main fear was that Abu Nidal's people, present under cover in several European cities, would catch up with him and take him forcibly back to Libya. Penniless and vulnerable, he needed protection. It was therefore pretty well inevitable that he should gravitate to the PLO, the only organization he could think of that had a strong interest in learning more about Abu Nidal.

But after Jorde had told his story to PLO intelligence, Abu Iyad no longer trusted him and suspected that he was a plant. Jorde was so glib, so skillful at spinning a yarn, that Abu Iyad thought it prudent to keep him on ice for a few months, probing into his background and testing his story against that of other defectors from Abu Nidal's outfit.

It was about this time that I met him. He was anxious to please and yet was edgy, like a man on probation, suspended between the organization he had fled from, which he feared was pursuing him, and the organization he hoped to join, which was wary of him. Perhaps Abu Iyad thought that an independent "debriefing" by me would tease the truth out of Jorde—or would at least provide one version of the truth, which PLO intelligence could then compare with the one Jorde had given them. I don't know the answer to that puzzle, and Abu Iyad is beyond questioning.

Most of the defectors I met lived in fear. Our meetings took place over several months in PLO safe houses in Tunis and its suburbs, reached after long car journeys, usually at night. Invariably, the men I interviewed had guns within easy reach (on the table next to my tape recorder, or tucked casually into the cushions of a chair) and were accompanied by young bodyguards, men much like Jorde, armed with submachine guns. When they were not in the kitchen making coffee, to see us through the long sessions, they lolled in the corridor or on the balcony, where they could keep an eye on the approach roads.

In 1990–91, my research took me to small hotels in Cyprus and Malta, to Paris and Marseilles, to Italy, Austria, and Greece, and to the offices and apartments of a number of men and women in Western capitals concerned with counterterrorism. To all of these I am grateful, although I cannot name them.

My aim in the narrative that follows is to paint as accurate a portrait as possible of Abu Nidal and of the clandestine outfit he has headed for the past seventeen years. No organization, even a legitimate one, likes to be investigated by outsiders. And this one, which is anything but legitimate, is no exception. Its very nature is covert. If they talk, its members and ex-members risk death. But splits and defections have opened a small window, allowing one a glimpse of what goes on inside.

Of all the men of violence in the contemporary Middle East, Abu Nidal poses the most intriguing riddles. Why does he kill? On whose orders? To what effect? How has he managed to survive for so long with half the world's secret services at his heels? Why has Israel never attacked him, as it has other Palestinian factions? No career in recent years throws more light on the Middle East's secret wars, in which dirty tricks abound and in which things are rarely what they seem.

This is not a pretty tale. It is a journey into a violent and distasteful underworld where principles and common pity are unknown and where death waits at every corner.

chapter

3

CHILDHOOD TRAUMAS

Eager to check out Abu Iyad's theory, I set out on the trail of Abu Nidal, digging into his past, questioning everyone I met who knew him, and trying to understand his evidently complex personality.

Abu Nidal is, I discovered, a man of nondescript appearance (although several sources mentioned his bald head, bright eyes, and good teeth), simple education, and poor health who suffers from stomach ulcers and angina. He dresses shabbily, most often in a zip-up jacket and old trousers. He has few of the obvious vices: He does not gamble, run after women, hanker after luxuries or even after comfort. He has hardly a family life to speak of. Whiskey, which he drinks nightly in large quantities, appears to be his only solace.

His long sojourn underground for nearly twenty years, something of a record in the world of clandestine operations, has made him shy of human contact. A fantasist with little regard for truth, he lives in a world of violence, delusion, and fear and, like other practitioners in the murky world of intelligence, is addicted to secret knowledge and secret power. A master of disguises and of subterfuge, trusting no one, lonely and self-protective, he lives like a mole, hidden away from public view. He seems to be a mine of contradictions: both quick and very cautious, both daring and cowardly.

Yet even his enemies concede that it has taken great abilities to create his disciplined and widely feared instrument of terror. A canny administrator with a sound financial brain, he has amassed a fortune, reportedly running into hundreds of millions of dollars. Ex-colleagues say that he is capable of hard work and clear thinking over long periods and that he is an undoubted leader who, though inspiring loyalty and dedication, rules his far-flung organization through fear.

Once upon a time, at the beginning of his career, Abu Nidal was famous for his fiery and unbending nationalism. Now he is notorious for his murders. Some say that in his middle fifties, he has come to savor his reputation as an outlaw and a killer, that it is a case of patriot turned psychopath. To kill repeatedly and on a large scale, to be awash in blood, is not a normal human condition. Such an aberration is usually found only in situations of great stress, when a community blinded by hate and fear attacks another, in times of war, or when an individual personality is profoundly disturbed.

THE LOSS OF A MOTHER

If Abu Nidal seems like a classic case of a split personality, his unhappy and insecure childhood, which several of his acquaintances mentioned, may go some way toward explaining it. He was born in May 1937 in Jaffa, an ancient Arab port on the Mediterranean coast of what was then Palestine. His father, Khalil al-Banna, was a solid citizen whose fortune lay in orange groves that stretched south of the town in luxuriant and sweet-smelling plantations. Each year he supervised as his citrus crop was packed in wooden crates and shipped to Europe, on a shipping line from Jaffa to Liverpool that had been opened in the 1890s.

Hajj Khalil was a patriarch. By his first wife, he had had eleven children, seven boys and four girls, who lived in a spacious, three-story house built of dressed stone, which was situated close enough to the shore for the children to skip down for a dip in the sea after school. To escape the humid summer heat of the coast, Khalil al-Banna bought another house in a mountain village further up the Mediterranean. It lay in the north of Syria, in the striking hill country above the port of Alexandretta (which was ceded to Turkey, against Syria's will, by the French on the eve of the Second

World War). Many of the inhabitants of these coastal mountain villages were and remain members of the Alawite sect, a heterodox offshoot of Shi'ite Islam. To bring in much-needed cash, these dirt-poor villagers were often forced to hire out their daughters as domestic servants to middle-class families in the region. One summer the Banna family brought home to Jaffa a handsome young Alawite girl of sixteen. Khalil al-Banna became infatuated with her and, in his old age, married her, to the outrage of the rest of his family. His twelfth child, the future Abu Nidal, was the son of the family maid. He was named Sabri.

From the beginning, Sabri's position in the household was uncomfortable. He was scorned by his older half-brothers and -sisters. Worse still, when his father died in 1945, his mother was eventually turned out of the house and so he lost her too. Aged eight, Sabri remained in the parental home, but there was no one to care for him, and such neglect meant that he received virtually no education. He dropped out of school after the third grade and to this day, to his embarrassment, continues to write with the untrained hand of a child, a source of much anguish.

Arabs have their own particular snobberies, often to do with pride of family, which is one reason that cousin so often marries cousin. But there was little to be proud of in being the son of a poor maid from a downtrodden sect—until, that is, Hafez al-Assad, himself an Alawite of peasant stock, came to power in Syria in 1970. Abu Nidal then tried, as we shall see in due course, to ingratiate himself with the Syrian leader by invoking this maternal ancestry.

Abu Nidal has since made it up with the members of his father's family, some of whom live under Israeli rule in the occupied territories. A half-sister lives in Nablus, on the West Bank; he sends her money from time to time in various roundabout ways. A half-brother, Muhammad al-Banna, was a prominent fruit-and-vegetable merchant who, until his death five years ago, was on good terms with the Israeli occupation authorities. Several of his nieces, of whom he has at least a score dispersed around the Arab world, are married to members of his organization. But who can tell how the loss of a mother and his early humiliation and rejection affected him? However, his cruelty and the need to dominate those around him point to a grievance against the world that may be connected with the pain he suffered as a child. Those who know him well say that he despises women, and there is little room for them in his all-male organization. His members' wives are kept in isolation and in ignorance of their husbands' activities. They are not even allowed to befriend and visit one another, as is customary among the other Palestinian groups. His own wife, as we shall see, a patient, long-suffering woman, has for years been kept away from society, without friends.

THE SHOCK OF EXILE

Abu Nidal's bitter and vengeful personality was very probably shaped by the slights he suffered as a child but also by the impact on him of the disaster that overtook his family, and the whole of the Palestinian community, as a result of massive Jewish immigration into Palestine, culminating in 1948 with the establishment of the state of Israel.

What happened in Palestine in 1947–48 is one of the most contentious subjects in modern history. This book is hardly the place to rehearse the old polemics or to set out the rival versions of history as seen by Arab and Jew. Monstrously persecuted by Hitler, the Jews needed a homeland and the British promised them one. In November 1947, the United Nations General Assembly passed Resolution 181, partitioning Arab Palestine into an Arab and a Jewish state, a resolution that the Zionists considered international sanction for a country of their own and which the Arabs rejected. Jews claim, moreover, an emotional attachment to the land of their historic ancestors. But the *way* the state of Israel was created, with the violent expulsion or stampeding of its Arab inhabitants, left much to be desired and has been a source of furious controversy ever since. Dispossessed Palestinians, who had enjoyed almost uninterrupted tenure of their land for thirteen hundred years, suffered a great shock from which they have been unable or unwilling to recover.

In the 1930s many a Palestinian child, like the young Sabri al-Banna, was brought up on tales of heroic deeds by Arab fighters who tried to stem the remorseless tide of foreign immigrants who were buying Palestinian land from Arab landowners, dispersing the Arab tenants and laborers. Jaffa, where he grew up, had a tradition of militancy. A Jewish attempt in 1935 to smuggle weapons through Jaffa port was one of the first incidents that roused the Arabs to take up arms against the Jews and their British protectors. Arab irregulars clashed with British troops. Their leader, Sheikh Izz al-Din Qassam, a devout cleric turned guerrilla fighter, was killed. Palestinians consider him the father of their armed resistance. His death was one of the sparks that ignited the great Arab revolt of 1936–39, which the British put down with terrible ruthlessness, killing thousands of Palestinians and interning tens of thousands. Palestinian protest at the influx of Jews was crushed for a generation. Living cheek-by-jowl with Tel Aviv, its brash, rapidly growing neighbor, Jaffa was caught in the grip of these violent events. Thousands of Arab peasants, evicted from the land as it passed to Jewish owners, set up miserable shantytowns around the port. Hostility between Arab and Jew, in Abu Nidal's youth, was an inescapable fact of daily life.

When the Arabs rejected the 1947 UN partition plan and civil war broke out between the Arabs and Jews, Jaffa found itself under siege. Surrounded by Jewish territory, it was an Arab enclave that the Jewish high command was determined to capture. Sniping escalated into running battles and then into mutual atrocities. In a notorious incident early in 1948, two Stern Gang terrorists disguised as Arabs drove a truck full of dynamite hidden under a pile of oranges into the town and blew it up, causing over a hundred casualties. Such terror tactics were repeated in many parts of Palestine as the Zionists raced to seize as much territory as possible before Britain's withdrawal on May 15, 1948, which, they feared, would herald the entry into Palestine of regular Arab armies. In Jaffa, the fighting shut down schools, factories, the bus service, and the citrus industry, the Banna orange groves and packing plant included.

The hugely successful Zionist strategy was to mount surprise attacks on Arab cities with mortar and rocket bombardments; to harry the Arab population with psychological warfare from loudspeakers and clandestine radio stations operated by the Hagana, the underground Jewish militia; and, in the countryside, to stage massacres in isolated villages such as Deir Yassin and Kolonia, calculated to stampede the rural population off the land. Several thousand Arab civilians were slaughtered in different parts of the country, leading to the panicked flight across the borders of some 750,000 others. It was then that the intractable Palestinian refugee problem was born. For years, much of the information about these killings was deliberately suppressed, but word has lately been filtering out, thanks mainly to Israeli researchers and historians, who have been probing into the events of the period.*

In Haifa, Acre, and Jaffa, scores of Palestinian families, under fire from Jewish snipers, were drowned in the rush to escape by sea to Gaza or Beirut. As soon as the Hagana seized Jaffa on May 14, 1948, it was cleaned out by looters from Tel Aviv and then quickly settled by thousands of Jews. Of an Arab population of 75,000, only 3,000 remained. The Banna plantations were confiscated by the Israeli government. The wild scramble of the Palestinians to get out was matched only by a Jewish scramble to seize their property. As late as 1953, a third of Israel's Jewish population was living on land taken from Palestinians.

A few weeks before the fall of Jaffa, the once proud and prosperous Banna family fled south to the small town of Majdal, where they hoped they would be safe, but they were soon driven out again by the advancing Israelis. Fleeing still further south to Gaza, then under Egyptian military occupation, they found shelter at last in the al-Burj refugee camp, where, packed together in tents, they spent a wretched year, including the very cold winter of 1948–49. They then moved on again to the city of Nablus, in the West Bank, then under Jordanian rule and temporarily out of reach of Israeli guns. In time, some of Khalil al-Banna's sons and daughters were able to scratch out a modest living. They were the lucky ones. Years after the 1948 catastrophe, most Palestinian refugees were still living in tents, still awaiting the miracle that would return them to their homes. Today in the camps, breeze blocks have replaced the canvas tenting, but the refugees are still there, their numbers swollen by natural increase and new wars. Attachment to their lost land and hatred for those who displaced them remain their dominant emotions and have intensified with the passing years.

Israelis are rightly proud of their state building and of their military prowess, but as many would now acknowledge, their "war of independence" was, like most wars, a brutal and often criminal affair. They won it because the military balance was crushingly in their favor. The propaganda version in which a helpless Jewish

*To cite a single example, on August 24, 1984, the Israeli daily *Hadashot* published an account of a previously unreported massacre at the village of Dweima on October 28, 1948, in which an estimated 500 men, women, and children were killed by a regular Israeli army unit.

community miraculously defeated overwhelming Arab forces is a myth and has been exploded by such Jewish historians as Simha Flapam, in his *The Birth of Israel: Myths and Realities* (1987), and Benny Morris, in *The Birth of the Palestinian Refugee Problem: 1947–1949* (1987). Furthermore, in a lecture delivered in 1990 in Jerusalem, Benny Morris, of the Hebrew University, reported that in the late 1940s and early 1950s, Israeli soldiers and civilians killed thousands of unarmed Palestinians who tried to reenter the country to pick their crops or recover their lost property. Soldiers "used to shoot them on sight," and settlers on kibbutzim would booby-trap water pumps to prevent Palestinians from removing them. The bodies of Palestinians killed in this way would then be booby-trapped in turn to kill anyone who tried to take them away for burial. Such incidents are a reminder of the brutalities the Palestinians suffered and, in the West Bank and Gaza, continue to suffer.

The Israeli state was built on the utter ruin of Arab Palestine and the uprooting of its population—a people that had had no hand in the frightful persecution of the Jews in Europe. Many in the West still see the Jews as victims of a thousand years of persecution, culminating in the obscenity of the Holocaust. But there can be no understanding of Abu Nidal and other angry Palestinians like him unless the impact on them of Israel's victory in 1948 is recognized. These men and women were made homeless, robbed of everything they possessed, forgotten by the world, and constantly taunted by the triumphalism of the victors. The mass exodus of Palestinians from their homeland gave the Israelis their real start in life, but for the losers it remains the supreme tragedy of their history, blotting out the horizon like an impenetrable cloud. To many Palestinians, the Israeli is a murderer and a thief, a brutal conqueror with neither conscience nor humanity.

What happened in 1948 was not the end of a process but the beginning. The repression of Palestinians, the expropriation of land, the building of settlements, the appropriation of scarce resources such as water—all these continue to this day, breeding in the victims of these policies an explosive mixture of rage and despair. However reluctant Israelis and Jews may be to acknowledge it, the terrorism of Abu Nidal and those like him is a reaction to the Jewish victory, which has condemned the Palestinians to a half life of helplessness, insecurity, and uncertain identity.

Perhaps none of this would have happened had the Arabs

accepted the UN proposal in 1947 to partition Palestine into an Arab and a Jewish sector, but they didn't and the result has been more or less unending misery and violence.

From a profound sense of grievance, an obsession with revenge has flowed ineluctably: What was taken by force can only be regained by force. This is the gut feeling of many Palestinians. No middle ground, compromise, or peaceful solution can be entertained. When I first started examining Abu Nidal's career, I felt that this maxim had blinded him to political realities and led him into a life of purposeless terrorism and crime.

YOUTHFUL AGITATOR

Abu Nidal's early teens in the West Bank city of Nablus were difficult. He scraped by on charity from his half-brothers, themselves struggling to survive. He took odd jobs as errand boy and electrician's assistant but deeply resented, as he made plain to friends later in life, his ragged clothes, empty stomach, and lack of education. He tried to attend a government school for a few months, but with no money to support him and having missed so many years already, he simply could not catch up. He faced ridicule, which added to his resentments. However, he was clever and ambitious, and attempting to read on his own, he came upon a semiclandestine news sheet, *al-Yaqzah* (*The Awakening*), which the local Jordanian branch of the Ba'ath party published occasionally on the West Bank.

The Ba'ath in Jordan was an offshoot, in fact the first such offshoot in the Arab world, of the mother party that two Syrian schoolmasters had founded in Damascus in the late 1940s. When Arab feebleness and disarray were exposed by the disaster in Palestine, young people looking for a way forward flocked to join the Ba'ath, with its exciting, if somewhat incoherent, program of Arab "rebirth." It was to become the great nationalist party of the period. The West Bank, and the city of Nablus in particular, packed as it was with embittered refugees, was fertile ground for Ba'athist ideas, especially in the turbulent years that followed the assassination of King Abdallah of Jordan in 1951—killed by a Palestinian for his collusion with Israel during the 1948 war and his proposal to accept its existence after the war. His mentally ill son Talal succeeded him but was soon deposed as unfit to rule. His grandson, the young Hussein, then seventeen, was still untried.

The Ba'ath in Jordan had not yet been given a license to function legally as a political party and was still more or less underground, playing cat-and-mouse with the authorities. But in violent demonstrations, it demanded a greater say for Palestinians in the kingdom's affairs. It also demanded that Jordan end its relationship to Britain, which the Palestinians felt had betrayed them to the Zionists. In 1955, the Ba'ath campaigned to keep Jordan out of the British-inspired Baghdad Pact, and in 1956, during the Suez war, it wanted King Hussein to side with Egypt's Nasser, the nationalists' hero then fighting for his life—and for Arab independence—against Britain, France, and Israel. This Ba'ath was the party that the young Abu Nidal joined when he was eighteen. It was his first taste of radical politics.

But this political experience was short-lived. In April 1957, a group of nationalist officers tried to seize power in Amman but were faced down by Hussein and his loyalist Bedouin troops. The would-be putschists were locked up or sent into exile. The Ba'ath and other radical parties called a congress in Nablus to demand that the officers be reinstated, that the king's advisers be sacked, and that Jordan realign itself away from Britain and the United States and toward Egypt. Agitating, demonstrating, and facing police gunfire, the young Abu Nidal lived every moment of these dramatic events. But the nationalist dream soon faded. Stiffened by Western help, Hussein reasserted his authority, smashing the Ba'ath by mass arrests. Its offices were closed and its paper suspended. Its top men, including the party leader, Abdallah Rimawi, fled to Syria, while young militants like Abu Nidal chose to lie low.

A year later, as Hussein's grip tightened and the Ba'ath party's prospects dimmed, a thoroughly disgruntled Abu Nidal, nursing a hatred for the Hashemites second only to his combined hatred of Israel, Britain, and the United States, went to seek his fortune in Saudi Arabia—one among tens of thousands of young Palestinians who, to escape the stinking, overcrowded refugee camps, headed for the oil-rich kingdom. He made his way to Riyadh and, with a friend, Abu Fadi, set himself up as a housepainter and electrician, trades in which he had dabbled in Nablus. By 1959 the two partners had managed to open a shop on al-Wazir Street, in the Saudi capital.

But distance from Palestine did not blunt Abu Nidal's feelings. On the contrary, the further away he was from the lost homeland, the more he dreamed of "the return," the obsessive idea that filled the minds of countless Palestinians. He still considered himself a Ba'athist—the party had been his school during the Nablus years. But in Saudi Arabia it presented few attractions: It was a puny underground movement, a dozen young men who held meetings in a cellar. In any event, Nasser, who was suspicious of the Ba'ath, had forced the Syrian mother party to dissolve itself at the time of the Syrian-Egyptian Union of 1958, plunging the movement into confusion, which spread to its branches throughout the Arab world. Abdallah Rimawi, head of the Jordanian Ba'ath and the man Abu Nidal had looked up to in his young manhood, left the movement and took refuge in Cairo.

Abu Nidal, in turn, left the Ba'ath, to find another outlet for his restless energies. In his early twenties, already conscious of his latent abilities, he saw himself as something of a leader, seeking to impress others by spinning yarns about his own achievements. He was a fabulist, playing games with the truth, a trait that would grow more pronounced. In Riyadh, gathering around him a group of young men, he founded his own little faction and, in the spirit of the times, gave it the grandiose name of the Palestine Secret Organization. He dreamed of dispatching emissaries throughout the region, of sprouting offshoots, of carrying the fight into "usurped Palestine" itself. Beirut was his first target. It was then considered the political and publishing mecca of the Middle East, the one Arab capital where speech was free enough and the secret police comparatively benign. So in the early 1960s, Abu Nidal staked his savings on sending two young men to Beirut to set up a branch of his secret faction. But his envoys gave up—one became a student, the other went into business—and the venture collapsed.

In striving to get started in the resistance business, Abu Nidal was not unique. In the late 1950s and early 1960s, many Palestinians working in Arab countries, as well as Palestinian students in Europe, attempted in a more or less clandestine fashion to set up their own political organizations. Dozens of groups emerged, although few survived for long. The prime inspiration was the trauma of exile, the suffering of their families, the need to break free from the shackles of Arab host countries—and the burning desire to hit back at Israel.

Of all these organizations, by far the most important was Yasser Arafat's Fatah, which emerged in Kuwait in 1958–59 and was soon to grow into the parent of all Palestinian fighting movements. Fatah had recruits wherever Palestinians were to be found—including Saudi Arabia, where Abu Nidal, a proven activist, was inevitably drawn into the net.

Abu Nidal did not join Fatah as a humble foot soldier. Having run his own "group" and passionately committed to the cause of the resistance, he entered a rung or two higher up on the organizational ladder. He had a head for figures, and his business was doing well. He was lively and entertaining company. He seemed well launched into life. On a visit to Nablus, he met and married a girl, Hiyam al-Bitar, from a good Jaffa family exiled like his own. She was better educated than he was, had been to school and had learned French. But, to his taste, she was agreeably docile, halfway between a traditional Arab wife and a modern woman. She was to bear him a boy and two girls.

In Saudi Arabia, Abu Nidal had been no more than an armchair guerrilla—plotting, talking, dreaming of great deeds, but not actually doing very much. The 1967 war—after 1948, the second traumatic date in the Arab calendar—changed all that. In a lightning preemptive campaign, Israel shattered the armies of its Arab neighbors, seized East Jerusalem and all that was left of Arab Palestine, as well as Egypt's Sinai Peninsula and Syria's Golan Heights, and emerged as the region's superpower, evidently stronger than any combination of Arab states. The West Bank and Gaza, with their teeming Palestinian populations, became the occupied territories, as they remain today. The blow to the Arab psyche, to Arab self-confidence, was colossal. The gangrene of hate ate deeper, as did the thirst for revenge.

Demonstrating against the war and its disastrous outcome, Abu Nidal and his friends were rounded up by the Saudis and expelled as dangerous subversives. But Abu Nidal could not return to the West Bank. His Nablus home had been overrun by the Israelis. The only possible destination was Amman, where Palestinian guerrillas were preparing to fight an enemy whose forward positions had now reached the Jordan River.

A Palestinian acquaintance, Abu Ali Shahin (who was later to spend many years in Israeli jails), remembers Abu Nidal at that time. "He was very fanatical," he told me. "He wanted to go and fight. He didn't believe in religion or Ba'athism or Marxism or anything else. There was no way to recover Palestine except by shedding blood. The gun was his ideology and his ideology was the gun. The gun, only the gun!"

chapter

4

A BLACK SEPTEMBER

"The gun, only the gun!"

Abu Nidal's call to arms after the 1967 war was no more than the standard rhetoric of the time. Traumatized, like practically every other Arab, by Israel's victory, expelled from Saudi Arabia for political agitation, he moved his young family to Amman.

At this time, there were hundreds of thousands of exiled Palestinians like himself who had been waiting for two decades for the Arab states and the United Nations to reverse the harsh verdict of 1948. But now, stricken by another immense disaster, the majority of them united around two basic principles—first, that the "lost homeland," the object of their painful yearning, could be recovered only by armed struggle; and second, that any negotiation with a triumphant Israel could only spell surrender and had therefore to be rejected out of hand.

Taking up arms against Israel was seen as an essential, morale-boosting formula for national salvation—a philosophy in tune with that of other third world liberation movements of the 1960s. But what sort of "armed struggle" could the Palestinians seriously wage against Israeli power?

In Riyadh before the June 1967 war, Abu Nidal's "resistance" had taken the form of excited late-night discussions with fellow members of his Fatah cell. If only the Arabs could mobilize their great potential, they must surely triumph. This was the recurring theme. How could a handful of alien settlers overcome the Arabs' teeming millions? The Arab world was a chained elephant confronting an Israeli mouse: Fatah's task was to break the elephant's chains and release its strength.

Such metaphors did wonders for the morale, but Abu Nidal had had no military training and no experience of any sort of armed conflict. His war talk was far removed from the reality of his situation. By day, he was a manager, a pen pusher. His electrician's shop in Riyadh had grown into a small contracting business. He had made money and had handled it sensibly. On arrival in Jordan, therefore, he did not, like many others, head for one of the ramshackle camps that Fatah was setting up on the Jordan River, within gunshot of the enemy, but installed his family in a decent house in Amman. He had a sense of organization, sorely lacking in much of the chaotic and quarrelsome guerrilla movement, and he could work around the clock.

Within a very short time, he had founded a trading company called Impex, whose offices in central Amman soon became a sort of clandestine Fatah "front," a place where people could meet when they came into town and where funds for the guerrillas and their families could be received and paid out. For all his talk of revolutionary violence, Abu Nidal was by nature orderly and methodical, a bureaucrat of armed struggle rather than a fighter, qualities that were noticed and appreciated by Yasser Arafat and other Fatah leaders.

It was in those early months in Jordan that he met and was befriended by Abu Iyad, Fatah's long-serving intelligence chief. In one of our talks, fluent and slightly ironic as ever, Abu Iyad told me that he had first heard the name Sabri al-Banna soon after the June war.

"He had been recommended to me as a man of energy and enthusiasm, but he seemed shy when we met," Abu Iyad recalled. "It was only on further acquaintance that I noticed other traits: He was extremely good company, with a sharp tongue and an inclination to dismiss most of humanity as spies and traitors. I rather liked that! I discovered he was very ambitious, perhaps more than his abilities warranted, and also very excitable. He sometimes worked himself up into such a state that he lost all powers of reasoning."

Abu Iyad enjoyed the younger man's readiness to criticize

everything and everybody, not least Yasser Arafat. With the cheekiness of youth, Sabri al-Banna, who now adopted the alias Abu Nidal, behaved as if he were Arafat's equal, because, before joining Fatah, he had been the boss of a tiny Palestinian outfit. Abu Nidal dared say things for which Abu Iyad and other Fatah leaders had a sneaking sympathy—notably, that Arafat was a dictator who was inclined to rush into impulsive decisions without first consulting his colleagues.

Abu Nidal often drove down to the Jordan valley to visit Abu Iyad at Karameh, a village where Fatah had set up a military base and from which it attempted, somewhat incompetently, to infiltrate men across the river into the occupied West Bank. Karameh was squalid, and Sabri was appalled at the wretched conditions in which Yasser Arafat and Abu Iyad lived. Why did it have to be such a shambles? In contrast, when Abu Iyad paid Abu Nidal a return visit in Amman, he would stay at his clean and comfortable house, have a square meal, take a shower, get a good night's sleep, and play with his host's two young children, Nidal and Badia.

Abu Nidal had no taste for the romantic heroics of the fedayeen or for their extraordinary capacity for getting themselves killed. Abu Dawud, a giant some six feet six inches tall, who would eventually in 1970 command all of Fatah's guerrilla forces in Jordan, remembers that in those days Abu Nidal carried a pistol but was never known to have fired it. In skirmishes in Amman between Hussein's troops and the guerrillas Abu Dawud was out fighting, but Abu Nidal stayed safely indoors, never leaving his office, let alone taking part in the street battles. To a tidy mind like his, such wild and unplanned clashes against superior forces were sheer madness.

By late 1968 or early 1969, Abu Nidal had persuaded Abu Iyad that his talents lay in diplomacy rather than guerrilla warfare and had secured a posting as Fatah's representative to Khartoum.

In the Sudan, Abu Nidal worked hard and intelligently, made contacts across the spectrum of local politics and was soon on good terms with the new regime of Ja'far al-Numeiri, the thirty-five-year-old colonel who, in the summer of 1969, had seized power in Khartoum. It was Abu Nidal's first proper job for the Palestinian cause and a spur to his ambition.

Why did Abu Nidal leave Amman? The question has long been pondered in Palestinian circles. Abandoning his trading company,

Impex, and his Fatah comrades, he ducked out just when the guerrillas in Jordan were coming under intense pressure from both Israel and King Hussein—a move that later earned him the charge of cowardice. Perhaps he was simply more careful than others.

THE STRATEGY OF TERROR

A history of recurrent defeat forced Palestinian leaders, Abu Nidal among them, to think hard about the strategy of armed struggle—the attempt to send guerrillas on sabotage missions inside Israeli territory—which they adopted with blithe amateurishness in the mid-1960s. Israel's counterstrategy was to lash out ferociously not only against the guerrillas themselves, on the principle of an eye for an eyelash, but also against the Arab countries that gave them sanctuary. Inevitably, the host countries turned on the guerrillas, as happened in Jordan and later in Lebanon: Made to choose between helping the guerrillas and sparing themselves Israeli reprisals, the Arab states not unnaturally put their own security first.

Abu Nidal seems to have had doubts about the way the Palestinian struggle was being conducted. Rather than open confrontation, he preferred the indirect approach, preparation in the shadows, the blow struck when and where the enemy least expected it.

How did this strategy evolve? Under the pressure of events, his ideas seem to have taken shape gradually between 1968 and 1973, by which time Abu Nidal had developed the tactics and the methods—in a word, the terrorism—for which he was to become infamous.

Men who knew him then report that he was much influenced by, and in fact modeled himself on, right-wing Jewish terrorist movements. He was in particular much impressed by the Irgun, the brainchild of the Russian-born agitator Vladimir Jabotinsky, who called for the unabashed use of force—an "iron wall"—against the Arabs to establish full Jewish sovereignty over both banks of the Jordan, an agenda adopted by his loyal disciples Yitzhak Shamir and Menachem Begin. Abu Nidal was also struck by the Irgun's more extreme offshoot, the Stern Gang, which under Shamir and others played a crucial role in unnerving both the Arabs and the British in the struggle for the Jewish state. During the Arab rebellion of 1936–39, the Stern Gang was the first to introduce terrorism to the Middle East by exploding bombs on buses and in Arab markets and, in November 1944, by assassinating Lord Moyne, the British resident minister in the Middle East. The Irgun also used terror against British and Arab targets. Its most eye-catching and notorious exploit was blowing up the King David Hotel in Jerusalem in July 1946, where the British had set up their headquarters. More than a hundred people died in the attack. By today's debased standards, such carnage might seem relatively small scale, but the shock at the time was colossal, and Abu Nidal is said to have been much affected by these acts when he learned about them later, as a young man.

His former comrades told me that in the late sixties, Abu Nidal was forever brooding over the lessons to be learned from the loss of Palestine. Where had the Palestinians gone wrong? In the mid-1930s, they had risen in spontaneous revolt against massive Jewish immigration, but the British had crushed them, reducing the Palestinian community as a whole to helpless spectators for the duration of the Second World War. By contrast, tens of thousands of Jews served in Allied armies and learned how to fight (including the teachings of sabotage and terrorism, which some of them used to devastating effect in 1947–48 against the ill-prepared Arab population of Palestine and the rabble forces of the Arab states).

From 1948 to 1965, as Israel grew stronger and stronger, the Palestinians did nothing. It was not until 1965, seventeen years after the loss of Palestine, that Fatah started small-scale military incursions into Israel with the goal not so much of fighting Israel alone—Fatah knew that this was impossible—but of dragging the Arab states into a war that, it hoped, would restore Palestinian "rights." This, in turn, proved a gross miscalculation, not least of Arab military strength. Indeed, although the guerrillas inflicted no significant damage on Israel, they helped precipitate the Six-Day War. Early in 1967, they implicated their Syrian backers in their inept incursions, arousing fears that Israel would retaliate against Syria and try to topple its radical regime. Egypt's President Nasser, who posed as the leader of the Arabs, could not stand by and let this happen. Fearing that an Israeli attack on Syria might catch him unawares and suck him in, he sought to bring the crisis under his direct control by shifting its focus from Syria to Sinai, where he indulged in some saber-rattling of his own. With half his army in

Yemen (fighting the royalists in the civil war there), Nasser had no intention of attacking Israel. But he did challenge a vital Israeli interest by closing the Red Sea shipping lane to Eilat, a route Israel had opened in the Suez war of 1956. Israel seized on this *casus belli* and smashed Egypt, together with its Syrian and Jordanian allies, in its devastating preemptive attack of June 1967 (as William B. Quandt has explained in his *Decade of Decision* [1977] and as I have written about in *Asad of Syria: The Struggle for the Middle East* [1989]).

The disastrous experience of 1967 should have discredited the old guerrilla strategy, but the Palestinians were seduced into believing that despite the defeat of regular Arab armies, "armed struggle" could still be waged against Israel, on the Algerian or Vietnamese model, in the form of a popular liberation war. Young Palestinian recruits were sent, without much preparation, to set up "revolutionary cells" in the occupied West Bank, more or less in full view of the enemy. With no *maquis* to hide them, they were soon rounded up or killed. By early 1968, such ineffectual pinpricks had been virtually ended and Israel was ready to counterattack against guerrilla bases in Jordan—and then against Jordan itself, predictably creating grave tensions between the guerrillas and the king.

Two events in 1968 were of great importance in that they set the Palestinians off once more in the wrong direction. The first occurred in March, when an Israeli armored force of 15,000 men, with air support, crossed the river and attacked Fatah's guerrilla base, at Karameh in Jordan, with overwhelming strength. The base and much of the village were wiped out, with heavy losses. However, the guerrillas fought back bravely and, with help from the Jordanian army, managed to inflict significant casualties on the Israelis. At a time when Arab demoralization was total in the aftermath of 1967, the fact that the Arabs had actually put up something of a fight was hailed as a great victory. Half the population of Amman rushed out to Karameh to embrace the surviving guerrillas, and thousands flocked to join their ranks. Carried aloft on a wave of popular sentiment, the idolized guerrillas considered themselves demigods and swaggered about Amman and other cities, with scant regard for the local authorities. Not surprisingly, King Hussein saw their undisciplined posturings as a threat to himself and began cooperating secretly with Israel to contain them.

A second decisive event was the hijacking in July 1968 of an El Al passenger plane on a scheduled flight from Rome to Tel Aviv and its diversion to Algiers. Women, children, and non-Israelis on board were soon freed, but to Israel's rage, the remaining twelve Israeli men among the passengers were held for thirty-nine days and were only released in exchange for fifteen Palestinians detained in Israeli jails.

This was the first terrorist operation of its kind, the prototype for many others to come, and its mastermind was Wadi Haddad, a Palestinian revolutionary from Safad who had graduated as a medical doctor from the American University of Beirut. Outraged by the violence Israel had done to his people, he had vowed to use violence in return. With three American University friends and contemporaries—Syrian Hani al-Hindi, Palestinian George Habash, and Kuwaiti Ahmad al-Khatib, the last two medical doctors like himself—Haddad founded a political party, the Movement of Arab Nationalists (MAN), which was to develop offshoots in several Arab countries. Its banner was a three-word slogan, "Fire, Iron, and Revenge," and its philosophy was that until the Palestinians regained their rights, the whole world could burn.

Not long after Fatah embarked on "armed struggle," Habash and Haddad gathered the Palestinian members of MAN into a separate organization that became the Popular Front for the Liberation of Palestine (PFLP). Envious of the bigger and more solidly implanted Fatah, and unable to match Fatah's operations on the ground, the PFLP resorted instead to terrorist spectaculars, such as the El Al hijacking, which won it immense prestige among Arabs and set the pace for the resistance as a whole.

Had the first hijacked plane not been Israeli, such piracy might have been rejected by the Palestinians themselves from the very beginning. It needs to be recalled that in the twenty years from 1948 to 1968, the Palestinians had never considered attacking an Israeli, still less a Jew, outside Israel. Terror was not on their agenda. From 1965 onward, Fatah's "armed struggle" was directed at such targets as Israeli water pipelines and railway tracks. Fatah disapproved of hijacking and had no intention of following the PFLP's example. But because the PFLP's target had been an "enemy" plane, the Arab world was loath to condemn the hijacking.

After this first "success," Wadi Haddad went on to hijack planes of other nations and to establish relations with European and Japanese terrorist groups. An unexpected windfall was that airlines started to pay him large sums in protection money. For example, two international airlines paid Haddad $1 million a month each, monies that he turned over to his organization and that allowed the PFLP to acquire a measure of independence from its Arab sponsors.

In Jordan, meanwhile, the overconfident guerrillas started preaching sedition against King Hussein and calling openly for his overthrow. Excited by the precedent of Aden, where armed irregulars affiliated with MAN had forced the British out, then routed their local rivals and seized power, some guerrillas believed that power in Jordan, too, was theirs for the taking. The crunch came in September 1970, when, in a hijacking orgy, the PFLP forced no fewer than three passenger planes to land at a disused airstrip in Jordan. An outraged King Hussein determined to fight back. Stiffened by the United States and by a threat of intervention by Israel, he unleashed his tanks against the guerrillas and his air force against some Syrian armor that had crossed halfheartedly into Jordan in their support. In the running street battles and the shelling of the refugee camps, several hundred guerrillas were killed, another three thousand were captured, and some ten thousand Palestinians were wounded, most of them civilians. Such was the gruesome balance sheet of that "black" September.

At a stroke, the guerrillas lost their vital sanctuary in Jordan, from which they had dreamed of pushing Israel back from the Jordan River—and so liberating Palestine inch by inch. The dream and the strategy had now to be abandoned, plunging the whole guerrilla movement into distress and disillusion.

From distant Khartoum, Abu Nidal followed the unfolding drama as best he could. But in early 1970, unable to contain himself any longer, he turned up in Amman, several months before the disastrous September denouement. He was there by February, in time to witness one of the first serious clashes between the guerrillas and the army, and it profoundly affected him.

Both militarily and politically, it seemed to him that the Palestinians were set on the wrong course. Militarily, their "armed struggle" had been totally ineffective and had lost them the sympathy and backing of Jordan, the Arab country with the longest frontier with Israel. Politically, the Palestinian resistance was far from a disciplined or cohesive movement. Commando groups had formed, merged, disbanded, split, and changed their names in a bewildering dance that outsiders found incomprehensible. These groups were divided by personal hatreds and rivalries but also by divergent views on how to achieve the common objective of the recovery of Palestinian land and the establishment of a Palestinian state.

The Palestine Liberation Organization, the "umbrella" apparatus for the resistance movement as a whole, had been born out of the decisions of the first Arab Summit Conference, of January 1964, when Arab leaders, unable to do anything about a major water pipeline Israel was then completing to carry Jordan water to the Negev, decided to defuse Palestinian anger and frustration by giving the Palestinians an organization of their own. Ahmad Shuquairy, a loquacious Palestinian lawyer who had never carried a gun, was made PLO chairman and a Palestine National Charter was approved, calling for the destruction of Israel. It remained a dead letter until June 1967, when the defeat of Arab regular armies stimulated the emergence of Palestinian commando groups, of which Fatah was the best organized and the most powerful.

By 1969, Yasser Arafat had become PLO chairman and Fatah had gained control both of the PLO Executive Committee and of the Palestine National Council, the Palestinians' parliament-in-exile. Being far and away the biggest of the commando groups, Fatah could, and no doubt should, have imposed its will on the other factions and unified the resistance movement into an effective force. As it represented the reasonably pragmatic mainstream, it could have saved the Palestinians a lot of heartache had it done so. But for reasons that remain obscure, Arafat and his colleagues felt it best to accommodate within the PLO the various shades of Palestinian opinion, with the result that from the very beginning, the PLO was paralyzed by internal quarrels.

Arafat had to contend not only with George Habash's PFLP, founded in December 1967, which vociferously rejected any thought of a compromise settlement with Israel, but also with Nayif Hawatmeh's Democratic Front for the Liberation of Palestine (DFLP), a Marxist organization formed in 1969 by extreme leftist defectors from both the PFLP and MAN, dedicated to an anti-imperialist third world liberation struggle. Another group that was to give Arafat a lot of trouble was Ahmad Jibril's PFLP–General Command, formed in 1968 from a split in the PFLP. Jibril, a stalwart military man, had been an early commando, with a history of guerrilla activity stretching back to 1959. His blunt philosophy was that the Palestinians should spend less time talking and more time fighting. Supported by Syria and Libya, he specialized in suicide raids into Israel.

Arafat had also to wrestle with two pressure groups controlled, respectively, by Syria and Iraq, states that were not inclined to leave the all-engrossing and highly dangerous confrontation with Israel in Palestinian hands alone. Syria's outfit was known as al-Sa'iqa (the Thunderbolt), formed in 1968 with members from the Palestinian branch of Syria's Ba'ath party. Its Iraqi equivalent, a rival of al-Sa'iqa, was the Arab Liberation Front (ALF), formed in 1969 by Palestinians close to Iraq's Ba'ath party. And this was by no means the end of the story. Other groups, with varied sponsors and objectives, emerged in subsequent years to muddy Palestinian waters and render it virtually impossible for a clear strategy to emerge or for the PLO to project a coherent message to the outside world.

Prominent among the troublemakers whom Arafat failed to control was Abu'l Abbas, leader of the Palestine Liberation Front, a small offshoot from Jibril's organization, which enjoyed first Iraqi and then Libyan backing. Among its later exploits, all disastrous for the Palestinian cause, were the seizure of the *Achille Lauro* in October 1985 and the murder of a crippled Jew on board, and then, in May 1990, an abortive guerrilla raid on the Israeli coast at Tel Aviv, which caused the United States to suspend its dialogue with the PLO.

ENVOY TO BAGHDAD

None of this was to Abu Nidal's liking. Early in 1970, foreseeing the coming showdown with King Hussein, he started to pester Abu Iyad, and indeed anyone in the Palestinian leadership who would listen, to send him once more to represent Fatah abroad—this time in Baghdad. As it happened, at that moment Fatah badly needed someone to lobby the Iraq government. Iraq had some fourteen thousand men stationed in Jordan, elements of a short-lived Arab "Eastern Command" that had once included Egypt and Syria. The Fatah leaders were anxious to know if they could count on these Iraqi troops to side with them in the event of an all-out fight with Hussein. To sound out Iraqi intentions, Arafat and Abu Iyad had in July 1970 met secretly with two leading members of the Iraqi regime, Abd al-Khaliq Samirra'i, a member of the Revolutionary

Command Council, and the interior minister, General Salih Mahdi Ammash, at an Iraqi army camp near the Jordanian town of Zarqa. They had been given assurances that Iraqi troops would fight with them. But Fatah needed someone in Baghdad who could hold the Iraqis to this pledge, someone able and forceful enough to make personal contact with President Ahmad Hasan al-Bakr and his army commander, General Hardan al-Takriti. Abu Nidal seemed the right man for the job.

In late July, just two months before all hell broke loose in Amman, he took up his new post in Baghdad, leaving the anarchy of Jordan behind him and once again arousing the suspicions of some of his comrades that he was running away to save his skin.

But Abu Nidal failed in his mission. When King Hussein's tanks blasted guerrilla positions that September, the Iraqis did not move. The battles between the Jordanian army and the fedayeen raged on for ten days with the dead and wounded piling up in the streets, but Fatah's desperate cries for help were ignored in Baghdad.

Arafat narrowly escaped capture, but Abu Iyad and another prominent Fatah leader, Abu al-Lutf (Faruq Qaddumi), later known as the PLO's "foreign minister," were seized by the Jordanians and interned. To break their morale, their captors made them listen to a tape of a telephone conversation between King Hussein and General Takriti in which the Iraqi commander confirmed that, *in accordance with their prior agreement,* Iraqi forces would not intervene. Iraq had betrayed the guerrillas.

The Fatah leaders were soon to have another shock. Immediately after the September carnage, Abu Nidal began to attack them over the Voice of Palestine, their own radio station in Baghdad, accusing them of cowardice in battle and condemning them for having agreed to a cease-fire with King Hussein. The man Abu Nidal singled out for particular abuse was none other than Abu Iyad, his old friend and mentor, who had given him the job in Baghdad.

Abu Iyad told me that, in retrospect, he had come to believe that something important had happened to Abu Nidal in 1969 or 1970 to set him on this new and suspect course. He wondered whether Abu Nidal had been recruited in Khartoum by Iraqi intelligence or by the Mossad. It was a puzzle Abu Iyad wrestled with until the end of his life.

By 1971, as Abu Nidal continued his radio attacks on his Fatah comrades, Arafat and his chief military colleague, Abu Jihad, decided to expel him from Fatah. But Abu Iyad advised caution. He was the butt of Abu Nidal's wounding criticism, but he felt it would be wrong to lose such an able man to the Iraqis—that is, until they could get an explanation from him for his alarming change of attitude. Moreover, Iraq was likely to interpret Abu Nidal's expulsion from Fatah as a criticism of itself. Fatah had just clashed bitterly with Jordan, and Abu Iyad thought it should beware of quarreling with Iraq as well.

In 1972, Iraq invited Fatah to send a delegation to Baghdad to discuss their increasingly sour relations. The delegation consisted of Abu Iyad, Abu al-Lutf, and Abu Mazin (Mahmud Abbas). High on their agenda for the talks was Iraq's failure to assist them in Jordan in their hour of need. As Abu Iyad recalled, Abu Nidal met them at the airport, but Abu Iyad was angry with him and refused to shake his hand.

They were soon deep in discussions with Iraq's leaders, notably with Abd al-Khaliq Samirra'i, the man who had promised them that Iraqi troops would intervene on their behalf and who was understandably embarrassed because the promise had not been kept.

"He took us to see President Bakr," Abu Iyad told me. "On the way there he tried to prepare us for what to expect. 'You won't be able to stay very long,' he warned. 'The president is tired. Don't bother to embrace him when you greet him.' The first thing that struck me as we entered Bakr's office was that he didn't rise from his desk. Such discourtesy from an Arab ruler toward Palestinian leaders was unheard of! I could sense that Samirra'i was getting still more embarrassed."

By all accounts, it was a glacial meeting. As it drew to a close, Abu Iyad said, "Mr. President, it seems you are busy. Please allow us to take our leave. But before we go, may I just say that we were upset by the decision not to support us in Jordan—no doubt taken without your knowledge."

"It was *my* decision!" Bakr snapped back. "*I* personally supervised the withdrawal of Iraqi troops." At this Abu Iyad felt compelled to ask the president for his reasons, to which Bakr replied: "You in the Palestinian resistance have nine lives, like a cat. If they kill you, you can rise again. But we are a regime! In Jordan in 1970, there was a conspiracy to draw us into a battle in order to destroy us. And had we been destroyed, we would have been finished!"

"And that was it," Abu Iyad told me. "The whole meeting barely lasted ten minutes. Once outside the room, I took Abu Nidal aside, cursed him, and gave him a piece of my mind. 'Is this the regime you are defending?' I stormed. That evening I went to his house and had it out with him in the presence of his wife. I said he had tied himself too closely to the Iraqis. I had heard he had a special relationship with Sa'dun Shakir, then head of Iraqi intelligence.

"Abu Nidal flew into a rage at my accusation. 'I'm no one's agent!' he protested. But my doubts persisted. Before I came to suspect a possible Mossad link, I believed that Iraqi intelligence had contacted him when he was in the Sudan and that his eagerness to be transferred to Baghdad had not been entirely his own idea."

However, even after this visit, Abu Iyad advised his colleagues in Fatah that it would be better if they tried to contain Abu Nidal rather than expel him, not to risk pushing him even further into the arms of the Iraqis. As Abu Iyad admitted to me, he was still fond of him. But he was worried by what was happening to him. There was something about Abu Nidal that frightened him. He did not, however, share his anxieties with his colleagues.

The Fatah leaders had to face the grim fact that their man in Baghdad had switched allegiance. Instead of defending their interests, he had made himself the echo of Baghdad's views and sniped at them over the airwaves. Abu Nidal had become a painful thorn in their flesh, but as he now enjoyed Iraqi protection, they could not easily pluck him out.

BIRTH OF BLACK SEPTEMBER

The matter of Abu Nidal's indiscipline was dwarfed by the turmoil into which the whole Palestinian movement was thrown by its catastrophic clash with King Hussein, and which was to be the backdrop to the next stage in Abu Nidal's development. The battle for Amman of September 1970 had routed the guerrillas but also profoundly divided them. When, at the height of the fighting, the besieged Fatah's leaders grasped that the king was out to destroy them, they held a council of war and decided to disperse—in effect, to run away. Some went to Cairo or Damascus, others went underground. The instinct was to survive to fight another day.

But some commanders would not give up the fight, chief among them being the fearsome, if misguided, Abu Ali Iyad (not to be confused with Abu Iyad), who had won prominence as a guerrilla leader during the battle of Karameh. Before that, he had been Fatah's chief military instructor at its camp in Al-Hameh, near Damascus, where he had been responsible for training Palestinian recruits, some hardly more than fourteen or fifteen years old. These *ashbal,* or "tiger cubs," were in great awe of him because of his strict discipline and fierce appearance: He had lost an eye and damaged a leg in an experiment with explosives.

After the battle of Amman, Abu Ali Iyad would not run away. Determined to carry on the fight, he headed north with a group of his tiger cubs to the wild country around Jarash and Ajlun in Jordan, where there were woods and caves to hide in. It was a suicide mission. In house-to-house combat in Amman, the guerrillas had had a chance against Hussein's armor, but out in the open they were no match for it. Abu Ali Iyad was lame and practically blind. The terrain was rough. In the early summer of 1971, the king sent troops to hunt him down. Their orders were strict and no quarter was given. Palestinians say that tanks were driven over the bodies of wounded men, providing a sight so harrowing that some seventy of Abu Ali Iyad's cubs fled across the river and, waving white shirts, preferred to surrender to the Israelis rather than face death at the hand of Hussein's troops.

On July 23, 1971, Abu Ali Iyad was reported killed. However, such was the wildness of the place that his corpse was never found. A few days earlier he had sent a man down the mountain with a letter to the Fatah leaders, bitterly criticizing them for running away and ending with a phrase that was to become the rallying cry of the survivors—"We will die on our feet rather than kneel." Those of his tiger cubs who escaped the carnage broke up into small clandestine groups, acquired arms and explosives, and vowed to avenge him.

Four months later, on November 28, Jordan's prime minister, Wasfi al-Tal, who had been King Hussein's right-hand man during the onslaught on the guerrillas and a fanatical enemy of the Palestinians, was shot dead in Cairo, on the steps of the Sheraton Hotel. "At last I have done it. I am satisfied, I have spilled Tal's blood!"

one of his killers, Munshir Khalifa, was heard to say defiantly on his arrest. Khalifa was one of Abu Ali Iyad's cubs. With this assassination, the Palestinian terrorist campaign known as Black September was born.

That Tal had been made to pay for the slaughter of the Palestinians was a source of exhilaration in guerrilla circles. Spirits that had been downcast were now raised and a great impetus was given to violence. Some fighters, with little grasp of reality, imagined that Tal's disappearance would allow them to return to Jordan and resume their fight against Israel from there. But as it turned out, the Palestinians' resort to terrorism was not a prelude to further armed struggle but only a tawdry substitute for it. Tal's murder was an expression of Palestinian weakness and frustration rather than of real Palestinian militancy.

The resistance movement in 1971 was in utter disarray. It had been crushed by Israel on the West Bank and by Hussein's army on the East Bank. The rebellious Gaza Strip, teeming with hapless refugees, had suffered the same death and destruction. In that year alone, nearly a thousand "terrorists"—Israel's term for whoever dared challenge its rule—were killed or captured under the heavy hand of General Ariel Sharon. Elite Israeli commando units were unleashed against the civilian population. There were prolonged curfews, demolition of homes, torture, summary executions, mass detention of families of wanted men, and the destruction of orchards, the only means of subsistence.

Desperate for a safe haven, survivors from all these battlefields regrouped in southeast Lebanon, only to be pursued there by punitive Israeli raids. Every man's hand was against them. No one, it seemed, was ready to accept the Palestinian resistance movement as a serious political force. Maddened by the killing of their fellows, hounded on every side, but also, it must be said, excited by the media attention the early hijackings had received, some fighters from all the various Palestinian factions turned in 1972 to "foreign operations"—in other words, to terrorism. Their inability to hit the enemy on his home ground had convinced them that their only option was to seek targets abroad.

TERROR AND COUNTERTERROR

The dirty war of terror and counterterror between Israel and the Palestinians of 1972–73 was something of a new phenomenon, different in significant ways from the violence that preceded it and from the violence that was to follow. Before 1972, terrorist attacks on Israeli and foreign targets were the work not of Yasser Arafat's Fatah, which disapproved of such "adventurism," but of radical groups like George Habash's PFLP. Such, for example, was the PFLP attack on December 26, 1968, on an El Al Boeing at the Athens airport, in which one Israeli was killed. Characteristically, Israel responded two days later with a one-hour commando raid on the Beirut airport in which thirteen *Lebanese* civilian planes, more or less Lebanon's entire fleet, were destroyed.

And such again was the PFLP hijacking, on August 30, 1969, of a TWA Boeing on a flight from Rome to Tel Aviv and its diversion to Damascus. Two Israelis on board were quietly exchanged for two captured Syrian pilots, but Israel's response then took the familiar form of air raids, artillery barrages, and ground assaults against Arab and Palestinian targets. Reprisals became still more violent when Golda Meir took over as Israel's prime minister in March 1969, inaugurating a policy of "active self-defense," which meant seeking out and destroying Palestinians—before or in case they attacked. Such state terror, aimed at liquidating Israel's enemies, was a good deal more destructive than the disastrous strategy of haphazard terror pursued by the guerrillas, although it did not always find its mark. In July 1970, Mossad agents fired rockets into the Beirut apartment of Wadi Haddad of the PFLP but failed to hit their quarry.

In 1972–73, there was a significant change of pattern when, under the banner of Black September, Fatah radicals joined with Wadi Haddad and others in a widespread terrorist campaign. Three distinct trends were discernible: Some of these militants wanted to kill Israelis; others wanted to put pressure on King Hussein to release the three thousand Palestinian prisoners held in his jails since September 1970 and allow the guerrillas back into Jordan; still others wanted to attack American targets, especially airlines and oil companies, to punish the U.S. for its support of Israel. In the dirty war that followed, both Israel and its opponents, abandoning all restraint, resorted repeatedly to murder.

Black September made a great impact on Abu Nidal. He admired its operations. But he was not part of it—in fact, its angry young men ignored him. They did not want him to participate in their operations even though several of them were actually planned and launched from Baghdad, where he was based. He was already drinking heavily, seemed overly self-important, and they felt he might spoil any operation in which he took part. None of these avenging tiger cubs were later to join his organization. But their indirect influence on Abu Nidal was considerable. He resented being left out and was determined to force his way in. As a challenge of sorts, he threw himself into terrorism, as if to convince those Palestinians already engaged in it that he was stronger and more effective than they were. Undercover work, identifying the enemy's weak spots, and hitting him hard—all these accorded with his temperament and fitted in with the philosophy he was then evolving.

But by 1973, after the murders and counter-murders of the War of the Spooks, Fatah and Israel were ready to conclude an unofficial truce. Fatah was now in a stronger position to regain control over undisciplined Palestinian fighters still thirsting for revenge, partly because Muslim opinion in Lebanon had rallied massively behind the resistance after an Israeli commando raid in central Beirut in which three top Fatah leaders were killed. As a result the Palestinian movement felt more secure in Lebanon. For another, the October War of 1973 had opened up prospects for a peaceful settlement, taking the sting out of Palestinian frustrations and making terror seem largely irrelevent.

It is often said that Black September was a secret arm of Yasser Arafat's Fatah. The truth is more complex. Some Fatah commanders approved of Wasfi al-Tal's killing, the incident that launched the violent movement. But Black September was never officially authorized by Fatah, nor was it a structured organization at Arafat's command. It was more a kind of mutiny within Fatah, a protest by disgruntled fighters at what they considered the blunders and passivity of their leaders.

Angry, vengeful guerrillas, graduates of the same camps, often friends or relatives bound together by common loyalties and common hatreds, were not easily reined in. To bring these mutineers under control, the Fatah leadership had to provide them with political cover. Within Fatah, Abu Iyad defended the young terrorists, and did so as well for international consumption. For example, he justified the attack on the Israeli athletes at Munich—an operation that, perhaps more than any other, tarnished the Palestinians' reputation—with the specious argument that Israel had taken the Palestinians' rightful place at the games. Because of such ill-conceived pronouncements he has been considered the mastermind behind Munich. Whether or not he was directly involved in planning the operation is still a matter of controversy, but as he disingenuously remarked to me in Tunis in the summer of 1990, "Defense lawyers are often called upon to defend causes they don't believe in!"

One device Fatah adopted to tame Abu Ali Iyad's tiger cubs, aged at the time between seventeen and twenty-four, was to marry them off. An Arabic proverb says that marriage makes a man both prudent and thrifty. One of Wasfi al-Tal's killers is now married and the father of seven children.

THE FATAH CONGRESS

Meanwhile, in Baghdad Abu Nidal had become, despite his public row over the airwaves with his Fatah colleagues, very much a diplomat. As chief Fatah representative in Iraq in the early 1970s, he spent his days making contacts in the media, meeting Arab and foreign envoys, and improving his relations with the Iraqi authorities. The Iraqis thought he was good at his job—no doubt because he defended their point of view. But on the quiet, he was up to something quite different: stitching together, with like-minded men in Iraq and other Arab countries, a secret group inside Fatah opposed to Yasser Arafat.

The immediate backdrop to his conspiracy was the Palestinians' catastrophic defeat in Jordan and the subsequent dirty war with Israel, which, as is clear from the list I drew up at the start, took a heavy toll of Palestinian lives. Within the resistance movement, radicals and moderates were quarreling over what had gone wrong and how to proceed. Abu Nidal had already emerged as a leading radical at Fatah's Third Congress, the first big Palestinian postmortem on events in Jordan, which was held late in 1971 at Hammuriya, in the leafy outskirts of Damascus, some six months before Black September first made itself known when it hijacked the Sabena flight from Vienna to Tel Aviv. What the Fatah leaders did not know at this time was that Abu Nidal had already moved beyond verbal criticism and was actually plotting against them.

As the mainstream Palestinian leader, Arafat tried to steady his reeling followers at the congress by pleading for political realism and defending his cease-fire with King Hussein. It had been a clear mistake, he argued, for fringe groups like the PFLP to force a showdown with the king. Such a political miscalculation should not be allowed to recur, and now that the Palestinians had given vent to their rage by killing Wasfi al-Tal, any further violence would only play into the hands of their enemies.

Arafat's arguments were violently contested by a "leftist" group that included Abu Dawud, the intellectual Naji Allush, an admirer of third world revolutions—and Abu Nidal, who had become their chief spokesman. Far from making it up with the king, they clamored for a campaign of sabotage and terror to bring him down. He was the enemy of the Palestinian people! A war of "continuous explosions" should be waged against him. Rather than the old bankrupt strategy of armed struggle by ill-trained, poorly armed guerrillas, the resistance should go underground and launch military operations from clandestine bases. Abu Nidal was the most vocal exponent of these ideas.

Fatah was used to being racked by fierce disputes over policy and also over what were known, in the jargon, as "organizational questions," in other words disputes over how power was to be exercised. The resistance movement was in a state of almost permanent dissidence. Military officers had mounted a number of minor mutinies against Arafat, while some political cadres, rebelling against their leader's "personal style," castigated his mistakes and fallibilities, his reluctance to consult, and his tight grip on the purse strings, one of the ways he has maintained his power over the Palestinian movement. As has already been suggested, Arafat's closest colleagues were not unhappy to hear these criticisms, because they felt that they served as a healthy brake on Arafat's natural authoritarianism. Abu Iyad, himself on the left of Fatah, had considerable sympathy for the rebels. As he told me, he was not much upset by Abu Nidal's diatribes at the congress because he still thought of him as a sort of wayward disciple whose career he had launched.

The radicals were united on two issues: First, they demanded more democracy within Fatah, an issue on which they had majority support; second, they pressed for violent action against King Hussein—a policy that, after the disasters in Jordan, was rejected as "adventurist." Had they chosen to fight on the first issue, they might have won; but instead, they chose the second, allowing Arafat to steer the congress away from their incendiary views and gain the upper hand. It was the last Fatah congress Abu Nidal was to attend. But he had made his mark.

Shortly afterward, his radicalism and personal ambition were further stimulated when, as a Fatah representative, he led a three-man mission, which included his friend Abu Dawud, on a ten-day journey to China and North Korea, from March 28, 1972, to April 8, 1972. They flew from Kuwait to Shanghai, where a private plane took them on to Beijing. But as they approached the Chinese capital, they ran into a storm. Temporarily unable to land, they circled the city to Abu Nidal's increasingly vocal alarm. Not knowing any English, he could not follow the pilot's explanation. "Why are we doing this?" he hollered. "Why aren't we landing?" Suffering what appeared to be an attack of hysteria, he found he could no longer move his legs. To calm him down, Abu Dawud tried to engage him in a game of chess, but as Abu Dawud told me later, Abu Nidal remained hysterical until the aircraft finally came down.

Cut off from the world and still in the throes of its "cultural revolution," China received the Arab delegation as if they were the leaders of the whole Palestinian movement. Abu Nidal was gratified and remained on excellent terms with the Chinese for the next decade. His fanatical nature found considerable affinity with Maoism. His quarrel with the Soviets may also have contributed to the warm welcome he received from the Chinese. Abu Nidal had come to dislike the Soviet diplomats he met in Baghdad, and they in turn found him too reckless for their taste. Their main quarrel was over the boundaries of a future Palestinian homeland: The Soviets backed the 1967 boundaries, whereas Abu Nidal dreamed of those of 1948, preaching the destruction of Israel and the recovery of the whole of Palestine.

As Abu Dawud told me, in discussions with the Chinese, Abu Nidal made it his ingratiating habit to open with a violent diatribe against the Russians, which finally caused Prime Minister Chou En-lai to react. "I don't think you can survive without Soviet help," he chided him. "They are an important force on the international scene, and you must deal with them. But try to avoid becoming a part of their regional strategy."

The Palestinian delegation posed for photographs with Mao

Tse-tung and Chou En-lai before flying on to North Korea for talks, and more photographs, with Kim Il-Sung. Abu Nidal never returned either to China or North Korea, nor did he undergo training in either country, as is sometimes alleged. Still, the trip provided him with some new slogans and a heightened sense of his own importance.

As the head of Fatah in Iraq, Abu Nidal was officially on a par with Fatah's other representatives in Syria, Lebanon, Egypt, and Libya, the main Arab centers of its activity. But following the expulsion of the guerrillas from Jordan, the Iraqi job had become somewhat more important than the others. In Baghdad, Abu Nidal had managed to procure Iraqi documents for thousands of exiled fighters and their families. Iraq was a thoroughfare to the Persian Gulf and the place where Palestinian volunteers from the Gulf came for training in camps put at their disposal by the Iraqi authorities. Arms were stored there. Donations flowed in from ordinary Iraqis. Militancy and political radicalism were in the air under the Ba'athist regime of President Hasan al-Bakr and his formidable deputy, Saddam Hussein. Inevitably, some of Iraq's considerable prestige in Arab affairs rubbed off on Fatah's chief representative in Baghdad.

But with Jordan now lost to them, how were the guerrillas to fight Israel? Many Palestinian fighters believed that they had been unjustly thrown out of Jordan and that King Hussein should be coerced into letting them back in. Many of them still dreamed of waging guerrilla warfare against the Israeli-occupied West Bank, and between 1971 and 1973, the Palestinians attempted repeatedly to placate King Hussein. They appealed to Arab intermediaries like King Faisal of Saudi Arabia to intercede for them, asking to be allowed back to fight Israel in full coordination with the king, if he so wished. But Hussein was not inclined to trust men who had very nearly overthrown him and who had killed his prime minister. Wanting safe and peaceful frontiers with Israel, Hussein firmly rejected their overtures.

Such was the background to Abu Dawud's ambitious plan of February 1973 to lead a sixteen-man hit team into Jordan. In later accounts, the target was said to be the American embassy, but at the time the real aim was to strike at the king, or at least to scare him into releasing the hundreds of Palestinians who had been picked up on the streets and in the camps in 1970–71 and who had been held in jail without trial ever since. Abu Dawud's operation deserves recounting in some detail because of its impact on Abu Nidal's career.

In East Germany, Abu Dawud had learned the trick of taking a car apart and concealing weapons in the cavities of the chassis. Several vehicles were thus loaded up and driven into Jordan by members of his team. Abu Dawud let his beard grow and, posing as a Saudi on holiday, crossed the frontier uneventfully, accompanied by his "wife." In fact she was the wife of one of his team members and had volunteered for the job. In Amman, he immediately contacted a Fatah sleeper, a certain Mustafa Jabr—but unfortunately for Abu Dawud, Jabr had been "turned" by Jordanian intelligence.

"The moment I saw him," Abu Dawud told me later in Tunis, "I knew from the look in his eye that he was going to betray me. I took him by the collar and whispered, 'Look here, Mustafa, if you ever think of squealing, you're a dead man!' "

Sensing danger, Abu Dawud determined to strike within twenty-four hours. But Mustafa must have alerted the Jordanians first, because Abu Dawud was arrested on his way back from seeing him.

For four days Abu Dawud was beaten and questioned, but he gave nothing away. By coincidence, on the fourth day the Jordanians arrested a young man in an empty car whom they suspected of smuggling marijuana. He was a member of Abu Dawud's team and his car was laden with hidden weapons. The Jordanians decided to show Abu Dawud to this man to see if he recognized him. Abu Dawud was lying slumped on the floor, where he had fainted from pain.

"Do you know who this is?" they asked the young man. "Why yes," he replied. "That is Abu Dawud. I came here with him!"

They dragged Abu Dawud back to the interrogation room, determined to make him talk. He was beaten again, for six or seven hours a day, for an entire month. Meanwhile, from the boy's confession the Jordanians managed to round up all the members of the team, who had been waiting at various hotels for the signal to move. They lined them up and hauled Abu Dawud in front of them. His face was swollen and his arms and legs bruised and useless. He must have been pretty well unrecognizable.

Only one man knew where the weapons were hidden in the

cars, and he cracked after two weeks of torture. At that point, the game was up. Abu Dawud and his team were all condemned to death. Twice he was dressed in the red death-row suit and taken down for execution, but each time it was deferred at the last minute.

Abu Dawud never let his captors know that Mustafa Jabr had betrayed him, and pretended not to know him at all. Later, in order to trap Mustafa, Abu Iyad sent him word from Egypt that he wanted to mount a really big operation in Jordan to secure Abu Dawud's release. The Jordanians could not resist the temptation of finding out what Abu Iyad had in mind, so they sent Mustafa Jabr to meet Abu Iyad in Cairo. He was seized there by Fatah and smuggled out to Libya, where he was imprisoned. Three years later, in 1976, on a plea from his old father, Jabr was released and on his return to Jordan was appointed director of cultural affairs at the ministry of information, a post he may still be holding.

As Abu Dawud told me, "I was myself released far sooner as a result of numerous appeals on my behalf. The Kuwaitis agreed to pay King Hussein $12 million to save my head, and the ruling Soviet troika of Brezhnev, Kosygin, and Podgorni sent Jordan a tough telegram. In 1973, the king knew that war in the Middle East was coming within a very few weeks and he didn't want to hold prisoner hundreds of Palestinians during a conflict which he hoped to stay out of. This was probably what got me out.

"On September 18, 1973, a few days before the outbreak of the October War, we were all released under a general amnesty. The king himself came to my prison cell and told me I was free."

Such was the immediate background to Abu Nidal's first act of terror.

chapter

5

MADE IN BAGHDAD

On September 5, 1973, just two weeks before Abu Dawud's release, five armed Palestinians seized the Saudi embassy in Paris. They took thirteen people hostage and threatened to blow up the building if Abu Dawud was not released from his Jordanian jail.

After lengthy negotiations, the guerrillas agreed to fly out to Kuwait on a Syrian Airways Caravelle, taking some of their hostages with them. More talks followed at a refueling stop in Cairo, and still more at the Kuwait airport, where the gunmen transferred to a Kuwait Airways Boeing and flew over Riyadh, the Saudi capital, threatening to throw their hostages out of the plane if their demand was not met. But when the Saudi authorities insisted that they could not be held responsible for King Hussein's policies, the gunmen eventually flew back to Kuwait, where, after further lengthy negotiations conducted by Ali Yassin, the PLO representative, they surrendered on September 8, thus ending the three-day drama.

ABU NIDAL'S FIRST TERRORIST ACT

This operation was Abu Nidal's first act of terror, planned and directed by him from Baghdad. My sources told me that the man in operational control was Samir Muhammad al-Abbasi (code-named Amjad Ata), Abu Nidal's aide whom Jorde had caught sight of at the Libyan camp. Amjad Ata was married to one of Abu Nidal's nieces and was to become one of the leading killers in his organization. At the time of writing, he was living in Libya.

Abu Nidal was of course eager to secure the freedom of his friend and fellow radical Abu Dawud: On his release from jail shortly afterward, Abu Nidal offered him a job in the secret group he was then forming. But the larger aims of the Paris operation were more complex.

On September 5, the day of the attack on the Saudi embassy, fifty-six heads of state had assembled in Algiers for the Fourth Non-Aligned Conference, which was opened that day by the Algerian leader Houari Boumédienne, in the presence of UN Secretary-General Kurt Waldheim. But Iraq's president, Ahmad Hasan al-Bakr, jealous of Algeria for hosting it, disapproved of the Algiers conference. The Paris operation, which enraged both President Boumédienne and King Faisal of Saudi Arabia, was an attempt by Iraq and Abu Nidal to torpedo the proceedings. One of the captured guerrillas later confessed to the Kuwaitis that his orders had been to shuttle the hostages back and forth as long as the Non-Aligned Conference lasted.

Yasser Arafat, who was also in Algiers for the gathering, was deeply embarrassed. He issued a statement condemning the assault as a "plot against the Palestine revolution" and vowed to punish the culprits. Fatah insiders knew that Abu Nidal was the agent and Iraq the sponsor.

A few days later, Abu Iyad and another Fatah leader, Mahmud Abbas (Abu Mazin), flew to Baghdad to have it out with the renegade—but found they had to contend with Iraq as well. Abu Iyad told me that when Abu Mazin started to rebuke Abu Nidal for the Paris operation, an Iraqi official present at the meeting interrupted him brusquely. "Why are you attacking Abu Nidal?" he asked. "The operation was ours! We asked him to mount it for us."

"It was as blunt as that," Abu Iyad said. "Abu Mazin was so angry he got up and left the room. We all followed."

It was now clear to Arafat and his colleagues that their man in Baghdad had put himself wholly at Iraq's service.

DIPLOMACY VERSUS REJECTIONISM

So far, the ostensible reason for Abu Nidal's estrangement from Fatah was the dispute arising from the Jordanian debacle. But the October War of 1973 introduced an altogether more important subject of controversy. In the Arab world, the October War is still thought of as an Arab victory that erased the humiliation of 1967. Arabs prefer to remember the early successes, when Egypt and Syria caught Israel napping and stormed its defenses on the Suez and Golan fronts, rather than the later failures, when Israel regained the initiative. Having proved they could fight and having tasted even limited victory, many Arabs now felt that the time had come to end the conflict with Israel, which had absorbed their energies for over thirty years. The desire for peace was widespread and it involved Arafat's PLO. The despair that had produced the violence of Black September now gave way to optimism. Terrorism was out of fashion as Arafat and his lieutenants sought to muzzle the hotheads and prepare the PLO for a diplomatic role.

There were three distinct landmarks on the PLO's road from armed struggle to political action.

First, the Palestine National Council, meeting in Cairo in June–July 1974, adopted after much heated debate a ten-point political program that accepted the principle that the PLO should set up a "national authority" on any "liberated" territory. This vote by the parliament-in-exile is widely considered the first formal signal that the Palestinians were ready to give up their maximalist demands to retake Israel and make do with a "mini-state" in the West Bank and Gaza.

Second, at an Arab summit in Rabat, Morocco, on October 20, 1974, Yasser Arafat managed to wrest from the assembled Arab leaders, and especially from a reluctant King Hussein, an admission that the PLO would henceforth be the "sole legitimate representative of the Palestinian people." Not all Arab leaders were happy to give the PLO such exclusive authority, but they fell into line when they learned that a Palestinian hit team had arrived secretly in Morocco and was preparing to assassinate them all. In fact the operation was a bluff, dreamed up by Abu Iyad to put pressure on the assembled Arab leaders without doing them any physical harm. At the appropriate moment, Abu Iyad tipped off the Moroccan police and the team was rounded up, having served its purpose. The catchphrase "sole legitimate representative" on which Arafat insisted was intended to advance the PLO's claim to negotiate the recovery of the West Bank in place of King Hussein.

Third, fresh from this Arab success, Arafat addressed the General Assembly of the United Nations on November 13, 1974, and won a standing ovation. Once again, he was signaling his readiness to negotiate a political settlement with Israel.

Several strands may be identified in Arafat's thinking at this time. He believed that after the October War, the United States genuinely wanted an evenhanded settlement in the region and that Henry Kissinger could deliver one. As we have seen, even before the war, he had sent Kissinger no fewer than four messages seeking a dialogue. Arafat now believed that with Israel overwhelmingly strong and the Arabs defeated and divided, guerrilla warfare could not possibly result in statehood. Armed struggle had brought victory to the Vietnamese and the Cubans, but their victories had to be set against a long list of costly failures by other revolutionary movements: the Kurds in Turkey, Iran, and Iraq; the Polisario in the Western Sahara; other insurgent groups in Thailand, Malaya, the Philippines, Burma, El Salvador, and Peru. No one at that time would have believed that by 1991 the Eritrean People's Liberation Front in Ethiopia would prevail after one of the longest struggles of all. It was difficult, Arafat argued to his close associates in 1974, to win against the formidable defenses of a state. Surely the time had come for the Palestinians to go for a political solution.

Non-Palestinians cannot easily comprehend how unwelcome this pragmatism was to the rank and file. Romantic and irresponsible rejectionism, the refusal to make concessions, the insistence on fighting when there is no chance of victory have a long ancestry in the Palestinian movement, as David Gilmour points out in *Dispossessed: The Palestinian Ordeal from 1917 to 1980* (1980). Convinced of the justice of their cause, the Palestinians were rejectionists in 1917, in 1922, in 1936–39, in 1948—and with even greater conviction when they started their armed struggle, in 1965. How could any people be expected to surrender voluntarily the greater part of their country? Gilmour quotes a remark by the Irish nationalist leader Eamon de Valera: "The rightful owners of a country will never agree to partition." So whatever Arafat recommended, and whatever resolutions were passed by the Palestine National Council, a negotiated settlement with Israel offended those Palestinians who believed that only force could liberate Palestine and feared that political concessions would lead to a sellout. They were not yet ready to accept the unsatisfactory compromise of a mini-state.

The PFLP's George Habash, one of the most ardent advocates of continued armed struggle, broke with the PLO at this time and took the lead in setting up a "Front Rejecting Capitulationist Solutions," which came to be known simply as the Rejection Front. Formally launched at a conference in Baghdad in October 1974, with the backing of Iraq, Algeria, and South Yemen, it opposed all negotiations. The front provided an umbrella for those Palestinian factions that shared this view: the PFLP; the Syrian-backed breakaway group that its leader, Ahmad Jibril, named the PFLP–General Command; and Iraq's own creation, the Arab Liberation Front. Meanwhile, Wadi Haddad, leader of the PFLP's military wing, continued incorrigibly to mount terrorist operations, although by now his organization was so penetrated by half a dozen intelligence agencies that most of his plans were aborted. He eventually died, following a mysterious illness contracted in Baghdad. Some say he was given a poison pill supplied by another Arab government to make it seem that Iraq was to blame. Abu Iyad was particularly incensed by Wadi Haddad's continued hijackings. "Which madman," he would storm despairingly, "would want to trap the Palestine cause in an airplane? If the plane blows up, the Palestine cause might blow up with it!"

Abu Nidal was perhaps the most violent "rejectionist" on the Palestinian scene, but he never formally joined the Rejection Front, which may have been too overt for so passionate a convert to clandestine action. In any event, he was busy setting up his own secret organization, and in this he had the inestimable advantage of having become Iraq's favorite Palestinian protégé.

From the start, Iraq's Ba'athist leaders set themselves up as the main champions of the Palestinian rejectionists. Far from the scene of the Arab-Israeli conflict, untroubled by fear of Israeli retaliation, and with no Palestinian refugee problem to cope with, Iraq could afford this grand gesture. There were also personal factors involved. The Iraqi president, Ahmad Hasan al-Bakr, a simple soldier of nationalist convictions who was fond of declaring that his most cherished dream was to die fighting in Palestine, had an unbounded contempt for Yasser Arafat. The antipathy was mutual and dated back to an incident in early 1969, when Arafat (still only Fatah's official spokesman and not yet chairman of the PLO's Executive Committee) paid a visit to Baghdad accompanied by Abu Dawud. Their reckless driver crashed into a truck. Arafat's hand was broken and his ribs crushed, while Abu Dawud's face and eyes were badly hurt by flying glass. They were taken for treatment to a military hospital in Baghdad, where Bakr came to inquire after their health. After the customary exchange of civilities, a dispute broke out in the hospital room over the friendly relations—too friendly, in Bakr's view—that Fatah had entertained with the preceding Iraqi regime, overthrown a year earlier by Bakr and his Ba'ath party. Sharp words were exchanged—and a lasting chill ensued, which was to have considerable political consequences.

Accordingly, by early 1974, when Fatah was considering its switch from guerrilla warfare to diplomacy in the wake of the October War, Iraq's Ba'athist leaders invited Arafat to visit Baghdad again. Men like Bakr and his powerful second-in-command, Saddam Hussein, considered the Palestinian cause inseparable from their party's historic mission: They could not tolerate an independent PLO that was not under their direction, an attitude not very different from that of Hafez al-Assad of Syria. Thus, Bakr and Saddam Hussein pressed Arafat to move his men to Iraq and reject all political compromise. If he did so, they promised, he would have Iraq's full backing! But Arafat refused their offer and, instead, went to Cairo to win support for his "moderate" ten-point program at the June meeting of the Palestine National Council. Iraq was furious and launched a propaganda campaign against Arafat.

Abu Nidal was the first to benefit from these developments. Though he was Fatah's man on the spot, he was a known opponent of Arafat. Iraq's instinct in the circumstances was to give him a secure geographical base and use him against the man they now saw as a traitor. Indeed, had it not been for Iraq's quarrel with Arafat, Abu Nidal might not have split from Fatah but might, at most, have led a strong opposition movement inside it, leaving the balance of power among the Palestinians to decide the issue in due course.

Abu Nidal also became the beneficiary of the endemic rivalry between Iraq and Syria, which dated back to the great Ba'ath party schism of 1966, which over the years had hardened into enmity between the two Ba'athist states. Seen from Iraq, Arafat's Fatah, which by 1972 had established itself in Lebanon, just across the Syrian frontier, was now in Syria's orbit. Syria had also created al-Sa'iqa (the Thunderbolt) as its own wholly controlled Palestinian organization. Iraq felt the need for a counterweight in the form of a Baghdad-based Palestinian group.

What choice did it have? A possible candidate was the PFLP, run by George Habash and his trigger-happy colleague Wadi Haddad, but these were prickly, strong-minded men who could not easily be controlled. Another possibility was the experienced officer Ahmad Jibril and his militarily effective PFLP–General Command, but having started life in the Syrian army, Jibril tilted naturally toward Damascus. Then there was Abu Nidal: ambitious, active, wanting power over others, a *provocateur* of the first order—and in many ways already Iraq's man. He seemed ideally placed to oppose Arafat's errant leadership. Furthermore, he let the Iraqis know that many cadres in Fatah thought as he did: He meant, for example, such well-known men as Abu Dawud and Naji Allush and even his former mentor, Abu Iyad. Moreover, as a member of Fatah's Revolutionary Council, he was already some way up the Fatah ladder.

Arafat and his Fatah central committee were by now thoroughly outraged by the disloyalty of their man in Baghdad. Ever since 1971 there had been moves to sack him—moves that Abu Iyad had repeatedly blocked, in the belief that Abu Nidal might still somehow be saved. But now a decision could no longer be deferred. In the early summer of 1974, it was decided to send Abu Mazin to Baghdad, accompanied by Abu Iyad and Abu Dawud, to inform Abu Nidal that he was being replaced.

Abu Iyad told me later that even at this eleventh hour, he wanted to make one last attempt to save Abu Nidal. Before the interview, he and Abu Dawud conferred secretly with Abu Nidal to urge him to plead with Abu Mazin not to expel him. They coached him in how to put his case. When the meeting took place, Abu Mazin gave Abu Nidal the dressing-down of his life. But in reply, Abu Nidal grossly overplayed his act. He was so abject and groveling that Abu Iyad had to leave the room in embarrassment. Abu Mazin guessed that Abu Iyad had schemed yet again to block Abu Nidal's expulsion.

"Abu Mazin and I were very close friends," Abu Iyad told me, "but it was about the tenth time that I had taken Abu Nidal's side against a central committee decision. Abu Mazin was very angry and uncomfortable and that evening had the first signs of the heart problem that was later to trouble him."

But Abu Iyad could no longer stem the tide. On July 26, 1974, the Palestinian news agency WAFA reported that Sabri al-Banna, "known by his alias of Abu Nidal," had been removed from his post as Fatah representative in Baghdad.

ATTEMPTED MURDER OF ABU MAZIN

Even before the formal announcement, Abu Nidal sought revenge for his humiliation—and he did so by plotting Abu Mazin's assassination. The affair was both complicated and controversial, but it was to precipitate the final split.

In June 1974, Fatah intelligence came upon a letter written in Baghdad by a certain Mustafa Murad (code-named Abu Nizar)—a close associate of Abu Nidal—to two men in Damascus, instructing them to spy on Abu Mazin's movements in preparation for an attempt on his life. Thus forewarned, Fatah proceeded to round up Abu Nidal's known sympathizers among Palestinians in Syria and Lebanon; when Abu Nizar went to Damascus on a mission in July 1974, he was seized by Fatah and imprisoned in its jail at Hammuriyah, near Damascus.

Three months later, Abu Nizar was put on trial before a Fatah court. A gun, equipped with a silencer, which he confessed to having supplied, was submitted in evidence, together with sketch maps prepared by the conspirators showing the location of Abu Mazin's house. In early November, Abu Nizar was sentenced to eighteen months in jail, to be served at Hammuriyah. Abu Nidal, the alleged mastermind behind the attempted assassination, was sentenced to death in absentia.

The death sentence was confirmed at a meeting of Fatah's Revolutionary Council—in the teeth of strenuous protests from Abu Dawud and Naji Allush, the radical journalist, who thus showed where their sympathies lay. Abu Mazin, the intended victim of the assassination attempt, left the meeting in anger. But still not giving up, Abu Dawud pleaded that Abu Nidal be given a last chance to put his case. It was decided to invite him to Beirut for questioning, with Abu Dawud personally vouching for his safety. Such was the incestuous relationship between these comrades and former comrades that the breach was even then still not final.

Abu Nidal was a very careful man. It was, therefore, with considerable hesitation that he traveled to Beirut, where Abu

Dawud met him at the airport and took him to a safe house. Fearing a trap, he insisted throughout his visit that Abu Dawud never leave his side. To give Abu Nidal every chance to clear his name and return to the Fatah fold, Abu Iyad diplomatically wrote out the questions to be put to him—*and* the answers expected from him. But this scheming came to nothing. Abu Nidal was no longer willing to humble himself. With Iraqi backing, he was beginning to feel both powerful and destructive. Angrily, he returned to Baghdad. Both sides had passed the point of no return.

It may be, as some Palestinian insiders suggest, that Abu Nidal never really intended to kill Abu Mazin but merely to frighten him; and that Fatah's death sentence, in turn, was more for public consumption than a genuine attempt to bring him to justice. In any event, no effort was made to carry it out. If Fatah had truly wanted to kill Abu Nidal, it could have sent someone to Baghdad to do the job.

But the psychological impact of the sentence on Abu Nidal was considerable. It had the effect of driving him out of Fatah altogether and of making him cling ever more closely to Iraq. As an acquaintance put it, "For Abu Nidal, *self* is everything. When he feels personally threatened, he goes berserk."

THE SPLIT BECOMES FORMAL

Abu Nidal's reaction to the death sentence was to denounce Arafat as a heretic whose willingness to accept a peaceful solution of the Palestine question was a betrayal of Fatah's original ideals. In support of his accusations, he published the resolutions of Fatah's Third Congress, which Arafat had forced through. So incensed had Abu Nidal been by these resolutions that his first thought had been to call his new movement Fatah: The Fourth Congress, to indicate his total rejection of everything the Third Congress had approved. But on reflection, in October 1974 he settled for Fatah: The Revolutionary Council. He was, after all, a member of Fatah's Revolutionary Council, most of whose members were his friends and held hard-line views like his own: Arafat might control the top of the pyramid, but its base, as he believed, was solidly with him. He thought of himself as representing not just a splinter group but a majority within the Palestinian movement. And in true sectarian fashion, he took to referring sneeringly to Arafat's Fatah as Fatah: The Executive Committee. His was the legitimate face of Fatah, Arafat's the face of treachery!

Many Fatah members across the Arab world were attracted to Abu Nidal's stance and thought him a brave and principled politician who had stood up against a sellout. The fact that he was no outsider, that he had a background in Fatah, made cooperation with him easier.

His strongest card was that he was now a source of considerable patronage, because the Iraqis had turned over to him all Fatah's assets in Iraq. These included a training camp at Ramadi, west of Baghdad; a large farm where food for his men was grown; passports, a more precious commodity for stateless Palestinians than food; scholarships for study abroad; a radio station; a newspaper; and a stock of Chinese weapons worth $15 million, which Abu Dawud had ordered for his militia in Jordan but which never got further than Iraq when the September 1970 crisis erupted. Abu Nidal sold some of them off: It was the beginning of his fortune. He also became the recipient of the regular financial aid Iraq had given to Fatah: 50,000 Iraqi dinars a month, the equivalent at the time of about $150,000. In addition, as a special bonus to set himself up, Iraq gave him a lump sum of $3–5 million. All this represented real wealth and power. Within a very short time, Abu Nidal became "Mr. Palestine" in Iraq, dominating the entire Palestinian community there. Any Palestinian who needed anything at all from the Iraqi government had to go through him.

His main supporter in Iraq was President Ahmad Hasan al-Bakr, the man from whom his power truly derived. They shared an anxiety about the "dangers of the peace process" and held Arafat in contempt. Abu Nidal cleverly suggested to Bakr that because of the position he had taken, he risked being killed by Fatah, so from the start he enjoyed Iraq's sympathy as well as the assiduous protection of its intelligence service, whose chief, Sa'dun Shakir, became his close friend.

THE KILLING OF AHMAD ABD AL-GHAFUR

An event then took place that was to have a profound effect on Abu Nidal, propelling him down the path of violence, or at least giving him a pretext for taking that road. One of his closest friends was killed by Fatah in Beirut.

Ahmad Abd al-Ghafur (code-named Abu Mahmud), a fervent nationalist and rising Fatah cadre, was one of the first and certainly one of the most important members of the secret group that Abu Nidal had formed inside Fatah in 1972–73. In the 1960s, he had worked for an oil company in Libya, where he made money and acquired management experience. He also struck up an acquaintance with the young Libyan officers who, under the leadership of Colonel Muammar al-Qaddafi, seized power from the aged King Idris in September 1969. The following year, Fatah called him to Jordan to help manage its slim resources, and he proved to be good at it, dipping into his own pocket when the need arose.

But like many others, he was shattered by the slaughter of the Palestinians in Jordan in 1970. A dramatic change came over him. This once sober man joined Black September and became one of its most bloodthirsty members. He was determined, he declared, to cleanse Fatah of its "heretics" and wreak vengeance on all supporters of Israel. To Abu Iyad's alarm, as he later explained to me, Ahmad Abd al-Ghafur took to propounding a dangerous terrorist theory: The way to win support for the Palestinian cause was to send gunmen to shoot people at random in the streets of Europe and the United States. In court, the gunmen would declare that they had killed in order to bring an oppressed and persecuted people to the attention of the world.

In 1972, Ahmad Abd al-Ghafur broke away from Black September, moved to Lebanon and, while still linked to Abu Nidal, formed a fighting group of his own made up of men he was able to seduce away from Fatah. As he was popular in the refugee camps, he soon had a large body of followers and angered Fatah by mounting terrorist operations just when Fatah was trying to put terror behind it. One of his most notorious operations was an attack on December 17, 1973, at Fiumicino Airport in Rome, on a Pan Am Boeing 707 about to take off for Beirut and Tehran. Five fedayeen hurled incendiary bombs inside the aircraft, killing twenty-nine people, including Aramco employees and four senior Moroccan government officials who were on their way to Iran.

Then, in 1974, to Fatah's even greater alarm, word reached it that Ahmad Abd al-Ghafur and Abu Nidal were working more closely together and were considering merging their two organizations. The combination of Abu Nidal backed by Iraq and Abd al-Ghafur backed by Libya—two crazy and destructive men, as Arafat believed at the time, in the pay of two extremist regimes—represented an intolerable threat to the political course on which Arafat had embarked. Abd al-Ghafur had to be stopped, and Arafat's military chief, Khalil al-Wazir (Abu Jihad), gave orders for him to be killed. Fatah may also have felt the need to clip the wings of a rival organization that was becoming a significant force in Lebanon, an especially sensitive theater of operations for Fatah. So Ahmad Abd al-Ghafur was gunned down in the Ashrafiya district of Beirut in late 1974 by a certain Azmi al-Sughayyir, a Palestinian of murky background who had worked for the Israelis, then for the guerrillas. (He would eventually be killed in southern Lebanon, during Israel's invasion in 1982.)

Abd al-Ghafur's ideas did not die with him. One of his disciples, a Palestinian named Abu Mustafa Qaddura, took over his group and, with backing from both Libya and Abu Nidal, organized the hijack of a British Airways VC-10 at Dubai when it landed there on November 22, 1974, on a flight from London to Brunei. The four gunmen on board, who called themselves members of the Martyr Ahmad Abd al-Ghafur Squad, forced the plane to fly to Tunis, where one of their hostages, a German doctor, was shot and tossed out onto the tarmac. Their most pressing demand was for the release from Egyptian jails of the five comrades who had staged the attack on the Pan Am plane at Fiumicino in December 1973 and who were awaiting trial by the PLO.

President Sadat of Egypt appealed to Abu Iyad for help in negotiating with the gunmen and sent a plane to take him to Tunis. Abu Iyad recounted to me that when he first spoke to the gunmen from the control tower, they were violent and abusive, but he was gradually able to influence each one of them in turn, including their leader, who called himself Tony. They kept threatening to blow up the plane, but he persuaded them to release a few passengers at a time. "Let the passengers go, and then do what you like with the plane," he argued.

In the meantime, President Sadat agreed to release the five prisoners held in Egypt, who were flown to Tunis to join the gunmen on board the plane. Once the passengers had been freed and the gunmen, their comrades, and the crew were alone on board, Abu Iyad persuaded them to give themselves up in exchange for free passage to a country of their choice. When they chose Libya, Abu Iyad got President Bourguiba to agree to the transaction. He then contacted the head of Libyan intelligence at the time, Abd al-Mun'im al-Huni, and he too approved the plan. They agreed that on arrival in Tripoli, the gunmen would be handed over to the local PLO office.

But when Abu Iyad arrived in Tripoli a day later, he found that contrary to the agreement, the gunmen had been allowed to go on to Benghazi, where, in protest at the handling of the affair by the Tunisian government, they had actually been allowed to take over the Tunisian consulate. Qaddafi was clearly settling a few scores of his own—against Tunisia. Abu Iyad thought the whole thing a scandal.

"I raised the matter with Qaddafi," he told me. "Why had he not honored our agreement to hand the gunmen over to the PLO? I had, after all, saved his reputation by resolving the crisis peacefully. Had it ended violently, his connection with the gunmen would have been made public!

"He pretended ignorance of the whole business, but asked me who on the Libyan side was responsible for the blunder. I replied that it was his own intelligence people, Sayyid Qaddaf al-Damm and Abdallah Hijazi. He summoned them and scolded them in a schoolboy manner, with lots of giggles. He said he wanted the hijackers handed over to me on the morrow. They laughed, nodded, and left.

"On my way out, I quizzed al-Huni, the Libyan intelligence head, about the colonel's manner. Was this how he usually behaved? Did he not have enough authority over those men to make them take him seriously? Al-Huni turned to me: 'Don't be misled,' he said. 'Take it from me: He's a wolf in sheep's clothing.'

"It's a description of Qaddafi I have never forgotten," Abu Iyad said.

The incident illustrated the stress, embarrassment, and frantic maneuvers imposed upon Fatah and Arab regimes as they struggled to contain such terrorist operations. In turn, the operations themselves had, by this time, very little to do with defending the Palestinian cause and a great deal to do with squabbles between Arab states and among Palestinians themselves.

As Abu Iyad conceded to me, Fatah had made a terrible error in killing Ahmad Abd al-Ghafur. His assassination introduced violence into intra-Palestinian relations, which had so far been largely absent. The death of Abd al-Ghafur released a ferocious tide in Abu Nidal's nature and gave him an excuse for his own later murders of Palestinians.

Why did Fatah not rid itself of Abu Nidal as well? The answer must be that at this late stage, he was still being protected by Abu Iyad, as he himself told me:

"I used to believe there were two ways of dealing with him: One was to cut him down, as many wanted to do; the other was to win him over. In spite of everything, I still hoped to do so." He explained that Fatah could have killed Abu Nidal when he came to Lebanon in 1974, but they did not do it because at that time he was only calling for reforms. "If we were to kill everyone who called for reform of the PLO, we would have to slaughter thousands," he said with a laugh. "Anyway, we claimed that ours was a democratic movement, and this was a way of proving it."

Abu Iyad felt that Abu Nidal voiced significant criticisms of the PLO—criticisms that in some ways he shared. "I wanted to let him loose on our movement so that he could act as a corrective to trends of which I disapproved," Abu Iyad said, despite Arafat's conviction that Abu Nidal was dangerous.

It was a view he came bitterly to regret, and one he would eventually pay for with his life.

BEGINNINGS OF THE MILITARY COMMITTEE

Abu Nidal spent his first years in Iraq as head of his own organization in careful preparation for an international role. He set up an ultrasecret Military Committee and proceeded to equip it for "foreign work." From the start, he was more interested in such operations than in cross-border raids into Israel, the traditional expression of Palestinian militancy. Whether or not this was because he already had a link with the Mossad must be a matter of conjecture. It is a subject to which we will return in a later chapter, once his connections with Arab sponsors have been explored. Abu Nidal's argument at this time was that Iraq was a long way from Israel, and his enemy Yasser Arafat would never allow him a free hand in front-line areas. One of his earliest recruits, known as Basil (later to be a commander of Abu Nidal's forces in Lebanon), whom

I interviewed in Tunis, recalls him saying in 1973 that "the battlefield on the borders of the enemy" was closed to him. The argument was spurious because he did in fact have men in Jordan and Lebanon who, like members of other groups, could have struck into Israel if he had instructed them to do so. But this was evidently not his first priority.

Instead, he concentrated on smuggling arms into European countries and concealing them there. In 1973–75, when security at airports and land borders was not as strict as it was to become, the clandestine movement of arms was still relatively easy. For this traffic, Abu Nidal used Iraqi diplomatic pouches, secret compartments in cars, and containers on ships sailing from Iraqi ports. In some cases, arms were bought locally from extremist groups, and suitable places to hide them abroad were located and mapped on land that was not going to be farmed or developed; woods were preferred. Weapons were stored either in small quantities, enough to arm one or two men, or in so-called strategic dumps, which could be drawn on several times and then hidden away or locked up for further use. Such larger dumps were placed in the custody of a "resident," usually someone married to a local girl or otherwise enjoying good cover. Great care was taken to protect the residents and to conceal any information that might link them to Abu Nidal's organization.

In those early days the main arms dumps were in Greece, Turkey, Cyprus, Italy, and France—some of which are still there today and could in theory permit Abu Nidal to mount operations in Europe. According to Basil and other sources, Abu Nidal learned his terrorist techniques from Black September but also from Iranian revolutionaries who were then plotting to overthrow the shah, some of whom had trained with the Palestinians in Iraq.

At this stage Abu Nidal's Military Committee seemed a wholly Iraqi creation. He did Iraq's bidding and was rewarded with access to Iraqi funds, airlines, embassies, and diplomatic bags. His enemies were Iraq's enemies, his operations were dictated by Iraq, and his various institutions—the Military Committee and other bodies dealing with finance, external relations, and internal organization—seemed no more than extensions of Iraqi intelligence.

Yet Abu Nidal's vanity would not allow him completely to be anyone's agent. In his view, he had not been "recruited" by the Iraqis but rather had entered into a partnership with them, founded on his personal friendship with their leaders. They provided the logistics, he paid in "services rendered." As he confided to one of his associates, "When I take, I give." It was a principle that was to govern his relations with other sponsors over the years.

The attack on the Saudi Arabian embassy in Paris in September 1973 was Abu Nidal's first recorded operation and one clearly carried out on Iraq's behalf. In December of that year, he sent two Tunisian members of his still embryonic organization to disrupt the Geneva conference, stage-managed by Henry Kissinger after the October War. The plan was that they should invade the conference hall or gun down the delegates to indicate their rejection of any sort of peace settlement, to which both he and Iraq were virulently opposed. But his men never got a chance to act. The conference opened at the Palais des Nations on December 21, 1973, and, after ceremonial speeches, adjourned that same afternoon. Henry Kissinger had conceived it as a fig leaf to legitimize his secret objective of a bilateral deal between Egypt and Israel. It never became the forum, as many had hoped, for a wide-ranging multilateral negotiation to implement UN Security Council Resolution 242, which called on Israel to withdraw from occupied territories, in exchange for secure and recognized borders. Thus, Abu Nidal had to call off his operation and bring his men home.

WAR ON SYRIA

By 1976 Abu Nidal's organization was ready for more ambitious operations. The Lebanese civil war had broken out, pitting Muslims of that country and their Palestinian allies against the once-dominant Maronite Christians. The Palestinian guerrilla commander Abu Dawud soon found himself in the thick of things. Although he was still in Fatah, he was also cooperating secretly with Abu Nidal. In early 1976 he brought about fifty of Abu Nidal's men into the port of Sidon, on the south coast of Lebanon, to fight under his command alongside other Palestinian troops in the commercial district of Beirut.

By the spring of 1976, the tide of war had turned against the Maronite Christians, who found themselves besieged in the mountains by a combined force of Palestinians and radical Muslims. Fearing an Israeli intervention to save the Maronites, President

Assad of Syria sent his army into Lebanon in June 1976 to force the Palestinians to call off their offensive. But Arab opinion could not accept that an Arab nationalist regime like Syria's should turn its guns on Palestinians. The outcry against Assad was heard from one end of the Arab world to the other. Sadat broke off relations, while Iraq's Saddam Hussein sent troops to the Syrian border, calling Assad a madman whose ambition had immersed him in a bloodbath. (Just before Syrian troops marched in, Abu Dawud got Abu Nidal's men out; he knew the Syrians would give them no quarter.)

On Iraq's prompting, Abu Nidal then mounted a terrorist campaign against Syria code-named Black June—the month in which Syrian forces entered Lebanon. In July 1976, he had bombs set off at the offices of Syrian Airlines in Kuwait and Rome, and two months later, on September 26, four Abu Nidal gunmen burst into the Semiramis Hotel in central Damascus and took ninety people hostage. Traveling on Iraqi passports, the team had smuggled its weapons into Syria from Europe, via Turkey. Syrian forces stormed the hotel, killing one gunman and four hostages and wounding thirty-four others. The next day, the three remaining gunmen were hanged in public.

In October, Abu Nidal mounted attacks on Syrian embassies in Islamabad and Rome, and in December on the Syrian embassy in Ankara and the Syrian legation in Istanbul. A weapon used in several of these incidents was the small Polish-made WZ-63 submachine gun, whose folding butt and large magazine made it a terrorist's favorite. Bombs placed in public trash cans in Damascus caused alarm and resulted in ugly casualties. One of Abu Nidal's men, Ali Zaidan, who had taken part in the two Rome operations of July and October, was arrested by the Italian police and would spend five years in an Italian jail. He is now a member of Abu Nidal's Revolutionary Council and one of his main killers.

Less than a year later, on October 25, 1977, Syria's then foreign minister, Abd al-Halim Khaddam, narrowly escaped death at the Abu Dhabi airport when a gunman opened fire on him. The bullet missed him but killed Saif al-Ghubash, the United Arab Emirates minister of state for foreign affairs, who was standing at his side. The planner of this operation, and of the attack on the Semiramis Hotel, in central Damascus, was Fu'ad al-Suffarini (code-named Umar Hamdi), a long-serving director of Abu Nidal's office in Baghdad and a member of his Military Committee. (An earlier attempt to kill Khaddam in Syria in December 1976, widely attributed to Abu Nidal, was in fact the work of the Muslim Brotherhood, then beginning a campaign to overthrow Assad's regime.)

With these anti-Syrian operations, Abu Nidal was cutting his teeth and making himself useful to the Iraqis. But he had yet to develop his own distinctive style. So far he had been busy building up his organization and acquiring weapons and funds. He claimed he wanted to wage war on "Zionism" and "imperialism," but his only targets so far had been Arab—and were soon to be more specifically Palestinian.

Yet as he sank deeper into an underworld of violence, he told a friend of the damage to himself and to his family of the course he had chosen:

"In the 1970s, when we lived in Iraq," Abu Nidal said, "I enrolled my son Nidal at a school in Baghdad under a false name. One day he misbehaved in class, and the headmaster asked to see his father. He said the boy wouldn't be allowed back to school until the father had been to see him.

"Nidal didn't dare tell me about it. He knew I could not appear in public. So he asked the father of a friend of his to stand in for me. But it didn't work. The headmaster insisted on seeing me.

"One day Nidal came to me and said he wanted to give up school altogether! I soon learned why, and telephoned the headmaster to ask him to pay me a visit. I had to tell him who I was and confess that my son was registered under a false name.

"I'd caused shame and discomfort to my own son!"

THE SPONSORS

For seventeen long years, from 1974 to 1991, Iraq, then Syria, and finally Libya gave Abu Nidal a home, logistical support, and that most precious gift of all—security. Iraq's sponsorship lasted for over eight years, from 1974 to 1983; Syria's for six years, from 1981 to 1987; and Libya's continues (despite Colonel Qaddafi's denials) to this day.

There was a curious overlap in the early eighties, when Abu Nidal's organization, one of the most dangerous in the region, gradually transferred its operating base from Baghdad to Damascus, in effect evading the control of either sponsor. What made the situation still more strange was that except for some months in 1978–79, Iraq and Syria were deadly enemies, busily abusing and sabotaging each other, each claiming to be the fount of Ba'athist legitimacy and Arab nationalism.

But Abu Nidal has an outstanding talent for inserting himself into the narrow gap between contending parties. He thrives on Middle Eastern conflicts, not only between Israel and the Palestinians but between the Arab states and Fatah, between Iraq and Syria, between Libya and Egypt, between the Arabs and the West. He threatened the conservative states of the Gulf as well as European governments on both sides of the Iron Curtain, which often caved in to his blackmail to protect themselves from his terrorism. This was the shadowy, quarrelsome world he inhabited, the underbelly of politics. Because he was ubiquitous and violent, there were many attempts to penetrate his organization or simply to make contact with him, allowing him in return to extort what funds, facilities, or concessions he could get. He offered his sponsors valuable services but was never entirely their creature.

The Middle East is a place of almost perpetual conflict. Arabs and Israelis have waged great wars during just about every decade. Iraq and Iran engaged in a grinding eight-year struggle. The civil war in Lebanon lasted the best part of a generation and the war in the Sudan longer still. We are still living in the dark shadow of Iraq's invasion of Kuwait and the Gulf War, which brought devastation to both Kuwait and Iraq. But another form of warfare, covert and subterranean, is as characteristic of the region. It is waged not by conventional armies but by secret services, by terrorists and irregulars. This conflict touches every state without exception, to the extent that Middle East politics is as much about this form of warfare as it is about the overt kind—a fact that Abu Nidal has turned to his advantage, becoming a sort of nefarious spirit inhabiting the region's contradictions.

HIGH NOON IN IRAQ

Abu Nidal first flourished under the harsh reign of the Ba'ath party in Iraq. The Ba'ath had seized power in Baghdad in February 1963, when it distinguished itself, with discreet American help, by the wholesale slaughter of members of the Iraqi Communist party, then the strongest in the region. As Marion and Peter Sluglett suggest in *Iraq Since 1958* (1987), the CIA may have supplied the Ba'athists with lists of their Communist enemies. "It is certain," they write, "that some of the Ba'th leaders were in touch with American intelligence networks." When the rough and reckless Ba'athists had finished liquidating their enemies, they started quarreling among themselves, which allowed a cabal of nationalist army officers to overthrow them, in turn, in November 1963.

The party then went back underground, where it remained for the five years from 1963 to 1968. During this time it was purged and rebuilt by a young man of ruthless talents, then still in his late twenties, called Saddam Hussein. In July 1968, the party climbed back to power in a coup staged by one of its military members, General Ahmad Hasan al-Bakr, a well-known officer who had participated in the overthrow of the monarchy in 1968. Bakr had support in the officer corps, but his real underpinning came from Saddam's civilian wing of the Ba'ath.

For more than a decade, from 1968 to 1979, Bakr and Saddam Hussein, the soldier and the party apparatchik, ruled Iraq together, stamping out opposition, packing the army with their loyalists, controlling it with political commissars, and imposing Ba'athist rule in every corner of the country by means of a cruel and all-seeing security apparatus that was Saddam's own creation. From very early on, he was the regime's "strongman," with the title vice-chairman of the Revolutionary Command Council and with powers over everything and everyone.

Living in Iraq from 1970 onward, Abu Nidal had a ringside view of the growth of Ba'athist power and of the Iraqi state, funded by rising oil revenues after the 1972 nationalization of the Iraq Petroleum Company and the oil-price explosion the following year. Abu Nidal's support derived mainly from President Bakr rather than from Saddam Hussein. He was also close to Iraq's foreign minister, Tariq Aziz, and to Sa'dun Shakir, Saddam's cousin, who was then director-general of intelligence. Bred in a new Iraqi tradition of ferocity, Shakir undoubtedly had a sinister influence over Abu Nidal. Saddam, however, tended to make light of Abu Nidal, perhaps recognizing in him a smooth operator like himself. Abu Nidal was extremely touchy and Saddam's slights were not forgotten, and the two men were not on easy terms.

The mid-to-late 1970s were the high noon of Abu Nidal's Iraqi period. At that time, Iraq was the Arab world's bully and mischief maker: It planted secret Ba'athist cells across the region to stir up revolution; cozied up to Moscow; and proclaimed the most extreme views on Arab socialism, Arab unity, and the Arab-Israeli dispute in an evident bid to claim the leadership of Arab radicalism from its principal rival, Syria. After the October War of 1973, Baghdad condemned Arafat's attempted moderation as treacherous and denounced Syria's 1974 disengagement agreement with Israel on the Golan Heights, together with Assad's intervention in Lebanon two years later. Abu Nidal was encouraged to unleash his terrorists against Syria and the PLO.

But in 1978–79, following a change in Iraq's political climate,

Abu Nidal suddenly fell out of favor. The immediate occasion was the signing of the Camp David accords of September 1978, brokered by Jimmy Carter between Begin and Sadat. Saddam Hussein, who had not so far had a chance to cut much of a figure beyond Iraq's borders, seized on Sadat's "betrayal" to assert himself in Arab politics. He convened a summit in Baghdad that November to concert an Arab response to Egypt. He made it up with Saudi Arabia and the Gulf states, as well as with Syria, and sought to project a new image as an Arab and international statesman. A considerable obstacle to this program was his sponsorship of terrorism. Washington had long urged him to clean up his act. Thus, Abu Nidal's murderous outfit became an embarrassment to Saddam, and even on the purely Palestinian front, it was now more to his advantage to deal with Arafat, who was mainstream.

While the Baghdad summit was still in progress, Saddam called Arafat and Abu Iyad into his office in order to outline his new policy to them. Abu Iyad later gave me an account of what took place:

> "What are our differences?" Saddam queried. "Are you still upset because we didn't intervene to help you in Jordan in 1970 [a reference to the inaction of Iraqi troops when the guerrillas were being slaughtered by King Hussein's army]? We've already criticized ourselves for that unfortunate episode," he said grandly, "and we consider it past history.
>
> "Is it our support for Abu Nidal that angers you? I can tell you at once that we will sanction no further operations against you mounted from Baghdad. We will no longer take responsibility for his actions—and we have told him so.
>
> "But," he added with a dreadful smile, "don't expect me to hand him over to you!"

Once Saddam had edged out the ailing Bakr and assumed the presidency in 1979, Abu Nidal knew that his organization's days in Iraq were numbered. Not wishing to be the hostage of any one regime, he began making secret overtures to Syria and Libya. But just when he expected to be expelled from Baghdad, the outbreak of the Iran-Iraq war, in September 1980, gave him a reprieve. The war meant that Iraq needed international support more than ever, especially from the West and the rich Gulf states, and therefore ought to have gotten rid of Abu Nidal. But he was a valuable man for a regime at war to have in its service. The Iraqis needed weapons and intelligence. They needed an external arm, and Abu Nidal was ready to make himself useful. He offered to assassinate members of the Iraqi opposition abroad; he put himself forward as a covert channel of communication with Syria; internally, he kept an eye on potentially subversive enemies; and he involved himself as a middleman in the arms trade, from which he hoped to profit personally.

One of Abu Nidal's principal lieutenants at this time was Abd al-Rahman Isa, the defector I had hoped to interview in Algiers, but whose taped debriefing was made available to me by Abu Iyad. From these tapes I learned that Abu Nidal had in 1980 or 1981 promised the Iraqis that he could obtain T72 tanks from Poland, where he had good contacts: "Saddam Hussein considered this a tremendous service," Isa told Abu Iyad, "a service that in fact delayed our eviction from Baghdad by two to three years!" The Iraqis made a down payment of $11 million, which Abu Nidal placed in a private Swiss account. But then the Iraqis changed their minds. It was no longer tanks they wanted but artillery. Abu Nidal could not help there, but according to Isa, he never returned the money, which was another reason for his eventual departure from Baghdad.

THE LEBANESE IMBROGLIO

During this same period, the late 1970s and early 1980s, when Abu Nidal was struggling to hang on in Iraq, there arose a crisis inside his organization. He was to come out of it harsher, more secretive, and still more violent. The turmoil started in Lebanon in the wake of Operation Litani, Israel's invasion of March 1978.

Israel announced that its invasion of Lebanon was a response to a Palestinian attack that month on its Mediterranean coast, when a small force of guerrillas landed from two rubber dinghies and hijacked two civilian buses. In the shootout, nine guerrillas and thirty-seven Israelis were killed. But in scope and destructiveness, the Israeli invasion dwarfed the incident that had provoked it. Israel occupied the whole of South Lebanon up to the Litani River, sending a panic-stricken population fleeing northward toward Beirut. Some two thousand Lebanese and Palestinians were killed and an estimated two hundred thousand displaced from their homes.

Angry at Israel's disproportionate violence, President Jimmy Carter told Menachem Begin to pull his troops out and lent American backing to UN Security Council Resolution 425, which called for a cease-fire and put a UN buffer force, baptized UNIFIL, between Israel and the PLO. The Israelis left three months later, but only after creating a buffer zone of their own inside Lebanon under a local Christian proxy, Major Sa'd Haddad.

The decision to accept the cease-fire with Israel split Fatah's high command. Arafat agreed to it after discussions with the UN secretary-general, Kurt Waldheim. But more militant members of the movement, including Abu Iyad, were determined to harass Israel's invading army. Abu Dawud, an ever willing firebrand, was ordered to assemble some men and send raiding parties against Israeli positions on the southern bank of the Litani. Looking for men to swell his force, Abu Dawud contacted Abu Nidal in Iraq, who supplied travel documents, tickets, and money for a Baghdad contingent some 150 strong. From his own stores in Beirut, Abu Dawud drew uniforms and weapons for the newcomers and sent them south. The incident illustrated Abu Dawud's ideological ambivalence: He was a prominent Fatah militia commander, yet he was also on the fringe of Abu Nidal's underground.

When Arafat heard what had happened, he interpreted it as a huge conspiracy against himself. Not only was his authority being flouted over the cease-fire, but he faced, or so he believed, a mass penetration of Fatah's ranks by Abu Nidal. His military commander, Abu Jihad, was instructed to arrest the "infiltrators." At this crucial moment, Abu Dawud was taken ill with food poisoning and had to be hospitalized. In his absence, Fatah disarmed and interned Abu Nidal's men. It was not an entirely straightforward task. Skirmishing broke out at several camps and there were casualties on both sides. At one point Arafat's loyalists came to suspect, with good reason, that Abu Iyad was siding with Abu Dawud and very nearly turned their guns on *his* men in Beirut. An intra-Palestinian bloodbath was narrowly averted.

After a long and stormy confrontation, Arafat and Abu Iyad made it up, and Abu Iyad went to interrogate the arrested men one by one: Some he won over to Fatah, but a good number were jailed. When he heard the news, Abu Nidal in Baghdad went wild with rage. He had lent 150 of his best fighters to Abu Dawud and now held him responsible for what had happened to them. He declared that his "martyrs" had been punished for refusing to follow Arafat's path of surrender to Israel, and he vowed to avenge them.

Suspicious as ever, he smelled a plot. Why had Abu Dawud asked him to send men to Lebanon? Was it a trap? Was Abu Dawud two-timing him with Abu Iyad? To put him to the test, he proposed a characteristically byzantine plan: He would lend Abu Dawud one of his men as a bodyguard for a few weeks—long enough for Abu Iyad, a frequent visitor at Abu Dawud's house, to get used to seeing him around. Then one day, on a prearranged signal, this man would kill Abu Iyad, and Abu Dawud would at once gun down the assassin and so destroy all evidence of the conspiracy. (It was, as has been seen, by a similarly devious scheme that Abu Iyad eventually met his death in January 1991.)

Abu Dawud indignantly rejected the plan. It was cowardly and immoral. But Abu Nidal took his refusal to cooperate as confirmation that Abu Dawud had deliberately led his men into a trap. In turn, when Abu Iyad heard of the proposed conspiracy against himself, it was enough to arouse his own doubts about Abu Dawud's ultimate loyalty. Of such tortuous stuff are Palestinian resistance relationships made!

As I learned, Abu Nidal and Abu Iyad then indulged in tit-for-tat assassination attempts against each other. In April 1980, a bomb was thrown at a car in which Abu Iyad was thought to be traveling in Belgrade. When that attempt failed, Abu Nidal sent three assassins to kill Abu Iyad in Beirut. Two of them, armed with rifles, waited on the roof of a building opposite his office for a signal from a third in the street below to open fire. This third man, a youth named Nabil, was spotted at his lookout post—in a barber's shop near Abu Iyad's office: The barber was in Abu Iyad's pay. When arrested by Abu Iyad's security men, he was found to be carrying a pistol. He was brought before Abu Iyad, who dismissed his guards and sat down alone with him.

"You really want to kill me?" he asked.

"Yes," the youth replied.

"Why?"

"Because you are a traitor! You are part of the leadership that has betrayed us." Nabil spat out the familiar line with which Abu Nidal brainwashed his members.

Abu Iyad put his loaded pistol on the table in front of Nabil.

"If you're convinced I should die, then shoot me."

Nabil pushed the gun away and broke down. He was a confused young man whose certainties crumbled when he found himself face to face with his intended victim. After a while, he gave away his accomplices, who in turn revealed the addresses of Abu Nidal's safe houses in Beirut and the names of the men who ran them. The PLO seized the buildings and arrested the members. To Abu Nidal's fury, about $1 million worth of property fell into PLO hands.

Determined to have done with the threat from Abu Nidal, Abu Iyad then sent a twenty-five-man team to kill him in Baghdad. Machine guns, hand grenades, and wireless communication equipment were smuggled in. After monitoring Abu Nidal's movements for several weeks, the team decided to ambush his car on a bridge over the Tigris River, which he crossed almost daily. However, a few days before the planned attack, Iraqi intelligence spotted five members of the team behaving suspiciously on the bridge. They were followed to their lodgings and arrested. The others scattered and the operation was called off. The five were condemned to death, but sentence was never carried out. Some years later, Abu Iyad managed to have them freed. "Two of them are now my bodyguards," he said with a smile as he told me the story. "You might have seen them as you came in."

By this time, the once friendly relations between Abu Iyad and Abu Nidal had turned to pure hatred. For years thereafter, Abu Nidal ran a column in his magazine in which Abu Iyad was always referred to as "the son of the Jewess."

THE COUP D'ÉTAT OF NAJI ALLUSH

In mid-1979, at the height of his murderous feud with Abu Iyad, Abu Nidal was struck down by a heart attack and had to be rushed to Sweden for surgery. The Iraqis generously paid the bills. To this day, when seeking to win sympathy, Abu Nidal is liable to unbutton his shirt and display his scars.

While he was convalescing, he handed over command of his organization to Naji Allush, a shy, plumpish, sweet-toothed intellectual of Christian parentage, normally resident in Beirut, who had joined the organization some eighteen months earlier with the high-

sounding but empty title of secretary-general. Allush was a radical member of Fatah and the head of the General Union of Palestinian Writers. In Arab circles, he was known as a left-wing thinker and publicist who preached that the Palestinians should model their struggle on the revolutionary experiences of Cuba and Vietnam. Sharing with his friend Abu Dawud a gut dislike for compromise and an enthusiasm for armed struggle, he had been attracted by Abu Nidal's criticism of Arafat.

However, Allush's real ambitions lay in Lebanon, where he dreamed of founding a press, a newspaper, even in time a political movement. Believing that he could do so with Abu Nidal's backing, he joined him. Abu Nidal, too, wanted to establish a clandestine presence in Lebanon and thought that Allush could provide him with the cover he needed. He may also have liked the thought of having an in-house ideologue in his employ. Like many self-taught people, he had an exaggerated respect for intellectuals. So Allush became the organization's figurehead. In practice he had no authority whatsoever—no access to the organization's funds or to its weapons, still less to its ultrasecret Military Committee, which was responsible for foreign operations. All these remained firmly in Abu Nidal's hands.

When Abu Nidal fell ill, Allush moved from Beirut to Baghdad, expecting to take command. But this only sharpened the contradictions between him and the rest of the shadowy outfit. From his sickbed, Abu Nidal continued to issue a torrent of peremptory memos and instructions—including one abruptly sacking two of his most dedicated followers, who were the bedrock of his movement, one a chemist called Imad Malhas (code-named Umar Fahmi), the other an accountant, Salah Isa (code-named Faraj). Suspecting them of disloyalty, Abu Nidal insisted they not only be dismissed from the organization but expelled from Iraq.

These orders appear to have greatly exasperated Allush. He disliked Abu Nidal's dictatorial ways, which left *him* no meaningful role to play. In spite of his title, he had never felt in charge. He shuddered at the organization's practices, its arrests, interrogations, and torture, which he now heard more about. Above all, he thought it wrong to murder Palestinians simply because one disagreed with them politically. His grievances had been building up for some time, but now came explosively to a head when he decided to mount a coup d'état.

But being neither cunning nor assertive, Allush missed his chance. Instead of expelling Abu Nidal and boldly taking over the organization, a move that in the absence of the chief had a good chance of success, Allush decided instead to break away altogether. Taking a handful of top people with him, he founded a new organization, called the Popular Arab Movement. Within a year or two, it had withered into insignificance. He had in effect surrendered to Abu Nidal what was left of the organization. Most members further down the hierarchy were barely aware of the ructions at the top: Allush was a remote figure; Abu Nidal was the leader from whom they got daily instructions. They stayed put. A few of the more sophisticated cadres, including some student members in Europe, drifted to Allush's side, but where and when he could, Abu Nidal exacted revenge. His representative in Spain, Nabil Aranki, was killed on March 1, 1982, for having sided with Allush.

An internal negotiating committee tried at the start to patch things up between Allush and Abu Nidal, but the latter was unforgiving. He launched a blistering attack on Allush, accusing him of stealing arms, of embezzling $400,000, of being a Vatican spy—for it was one of Abu Nidal's enduring obsessions that a dangerous papist conspiracy was at work in the region and in the Palestinian movement in particular.

Before this crisis, Abu Nidal had not been a wholly clandestine figure. In addition to being the boss of a secret outfit, he was also something of a diplomat and politician, receiving visitors at his house and dealing with people face-to-face. But after his heart attack and the Allush split, he became a recluse. When his doctors recommended that he take a glass of whiskey in the evenings, he started doubling the dose, and then doubling it again, until whiskey became an addiction, no doubt contributing to his suspicious and vengeful inclinations. He closed his door and tightened his security. His organization became more difficult to penetrate and his operations harder to monitor—as Fatah and his other enemies, including Western intelligence agencies, discovered to their chagrin. As a result of these upsets, 1979 was a relatively inactive year for him.

Abu Nidal was shaken by Naji Allush's split, but he recovered quickly. After all, he still controlled the money and the arms. His Military Committee was watertight, its secrets safe. Having lost some old-guard radicals, he took the opportunity of replacing them with men he could wholly control, small fry with little political

experience whom he turned into killers and fanatics. One way or another, he was able to contain the Allush upheaval and stabilize his organization.

THE MOVE TO DAMASCUS

After his heart operation in 1979, Abu Nidal could no longer bear the fierce summer heat of Baghdad and took to spending several months a year in Poland, where he moved his family into a large villa some sixty kilometers outside Warsaw. He did not speak a word of Polish, or indeed of any other foreign language, but his children went to Polish schools and his daughter, Badia, acquired fluency in the language. He settled in Poland more or less permanently between 1981 and 1984, only rarely visiting the Arab world and communicating with his colleagues by courier. It was a period of convalescence and retrenchment.

Calling himself Dr. Sa'id, Abu Nidal posed as an international businessman, and for the first year of his stay the Polish authorities did not know who he was. His cover was a Warsaw-based company called SAS, which had branches in East Berlin and London and through which he traded with Polish state companies. One deal the company made was to purchase four thousand Scorpion submachine guns. Desperate for foreign exchange, the Poles chose not to inquire too closely about the destination of the weapons.

Abu Nidal's relationship with Poland dated back to contacts he had made with the Polish embassy in Baghdad in 1974. As his quarrel with Fatah deepened, so he used bribes and the arms trade to strengthen his ties with Eastern Europe. For a while, Faraj (the accountant he dismissed in 1979) was in charge of relations with Poland, distributing gifts and commissions to officials, some of them in cash on a monthly basis. In the late 1970s, Abu Nidal deposited $10 million in a Polish bank, greatly improving his status in that country.

He had settled in Poland in 1981 because he no longer felt safe in Iraq. The Iraqi authorities had signaled their changing attitude toward him in a number of unfriendly moves. They had informed him that from January 1, 1981, they would no longer issue Iraqi passports to his members, with the result that some 120 men whose passports had expired found themselves in difficulty. At the same time, Iraqi intelligence started monitoring conversations at Abu Nidal's Baghdad offices, forcing him and his colleagues to go to the Ramadi training camp, outside Baghdad, when they wished to escape this irksome surveillance. It was a considerable inconvenience.

It was very probably these developments that, early in 1981, caused Abu Nidal to instruct his close aide Abd al-Rahman Isa to sound out the Syrians about the possibility of a move to Damascus. Between January and May 1981, Isa went five times to Damascus at the head of a small delegation for discreet talks with General Ali Duba, head of military intelligence; General Muhammad al-Khuly, head of air force intelligence; and Foreign Minister Abd al-Halim Khaddam. The Syrians wanted a detailed explanation of Abu Nidal's anti-Syrian operations, including the attempt on Khaddam's life. Syria was holding half a dozen of his members in jail, on suspicion of having been involved in sabotage in Damascus in the 1970s. For his part, Abd al-Rahman Isa took the Syrians to task for their intervention against the Palestinians in Lebanon and for standing by while Maronite militias besieged the Palestinian camp of Tal al-Za'tar and then massacred many of its inhabitants. But finally it was agreed to let the future be a test of their good intentions toward each other. More immediate interests were involved.

Abu Nidal needed a new sponsor and hoped to develop with Syria the same intimate relationship he had once enjoyed with Iraq. He instructed Isa to ask permission to open offices in Damascus. Syria, for its part, had two main objectives in dealing with Abu Nidal: First, it saw him as a potential ally in the bitter war it was then waging against the Muslim Brotherhood—a war of militant Islamic terror and Ba'athist counterterror that had developed into the gravest challenge Assad's regime had yet faced. Terrorists of the Muslim Brotherhood had started their campaign of bombings, assassinations, and attempted insurrection in Syria in 1977 and were to pursue it ruthlessly until 1982, when, in a gory finale, the regime rooted them out and crushed them, together with thousands of innocent civilians, in the central Syrian city of Hama, which the rebels had made their stronghold.

In early 1981, when Abd al-Rahman Isa made his approach to Syria, the regime's war against its internal Islamic enemies was at its peak, and Syria's relations with its neighbors Jordan and Iraq, which were known to be providing the Muslim Brotherhood with arms, funds, training, and sanctuary, were at an all-time low. Abu Nidal seemed well placed to supply intelligence about both the Muslim activists and their backers in Amman and Baghdad, as well as to strike at their leaders, some of whom were operating from Europe. Abu Nidal had learned a good deal about the Muslim Brotherhood in Baghdad and had even trained some of their men at his base at Hit, 300 kilometers north of Baghdad. All this information he was now proposing to trade with the Syrians.

Second, Syria saw Abu Nidal as a useful instrument with which to deter King Hussein of Jordan and Yasser Arafat from private dealings with Israel. Assad had for years been sparring with the two men on this issue. He feared that if Jordan and the PLO negotiated a separate peace with Israel, Syria would be isolated and militarily at Israel's mercy. Assad believed fervently that the only peace with Israel worth having was a comprehensive one, in which Israel withdrew from all the Arab territories it had seized in 1967, and that the only way to make Israel come to the negotiating table was for the Palestinians, Jordan, and Lebanon to fall in behind Syria and confront Israel as a united bloc. Assad felt that recruiting a notorious hit man like Abu Nidal was a way of putting pressure on both the PLO leader and the Jordanian monarch to accept Syrian leadership on these issues.

But the Syrians were far more cautious than the Iraqis in their dealings with Abu Nidal. Ahmad Hasan al-Bakr had embraced him, set him up in business, and given him access to Iraqi facilities, whereas Assad refused to meet him, and he insisted that the relationship be kept within strict intelligence bounds and be reviewed at intervals. In the meantime, Abu Nidal's organization was to be allowed no overt political activity and no training camp. The link with Abu Nidal was to be maintained by Muhammad al-Khuly's air force intelligence rather than by Ali Duba's military intelligence, which handled relations with all other Palestinian groups. Assad had not been impressed by ingratiating letters Abu Nidal had sent him, in which he reminded the Syrian leader that his own mother had been an Alawite, a member of Assad's own sect, and that he should therefore be considered not just an ally but a kinsman.

On his fourth visit to Damascus, Abd al-Rahman Isa presented the Syrians with a working paper of a page and a half, signed by Abu Nidal, which set out the main lines of their prospective understanding. The Syrians promised to respond. A month later, on Isa's fifth visit, in the spring of 1981, he and his delegation were summoned to General Khuly's office, where, as Isa later told Abu Iyad, they were warmly received. "Our leadership has decided that Syria should be your country, so welcome to it!" Khuly declared. "Move here as and when you please. But I would suggest that at the start, your presence should be kept secret. Let us hope that the relationship between us will go from strength to strength."

In this friendly climate, Abu Nidal paid his first visit to Syria on June 11, 1981, and, to his considerable satisfaction, was met by General Khuly on the Iraqi-Syrian border and escorted to Damascus for a five-day visit. Abu Nidal was now officially under Syrian auspices. Isa was left to search for suitable premises and appealed to Abu Nidal for the money to buy a five-story building in the Sha'lan district of Damascus. Isa moved into a small room on the top floor with his wife and children and for several months shared the rest of the building with the organization's members, until General Khuly found them an apartment.

Soon Isa was given permission to set up a radio link with headquarters in Baghdad, and the Syrians also helped him monitor Fatah's radio communications. Members of the organization were allowed to carry light weapons for purposes of self-defense. More buildings and vehicles were acquired and more cadres drafted in. There was a lot to do: internal administration; contacts with Arab and foreign embassies; spreading the word in the Palestinian camps; liaising with the organization's members in Lebanon and Jordan; and of course, starting up intelligence work. A branch office was opened in Der'a, on the Syrian-Jordanian frontier, from which to run agents and smuggle weapons into Jordan. A group of very young recruits, aged fifteen to seventeen, was sent to Iraq for training. In November 1981, the organization opened a real estate agency in Damascus, as a cover for acquiring suitable apartments and offices, and in December it bought two heavy trucks to work the Baghdad–Damascus road and a refrigerated vehicle to work the Amman–Damascus road, commercial investments that could, when needed, be put to other uses. By the end of 1981, Abu Nidal had some 120 full-time workers in Syria and Lebanon.

EXPULSION FROM IRAQ

Although the Iraqis did not like Abu Nidal's growing involvement with Syria, their own relationship with him dragged on until 1983. The last straw was the murderous operations he mounted for purposes of extortion and blackmail against both the United Arab Emirates and Jordan. The Emirates were one of Iraq's paymasters in the Iraq-Iran war, while Jordan's port of Aqaba had become its lifeline to the world. Iraq came under great pressure to have done with Abu Nidal once and for all.

On November 4, 1983, Abu Nidal (then on a brief visit to Iraq from Poland) and two of his top officials were summoned at short notice to a meeting with Tariq Aziz, Iraq's foreign minister. Abd al-Rahman Isa, Abu Nidal's intelligence chief, witnessed the scene and related it later to Abu Iyad in his taped debriefing. Aziz was unusually brusque with them. "Our leadership," he declared, "has been discussing your presence here. President Saddam has come to the conclusion that you have become a dangerous burden to us. You have not kept to our agreements. At a time when we are engaged in a national battle, you have attacked our allies. Your organization has just one week from today to clear out." Then, turning to Abu Nidal and rudely jabbing a finger at him, he said: "As for you, *you* are to leave Iraq the minute you step out of this office!"

The humiliation of this dismissal enraged Abu Nidal. Given to fanatical prejudice, he worked himself up into a frenzy of hatred against Christian-born Tariq Aziz, whom thereafter in his publications he regularly accused of being in league with the pope to destroy the Arabs. Abu Nidal had actually been expecting the eviction for months, and he had deliberately stayed abroad for extended periods so as not to be in Baghdad when word of it came. But the Iraqis had cunningly waited for his return, to serve the notice on him in person. Apart from relishing his humiliation, they might perhaps also have feared that had he been absent from Baghdad at that time, he might have ordered his men to put up a fight before leaving. The Iraqis knew that he was perfectly capable of sacrificing his members so long as he himself was safe.

In the district around the Ramadi training camp, Abu Nidal's organization had made many Iraqi friends, largely by providing local services such as improving the water and electricity supply. On feast days, as many as twelve thousand people might attend celebrations at the camp. That is why the Iraqis feared that if it came to a confrontation, some of these could have been recruited and armed. While the war with Iran was raging, even a small internal uprising could have done the regime great harm.

The organization's departure was soon complete. Furniture from the various houses and offices was sold off. Half the weapons from the training camp were trucked to Syria for storage and the rest given to Iraq as a contribution to its war effort. The Iraqis allowed Abu Nidal to keep a small office, manned by two lowly cadres, to handle matters concerning members held prisoner in Iraq and families of men who had died there while in the organization's service.

On being thrown out, Abu Nidal was bold enough to complain that Iraq owed him $50 million in compensation for the properties he was giving up, although all of them had in fact been bought with Iraqi money. In numerous communiqués, from 1983 to 1987, he kept up a steady volley of invective against Baghdad on account of the money he claimed it "owed" him. It was true that he had greatly improved a large tract of land at Hit, in the north, which the Iraqis had given him. "It was," one of his group's members remarked, "just about the best developed piece of land in that whole country!" It was unfortunate, however, that when the Iraqis recovered it, they found, as well as improvements, twenty-six corpses buried under the trees, the grisly remains of those members he had murdered.

CONSOLIDATION IN SYRIA

The expulsion from Iraq caused Abu Nidal's organization to focus its attention and its hopes on Syria. Members poured into Syria, some with the permission of air force intelligence, most of them incognito, posing as ordinary Arabs who wished to reside there. Members who, in the years of tension with Iraq, had dispersed to Eastern Europe now set up house with their families in Damascus.

At first, the Syrians decided that the organization could rent only a limited number of buildings, but such restrictions soon went by the wayside. Abu Nidal's tactic was to acquire apartments as private residences and then turn them into offices. It was all done secretively. No sign was put up or guard posted at the door. Eventually, he began to purchase houses and flats, often registering them in the names of his members' wives. Some forty offices and about a hundred apartments were secured in this way, as well as a number of outlying farms. Perhaps because of his upbringing as the son of a Jaffa orange grower, Abu Nidal preferred country properties. Though Syrian security had monitored some of these activities, it did not grasp their scale.

The organization's main headquarters, in the Sha'lan district of Damascus, was expanded to house a prison, a technical unit responsible for forging passports and other documents, and the offices of the Intelligence Directorate, where weapons were hidden away in cavities in the walls or under the floors. Closed-circuit television provided a permanent watch of the surrounding streets. In addition, a press was bought on which to print pamphlets and magazines; a travel agency, secretly owned, booked flights for members and issued air tickets; an estate agency looked after Abu Nidal's expanding real estate interests; and a news agency, called Dar Sabra, served as a front for intelligence gathering. But at this stage, the Syrians did not permit the organization to open a training camp, nor were they forthcoming with weapons and military stores. (This contrasted with their treatment of other Palestinian factions, notably Ahmad Jibril's PFLP–General Command, which was allowed to build up a considerable military establishment.) The Syrians did not provide Abu Nidal with funds, either. If anything it was really the other way around: To ease his entry into Syria, Abu Nidal arranged for well-placed Syrian officers and officials to be given gifts of cars and fancy guns and to be lavishly entertained at the best hotels. During the time Abu Nidal was living in Poland, this expansion into Syrian life was directed by Abd al-Rahman Isa, the organization's head of intelligence.

As we have seen, Syria was mainly interested in using Abu Nidal internally against the Muslim Brotherhood and externally against King Hussein and Yasser Arafat, whose initiatives on the so-called peace front made Assad nervous. But by the spring of 1982 the Muslim Brotherhood had been defeated and Abu Nidal's services against it were no longer required. Jordan's King Hussein had become the main target.

With Syrian encouragement, Abu Nidal was to wage a terrorist war against Jordan for nearly two years, from October 1983 to the summer of 1985. It was to be the only substantial service he rendered the Syrians.

THE SYRIAN-JORDANIAN WAR

There were several strands to the quarrel between President Assad and King Hussein, but two deserve special mention. Assad had been angered by the support—in the shape of funds, training facilities, and safe haven—that Jordan had given terrorists of the Muslim Brotherhood in their war against Damascus from 1977 to 1982. However, by 1983–85, his main subject of disagreement with Hussein was over strategy vis-à-vis Israel, and in particular a dispute over how to recover the Arab territories Israel had conquered in 1967. King Hussein thought that he could win at least some of them back through negotiations with Israel, in which *he* would represent the Palestinians as well as himself. Assad's view was that only a solid Arab front, which included Syria, could have any chance of making Israel yield. If Hussein ventured alone into negotiations, Jordan would be gobbled up and the whole Arab camp considerably weakened.

This particular argument had a long history. Assad had fought the 1973 October War together with Sadat in the hope of loosening Israel's hold over the occupied territories and forcing it to the conference table. But Israel had gained the upper hand, defeating Egypt so decisively that it was Sadat who was forced to conclude a separate peace, leaving Syria and its neighbors Lebanon, Jordan, and the Palestinians exposed to Israeli power. From then on, Syria's concern was to prevent Israel from picking off the lesser players and bringing them into its orbit. If Syria could expand its own influence on the players, so much the better, Assad felt.

For years, Hussein had come under sustained Israeli pressure to "solve" the Palestine problem in direct negotiations. Israel sought to offer Hussein the job of policing the Palestinians in the occupied territories while retaining sovereignty for itself, together with control over land, water, and security. Hussein's counter-strategy was to press for a Jordanian-Palestinian federation, which, he felt, would give Israel the security it needed while providing the necessary outlet for restless Palestinian aspirations.

In 1983, Hussein set about trying to convince Arafat to let him talk to Israel on behalf of both of them. To prepare the ground, the king freed Palestinians from his jails, held frequent meetings with Arafat, promoted his plan in London and Washington, and restored diplomatic relations with Egypt, broken off at the time of Camp David.

Assad's worst fears thus aroused, it was then that Abu Nidal unleashed his hit men against Jordan. The Syrians were careful to stay in the background, not wishing to be obviously implicated in terrorism. They did not agree to joint planning with Abu Nidal, nor did they give him explicit directives to hit specific targets. They merely let fall suggestions, leaving the rest up to him. After all, it was *his* job to sniff out whom the Syrians hated most at any given moment. For this reason, Abu Nidal mounted his operations under different aliases. Then he waited to see: If the Syrian reaction was favorable, he would acknowledge the operation as his own; if the reaction was negative, he could just as easily disown it.

The results of his efforts were soon to appear in a frightening display of pyrotechnics that brought into play his wide network of arms caches, sleepers, residents, and killers. In October 1983, the Jordanian ambassador to New Delhi was assassinated and his colleague in Rome wounded, in separate gun attacks; in November, a Jordanian official was killed and another seriously wounded in Athens, and three explosive devices were found and defused in Amman; in December, a Jordanian consular official was killed and another wounded in Madrid. In March 1984, a bomb exploded outside the Intercontinental Hotel in Amman, and in November of that year the Jordanian chargé d'affaires in Athens narrowly escaped being shot when his attacker's gun jammed. In December, the Jordanian counselor in Bucharest was shot dead. In April 1985, there was an attack on the Jordanian embassy in Rome and on a Jordanian aircraft at Athens airport. In July, the Madrid office of Alia, the Jordanian airline, was machine-gunned, and in Ankara, the first secretary of the Jordanian embassy was shot dead.

This last operation was particularly costly for Abu Nidal. The Turks and the Jordanians got together, pooled their intelligence, and smashed his networks in both countries. Sixteen Palestinians, most of them members of his organization, were expelled from Turkey.

Syria in turn did not escape retaliation, almost certainly by Jordanian intelligence. In December 1984, a Syrian attaché in Athens was attacked but drove off his assailant. In April 1985, the Rome office of Syrian Arab Airlines was bombed and three employees wounded; an attempt was also made to kill a Syrian diplomat in Geneva. In May, his colleague in Rabat was shot, while in June a bomb was defused outside the Syrian embassy in London. In July, large car bombs exploded in Damascus outside the offices of the

Syrian Arab News Agency and the ministry of the interior, causing dozens of casualties. Of course, neither Assad nor Hussein would admit that they were waging a terrorist war against each other, but as their differences were well aired, it was public knowledge.

By mid-1985, Hussein decided the time had come for a truce. To Assad's satisfaction, Hussein publicly admitted the help he had given the Muslim Brotherhood and renounced all plans for direct negotiations with Israel toward a partial or separate settlement. Hussein even called on Assad in December 1985, his first visit to Syria since 1979. In keeping with this brotherly reconciliation, the Syrians made it clear to Abu Nidal that Jordanian targets were now off limits. A red line was put in place.

Like Iraq before it, Syria warned Abu Nidal that he was on no account to mount operations against Saudi Arabia. Damascus could not afford to offend one of its main benefactors: During the whole of the organization's stay in Syria, no attacks were made on Saudi targets.

But, as Abd al-Rahman Isa revealed to Abu Iyad in his taped debriefing, the Syrians did manage to get Abu Nidal to play a trick on the Saudis. As Isa recounted: "On one occasion the Syrians asked the organization to smuggle a quantity of arms and explosives into Saudi Arabia, to bury them in a suitable spot, and then give the Syrians the maps. Once the arms were in place, and making much of their concern for Saudi security, the Syrians told Riyadh that their intelligence had just uncovered a plot by a group of radicals to carry out sabotage operations in the kingdom. And here were the maps showing the exact location of the weapons! Lo and behold, the Saudis dug them up—and handsomely rewarded the Syrians for the tip-off."

MILKING THE RICH

While working for Syria, Abu Nidal also worked on his own account—in order to replenish his coffers. Syria was no rich sponsor about to put millions of dollars his way: The Syrian view was that giving him a home was reward enough. So by means of violence or mere threats of violence, Abu Nidal took to extorting money from the oil sheikhdoms of the Gulf. There was no pursuit of Palestinian interests in this blackmail. The superpatriot had become a highway robber.

Sheikh Zayid bin Sultan, ruler of Abu Dhabi since 1966 and first president of the United Arab Emirates (the federal state of the lower Gulf created in 1971), was well known for his generous donations to all manner of causes, the Palestinian cause among them. However, for Abu Nidal it was a source of constant frustration that he had not benefited from the sheikh's munificence. This was no oversight on Zayid's part, since one of Abu Nidal's gunmen had killed the Emirates' secretary of state, Saif al-Ghubash, at the Abu Dhabi airport in October 1977. The intended target, it is true, had been Syria's foreign minister, Abd al-Halim Khaddam, who was standing at Ghubash's side, but this hardly tempered Sheikh Zayid's indignation. Abu Nidal made repeated attempts to intimidate the sheikh into buying him off, but to no avail. Sheikh Zayid refused to be cowed.

Abu Nidal's approach was blunt. His habit was to send Gulf rulers threatening messages recorded on tape in his own voice. At first, the messages might be almost civil, on the lines of: "We are a revolutionary movement dedicated to the fight against Zionism and imperialism. We understand that you give money to the traitors of the PLO. We demand that you give us our own money or at the least a share of theirs! If you do not comply within six months, we will consider you our enemy and take action accordingly." If there was no response, the tone would soon become harsher and the message plainer: "I will kill you! I will kidnap your children and your princes! I will blow you up!"

When Sheikh Zayid still would not yield, Abu Nidal resorted to terror. On September 23, 1983, a Gulf Air Boeing 737 bound from Karachi to Dubai crashed in a mountainous region fifty kilometers from the Abu Dhabi airport, killing all 111 passengers and crew. A few days later, a news agency in Paris received a call on behalf of the "Arab Revolutionary Brigades," claiming responsibility. A defector from Abu Nidal's organization confirmed to me that the organization had put a bomb on board the aircraft and that the Brigades were a fiction Abu Nidal had invented for the occasion.

On February 8, 1984, the United Arab Emirates ambassador to Paris, Khalifa Ahmad Abd al-Aziz, by all accounts a good man and a patriot, was shot dead by a lone gunman outside his flat near the Eiffel Tower. Once again the fictional Arab Revolutionary Brigades claimed responsibility. And they struck again on October 25, 1984, when the UAE deputy chargé d'affaires in Rome, Muhammad al-Suwaidi, came under fire at the wheel of his car. He was critically wounded and his Iranian girlfriend, sitting by his side, was killed.

For the Emirates, this was the breaking point. Abu Iyad, whose business it was to keep abreast of such matters, later told me that under great pressure from such criminal attacks, Sheikh Zayid finally agreed to pay Abu Nidal $17 million, in three installments—$10 million; $5 million, and $2 million.

Abu Nidal considered Kuwait one of his most important "stations." Not only was there a large Palestinian population there, but in the 1980s, he also began to transfer large sums of money to Kuwaiti banks, when he feared that Western governments might try to seize his assets in Europe. To protect his interests in Kuwait, Abu Nidal resorted to his usual method of putting physical pressure on the Kuwaiti authorities. In May 1982, two of his members were arrested for bringing in large quantities of explosives from Iraq and were sentenced to long terms of imprisonment. On June 4, the first secretary at the Kuwaiti embassy in New Delhi was killed; this was followed on September 16 by the assassination of the first secretary at the Madrid embassy, and on the same day an unsuccessful attempt was made to kill the Kuwaiti consul-general in Karachi.

To spare themselves such headaches, the Kuwaitis started a secret dialogue with Abu Nidal and agreed to pay him a monthly stipend. He was even allowed to keep a clandestine representative in Kuwait to oversee his deposits and carry out intelligence tasks. According to my sources, the last person known to hold the post, in the late 1980s, was a certain Nabil Uthman (code-named Hamza Ibrahim).

Whenever the Kuwaitis attempted to harden their position and arrest or expel his members, Abu Nidal would remind them just what he was capable of. On April 23, 1985, Ahmad al-Jarallah, editor-in-chief of two Kuwaiti dailies, *al-Siyassa* and the *Arab Times,* narrowly escaped death when a gunman opened fire on him outside his offices. Once more the elusive Arab Revolutionary Brigades claimed responsibility. Less than three months later, on July 11, the same Brigades bombed two seaside cafés in Kuwait City, patronized almost exclusively by Kuwaiti families rather than by Palestinians. Nine people were killed and eighty-nine were wounded. This was another example of terror for purposes of extortion. It was certainly not calculated to improve Kuwaiti-Palestinian relations.

THE MUTINY IN FATAH

Early in 1982, Abu Nidal's intelligence chief, Abd al-Rahman Isa, was joined in Damascus by another senior cadre who had distinguished himself on the military side of the organization. His name was Mustafa Murad (code name Abu Nizar), a tall, bald man with a round face, fair skin, and a polite, cheerful manner, who was soon to be promoted to become Abu Nidal's deputy. His orders from Abu Nidal were to start infiltrating men from Syria into Lebanon to set up an independent base there.

At first, this had to be done in small numbers and with very great care. Lebanon was a Fatah stronghold. If any of Abu Nidal's men were discovered there, they risked being put to death. For this reason, the early infiltrations were made under the wing of a small Lebanese political faction that Abu Nidal had befriended. Called the Party of Socialist Action, it was an armed Marxist offshoot of the PFLP, one of the many fighting groups that had emerged in the ideological free-for-all of Lebanon. (Its leader, Hashim Ali Muhsin, was to die in a Bulgarian hospital in 1988.) It agreed to lend its name to Abu Nidal's men and gave them the run of its camp in the Bekaa Valley.

Israel's second invasion of Lebanon, of June 1982, was a great boulder thrown into the Palestinian pond, a far greater disturbance than the more limited 1978 incursion. Fatah's control over Lebanon was broken. Its forces were expelled or dispersed. By 1983, thousands of men found themselves adrift in the Bekaa Valley or in and around the northern refugee camps. All over the country, Palestinian families buried their dead and struggled to rebuild shantytowns ravaged by Israeli bombardment. The Israeli invasion also posed a great threat to Syria, stretching its resources and its attention to the limit. Syria was in desperate need of allies and proxies to stem the Israeli advance, and it was not fussy about who they were. Here was Abu Nidal's opportunity. His men could now begin to trickle into Lebanon from Syria more confidently and in greater numbers and set up their own camps under their own name. Emerging from the clandestine cocoon in which it had wrapped itself in Iraq, the organization started to make itself known.

An event then took place that was also hugely to Abu Nidal's advantage. A group of Fatah officers, based in Lebanon and Syria, rose in rebellion against Arafat in the spring of 1983. Three Fatah colonels—Abu Musa, Abu Salih, and Abu Khalid al-Amli—had been outraged by Arafat's decision to evacuate Beirut in September 1982 rather than carry on the fight against Israel, and they resented the protection he had given to a number of cowardly officers who had failed the test of battle. Such a one was Colonel Isma'il, the commander of Fatah's forces in South Lebanon, who, when Israel marched in, had gotten into his car and driven off to the Bekaa without even bothering to inform his troops. Instead of court-martialing him, Arafat had actually promoted him.

Beyond these specific issues was the old quarrel that had divided Fatah since 1974: armed struggle versus diplomacy. The mutineers were suspicious of Arafat's flirtation with "peace plans" and of his talks with King Hussein to establish a common negotiating stance. They wanted Arafat to sack the cowardly officers; to share power with them in a "collective leadership"; to smuggle back into Lebanon the Palestinian fighters who had been dispersed abroad; and to opt unequivocally for armed struggle rather than political compromise.

When, in May–June 1983, the rebels attacked Fatah's arms depots in the eastern Bekaa and seized supply lines from Syria, Arafat hurried to rally his supporters. But Syria's President Assad, who had no love for him and no confidence in the plans he was cooking up with King Hussein, threw his weight behind the rebels. Screaming foul, Arafat accused Syria of taking sides, whereupon he was unceremoniously expelled from Syria on June 24, 1983—a move that dramatized the Assad-Arafat breach, underlining Assad's ambition to wrest the key to a solution of the Palestine problem from an independent PLO.

Abu Nidal had by this time built up a sizable enough force in the Bekaa to fight alongside the Fatah rebels against Arafat's loyalists. Calling in more guerrillas from Syria, he also took part in Arafat's dramatic finale at the northern Lebanese port of Tripoli in December 1983, when, under heavy shelling from the Fatah mutineers and their allies, the PLO leader was forced out of Lebanon altogether. To reward Abu Nidal for helping defeat Arafat, the grateful Syrians now allowed his organization to set up an official presence and operate in the Bekaa and in northern Lebanon.

In Damascus, Abu Nidal's organization's prestige was high. It was given all sorts of facilities, with air force intelligence remaining the main conduit for Syria's favors. Inside the organization, the link with this intelligence service was described as the "central relationship" and was given very special attention. Abu Nidal appointed one of his nephews, Abd al-Karim al-Banna (code name Husam Mustafa), a graduate of the Baghdad College of Law and Politics, to take charge of it.

Soon Abu Nidal's members were allowed to fly in and out of Damascus airport simply on the strength of a telex from air force intelligence, a very special privilege, since other Palestinian groups needed the permission of *al-dabita al-fida'iyya,* a department of military intelligence renowned for its strict handling of guerrilla affairs. For road travel between Syria and Lebanon, air force intelligence gave the organization a dozen cars with official number plates, which allowed its members to sail across the border with no other formality than giving their code names. Members of other Palestinian groups had to produce genuine identity cards with their photographs on them.

Such an easygoing system was open to abuse—and Abu Nidal was quick to abuse it. The cars provided by air force intelligence proved a dangerous loophole. They were used to transport to Lebanon, against their will and without the Syrians' knowledge, dozens of people arrested or kidnapped by the organization in Damascus. The victims would usually be told they were being sent on a training course, only to be murdered in the Bekaa. If their families or the Syrians made inquiries, the organization would tell them that they had been sent abroad on a mission. If someone refused to go quietly, he would be drugged and carried to Lebanon in the trunk of a car. On occasion the organization killed its victims in Syria and buried them on one of its farms. Cars returning from Lebanon were used to smuggle weapons back into Syria in secret compartments. Routine checks by the Syrians at the border revealed nothing.

Members of the organization who were selected to take part in foreign operations were taken to Lebanon for training in an air force intelligence car, then brought back and sent on their mission from the Damascus airport. If they were arrested abroad, a Syrian stamp would be found in their passports, showing that Damascus had been their point of departure. Under interrogation, they would confess to having been trained in the Bekaa, thus suggesting that they had been under Syrian control. In each case, Syria would be blamed. Abu Nidal's strategy was to leech on to the host country he was in—offer it his services so as to seem indispensable and then implicate it in his violence so as to render it vulnerable to future blackmail by him. "Betray me," he was saying in effect, "and I reveal all."

Abu Nidal benefited from the Fatah mutiny and benefited again from the mutiny's collapse. The rebel colonels started squabbling among themselves almost immediately after their coup. Months before the mutiny, in 1982, Abu Nidal had secretly met Colonel Abu Khalid al-Amli in Prague, given him half a million dollars, and discussed with him plans to oust Arafat. They agreed to form a joint command in which Abu Nidal would figure prominently. But Colonel Abu Musa knew nothing about these arrangements and, anyway, did not want to be associated with what was considered a terrorist outfit. Tiring of these quarrels, Abu Salih, himself a candidate for the leadership, went to Beirut, quit politics, and withdrew from the fray.

Meanwhile, as the colonels quarreled, their common enemy, Arafat, was far from finished. He had been expelled from Beirut by the Israelis, from Damascus by the Syrians, and from North Lebanon by the Fatah rebels. He had nevertheless managed to preserve his freedom of maneuver by strengthening his links with Egypt and Jordan. In the occupied territories, he was still the supreme symbol of Palestinian nationalism. The more the mutiny came to look like a Syrian plot to down him, the less popular support it got. In due course, the anti-Arafat rebellion collapsed in acrimonious exchanges. Short of money, of organization and coherent leadership, it would fail to become an effective Palestinian rallying point.

Here was Abu Nidal's opportunity to fill the vacuum. He had arms; he had money—he could even pay in dollars; and he had Syrian air force intelligence facilities, which gave him great freedom of movement. Men who had defected from Arafat's ranks in 1982–83 to join the Fatah rebels defected again to Abu Nidal's group, including several hundred of Abu Salih's best fighters.

Most of these changes took place more or less spontaneously, under the pressure of events, while Abu Nidal was away in Poland. He did not view the changes with much enthusiasm. His instinct was *not* to come aboveground and into the open. Moreover, some of the new men who joined at this time had no sympathy for his terrorist methods or his ties with Arab intelligence services. Now that they were within gunshot range of Israel, they could see no point in his terrorist operations in Europe and further afield.

To keep an eye on things, Abu Nidal visited Syria from Poland a number of times in 1984—unbeknownst to the Syrians. He simply entered under a false name, with a Libyan passport. Because of the good relations between Syria and Libya at the time, Libyan passport holders could enter Syria with no questions asked. Or perhaps the Syrians simply preferred not to know.

chapter

7

THE COLONEL'S CRONY

On a cold, bright day in February 1984, two Arabs were having a long confidential conversation over lunch in a hotel in Sofia, the Bulgarian capital. One was a Palestinian, a small, round, dark-skinned man who walked with a slight limp, the result of beatings he had suffered in Jordanian jails in 1970. This was Abu Nidal's long-serving intelligence chief, Abd al-Rahman Isa. The other was a tall, elegant, sharp-witted Libyan, Ibrahim al-Bishari, Qaddafi's head of external intelligence (and, at the time of writing, his foreign minister). They had come to prepare the ground for a meeting of their principals.

Abu Nidal and Qaddafi were not yet personally acquainted, but they had had dealings with each other over the years and their relationship had known a number of false starts. However, it was only a matter of time before these two mavericks of Arab politics, two men who lived by their own rules, gravitated toward each other. They had much in common—a neurotic suspicion of the outside world, an inferiority complex—but they also shared the belief that they were men of great destiny. Qaddafi, ruler of a handful of desert tribes on the Mediterranean seaboard, was convinced that he was born to leave his mark on Arab history. (In an interview in the late 1970s, I heard him say without a hint of irony that the model of society he had outlined in his *Green Book,* a small volume of eccentric maxims, should serve the whole of humanity.) In turn, Abu Nidal, a professional subversive who made it his business to challenge the established order, saw himself as the natural leader of world revolution. Behind their usually calm and reserved exteriors, both men were also extremely aggressive, ever ready to pounce.

A MEETING OF MINDS

In May 1984, accompanied by the faithful Isa, Abu Nidal traveled from Warsaw to Tripoli, the Libyan capital, for his first encounter with Qaddafi. It took place in the multicolored Arab tent, pitched incongruously among the billets and guardrooms of the Bab al-Aziziyya barracks, that serves as the Libyan leader's office and reception room. By all accounts, they got on famously and their talks lasted for hours. It was a meeting of like minds.

Qaddafi's paranoia, his sense of being under siege, was more than usually acute at this time. A few weeks earlier, one of his security men inside the Libyan People's Bureau in London's St. James's Square had crazily opened fire from a first-floor window on a crowd of anti-Qaddafi demonstrators, killing a young British policewoman, Yvonne Fletcher. Britain broke off diplomatic relations and, after a nine-day siege of the People's Bureau, expelled the whole of its staff. Several Western leaders called for a joint strategy to combat Libyan-sponsored terrorism, prompting Qaddafi to retort defiantly that he would "hurt" countries that conspired against him. "Each country has its sensitive areas where we can put pressure!" he warned.

In security matters, Qaddafi's mind was parochial: His attention was focused on the small pockets of Libyan exiles—defectors from his Free Officers movement and from his diplomatic service, students who failed to return home, and the like—most of whom had taken shelter in the United States, Britain, Egypt, Morocco, or the Sudan. There and elsewhere, they had formed opposition movements, ranging from the democratic to the Islamic, all largely ineffective, with names like the National Front for the Salvation of Libya; the Libyan Constitutional Union; the Libyan Democratic National Rally; and the Islamic Association of Libya. From time to time, Qaddafi sent hit men to disrupt and intimidate them and, between 1980 and 1984, managed to have no fewer than fifteen exiles murdered. His main fear was that one or another of these groups would one day secure the backing of a foreign government to mount a coup against him.

It so happened that the international outcry over the killing of Yvonne Fletcher encouraged one of these opposition groups, the National Front for the Salvation of Libya, to try to topple Qaddafi—a bid that, by coincidence, reached its climax when Abu Nidal was in Tripoli meeting with the Libyan leader. The head of the National Front's military wing, a former Libyan officer called Ahmad al-Hawwas, had managed to infiltrate a group of armed men into Libya and to entrench them in a building immediately opposite the entrance to the Bab al-Aziziyya barracks. But Hawwas himself was not so fortunate. He entered Tunisia on a Sudanese passport, preparing to join his men in Tripoli, but Libyan intelligence was tipped off and he was intercepted and killed at the Tunisian-Libyan border. His armed cell in Tripoli was discovered. It was attacked by the Libyan army and overwhelmed.

Abu Nidal had spent long hours with Qaddafi a day earlier, and was actually in a nearby guest villa, waiting to take his leave of Libya's intelligence chiefs before driving to the airport, when the shooting broke out. According to Abd al-Rahman Isa, who witnessed the scene, the gun battle threw Abu Nidal into a total panic. "Get me out of here!" he shouted. He calmed down only when he managed to fly out of Libya a day later. This master terrorist, who glibly sent men to their death and who had just sold his services to Qaddafi, was terrified of being exposed to any violence.

The National Front's attack, abortive though it proved to be, helped convince Qaddafi that he needed someone to take on the external enemies of his revolution, the "stray dogs" as he referred to them, as well as the "imperialists" who were giving them protection and support. Abu Nidal was obviously his man. The colonel was impressed by Abu Nidal's reputation as a ruthless operator with a worldwide organization at his command—and Abu Nidal was never modest in trumpeting his capabilities.

Many Arab states have tried to recruit Palestinians into their intelligence. Dispersed about the world, skilled and educated but not always finding it easy to make a living, they are often open to recruitment. For Qaddafi, a Palestinian on the trail of a dissident Libyan in Europe or the United States might be less suspect than another Libyan. In their pursuit of exiles, his own Libyan agents had often proved incompetent and had blackened his name in foreign capitals. He now needed a professional.

When, in earlier years, he had been on good terms with Arafat, Qaddafi had tried to get Fatah to do his dirty work for him, but Fatah had turned him down. The very last thing the PLO leaders needed was to be further tarnished by providing Qaddafi with "death squads." George Habash's PFLP and Ahmad Jibril's PFLP–General Command had also been approached, but they too had enough sense to refuse Qaddafi's contract. Abu Nidal, on the other hand, had no such inhibitions. In exchange for protection and facilities, he was ready to render whatever services were asked of him. He had worked for the Iraqi government against the Communists, against moderate Palestinians, and against Syria; he had worked for Syria against King Hussein. He was now ready to work for Qaddafi against the Libyan opposition and to stage spectacular operations for him against American, British, and Egyptian targets.

Qaddafi felt he needed Abu Nidal. Abu Nidal, in turn, needed Qaddafi. His relationship with Syria had not fulfilled his expectations, and his expansion into Lebanon was starting to cost him a great deal of money. He reckoned that a move to Libya might, at a stroke, solve both problems. So Abu Nidal, in 1984–85, latched on to Qaddafi with great eagerness, treating him with sycophantic respect, giving him presents of inlaid swords whose blades he had had inscribed with fulsome tributes to the "Arab hero."

THE WAR OF THE CAMPS

The changes being wrought in his organization in Lebanon posed problems for Abu Nidal. To accommodate the new recruits who had flooded in after the collapse of the Fatah mutiny—to feed, clothe, house, and arm them—his organization had created a People's Army Directorate, with branches all over Lebanon. As Israel's armies, harried by the Lebanese resistance, fell back toward the border, Abu Nidal's men pushed south as far as Sidon, adding all the while to their numbers as they went along. The original tightly knit, secretive terrorist organization had suddenly come aboveground and rejoined the Palestinian mainstream. While Abu Nidal was abroad in Poland, his organization had taken on a different life and character, presenting him with a number of critical choices: What sort of movement did he wish to command and what sort of leader did he wish to be?

The main impetus for the organization's transformation was the so-called War of the Camps, a pitiless struggle between Palestinians and Shi'ites, which lasted from 1985 to 1987, leaving countless thousands dead, wounded, or uprooted from their homes. Traditionally the underdogs of Lebanese society, the Shi'ites of South Lebanon and the Bekaa Valley were victims of exploitation and neglect. They endured still worse suffering when Palestinian guerrillas moved into Lebanon and brought down ferocious Israeli reprisals on their own heads—and on those of the unfortunate Shi'ites living alongside of them. As a result of Israeli bombing, tens of thousands of Shi'ites abandoned their villages and fled north to shantytowns around Beirut.

This unhappy situation led to Shi'ite mobilization under the Imam Musa al-Sadr, a charismatic cleric of Iranian-Lebanese descent who founded his Movement of the Disinherited in 1974, followed in 1975 by a self-defense force called Amal (Hope). As fellow sufferers, Shi'ites and Palestinians were natural allies, but there were tensions between them: The Shi'ites blamed the Palestinians for their plight, so when Israel invaded Lebanon in 1982, many Shi'ites welcomed them as deliverers from the Palestinians and their women even threw rice at the invading Israeli soldiers in a gesture of welcome.

But the Israelis soon outstayed their welcome. And when they sought to impose Maronite rule on the country, the Shi'ites moved into outright opposition. Turning to Syria and Iran for help, they harassed and ambushed the Israelis, eventually forcing them back toward their frontier. The Shi'ite spirit of martyrdom made them particularly adept at suicide attacks, which took a heavy toll of Israeli lives. And once the Israelis had fallen back on their self-styled "security zone" in South Lebanon, the Shi'ites moved in to fill the vacuum. They were determined to recover their villages and fight off all newcomers—including the Palestinians. They could no longer accept the return of an armed Palestinian presence, which, they feared, would start the whole cycle of Israeli reprisals and Shi'ite suffering again.

So when Arafat started infiltrating men back into Lebanon in the mid-1980s and rearming the refugee camps—from his point of view a justifiable measure of self-defense—Amal laid siege to the camps and attempted to subdue them. The Palestinians put up stiff resistance. They even carried the fight into the enemy camp by shelling Shi'ite suburbs of Beirut. Violent battles ensued in May–June 1985. The War of the Camps had begun. Shi'ites and Palestinians believed their very survival was at stake. No quarter was given, and each round of fighting had its brutal accompaniment of slaughter. Defenseless civilians perished in large numbers during this terrible confrontation.

Over the next two years, the fighting would die down only to flare up again, because the fundamental problem was not resolved: The Shi'ites wanted to be masters in their own house. They could not tolerate a Palestinian force able to act independently. For its part, Syria too could not tolerate the restoration of Palestinian power, which might challenge its own position in Lebanon or expose it to danger from Israel. As Lebanon was vital to Syria's security, Assad supplied the Amal group with arms—including tanks—with which to control the Palestinian camps. But Arafat, too, needed to protect his civilians. He was also anxious to show that the PLO was still a force to be reckoned with and that Israel's attempt to smash it had failed.

Such was the dilemma confronting Abu Nidal's organization in Lebanon: Should it side with its Syrian patron against the Palestinians? Or should it defend the Palestinian refugee camps besieged by the Syrian-backed Shi'ites?

In fact the organization had no choice, because events had already dictated its position. Its very success, since the Fatah mutiny of 1983, in drawing into its ranks hundreds of Palestinian fighters and dozens of political cadres, meant that it could no longer stand by and watch Amal wreak havoc on the refugee camps, and it went to their defense. The War of the Camps was in fact the catalyst that drew the organization out of its shell and caused it to fight beside Arafat's men. The years of hatred and blood that separated them were set aside. This unexpected alliance was spontaneous, forged in the heat of battle and decided by the organization's rank and file, without waiting for word from Abu Nidal.

These dramatic developments owed a great deal to one man, Atif Abu Bakr, who defected from Fatah to join Abu Nidal's organization in 1985 (and whom I interviewed over several weeks in Tunis after his break with Abu Nidal). As has been mentioned, he had served as a PLO "ambassador" in Eastern Europe from 1974 to 1984 and was well known as a highly articulate political ideologue and poet. Always a radical, Abu Bakr had watched Arafat's slide toward concession and compromise with growing alarm. For him the breaking point came in November 1984, when Arafat called a meeting of the Palestine National Council in Amman, apparently signaling his acceptance of King Hussein's ideas for a settlement with Israel. A few months later, in February 1985, Arafat and Hussein signed an agreement that seemed to give the king a mandate to negotiate with Israel on the Palestinians' behalf. The radicals were outraged at what looked like a sellout. Abu Bakr went to Syria, resigned from the PLO, and joined Abu Nidal's organization—one of many to do so at the time.

For Abu Nidal's organization, Atif Abu Bakr was a very considerable catch. Not since the days of Naji Allush could it boast of an intellectual of any stature. Within a very short time Abu Bakr was assigned to the organization's top institution, its Political Bureau, and was appointed head of the Political Directorate, as well as official spokesman.

But what Atif Abu Bakr really became was the spokesman for the new spirit that swept through the organization in Syria and Lebanon in the mid-1980s, at a time when Abu Nidal, flitting between Warsaw and Tripoli, was engrossed in other things. In his absence, a reconciliation began to take effect between comrades who, ever since the great Fatah split of 1974, had been bitterly at odds. Past feuds were set aside, and recent defectors from Fatah like Atif Abu Bakr could embrace old defectors like Abu Nizar. Were they not, after all, sons of Fatah? Did they not spring from the same root? Together, Atif Abu Bakr and Abu Nizar drew into the new-style organization many men, both cadres and fighters, who had lost their bearings in the various Palestinian splits and rebellions. Committing these men to the defense of the camps against the assaults of Amal created an atmosphere of revival, of true nationalist struggle.

A new joint command was set up. Breaking with the past, it wanted to put an end to intra-Palestinian killings; to give up "foreign operations"; and to build bridges to Fatah, the mother organization from which it had strayed. These men had no love for Arafat, but who actually was in charge no longer mattered. What was important, Atif later told me, was to rebuild a united resistance movement. Propaganda against Fatah, once the staple ingredient of the organization's communiqués and publications, was abandoned and the old accusatory language was dropped. In Abu Nidal's magazine, the PLO, which had hitherto been considered irredeemably treacherous, was now described as a "Palestinian house" that all those could enter who wished to confront the common enemy. Such were the views that Atif Abu Bakr passionately promoted.

A parallel change took place on the military side. Swollen with new recruits, the People's Army formed five regional commands, covering Lebanon from far north to far south. Still financed (by now rather reluctantly) by Abu Nidal, it became a very visible body, creating infrastructures that could provide its fighters with food, uniforms, and weapons, as well as medical services and political education. Instead of the assassin armed with a bomb or a sniper's rifle, the organization now had men who could drive armored vehicles or could fire missiles, former Fatah officers with years of experience behind them and considerable military skills. The People's Army became the second largest Palestinian fighting force in Lebanon, second only to that of Fatah itself. It was estimated that in 1986 it was costing about $1.5 million a month to run. Instead of being a small, closed, clandestine outfit that Abu Nidal could direct by remote control, the organization was developing into a mass movement with its own strong leaders and cadres. A new power base was being formed inside Abu Nidal's outfit.

Swept along by their own enthusiasm, the reformers believed that Abu Nidal would welcome the chance to lead a now popular and powerful faction that had won a new acceptance among Palestinians because of the "national role" it was playing. But they had forgotten the nature of the man and did not yet grasp what he was up to in Libya. They were very soon to be disabused. As we shall see in due course, Abu Nidal was to use the move to Libya to destroy them.

Abu Nidal felt that the transformations that had occurred in Lebanon were a grave personal threat to him, so he conspired to reverse them and return the organization to its old fanatical mold. He had by now given up Poland and was traveling back and forth between Tripoli and Damascus—but it was in Tripoli rather than Damascus that he felt wanted, appreciated, and at ease. His movements to and from Syria were undertaken with Libyan aid and approval, with Libya supplying the carrier, the money, and the passports. And astonishingly enough, they were usually undertaken without the knowledge of the Syrian authorities. The man who escorted him in and out of Syria was Muftah al-Farazani, a Libyan intelligence officer and head of the Libyan People's Bureau in Damascus, who was in direct touch with Libya's intelligence chiefs, Ibrahim al-Bishari and Abdallah al-Sanussi (the latter a particularly powerful figure because of his marriage to Qaddafi's sister-in-law).

What Abu Nidal always looked for was a secure base in an Arab country and, with it, the protection of an Arab intelligence service to complement his own elaborate arrangements. When this was not forthcoming, he preferred to withdraw from the Middle East altogether and to live as a recluse abroad, as he did when he went to Poland in 1981, between his falling out with Iraq and his organization's move to Syria.

DISAPPOINTMENT WITH SYRIA

A key to Abu Nidal's longevity as a terrorist is the extraordinary attention he pays to his personal security. Watchfulness has become second nature, together with a morbid suspicion of everyone and everything. Constantly on the move, he can congratulate himself on never having been caught. He is skillful at disguises, cultivates a nondescript appearance, and travels on an array of Arab passports, some forged and some genuine, preferably ordinary rather than diplomatic ones, because they attract less attention. His bodyguards are totally loyal, and he has known them for years. While parts of his organization are overt and more or less visible—in Lebanon he even boasts an official spokesman—he himself remains well in the background, his exact whereabouts at any one time known only to a handful of his associates. It is part of his passion for secrecy that in the course of a long career, he has given only five interviews—in 1974, 1978, and three times in 1985, which, for a man of his undoubted conceit, suggests a measure of self-denial. (However, petty vanities show through: Although he had little formal education, he likes to be called Doctor—Dr. Sa'id in the early days, and later Dr. Muhammad.)

In the early 1980s, Syria had taken him in and protected him. But the Syrians disappointed him. Even when his organization was well established there, Syria never made him feel as secure as he had felt in Iraq. In Damascus, he was not allowed to meet let alone befriend Syria's political leaders, nor could he match the close relations he had once enjoyed in Baghdad with President Bakr and Foreign Minister Tariq Aziz. He tried repeatedly to get himself officially invited to Damascus, but the Syrians continued to be evasive. Despite the services he rendered them in the terrorist campaign against Jordan, Syrian leaders refused to receive him in person. Theirs was no intimate, formally acknowledged relationship: There was no joint operations room; he had no access to Syrian embassies and diplomatic pouches. A strict ceiling was put on his activities. His organization's contacts remained restricted to General Muhammad al-Khuly's air force intelligence, the more disreputable, strong-arm end of Syria's intelligence apparatus. When he proposed coordinating anti-Iraqi operations with Syria's external intelligence service, headed at the time by General Adnan al-Hamadani, the Syrians declined.

What Abu Nidal found particularly frustrating and offensive was the Syrians' refusal to recognize that he had any *political* legitimacy. No doubt wishing to distance themselves, at least outwardly, from terrorism, they wanted their relationship with him to remain deniable. Syria's veteran defense minister, General Mustafa Tlas, once went so far as to dismiss Abu Nidal as a CIA agent, while President Assad himself could tell foreign visitors in all candor that he had never even *seen* Abu Nidal. Such circumstances were not calculated to reassure him. On the contrary, Abu Nidal felt threatened, haunted by the thought that in a bid to improve their relations with the West, the Syrians might betray him to the Americans. On his occasional furtive visits to Damascus, it was clear to him that the Syrians preferred not to know he was there.

Far away most of the time in the Polish countryside, he could not fully grasp what was going on inside his organization, and his secret policeman's mind brooded over the possibility of conspiracies hatching against him. He insisted on being kept informed of the most minute and trivial details.

Once a week, a special messenger would arrive in Poland from Damascus, carrying the organization's mail for him to study and respond to. His colleagues Abu Nizar, Abd al-Rahman Isa, Dr. Ghassan al-Ali were shouldering the daily burden of running an increasingly complex machine. Men had to be trained and briefed and sent on missions. The work of foreign stations had to be monitored. Funds had to be accounted for and archives kept up to date. The growing militia in Lebanon had to be supplied. Accordingly, the letters Abu Nidal sent back to the leadership in Damascus caused great irritation and rumblings of discontent. He would bombard his hard-pressed colleagues with bullying memoranda. Why, he wrote on one occasion, is so-and-so spending so much on apples? The return to Damascus of the weekly messenger was an anxious moment for members of the leadership as they wondered what further importunate demands their chief might make on them.

From time to time, to catch up on fast-moving events, Abu Nidal would summon his top aides to a conference at his house outside Warsaw. His harangues would be recorded on tape and would, on his instruction, be played back to those members of the command who had remained behind in Damascus. Abu Nidal's tactic was invariably to be bad-tempered and critical, to set one man against another, to play on differences between them, to reveal what X had said about Y, to stir up trouble. The return of his colleagues to their work in Damascus was always ridden with tension.

In early 1985, alarmed at the growth of his organization in Lebanon, Abu Nidal decided to return permanently to the Middle East. He moved his wife and children to Damascus and took a ground-floor apartment in the same building as his chief military colleague, Abu Nizar. But not daring to remain long in any one place, for fear of drawing attention to himself, he moved again within a few months to the small town of Zabadani, some forty minutes by road from Damascus, where, away from the public gaze, he bought two adjoining houses set in a large field. For added protection, he hired half a dozen Alawite peasants, said to be relatives of his mother, to work the land and look after the property. Abu Nidal's wife, Hiyam, did not like the isolation, especially as he was away a good deal, traveling continuously between Poland and Libya.

Late in 1985, a violent incident took place that was to have a dramatic impact on their relationship. Hiyam and her brother, Hussein al-Bitar, who lived in Jordan, jointly owned a substantial house and garden in Amman that was valued at a million dollars. Although the property was registered in their names, Abu Nidal claimed it was his, and he may indeed have helped finance its purchase. A bitter family quarrel ensued. Tiring at last of the arguments, Abu Nidal decided to resolve the matter once and for all—by killing his brother-in-law.

Because relations between Jordan and Syria had by now been patched up, he thought it wiser to mount the operation from Kuwait rather than from Damascus. Accordingly, three assassins, traveling on Jordanian passports, were sent into Jordan from Kuwait. On November 24, 1985, Hussein al-Bitar and his five-year-old son, Muhammad, were murdered. In a characteristic communiqué, Abu Nidal brazenly claimed that Bitar had been killed because he worked for Jordanian intelligence and supported Yasser Arafat.

These killings led to a traumatic emotional separation between Abu Nidal and his wife. She demanded a divorce, but he would not consent to it. They continued to live in the same house but began to lead separate lives. Inside the organization, some people said that she stayed because of the children, others that she put up with him because a good deal of the organization's money was deposited in banks in her name. In any event, she started traveling, taking their three children on trips abroad, often to Austria and Switzerland, simply to get away.

THE MOVE TO LIBYA

It was about this time that Abu Nidal moved triumphantly to Libya. His relationship with Qaddafi really took off in 1985, but it had not always been cloudless between them before.

A decade earlier, in 1975, Abu Nidal had sent some junior cadres, mainly students and teachers, to live covertly in Tripoli and Benghazi, where they were to spread the word and distribute his literature. In 1977, when Libya and Egypt came to the brink of war, these people supported Libya and some even volunteered to be sent to the front, a display of loyalty that induced the Libyans to allow Abu Nidal's organization to open an office on Umar al-Mukhtar Street in Tripoli.

Perhaps more to the point, Qaddafi was then on poor terms with Fatah, and especially with Abu Iyad, following a row they had had when they were both being entertained by President Boumédienne in Algiers. Qaddafi had urged Fatah to adopt his *Green Book* as its ideological bible. But Abu Iyad, as he told me later, could not help laughing at the suggestion. "It's no book at all," he told Qaddafi. "Whoever wrote it for you did you a great disservice!" Qaddafi was so angry that in 1977–78 he cut off his aid to the PLO, which was then running at $12 million a year in cash and another $50 million in stores and equipment. Another, perhaps more important, source of coolness was Fatah's refusal to fall in with Qaddafi's request to kidnap or kill a prominent Libyan opposition figure, Abd al-Mun'im al-Huni, one of the original Free Officers and a former head of Libyan intelligence, who had fallen out with Qaddafi and taken refuge in Egypt and whose head the colonel wanted.

So for a moment in 1977–78 Abu Nidal's people were in favor in Tripoli. But this did not last long. When, as we shall see, Abu Nidal started killing PLO moderates in 1978—Sa'id Hammami was killed in London in January and Ali Yassin in Kuwait in June—Fatah retaliated by attacking the organization's Tripoli office in July, killing two of Abu Nidal's men. (It was said that this was done with the complicity of Libya's minister of the interior, Colonel Khwaldi al-Humaidi, whose sympathies were with Fatah.) The Libyans decided to close down the organization's office and evict its members. Cells they had formed were dismantled. To try to patch up relations, Abu Nidal paid a flying visit to Tripoli on December 30, 1979, to see Libya's prime minister, Abd al-Salam Jallud, but he was not invited to see Qaddafi. In spite of his tiff with Abu Iyad, Qaddafi had no interest in seriously alienating Arafat or in muscling in on Iraq's turf, for Abu Nidal was, at that time, thought of as an *Iraqi* creature.

Abu Nidal had to wait until 1982 for another chance to make his mark in Libya—and once again it was as a result of a breakdown in Libyan-Fatah relations. During Israel's siege of Beirut, when the Palestinians were holding out under intense bombardment, Qaddafi sent Arafat a now famous telegram in which he urged him to commit suicide rather than allow Israel to expel him. Arafat replied that his fighters were ready for the supreme sacrifice provided that Qaddafi joined them. Acidly, he added that his present circumstances would not have been so desperate had Qaddafi delivered the weapons he had promised. Affronted, Qaddafi cooled toward Arafat, and when the Fatah mutiny occurred in 1983 and a Syrian-based "National Salvation Front" emerged, grouping most of Arafat's Palestinian opponents, Qaddafi was quick to lend

assert his leadership of radical movements throughout the area. This was the body through which other Palestinian factions, such as Ahmad Jibril's or Abu Musa's, were obliged to deal with the Libyan government. In contrast, Abu Nidal's organization dealt direct with Libyan intelligence. It was the only Palestinian organization to do so.

Abu Nidal was quick to grasp that Libya had very poor resources for intelligence gathering. Staffed by badly trained amateurs, its networks were virtually useless. Its officers were lazy and easily became dependent on others to do the work for them. As one source put it: "If you said to the Libyans, 'I will get you information about Chad,' they would stop all inquiries of their own and wait for you to hand them a file on a plate." So in addition to the surveillance, harassment, and assassination of the Libyan opposition abroad, Abu Nidal put his organization to work collecting information on Libya's behalf. Immersing himself in the task, he was soon to gain virtual control of Libya's intelligence apparatus.

For Abu Nidal, the years 1985–87 were a time of fruitful ambiguity in which he found himself situated between Syria and Libya. But there was no doubt which of the two he preferred. Qaddafi had invited him into the very heart of the Libyan system, where Abu Nidal loved to be. The Libyans allowed him to organize and proselytize in the resident Palestinian community, to conduct an energetic publicity campaign for his organization—in short, to be politically active.

Qaddafi and Abu Nidal had now become partners. Insiders who attended their many meetings at this time reported that they hugely enjoyed each other's company and happily spent their time together abusing their enemies—before plotting how best to destroy them.

it his support. Conditions were now propitious for Abu Ni
reentry into Libya.

This was the background to his arrival there in 1985. No
was done properly. Abu Nidal began by appointing Hamdan
Asba (code-named Azmi Hussein), a cadre from the Intellig
Directorate, as his personal liaison officer with Libyan secu
Asba was followed in Tripoli by Ali al-Farra (code-named
Kamal), one of Abu Nidal's most trusted associates: His reside
in Libya signaled that Abu Nidal had now made Libya his princ
base. More cadres from other directorates were soon in pl
Libyan planes and embassies, passports, diplomatic pouches,
communications were put at Abu Nidal's disposal. And as
relationship expanded and grew warmer, Qaddafi gave Abu Ni
villas and apartments in Tripoli, housing outside the capital,
two farms—all free of charge. Most of these properties had b
expropriated from members of the Libyan opposition who had f
abroad.

The Libyans were generous with air tickets, travel expens
and hospitality of all sorts, putting up in hotels or private vil
members who were passing through. A year later, in 1986, Liby
intelligence also provided the organization with international te
phone lines, then a precious commodity because, after the Ame
can attack on Libya of April 1986, direct dialing was discontinu
and all outgoing calls had to be routed through an operator. T
Libyans not only provided the lines but also paid the bills.

More significantly, from 1985 onward the Libyans helped t
organization transport weapons into Libya to store them ther
also, to transport weapons *out of* Libya and hide them in caches i
Europe, Africa, and Asia. In some cases arms were handed by th
Libyans to members of the organization when they were already o
board aircraft at Tripoli airport; in other cases, arms were sen
abroad by Libyan diplomatic bag and handed to members of th
organization at Libyan embassies. For all practical purposes, Ab
Nidal had ceased to be an independent operator. His main place
of residence and of work, as well as those of his organization, and
the facilities that made his sort of work possible were gifts from
Libyan intelligence. He had become so closely involved with Libyan
intelligence that it had become impossible to tell them apart.

A pet idea of Qaddafi's was the National Command of Arab
Revolutionary Forces, which he set up at this time in an attempt to

chapter

8

MURDER OF THE MODERATES

> Ben-Gurion said that whoever approaches the Zionist problem from a moral aspect is not a Zionist.
> —Moshe Dayan

> The PLO? A bunch of traitors penetrated by a few patriots.
> —Abu Nidal

As I charted Abu Nidal's career in Iraq and his subsequent moves to Syria and Libya, he seemed to me at first a classic case of a Palestinian faction leader who, in search of safe haven, had turned mercenary, and then, in search of financial independence, had turned gangster. I reviewed the information I had gathered. Iraq had "created" him when it wanted the leadership of Arab radicalism but had dropped him during its war with Iran. Syria had taken him on to fight its terrorist war against Jordan but had lost him to Libya, which had used him against its "stray dogs" and other external enemies. All three Arab "sponsors," hostile to an independent PLO, had also used Abu Nidal to keep Arafat in check.

Abu Nidal himself posed as the supreme rejectionist, a diehard opponent of the negotiated settlement with Israel that the "capitulationist" Arafat had been angling for since 1974. But it was evident that he was also running an extortion racket, with little reference to the Palestine cause. In fact most of his operations seemed to do the Palestinians harm. The man was a puzzle. I couldn't understand what drove him.

Widening the scope of my inquiries, I left Tunis and its hothouse politics of defectors and guerrilla fighters to consult sources in Europe and the Middle East. I interviewed intelligence and police officers, as well as journalists and politicians, people who for one reason or another had a professional interest in the Israeli-Palestinian war because some of its battles had been, and continue to be, fought on their territory. What view did they have of Abu Nidal and his organization?

I heard two quite different explanations. The conventional view was the one Abu Nidal advanced—that he represented one extreme pole of the internal Palestinian debate, which had raged for twenty years, about whether a compromise with Israel was possible or even desirable. But a second opinion put forward by some of my sources was more sensational—and more in line with Abu Iyad's allegations: Abu Nidal was a tool of the Israelis, either because his organization had been penetrated by the Mossad (much as the Mossad had penetrated every other Palestinian faction, at one time or another, over the past twenty-five years) or because he himself had been recruited. The argument was usually stated like this: In theory, Israel and Abu Nidal are bitter enemies; in practice, their anti-PLO objectives and operations are so similar as to suggest an operational relationship.

In this view, Abu Nidal was less a product of intra-Palestinian disputes than of Israel's long-running war against the Palestinians. Whatever jobs he might have done for Arab sponsors, and they had been numerous and nasty, he had done many other jobs from which Israel alone appeared to "benefit."

Hard evidence remained scant, but as I discovered, the subject was gossiped about a good deal. A senior Jordanian intelligence officer, now retired and living in Amman, told me, "Scratch around inside Abu Nidal's organization and you will find Mossad." Much of this man's career had been spent liaising with Israeli intelligence and running agents against Palestinian organizations. It is not widely known that Israel and Jordan worked together from the late 1960s to contain what they saw as a common threat from the Palestinian guerrillas. The Jordanian intelligence officer supplied no evidence to support his remarks, but his view is typical of the widespread gossip that surrounds this supposition in Mideast intelligence circles.

The grave crisis of 1970–71, in which King Hussein put down the Palestinian rebellion, greatly strengthened the Israeli-Jordanian intelligence relationship. As my Jordanian source explained, the guerrillas shook King Hussein's throne; they called on Syrian tanks for support; they assassinated Hussein's prime minister, Wasfi al-Tal. It was not surprising that Hussein should look to Israel as a counterweight to Syria during the crisis itself, and afterward coordinate with it the intelligence war against the fedayeen.

Most Palestinians thus found themselves controlled by two powers, Israel and Jordan, whose excellent intelligence services wanted to contain Palestinian militancy and penetrate the various Palestinian groups beyond their borders. When the Black September terrorist movement emerged in the early 1970s, Israel, Jordan, and other affected states had a further strong incentive to plant agents in Palestinian networks and training camps to monitor, and if possible abort, hostile operations.

The intriguing hint dropped by the Jordanian intelligence officer about a Mossad–Abu Nidal connection was put more strongly by some of my other sources. A German security officer engaged in counterterrorism, whom I interviewed in London in April 1990, told me, "Israel needs to control men such as Abu Nidal. It *must* neutralize him. If it can make use of him, so much the better. Any intelligence service would do the same if it could." But this, of course, was still only an opinion based on a general observation. Then a French government expert on international terrorism, with considerable Middle East experience, said to me in the course of a long interview in 1991, "If Abu Nidal himself is not an Israeli agent, then two or three of his senior people most certainly are. Nothing else can explain some of his operations. But," he added, "the tracks are well covered and proof will be hard to find."

Among such people it was widely assumed that there was some overlap, some common ground between Abu Nidal and the Mossad. Some thought the penetration was at a low level; some believed that senior men had been recruited, perhaps even Abu Nidal himself and members of his extended family.

A former CIA officer, who had served as station head in several Arab countries and whose attitude toward the Arab-Israeli conflict was detached and professional, was more explicit: "It's as easy," he said, "to recruit the man at the top as it is someone lower down the ladder. It's quite likely that Mossad picked up Abu Nidal in the late 1960s, when it was putting a lot of effort into penetrating the newly formed Palestinian guerrilla groups. My guess is that they would have got him in the Sudan when he was there with Fatah in 1969. Once they had set him up, funded, and directed him, he would have had nowhere else to turn. If he had tried to quit, he would have been a dead man.

"The British could not have done it, or the French, or the Americans. Only Israel would have had the professionalism and the motivation to nurture and control him over twenty years."

This sort of argument from an intelligence professional sounded plausible, but once again proof was absent. On the whole I tended to discount Palestinian evidence on this subject as surely biased. One Palestinian who had had plenty of time to study Israeli methods was Abu Ali Shahin, a veteran guerrilla fighter who was captured by Israel in the West Bank in 1967 for setting up a clandestine cell and who spent the next seventeen years in Israeli jails—the first thirteen years and ten months, he told me, in solitary confinement.

When I interviewed him in Tunis in August 1990, I found him to be a small, strong man of about sixty, with a thick mustache, round glasses, and patient, fathomless eyes. His hatred for Israel ran deep, but nevertheless he seemed capable of objective judgments. Once he was out of solitary confinement, he was able to question other prisoners about their experiences. "Israel," he told me, "makes great efforts to 'turn' prisoners in jail, using all sorts of pressures and inducements. It also recruits Palestinian students who leave Israel to study at Arab universities, most of whom are instructed to penetrate Palestinian organizations and report back. Israel has a permanent interest in penetrating Palestinian groups, Abu Nidal's organization among them."

THE NEED TO PENETRATE

The principle of penetration is well established. It is a commonplace of intelligence work that effective counterterrorism or counterinsurgency vitally depends on intelligence from inside the enemy camp.

Ever since it resorted to armed struggle in the mid-1960s, the Palestinian guerrilla movement has been too dangerous to be left alone. All the major players in the region, and a good many outside it, have found it necessary to monitor and control its activities—in other words, to try to penetrate it.

Some guerrilla groups are penetrated almost openly. In Fatah, for example, can be found a pro-Iraqi faction, a pro-Egyptian faction, a pro-Syrian faction—and, if not a pro-Israeli faction, then a good many Israeli agents. Abu Nidal's organization, jealous of its secrets, is harder to penetrate, but for obvious reasons, Iraq, Syria, Jordan, Egypt, Fatah, and Israel all seek to penetrate it and, probably, have often succeeded. Penetration agents from most of the Arab countries abound in all the Palestinian groups.

Arab states need to control the Palestinians for three main reasons. The first is security. Because Israel usually responds to Palestinian attacks by retaliating violently against Arab countries that shelter Palestinians, Arab states need to keep abreast of Palestinian activities to protect themselves against reprisals. The second is prestige. The ordeal of the Palestinians is so large a part of contemporary Arab consciousness that every Arab ruler wants to be seen as the Palestinians' champion. The third reason has to do with inter-Arab feuds. The Palestinians are so often used by Arab regimes against one another that at one time or another, most Arab states have sought to control the PLO. When they have failed to do so, states like Syria or Iraq have set up their own Palestinian factions to use against their rivals or against the PLO itself.

But no state in the region is more obsessed with the Palestinians than Israel. As a former Israeli intelligence officer explained to me, Israel has targeted Palestinian groups of all political colors for the past quarter of a century. To have done otherwise would have been self-destructive neglect of national responsibility.

For this purpose, Israel has mainly drawn on the large Palestinian population that came under its rule after the Six-Day War of 1967, over which it exercises powers of life and death. Whether bought or coerced, Palestinian agents have been taken on in large numbers by the Shin Bet, Israel's security service, and by the Mossad, its intelligence service, and have been used both to crush resistance in the occupied territories and to infiltrate guerrilla groups outside. Ze'ev Schiff, a respected Israeli military correspondent, reported in the Israeli daily *Ha'aretz* on August 21, 1989, that informants or collaborators in the territories—the sort of people who, during the *intifada,* have been the victims of often savage killings by fellow Palestinians—were estimated to number about five thousand.

As early as 1967, an Israeli recruitment drive for Palestinian agents was aptly named Operation Flood because of the large numbers netted. "The Israelis go in for quantity," my Jordanian intelligence source told me. "They try to recruit almost every Palestinian student traveling to an Arab country. This way they can't lose. If a student agrees to work for them, they have gained an informer. If he refuses, they don't let him back into the occupied territories and they are therefore rid of yet another Palestinian!" These young Palestinians come under great pressure. Unless they cooperate, they risk not seeing their families again. Often, they are the only breadwinner in the family and simply have no choice but to return. So they start reporting to the Mossad through the post-office box addresses they are given.

Thanks to information from such agents, Israel was able, in the late 1960s, to stifle at birth the guerrilla war the Palestinians hoped to wage against it and to keep on top of the Palestinian problem ever since.

DEATH OF AN AGENT RUNNER

In Cyprus in the spring of 1991, and after elaborate negotiations, I was able to interview a retired Fatah intelligence officer, a tall, thin man with a long nose and doleful eyes, who claimed he had lured a Mossad agent runner, Baruch Cohen, to his death in Madrid in 1973. Cohen had set up a Europe-wide network of Palestinian student informers, which he used to penetrate guerrilla movements.

The Fatah officer first explained how the trap had been baited. In 1972, when he was studying in Spain on a stipend from his brother in Kuwait, Fatah had instructed him to write to his parents in the occupied territories to say that he was so short of money that he was thinking of giving up his studies. Fatah knew that Mossad censored the mail and, on learning of his financial straits, would consider him a potential recruit. Sure enough, shortly afterward, in October 1972, the Palestinian was telephoned by a man calling himself Sami Haddad, who, speaking to him in Arabic with a

Jerusalem accent, said he was a friend of his brother in Kuwait. They arranged to meet at the Plaza Hotel in Madrid.

"He was a small, kindly man," the former Fatah officer told me, "and he began merrily enough, joking and talking, telling me how much of a financial burden I was to my brother and mentioning the complaints I had made to my parents. I talked to him as if I really believed he was a family friend. Then he turned serious and suddenly told me that he belonged to Mossad. He asked me to work for him."

Although the Palestinian had been set up to solicit just such an approach, his feelings got the better of him. He had left the West Bank before the 1967 war and had had no previous contact with Israelis. He leaped to his feet and said he could not continue the conversation.

"Sit down!" Sami Haddad said scornfully. "I have a letter for you from your father."

"You're a liar! My father can't write."

The letter was written in the hand of his younger brother, a boy in sixth grade who used to write his father's letters for him.

"Your family is in our power," Haddad told him. "You are responsible for their lives. If you want them to stay alive, you had better do as I tell you."

Pretending to be suitably intimidated, the Palestinian agreed to supply Haddad with the information he wanted—which was mainly about the activities of Palestinian students and student groups in Spain and about the PLO office in Madrid. He reported to him regularly about these matters over a three-month period.

At one of their secret meetings, Sami Haddad told the Palestinian that he had been recalled to Tel Aviv to investigate the Red Front, a spy network of left-wing Jews and Arab nationalists said to be in Syria's pay. But according to the retired Fatah officer, Fatah agents in Madrid, who had been keeping Haddad under surveillance, learned that his real destination was not Tel Aviv but Brussels, where he was based at the Israeli embassy. They also discovered that his real name was Colonel Baruch Cohen and that he had been involved in the murder of two PLO representatives in Europe—Wa'il Zu'aitar, in Rome in October 1972, and Mahmud al-Hamshari, in Paris in December. My informant told me that Fatah then decided to kill Baruch Cohen on his return to Madrid.

The Palestinian met Cohen again in mid-January, when Cohen

instructed him to go to Lebanon in order to penetrate one of the Black September cells operating from Beirut. They agreed to meet again on January 26 to go over the details at La Palmera Café, on Jose Antonio Street. But this time the Palestinian had brought along an accomplice armed with a pistol, who waited at a newspaper kiosk near the entrance to the café. When Cohen stepped out of the café, he was gunned down at close range. The two Palestinians escaped.

But such PLO successes were rare. Abu Iyad told me they had managed to kill six Mossad agents over the years but had lost many more men themselves. It was, he said, an unequal struggle.

FROM PENETRATION TO MANIPULATION

As the Baruch Cohen case showed, Israeli penetration of Palestinian organizations was common, but it was clearly not the whole story. Most intelligence sources I consulted agreed that it was standard practice to use penetration agents not simply to neutralize or destroy the enemy but to try to manipulate him so that he did one's bidding without always being aware of doing so. If the exercise was successful, the enemy's organization became an unwitting extension of one's own. For practioners of counterespionage, this was the stuff of dreams.

Israel, my intelligence sources argued, was bound to see an extremist Palestinian like Abu Nidal as someone to be provoked or manipulated because of the damage he could do inside the Palestinian movement. His rejectionist views made him an obvious instrument to use against Arafat and the PLO. If he could be encouraged to kill Arafat loyalists, so much the better.

Gérard Chaliand, a French expert on irregular warfare, explains in his book *Terrorism: From Popular Struggle to Media Spectacle* (1978) how a state can sometimes play on the internal contradictions of a guerrilla or liberation movement by manipulating even a small fraction of it. He cites the example of PIDE, the Portuguese secret police, which engineered the assassination of Amilcar Cabral, leader of the anti-Portuguese movement in Guinea-Bissau and Cape Verde, by manipulating members of Cabral's own PAIGC party. The Black Guineans were promised independence on the condition that they got rid of the half-caste Cape

Verdians, of whom Cabral was one. There are numerous examples of such devious tactics in the struggles waged by intelligence services against insurgents in many parts of the world.

But the fact that manipulation of liberation movements has occurred elsewhere does not amount to evidence in the case of Abu Nidal. Nonetheless, it gave me a lead. I determined to take a closer look at the spate of murders of moderate Palestinians, focusing in particular on five well-known Palestinian "doves"—Hammami, Yassin, Qalaq, Khudr, and Sartawi—killed in London, Kuwait, Paris, Brussels, and Portugal between 1978 and 1983, allegedly by Abu Nidal. Was there any evidence, I wondered, of an Israeli involvement in these killings?

There was plenty of evidence of Israeli penetration of Palestinian groups, but as the retired Israeli general in military intelligence had told me, manipulation was another matter.

THE BOMB AND THE BULLET

Throughout their recent history, many Palestinians have been killed by both Israel and their fellow Arabs. In more than forty years of bloodletting, Palestinians have died in the 1947–48 war that led to the creation of Israel; the 1967 war, in which Israel conquered the rest of Palestine; the showdown with King Hussein of Jordan and the "pacification" of Gaza by General Ariel Sharon, both in 1970–71; the battles in Lebanon against the Maronites and against Syria in 1975–77; Israel's two invasions of Lebanon, in 1978 and 1982; the intra-Palestinian fighting at the time of the Fatah mutiny of 1983; the War of the Camps between Palestinians and Shi'ites in 1986–87; Israel's repression of the *intifada* from 1987 onward and its repeated bombing of Palestinian settlements and positions up to the present time; and of course, the punishment inflicted on the Palestinians, in Kuwait and elsewhere, for their stance in favor of Saddam Hussein during the 1991 Gulf war.

In addition to these "battlefield" deaths, the resistance has suffered many assassinations. As was clear from the list I drew up at the start, many of its brightest people have been gunned down or blown up in cold blood either by Israel or by Abu Nidal. Yasser Arafat has so far escaped assassination—although he has had a number of narrow escapes, notably during the Israeli siege of Beirut in 1982 and, again, in 1985, when Israel bombed his Tunis headquarters. In the meantime, the murder of so many of his associates has crippled the PLO.

I started by reviewing the political background to the murder of the moderates. Abu Nidal's split from Fatah, the most damaging factional dispute in its history, occurred in October 1974, at a crucial moment in the fortunes of the resistance movement. Yasser Arafat had persuaded Arab leaders to recognize the PLO as the "sole legitimate representative" of the Palestinian people; he had tamed Black September activists and largely put an end to PLO terrorism; he had gone on to address the UN General Assembly and won observer status for his organization. His efforts to persuade his followers to substitute political action for armed struggle strongly suggested that he wanted a peaceful settlement with Israel.

As we have seen, for both Israeli and Palestinian hard-liners this program was a deadly threat, and over the following years, Arafat found himself caught between two fires, neither of them friendly.

The Israeli right considered that any concession to Palestinian nationalism undercut the legitimacy of the Zionist enterprise and threatened the integrity of the "land of Israel." What such hard-liners found especially dangerous was that Arafat had managed to alter the world's perception of the Palestine problem from an Arab-Israeli border conflict, involving some displaced refugees, to a struggle for self-determination by a national liberation movement. The more sympathy Arafat won for the PLO, the higher his international profile, the more urgent it became for Israel and its friends to stop him.

When the Labor party's Yitzhak Rabin was prime minister, Israel's attitude toward the Palestinians was negative enough: Rabin had no interest in encouraging PLO moderates and opposed the establishment of a Palestinian state. But the policy became one of violent and unflinching rejection once Menachem Begin came to power in May 1977. However strenuously Arafat sought to steer his movement toward moderation, Begin was determined to give him neither an ounce of recognition nor an inch of territory. Begin, and his successor Yitzhak Shamir, saw Palestinian moderates as their real enemy because, by mobilizing international and Israeli opinion in favor of a peace settlement, they risked forcing Israel into negotiations that might lead to territorial concession.

Israel has made no secret of its utter refusal to deal with the

PLO, as successive American administrations have discovered in their efforts to promote Middle East peace talks. In 1986, Yossi Ben-Aharon, the influential director-general of the prime minister's office and Yitzhak Shamir's political adviser, was candid about Israel's policy toward the PLO.

> There is no place for any division in the Israeli camp between Likud and Labor. There is in fact cooperation and general understanding, certainly with regard to the fact that the PLO cannot be a participant in discussions or in anything. . . . No one associated with the PLO can represent the issue of the Palestinians. If there is any hope for arrangements that will solve this problem, then the prior condition must be to destroy the PLO from its roots in this region. Politically, psychologically, socially, economically, ideologically. It must not retain a shred of influence . . .

Israel's strategy to destroy the PLO by all possible means has included sending specially trained commando units to assassinate Palestinian leaders and waging a full-scale war in Lebanon in 1982 to liquidate Arafat's organization physically. It was therefore not implausible that if it could, it would use Abu Nidal to kill key men in Arafat's camp. An alliance of rejectionists was not inconceivable.

Just as Israel considered the PLO a menace to be rooted out, so Abu Nidal branded Arafat a traitor for considering the "surrender" to Israel of 80 percent of Palestinian territory, condemning most Palestinians never to return to their original homes. Before 1974, Abu Nidal had been a rallying point for Arafat's left-wing critics within Fatah. After 1974, he became something more deadly: He split the Palestinian movement, identified it with terrorism, and then silenced the moderates by killing them.

He justified his position to his followers by preaching that Arafat and his Fatah colleagues were the "enemy within"—an enemy that, he said, was more dangerous to the Palestinian revolution than the external Zionist enemy. Fatah, he thundered, was run by traitors who threatened to wreck the revolution by working for a "peaceful solution" with Israel. It was absolutely essential to prevent any such "surrender." The treacherous "enemy within" had to be struck down.

In their parallel anti-PLO activities, to what extent did Israel and Abu Nidal act independently of each other and to what extent were their efforts coordinated? This, my intelligence sources said, was the puzzle every service was anxious to crack.

I reflected that in the murders of the Palestinian moderates, alternative explanations could be found. For example, if Abu Iyad's suspicions were correct, Abu Nidal may have killed Palestinian doves because Israel wished to eliminate Palestinian moderates who had made an impression on Western leaders; but he may also have killed them because he believed they were traitors who consorted with the Israeli enemy.

It could be argued, however, that the successful manipulation of an apparently hostile organization was usually possible *only under the cover of an alternative explanation.* If some of these moderates had not been abused and vilified in Abu Nidal's own magazine as traitors to the Palestinian revolution, killing them, if the killings were indeed manipulated from outside, could not have been justified by Abu Nidal as the apt response to treachery.

Moreover, Abu Nidal's violence made it easier for Israel to depict *all* Palestinians as terrorists and murderers and to define the PLO as an outlaw group with which no peaceful dealings could be contemplated. This fitted in well with the Israeli view that the PLO should never be allowed to escape from the terrorist stigma or be accepted as a partner in the peace process. "How can you negotiate with a man who wants to kill you?" was a familiar Israeli query.

THE CAMPAIGN OF MURDER

On January 4, 1978, a single bullet to the head killed Sa'id Hammami, Arafat's dovish "ambassador" to London. The lone gunman spat at him and called him a traitor as he fired, and ran off. A few weeks earlier, in November 1977, Egypt's President Sadat had visited Israel—a bold initiative hailed in the West as a breakthrough but condemned by many Arabs as a betrayal. Arafat, too, condemned Sadat, but so hesitantly that Arab rejectionists suspected him of wanting to go to Israel himself. Everyone knew that he had encouraged Hammami, his man in London, to put out peace feelers to the Israeli left. For Abu Nidal and his Iraqi backers, such contacts were treachery and Hammami deserved to die.

Hammami was one of the most eloquent Palestinian advocates of peaceful coexistence between Palestinians and Israelis. From

1975 onward, he had held a series of meetings with Israeli peace campaigners, notably with the editor and writer Uri Avnery, whose book *My Friend, the Enemy* (1986) gives a moving account of these furtive but unfruitful encounters.

Hammami's was the first in a series of terrorist murders that, over the next five years, killed the most thoughtful and persuasive Palestinian spokesmen in the West. Clearly, now that Arafat was ready to talk peace, someone was out to wreck his diplomacy and leave him powerless. As a result moderates in the Palestinian movement were scared into silence. Few now dared pursue contacts with the Israeli left: The hit-and-run attacks had shown how vulnerable these PLO doves were, and that protecting them was hardly a priority of European police forces.

Nevertheless, the British police established that Hammami's killer was Kayid Hussein (sometimes known as As'ad Kayid), a Tunisian member of Abu Nidal's organization, registered in London as a student.

On February 13, 1978, a little more than a month after Sa'id Hammami's murder, a meeting was held in London to honor him. One of the speakers was Claude Bourdet, a leading member of the wartime French resistance, founder of the underground paper *Combat,* and no stranger to intelligence operations. He concluded his address with the following words:

> Could it not be that the masterminds behind Sa'id's death—not the people who pressed the trigger and protected the murderer, not even the people who ordered the murder, but possibly those who, by cunning and deceit, by subtle intoxication of less subtle brains—contrived a situation where the organizers of the murder were led to believe that they were doing a service to the Arab, to the Palestinian cause . . .
>
> There are many ways of provoking a killing. Other than *doing it.* Other than *ordering it.*
>
> It would not be the first time in history that extreme radicals are manipulated by foreign agents—in ways they themselves are unable to understand.

Bourdet's suggestion that Hammami's killer might have been manipulated by foreign agents is, of course, pure conjecture, but the foreign agents he had in mind were the Israelis, as he told some of those who attended the memorial service. Here was an experienced Frenchman, I reflected, who shared Abu Iyad's suspicions.

Both Arab and Israeli rejectionists had reason to want Hammami dead. Abu Nidal and Iraq's leaders detested him for his language of reconciliation. I learned from Abu Bakr that in the months before Hammami's death, Abu Nidal's organization had demanded that he call a press conference to denounce Arafat. Hammami had refused. But Israel's hard-liners also loathed him for his advocacy of a two-state solution and his impact on British opinion. It was clear that Abu Nidal's man had done the deed with Iraqi approval. But had Israel, by manipulation, given the murderous process a nudge? So far as I could see, there was no evidence for it and the mystery remained unsolved.

On February 18, 1978, a few days after the service for Hammami, Abu Nidal struck again. Two of his men burst into the lobby of the Hilton Hotel in Nicosia and shot to death Yusuf al-Siba'i, editor of the Egyptian newspaper *al-Ahram* and a confidant of President Sadat, whom he had accompanied to Jerusalem. The aim was to punish Sadat and give him a taste of what he, too, might expect.

Defectors from Abu Nidal's organization told me in Tunis that the operation had been mounted by Samih Muhammad Khudr (code-named Zuhair al-Rabbah)—one of Abu Nidal's most dangerous foreign operatives, of whom more will be heard—in close coordination with Iraqi intelligence. This sounded plausible as Iraq was then taking the lead in ostracizing Egypt for its contacts with Israel.

Once they had killed Siba'i, the gunmen seized hostages at the hotel, then demanded and were given a Cyprus Airways plane, which flew around the region looking for a place to land. But on being turned away everywhere, the plane returned to Larnaca. In the meantime, Sadat had sent in a force of Egyptian commandos to overpower the gunmen and free the hostages. The Cypriots resented this foreign interference. When the Egyptians landed, they were engaged by the Cypriot National Guard, which killed fifteen of them in an hour-long battle. As Cyprus and Egypt exchanged bitter recriminations, the gunmen released their hostages and surrendered. It seemed to me a good example of Abu Nidal's disruptive abilities.

THE KILLINGS OF YASSIN AND QALAQ

A few months later, three more prominent PLO "ambassadors" were attacked. On June 15, 1978, Ali Yassin, Fatah's representative in Kuwait and a noted moderate, was shot to death in his home; on August 3, 1978, Izz al-Din Qalaq, PLO representative in France, a cultured, soft-spoken, and dedicated Palestinian who had made a considerable impression on French opinion, was murdered in Paris; and two days after that, on August 5, gunmen attacked the PLO office in Islamabad, killing four people but missing Yusif Abu Hantash, the PLO representative.

The PLO immediately blamed Abu Nidal and Iraq. The killing of Yassin aroused particular fury. "I never wanted to kill Abu Nidal until the day he murdered Ali Yassin," Abu Iyad told me. (He added that he had attempted to have him killed several times—on one occasion he actually took the weapons into Baghdad himself, on one of his official visits. But Iraqi intelligence guarded Abu Nidal as securely as it guarded President Bakr or Saddam Hussein.)

Yassin had been everyone's friend—he had been Abu Nidal's friend, too, and had even kept him supplied in Baghdad with cars and gifts of electrical appliances from Kuwait. To the Palestinian movement, his murder seemed wicked and incomprehensible.

To avenge Yassin, Fatah went to war, firing rockets at the Iraqi embassy in Beirut on July 17, 1978, and, two days later, storming Abu Nidal's office in Tripoli, Libya, killing two of his members. On July 24, Fatah planted a bomb outside the Iraqi embassy in Brussels, and on July 28 the Iraqi ambassador in London escaped an attempt on his life. On July 31, Sa'id Hammami's brother, Ahmad, tried to seize the Iraqi embassy in Paris, whereupon members of the embassy staff opened fire, killing a French police inspector.

Then, on August 3, 1978, Qalaq was killed in Paris (together with Adnan Hammad, brother of Nimr Hammad, the PLO representative in Rome, who happened to be paying Qalaq a visit). Qalaq's office was above a café. On his way up to his office, he waved to a student he recognized sitting at a table. It was his killer. When Qalaq realized that the student was coming up after him, he tried to barricade himself by moving a cupboard against the door. But the killer broke the door down and pushed the cupboard aside. As in the case of Hammami, the assassin was overheard calling him a traitor before shooting him and running off.

Qalaq's killer was the same Tunisian, Kayid Hussein, who had killed Hammami in London, who had then moved to Paris and registered in a language school. Who, I wondered, was responsible this time? Was it Iraq, or was some other party involved?

A partial answer was to emerge a few months later. Early in November 1978, an Arab summit was convened in Baghdad to condemn Egypt for signing the Camp David accords with Israel. For the occasion, Syria and Iraq were temporarily reconciled. As he prepared to leave for Baghdad, Syria's president, Assad, decided to take Arafat and Abu Iyad with him, so that they too could make their peace with Iraq's president, Bakr, and his deputy, Saddam Hussein, and put an end to the Iraqi-PLO war caused by Iraq's support for Abu Nidal's murders of PLO moderates.

Bakr gave a reception at his home for the visiting Arab delegations and was persuaded to invite Arafat, although he was still not on speaking terms with him. At some point in the evening, Bakr could contain himself no longer. According to an eyewitness (Khalid al-Fahum, a veteran Palestinian politician, who told me the story), Bakr marched up to Arafat and screamed at him: "All right! We killed Hammami! Yes, we did it. But as for the others, we were not involved. We had nothing to do with their deaths!"

It is hard to see what Bakr would have had to gain from lying. Killing opponents was something he and his deputy, Saddam Hussein, did every day. They were not shy about it. In denying responsibility for the killings of Yassin and Qalaq, Bakr was probably telling the truth. Abu Iyad later told me that Iraq's intelligence chief, Sa'dun Shakir, and the foreign minister, Tariq Aziz, also strenuously denied any Iraqi involvement in these killings and that he was inclined to believe them.

In 1987 when, as we shall see, Abu Iyad had a night-long confrontation with Abu Nidal in Algiers, arranged by Algerian intelligence, Abu Nidal would admit to killing Hammami, but he also repeatedly denied having had a hand in the murders of Yassin and Qalaq. Even inside his highly compartmentalized organization, defectors later told me, there was puzzlement about these murders, with different directorates blaming each other.

If neither Iraqi intelligence nor Abu Nidal ordered the killings, who did? Perhaps there was a hint here of outside intervention. Qalaq, in Paris, and Yassin, in the Gulf, were men who preached peace and urged a settlement with Israel—one that would involve

Israel giving up territory. They were both eloquent exponents of Israeli-Palestinian coexistence, of a two-state solution, ideas that were anathema to the Likud, the governing coalition in Israel. Certainly, they did not fit Begin's standard smear of the PLO as "the blackest organization—other than the Nazi murder organizations—ever to arise in the annals of humanity."

THE KILLING OF ALI HASSAN SALAMEH

Whether or not the Israelis had had a hand in the murder of Qalaq and Yassin, they were soon killing other Palestinians without the help of anyone. Within a few weeks of the Baghdad summit, on January 22, 1979, an Israeli car bomb in a Beirut street killed Fatah's security chief, Ali Hassan Salameh (also known as Abu Hassan), together with four of his bodyguards and five passersby. Another powerful blow had been struck in Israel's war against the PLO.

The rumor was that Israel was exacting revenge for Salameh's role in Black September operations five years earlier. The able young Salameh had been Abu Iyad's deputy in *rasd al-markazi,* the counterespionage outfit Fatah had set up in 1967, but he had broken with Fatah during the Jordanian crisis of 1970. He then took over one of Black September's "tiger cub" groups and managed to throw a small bomb at some oil storage tanks in Trieste on August 5, 1972—whereupon he was secretly contacted by a number of oil companies with offers of protection money. In fact, no further operations of the sort were being planned, but Salameh dutifully reported the offers to his former colleagues in Fatah, who took note of his honesty. This was one of the reasons that Arafat later brought Salameh back into Fatah and put him in command of his personal bodyguard, the unit that came to be known as Force 17.

The new, prestigious job in Fatah, together with optimism about a peaceful settlement after the 1973 war, led to a dramatic change in Salameh. On Fatah's written instructions, he began an intelligence relationship with the CIA station chief in Beirut, with the result that the former Black September terrorist who had once wanted to attack American targets now became the guardian of the American embassy in Beirut during the civil war and the overseer of the safe evacuation of American civilians in 1976. To complete his entry into the conservative *beau monde,* Salameh took as his second wife a stunning Lebanese beauty queen and a former Miss Universe, a Christian girl named Georgina Rizk.

U.S.-PLO relations grew closer still when Jimmy Carter decided to support the Palestinian "homeland" that Arafat himself was asking for. Salameh went twice to stay at CIA headquarters at Langley, Virginia, where he gave his hosts an in-depth personal assessment of Arafat, the first time CIA officers had heard such testimony from someone so close to the PLO leader. Salameh explained that the PLO was funded by Saudi Arabia, the Gulf states, and Palestinian capitalists—and not by Moscow—and that it was prepared to guarantee that a future Palestinian state would not be communist or terrorist or a dictatorship of any sort. The Palestinians, he told the CIA, were ready for friendship with the United States, and they were certainly not interested in destroying Israel.

According to my Western intelligence sources, Israel opposed this U.S.-PLO friendship. I was told that as soon as Israel learned of Salameh's contacts at Langley, the Israelis decided to kill him—not because of his earlier Black September activities but because he had become the PLO's liaison man with the CIA. (For a fictionalized account of Salameh's story, see David Ignatius's novel *Agents of Influence.*)

THE KILLING OF NA'IM KHUDR

After a pause, the killing of PLO representatives was resumed. Na'im Khudr, the PLO representative in Brussels, like Hammami, Yassin, and Qalaq, a prominent moderate, was shot dead on June 1, 1981. He happened to be the only Christian among PLO ambassadors, and an ex-priest in the bargain. Abu Nidal was generally blamed for the murder.

However, the former Mossad agent Victor Ostrovsky says bluntly that the Mossad killed Khudr. In his book *By Way of Deception* (1990), he writes: "On his way to work, a dark-complexioned man wearing a tan jacket and sporting a pencil mustache walked up to Khader [Khudr], shot him five times in the heart and once in the head, walked off the curb, climbed into a passing 'taxi' and disappeared. Although Arafat didn't know it then, the Mossad had struck."

Khudr was killed at a time when Menachem Begin, Israel's prime minister, was greatly concerned with Lebanon. Having removed Egypt from the Arab front line by the 1979 peace treaty, Begin now wanted to bring Lebanon into Israel's orbit—and thus neutralize Syria. The Mossad had for some years been grooming a Lebanese Christian warlord, Bashir Gemayel, to be Israel's proconsul in Beirut. In the spring of 1981, Begin began a series of aggressive maneuvers in Lebanon—the shooting down of two Syrian helicopters in April; the heavy air and naval bombardments of Palestinian positions in May and June—which he clearly hoped would draw the Syrians and the Palestinians into a fight. In fact he had to wait until June 1982, when an attempt on the life of Israel's ambassador in London gave him the pretext he needed for a war in Lebanon, which he hoped would allow him to realize his strategic plan.

Khudr, the PLO's man in Brussels, was one of several Palestinian leaders at that time who understood how vital it was *not* to give Begin reasons to invade Lebanon. Khudr had telephoned a diplomat at the Israeli embassy in Brussels, asking for a meeting to explore ways of defusing the dangerous Lebanese situation. But this was the last thing the Israeli government wanted to do, for as we have seen, the main fear of Israeli hard-liners such as Begin—a fear shared by his successors—is not PLO *militancy* but PLO *moderation,* which might, under pressure of international opinion, force Israel to negotiate and therefore make territorial concessions.

In his book, Ostrovsky says that Khudr was murdered by a Mossad hit man precisely because he was trying to prevent a war in Lebanon—a war the Palestinians feared but one that the Mossad and its political masters wanted, in order to destroy the Palestinians and make their man, Gemayel, president.

Ostrovsky is not a careful writer, hardly, it would appear, any sort of writer at all: He enlisted the Canadian writer Claire Hoy to help him with the writing. But no one, so far as I know, has ever denied that he worked for the Mossad or that his lengthy account, in the first part of the book, of his recruitment and training is anything but authentic. The Israeli government tried strenuously to suppress his book and sued him in New York to stop its publication. In *Israel's Secret Wars* (1991), two highly respected authors, Ian Black and Benny Morris, say that Ostrovsky's book embarrassed the Israelis. "If an intelligence agency cannot manage to keep its own innermost secrets . . . how effective can it be?" they write. It is therefore hard simply to dismiss Ostrovsky's claim that the Mossad killed Khudr.

Yet sources from inside Abu Nidal's organization assured me without doubt in the summer of 1990 that the man who actually gunned down Khudr in Brussels was not an Israeli but a member of Abu Nidal's organization. His name was Adnan al-Rashidi (code-named Hisham Hijah), and the murder weapon was smuggled into Belgium by a Tunisian, Muhammad Abu al-Jasim, and given to Adnan al-Rashidi by an unknown cut-out.

Assuming the defectors I interviewed were correct, here then was a possible case of the kind of collaboration between the Mossad and Abu Nidal that Abu Iyad had been trying to tell me about, assuming that Ostrovsky's Mossad assassin was in fact al-Rashidi. On this theory the Mossad had either planted its man in Abu Nidal's organization or, by complicities higher up the chain of command, had managed to influence Abu Nidal's target selection.

But there were still too many loose ends. The possibility that al-Rashidi was Ostrovsky's Mossad hit man depended too much on hearsay evidence and was far from watertight. Ostrovsky might have had a lapse of memory, or my defectors might have misled me. In any event, a single example of a possible Mossad–Abu Nidal link was not enough to prove the case. Maybe it had happened only once.

There was a further twist to the Khudr story, which made me even more skeptical. On August 29, 1981, three months after Khudr's death, two of Abu Nidal's gunmen stormed a synagogue in Vienna. They killed two Jews and wounded nineteen others. They were arrested and interrogated by the Austrian police. According to the Israeli writer Yossi Melman, in *The Master Terrorist: The True Story of Abu Nidal* (1987), the Austrians sent a photograph of one of the gunmen they had arrested to the Belgian police team investigating the Khudr murder. Eyewitnesses, who had seen Khudr gunned down in Brussels, identified his killer as one of the gunmen in the Vienna synagogue.

In the two years before the storming of the Vienna synagogue, Abu Nidal had attacked several other "soft" Jewish or Israeli targets in Europe. Most of these attacks had failed. On November 13, 1979, for example, an attempt to kill Efraim Eldar, the Israeli ambassador to Portugal, failed. On November 20, 1979, an attempt to bomb an exhibition about Jerusalem, staged at a Salzburg hotel by the local Jewish community, had also failed. On March 3, 1980, an attempt to kill Max Mazin, a prominent member of Madrid's Jewish community, had also gone wrong: In an apparent case of mistaken identity, the killer gunned down a Spanish lawyer, Adolfo Cottello, who happened to live or work in the same building.

If there was any truth to the rumors that Israel had penetrated and was manipulating Abu Nidal's organization, then these failures could have been deliberate. But on July 27, 1980, two grenades thrown by Abu Nidal terrorists at a group of Agudat Israel schoolchildren in Antwerp killed one Jewish youngster and wounded twenty-one others. And in Vienna, on May 1, 1981, Heinz Nittal, a prominent member of Vienna's Jewish community, head of the Austria-Israel Friendship Society and a friend of Chancellor Bruno Kreisky, was murdered.

If Israel had agents inside Abu Nidal's organization and influenced its target selection, why had it not stopped such criminal violence against Jews? It seemed to me wholly implausible that the Israelis would condone or overlook the killing of Jews. People accept that Palestinians kill Palestinians and that Russians kill Russians, but Jews are not known to kill Jews. There was a case in Baghdad in 1950—well documented in Abbas Shiblak's book *The Lure of Zion* (1986)—when Israeli agents bombed Jewish targets to stampede the Jewish population of Iraq into fleeing to Israel. But this was an isolated case. There was no way that I could see in which the attack on Jewish schoolchildren in Belgium could be fitted into the theory of Abu Nidal as an Israeli agent. Clearly, if the Israelis had penetrated his organization, they could not have controlled it entirely. It was possible of course that Abu Nidal, while unable or reluctant to attack Israeli targets, had targeted non-Israeli Jews to impress his Arab followers that he was nonetheless anti-Semitic and the Israelis could do nothing to stop him.

There was, however, a strange feature of the affair: The Israelis had done nothing to punish Abu Nidal. Attacks on Jews or on Israelis did not usually go unpunished. In fact, it was Israel's declared policy always to retaliate. It was a bewildering puzzle.

It seemed to me that the murder in Vienna of Heinz Nittal, a prominent liberal Jew who had expressed sympathy for the PLO, might be a somewhat different matter. By 1980–81, there were signs in the Jewish diaspora of mounting disenchantment with Begin and his aggressive hard-line tactics. Jewish personalities of international renown, like Nahum Goldmann, Philip Klutznick, Pierre Mendès-France, and Bruno Kreisky, were openly critical of Israeli policy. To men like Begin and his defense minister, Ariel Sharon, the Jewish-born and peace-campaigning Chancellor Kreisky, with his friendship for the PLO, his meetings with Arafat, and his advocacy of Palestinian statehood, was a traitor to the "greater Israel" cause. Even if Jews were not known to kill Jews, I reflected, it was just possible that Israelis might kill a Jew they thought was a traitor, and that is what Begin thought of Kreisky. So the Israelis might have sent Abu Nidal after Kreisky's friend, the dovish Heinz Nittal, as a warning as to what constituted acceptable Jewish behavior. Although pure speculation, this seemed to me not implausible.

THE KILLING OF ISAM SARTAWI

After the murders of Hammami, Yassin, Qalaq, and Khudr, Dr. Isam Sartawi was the only prominent dove left in the Palestinian movement, a perfect example of the species loathed equally by Israeli hawks and Arab rejectionists. He had repeatedly and publicly accused Abu Nidal of being an Israeli agent. In an interview with the distinguished French daily *Le Monde* on January 22, 1982, Sartawi was bold:

> Abu Nidal is not a maximalist serving the cause of the rejection front, but a renegade in the service of Israel. The Austrian security services have established, without any doubt, that a right-hand man of Abu Nidal not only killed the municipal councillor Heinz Nittal on May 1, 1981, and attacked the synagogue in Vienna in August, but also murdered, on June 1, Naim Khudr, the representative of the PLO in Brussels . . .
>
> Who but Israel could be interested in eliminating our leaders? Who was interested in discrediting the Palestinian resistance by committing crimes of such a scandalously anti-Semitic nature?
>
> We do not ask ourselves these questions anymore since the members of the Abu Nidal group whom we hold in Beirut have admitted to having been recruited by the Mossad in the occupied territories.

In great agitation, Sartawi repeated this charge to me when I interviewed him a year later in Algiers, at the Palestine National Council meeting of February 1983. He claimed that Fatah had arrested some of Abu Nidal's men in Beirut and that they had confessed to having been recruited by the Mossad in the West Bank. He was certain that Abu Nidal or the Mossad—or the Mossad *through* Abu Nidal—would try to kill him.

To make matters worse for him, at the PNC meeting Arafat had disavowed him and his dovish views, which were too extreme even for Arafat, and had not allowed him to speak. I well remember the scene, because I was standing beside Sartawi at the side of the hall. Faruq Qaddumi, the PLO's "foreign minister," delivered a hard-line political report that rejected everything Sartawi stood for. Listening to Qaddumi, a white-faced Sartawi turned to me and exclaimed (with doubtful syntax), "Are you now disgusted enough!" This once popular man was now alone. No one came up to talk to him. He may have known then that he was doomed—alone, out in the open without protection or political cover, and pursued by killers from both camps. In contacting the Israeli peace camp, Sartawi had acted under Arafat's instructions, but he may have gone too far.

On April 10, 1983, as Sartawi was chatting in the lobby of a hotel at Albufeira, Portugal, with other delegates attending a meeting of the Socialist International, an assassin killed him instantly with a shot to the head. A few hours later in Damascus, Abu Nidal jubilantly claimed responsibility for the death of "the criminal traitor Sartawi."

Whether or not Israel had had a hand in his murder, there was as usual an alternative explanation. A few months before his death, Sartawi had received a letter from Abu Nidal asking when he planned to meet his Israeli contacts in Vienna. Abu Nidal wanted to arrange to have them killed. Sartawi tipped off the Austrian police: Fatah was then cooperating with the Austrians, and with other European police forces, to frustrate Abu Nidal's terrorism. When two of Abu Nidal's gunmen flew to Vienna, they were arrested—and Sartawi helped the Austrians with their interrogation. Abu Nidal was enraged.

Sartawi had not always been a dove. For years he had been a close friend of Abu Nidal and had shared his rejectionist views. In 1948, his family had fled from Acre, near Haifa, to Iraq, where he began his medical studies, later becoming a heart surgeon in the

United States. But after the Arab defeat of 1967, he left America and joined the guerrillas in Jordan, fighting at Karameh in March 1968.

In 1969, Sartawi broke from Fatah and set up a group that he called the Action Committee for the Liberation of Palestine, with funding first from Iraq and then from Egypt, which led some Palestinians to believe that he had sold out to Arab intelligence services. At this stage of his life, both his language and his actions were extremely violent. In January 1970, he mounted an attack on a busload of El Al passengers at the Munich airport.

But by the early 1970s, Sartawi underwent a conversion and became for the rest of his life an ardent advocate of Arab-Israeli coexistence. He worked with PLO and Israeli peace activists and appealed to such people as Austria's Chancellor Bruno Kreisky and the king of Morocco. He argued that the Arabs could not challenge Israel with conventional military force or with guerrilla warfare. Such attempts were bound to fail. Only dialogue and links to forces inside Israel could bring peace to the Middle East, a peace that might at last give the Palestinians a state of their own.

In 1987, during a meeting between Abu Iyad and Abu Nidal in Algiers, Abu Iyad would bring up Fatah's main grievance: the long list of PLO men murdered by Abu Nidal—or, as he believed, by some secret hand inside his organization. Abu Iyad later told me what he and Abu Nidal had said:

" 'Why did you kill Isam Sartawi?' I asked him. 'He was your lifelong friend!' I told him I believed this was an operation in which the Israelis had pulled the strings. The whole affair stank of penetration and manipulation—the way the weapons had been smuggled in, the escape of the killer, the arrest of a young accomplice traveling on a false passport whom the Moroccans could not charge with the murder. 'I know Israel is playing games with you,' I told him."

Abu Iyad told Abu Nidal that he began to suspect Israeli penetration when a Moroccan intelligence officer had given him a list of Abu Nidal's members in Spain—nineteen names in all—and said his source was the Mossad. Abu Iyad then checked out the list himself and found it accurate: Seventeen of the men on it, most of them students, were still living in Spain; two had graduated and returned home.

Abu Iyad told me: "I was amazed by Abu Nidal's answer.

'Yes,' he had responded calmly. 'You are right. Israel has penetrated us in the past. I discovered this from my Tunisian and Moroccan members. Israel used to plant them on me. But let me tell you that I send my own North African members—the ones I really trust—to France to turn and recruit Israel's North African agents! The flow of intelligence is sometimes to my advantage. These people have supplied me with truly astonishing information.'

" 'Take for example the Sartawi case. They gave me all the detailed information I needed for the operation!' "

As he recollected their conversation, Abu Iyad could still hardly believe what he had heard: "Israeli agents were present in his organization. They had fed him information. He admitted it! His matter-of-fact tone astounded me. He added that he was trying to liquidate the Israeli agents one by one. That is what he said!" Though the admissions implied no more than penetration, Abu Iyad was convinced they also indicated collaboration between the Mossad and Abu Nidal.

Abu Iyad told me that he had thought about Israel's manipulation of Abu Nidal with North African agents. He knew for a fact that Khudr had been killed by a Tunisian member of Abu Nidal's organization. So had Hammami and Qalaq.

"We stopped terrorism in 1974," he insisted, "but the Israelis did not, although they convinced the world of the contrary. They continued to attack us. Sometimes they did so quite blatantly, as when they killed Abu Jihad in Tunis in 1988. More often they mounted operations that could be read in different ways. I must admit it confused us. On several occasions we weren't sure whether Abu Nidal or Mossad was responsible."

The Mossad agents that Abu Iyad had in mind were probably trained in Morocco, where the Moroccan government and the CIA run an unusual intelligence school that specializes in Palestinian affairs. I learned about this school from several intelligence sources, both Arab and Western. They told me that the CIA, which works closely with Israel on Palestinian matters, had brought the Mossad into the arrangement as well. The students are mostly young North Africans who are recruited in Europe and brought back to the Moroccan school to be trained as spies. They are put through courses on the various Palestinian factions, studying their leading personalities, their structure, ideology, and operations—so that by the end of the course, they are able to use the arcane jargon of these organizations. All the principal groups—Fatah, the PFLP, the Democratic Front, the PFLP–General Command, the Arab Liberation Front, and Abu Nidal's organization—are studied.

Once their course is completed, the youths are taken back to Europe and instructed to hang about in cafés, meet other Arabs, and speak to them in the language they have been taught. The hope is that they will eventually get taken on by the groups they have learned to mimic, so that the Moroccans, the CIA, or the Mossad can use them. Some of the graduates of the school become informers, some plan operations, and some are even schooled to become ideologues for the groups on which they are planted. Some are killers.

ABU DAWUD ESCAPES DEATH

There was one further case I learned about. It was an attempted murder rather than a murder, and it did not involve a dove. But it seemed relevant to my inquiries.

On July 27, 1981, a month before the attack on the Vienna synagogue, the prominent Fatah commander Abu Dawud narrowly escaped death in Warsaw. In Tunis in 1990, he gave me his account of the incident.

He had been Abu Nidal's friend, he told me, since their early days in Saudi Arabia but had broken with him over the killing of Yassin and the other PLO representatives. In July 1981, he had gone to Warsaw on Fatah's behalf for talks with the Polish authorities and booked in at the Hotel Victoria on Friday, July 27. But as it was too late to see anyone that day, he had gone to take a sauna in the health club before wandering upstairs to the café on the first floor. It was a quiet place, he said, but it was frequented by prostitutes.

"I noticed as I came in that the place was full of Arabs. I learned later that they were a party of thirty Iraqi intelligence officers on an official visit. Rather than sit at a corner table as I usually do, I sat at the first empty table I could see. I didn't want them to think I was trying to pick up a girl.

"I had just ordered a coffee and a bottle of mineral water when two men came bursting through the door. One pointed me out to the other, who rushed up and started firing at me when he was about six feet away. His first shot went through my hand. The next broke my jaw—I had to keep my mouth shut for five months while it was being rebuilt. A third and fourth went through the fleshy parts of my body.

"The Iraqi intelligence officers in the café pretended they had seen nothing and never offered to help me."

Abu Dawud chased the gunman as far as the hotel entrance but failed to catch him. Bleeding profusely, he collapsed on a sofa in the lobby and waited for nearly two hours for a Polish ambulance to take him to a hospital—where there was a further long wait before he received medical attention. The next day, the Poles moved him to a clinic that belonged to the ministry of the interior, where he stayed for ten days before going on to East Germany to convalesce. He later learned that the Poles had arrested his would-be assassin but had released him a day later on receiving a payment of $200,000 from Abu Nidal's Polish company, Zibado.

Abu Dawud continued his story: "The man who pointed me out in the café was one of Abu Nidal's boys. I recognized him. But who was my attacker? I was curious to find out. I didn't think he could be a Palestinian member of Abu Nidal's organization, because I knew most of them. I had trained many of them myself in various militias. And what was the motive? There seemed no obvious reason to kill me. Unlike Hammami, Abu Nidal couldn't accuse me of having dealings with the Israelis! So why me?"

About eleven months later, Abu Dawud happened to be in Iraq, where he took a room at the Baghdad Hotel. Hearing he was there and thinking that he had come to kill him, Abu Nidal sent one of his henchmen, Dr. Ghassan al-Ali, to sound him out. Abu Dawud pretended that he did not suspect Abu Nidal of involvement in the shooting. He asked after his health and said he would like to see him.

"Abu Nidal is a crafty devil!" Abu Dawud continued. "To put me to the test, he sent my would-be assassin to sit in the hotel lobby to see how I would react. There he was, large as life, a small, dark man with curly hair, reading a newspaper and wearing the same suit he had worn when he shot me.

"Some Palestinian friends had come to see me at the hotel, so I sounded them out discreetly about the identity of the man in the lobby. I learned that he was a Tunisian who posed as a businessman but in fact worked for Abu Nidal.

"There he was, eyeing me warily from behind his newspaper. I decided I would try and capture him. I approached, but he saw me coming and started running. I gave chase, but once again, as in Warsaw, he got away.

"The moment Abu Nidal heard what had happened, he left Baghdad for his farm in the north and did not reappear until he was certain I had left the country. There is no doubt in my mind of his involvement in the affair. No one else could have sent his man to point me out in the Warsaw hotel, and no one else could have bribed the Poles to let my attacker escape."

Abu Dawud asked everyone he could about the Tunisian who had tried to kill him. He told me that the Tunisian had been recruited by the Mossad in Paris, sent first to Israel for training and then on to the CIA's intelligence school in Morocco, where he was taught Abu Nidal's theories and jargon. He was then sent to Paris, where he was picked up by Abu Nidal's people and recruited.

Abu Dawud believed after an extensive investigation that the Israelis had planted the Tunisian on Abu Nidal. The real question in his mind was who in the organization had chosen to kill him and ordered that particular agent to mount the attack. He had no doubt that the Mossad had someone high up in Abu Nidal's organization, perhaps at the very top. I asked him who it was, but he couldn't tell me.

The interesting thing was, Abu Dawud added, that Abu Nidal did not tell even his closest associates that he had ordered the attack. Abu Dawud learned later that the secret was shared with only two people: the man responsible for selecting and researching the target—very probably Dr. Ghassan, of whom more will be heard—and the Tunisian hit man. The youth who had identified him at the hotel in Warsaw had been brought in at the last minute. He had worked as a courier for Abu Nidal and knew Abu Dawud well.

"My Tunisian attacker is now living in France," Abu Dawud told me. "I know this and so does French security. He has recently left Abu Nidal's organization."

Although I was still by no means satisfied with the evidence I had collected, it seemed to me that there were grounds to pursue the hypothesis that a terrorist outfit like Abu Nidal's was most dangerous not when it was operating on its own account but, as Claude Bourdet might have put it, when it was systematically manipulated by more sophisticated minds, with their own ruthless agenda.

chapter

9

THE ORGANIZATION

Researching the murder of the moderates left me with the suspicion that there might be something after all to Abu Iyad's allegations. At any rate, I could see how his obsession came about. The evidence was still fragmentary, but it had begun to look as if a number of Israel's North African agents might have had a free run of Abu Nidal's organization. They kept cropping up on murderous assignments. But who directed these agents? Abu Dawud's story, which I had no reason to doubt, suggested that the Mossad had a man, or perhaps several, at the very top of the organization. Thus, I shifted the focus of my inquiries. In interviews with Arab and Western intelligence contacts, with Abu Iyad, and with defectors back in Tunis, I set about trying to make a chart of Abu Nidal's organization to see who, if anyone, was in a position to direct these North Africans who, according to Abu Iyad, had killed Khudr, Hammami, and Qalaq and had tried to kill Abu Dawud. As I discovered, it was no easy task.

I had one important lead. Abu Iyad told me that French intelligence had asked him for information about a certain Sulaiman Samrin (code-named Dr. Ghassan al-Ali), a very senior man in Abu Nidal's organization who the French suspected was a Mossad agent. Who was Dr. Ghassan and what job did he do? How did he fit into Abu Nidal's elaborate structure? And how was the whole outfit run? My inquiries lasted several months.

• • •

Some men lead from the front, others from behind the scenes, some by making themselves accessible, others by being remote. Some men dominate through personal charisma, others through fear. Some owe their power to popular vote or to a party machine, others to the armed forces.

Abu Nidal rules by contempt—bullying, browbeating, and humiliating his colleagues. He dictates not only where they live and what work they do but also what brand of cigarettes they may smoke, how much meat they may consume, what toys their children may play with, what items—and certainly not *chocolate!*—they may buy at airport duty-free shops, and even what dresses their wives are allowed to wear.

Abu Nidal is especially contemptuous of the wives of the men who work for him. Once he tried to save money by buying women's underclothes in bulk for all his members' wives. A guard from the Intelligence Directorate measured the women for bras and panties, and only after great resistance from the women was the scheme dropped.

When he first started out in Baghdad in the early 1970s, Abu Nidal's main instrument was a clandestine "Military Committee" that planned and directed his terrorist operations. In due course, various administrative bodies coalesced around this secret core, but it was only in 1984–85, when Abu Nidal returned to the Middle East from Poland, that the organization finally took shape. Abu Nidal's model was Yasser Arafat's Fatah, but he also borrowed from what he knew of Israel's Mossad and of Action Directe, the French terrorist group. After he was thrown out of Syria in 1987, he had to make further organizational changes to take account of his dispersal between Libya and Lebanon.

Today, the organization comprises a number of executive directorates and committees through which the day-to-day work is conducted. Supervising them are three central institutions—a small Political Bureau: a somewhat larger Central Committee, of about twenty people; and a still larger Revolutionary Council. Of these three, the Political Bureau, a mere handful of men chaired by Abu Nidal in Tripoli, is the supreme decision-making body.

Hierarchically, directorates and committees are on the same level. The only difference is that directorates are bigger and comprise more than one committee. Both directorates and committees are usually headed by a member of the Political Bureau or Central Committee.

From defectors and other sources, I have been able to identify Abu Nidal's principal colleagues and gain some insight into the inner workings of the organization, of which the principal subdivisions are the Secretariat, the Intelligence Directorate, the Organization Directorate, the Membership Committee, the Political Directorate, the Finance Directorate, the Committee for Revolutionary Justice, the Technical and Scientific Committees, and the People's Army.

THE SECRETARIAT

Abu Nidal controls his organization through the Secretariat, a command-and-control unit that he runs himself and that keeps him informed of everything in the minutest detail. The Secretariat also keeps the organization's archives, but its main function is as a communications center: All communications between different parts of the organization and all documents passing between Libya and Lebanon are channeled through it. Five cadres work in the Secretariat's archives in the South Lebanon port of Sidon and another five in Tripoli, Libya. Their task is to note, transmit, and file and to keep Abu Nidal informed.

All this activity generates a great deal of paper—most of it carried back and forth under seal by special messenger. (Routine messages are also sent by radio, and in addition, a good deal of material travels between Libya and Lebanon, via Damascus, by Libyan diplomatic bag.)

The present head of the Secretariat is none other than Sulaiman Samrin (Dr. Ghassan al-Ali), the man whom, Abu Iyad told me, the French suspected of being a Mossad agent. The high-ranking defector Atif Abu Bakr described him to me as "one of the most violent and dangerous criminals in the whole organization." If Dr. Ghassan was in fact Israel's man, he was extremely well placed to manipulate the organization. He was the only person, except for Abu Nidal himself, who knew everything that happened inside the outfit. He virtually ran it.

Based in Lebanon with the title of first secretary of the Central Committee, Dr. Ghassan is a lean, dark chain-smoker of maniacal energy. He drinks heavily and has gray hair and large owlish glasses. He claims to be a karate expert and watches karate films on video. He has also read Marxist economics and discusses world events in those terms. He edits the organization's in-house magazine, *al-Tariq* (*The Path*), and is its principal contributor. He greatly influences Abu Nidal and considers himself his natural heir. In 1990–91, he filled the number-three position in the organization, after Abu Nidal and his deputy, Isam Maraqa (code name Salim Ahmad).

For all his power in the organization, Dr. Ghassan is also intensely unpopular and has even become an object of suspicion. He is aloof, elitist, insulting to others. But with Abu Nidal he is servile. Abu Nidal was once heard to call out, "Samrin, your sisters in Kuwait, those three whores, I hear they've done such and such . . ." and Dr. Ghassan nodded meekly.

Dr. Ghassan was born in the West Bank village of Silwan in 1946. He was a good student and was sent to study in Britain, where he graduated with a B.A. in chemistry and later was awarded an M.A. Although he calls himself Doctor, he has no such degree. He learned English well, married an Englishwoman, and had several children by her, including male twins. But in 1970 he went to Beirut to work for Fatah. He left his wife behind in Britain and eventually divorced her.

(One of his twin sons recently died violently. He fell in love with a girl who, like himself, was studying computer science at an institute in Sidon, in South Lebanon. But she rejected him. On April 18, 1990, he shot her and then killed himself. His death was reported in Abu Nidal's magazine, where he was referred to by his code name, Kamal Hassan, no doubt to prevent readers connecting him with his father. The true cause of death was not given. He was described as a martyr, killed by enemies of the Palestinian revolution.)

Dr. Ghassan's first job in the early 1970s was working on weapons development and radio communications in Fatah's embryonic Scientific Committee. When the committee moved from Beirut to Baghdad in 1974, because of the better facilities available there, Dr. Ghassan went as well—eventually transferring his allegiance to Abu Nidal when the latter broke from Fatah. Over the next few years, he rose to become head of Abu Nidal's Scientific Committee and then, attaching this committee to the Intelligence

Directorate, he moved across in the mid-1980s to head the Directorate's Committee for Special Missions, its terrorist arm.

It was in this capacity that he supervised the attacks on the El Al counters at the Rome and Vienna airports in December 1985, the hijacking of the Pan Am airliner at Karachi in September 1986, and the killings at the Istanbul synagogue that same month. But if Abu Iyad was right in believing he was the Mossad's man, how could he have done such things? It was a puzzle I could not explain. It was not conceivable that an Israeli agent would mastermind an attack on a synagogue. Yet there was no doubt in my mind that Dr. Ghassan had been in charge of the Special Missions Committee at that time. The strangest puzzle of all was that the Israelis had not retaliated against him or against the organization for these attacks on Israeli and Jewish targets—although, except in this case, they invariably sought revenge quickly and violently. This was clearly an area I needed to investigate further.

The working procedure in force at that time inside the organization was for the Committee for Special Missions to produce a list of potential targets, which Dr. Ghassan and Abu Nidal would then discuss, picking out the ones that attracted them. As a defector from the organization told me,

> Dr. Ghassan always seemed to favor the most extreme and reckless operations. He used to speak with the greatest admiration of the Khmer Rouge, the IRA, the Red Army Faction. These were the models he held up to us. He detested any form of moderation.
>
> On the Palestinian side of things, he was totally opposed to the efforts of men like Atif Abu Bakr to bring about a reconciliation with Fatah. Instead, he seemed to encourage Palestinian discord. I formed the impression that he was a nihilist who reveled in the language of blood.

Yet several of Dr. Ghassan's operations proved unsuccessful or were aborted at an early stage—which in itself aroused the suspicions of some of his underlings. There was, for example, an attempt in late 1986 to smuggle arms into Britain—an operation that he directed. A member of his Committee for Special Missions, a certain Dr. Ramzi Awad, who lived in Spain, drove a car into

Britain with a hidden consignment of arms. He passed through customs without difficulty and got as far as London, where he was suddenly stopped in the street and arrested. The British police had evidently been tipped off. Dr. Awad was given a twenty-five-year sentence.

Sources inside the organization report that on this occasion, no attack was being planned. Abu Nidal had merely wanted to hide guns in Britain—for future use. For once the weapons are in place, it is no great problem to forge a passport and smuggle a man across a border to mount an attack. The weapons Dr. Awad was transporting may even have been destined for another organization: Barter is common in the terrorist underground. A bomb in London might be swapped for a machine gun in Madrid. Ten forged passports in Amsterdam might be worth as many hand grenades in Rome. In anticipation of a deal, Abu Nidal liked to accumulate supplies in different centers. If one of his sponsors, say, needed arms in Berlin, Paris, or Athens, he liked to be in a position to oblige.

After the organization moved out of Syria in 1987, the Secretariat was of necessity divided between Lebanon and Libya. While Dr. Ghassan presided in Lebanon, his deputy, known as the second secretary, lived and worked in Libya. The present incumbent of this post is Samir Muhammad al-Abbasi (code-named Amjad Ata), whom Jorde saw in the Libyan camp—a tall, dark man of about forty (in 1991), who is married to one of Abu Nidal's nieces, Salima al-Banna, by whom he has a son and a daughter. As Abu Nidal's right-hand man and confidant, he is privy to many of his criminal secrets. Ata's position gives him ultimate control over the archives and over the training camp where Jorde spent many desperate months.

Amjad Ata is well prepared for these tasks. In the 1970s he was a hard-working cadre of the Military Committee in Baghdad, helping organize the hostage taking at the Saudi embassy in Paris and the clandestine movement of weapons to Greece—then one of the organization's main centers for arms storage and distribution. In Syria in the 1980s, he headed Abu Nidal's private office before being put in charge of the Libyan end of the Secretariat once Abu Nidal settled there in 1987.

Middle-level cadres of the Secretariat tend to be moved around fairly frequently, to limit possible damage from leaks and indiscretions. But this did not prevent a couple of catastrophic defections.

In December 1989, Muhammad Khudr Salahat (code-named Karim Muhammad), then in his late twenties, fled with his wife and two children to Algeria, where Algerian intelligence was said to have pumped a great deal of information out of him—but nothing, it would appear, about a possible Israeli connection.

Salahat had been hand-picked by Abu Nidal to look after a top-secret section of the Secretariat's files known as the private archive. What made matters worse was that he was a nephew of Abu Nidal's wife—a member of the family. He may have had a sense of grievance on account of an earlier episode in his career: He had spent a year in one of the organization's jails, on a charge of embezzling $125,000 from a larger sum that, for safekeeping, Abu Nidal had deposited in Salahat's name in a foreign bank.

A second damaging defection, in March 1990, was that of Arif Salem, one of the chosen few, the four or five people able to paint a complete picture of the organization. For three years he had occupied the sensitive post of secretary to the first secretary—the man who opened the mail, examined its contents, and decided which items he could deal with himself and which he should pass on to his chief. Before that, he had filled an almost equally sensitive post in the Membership Committee, which, as its name suggests, keeps all the members' files. Arif Salem defected to Jordan, and it is suspected that he may have been working for Jordanian intelligence all along. I reflected that since neither of these people is thought to have revealed to Algeria or Jordan an Israeli connection, they either did not know about it or there was none.

THE INTELLIGENCE DIRECTORATE

From the moment of Abu Nidal's breach with Fatah in 1974, his "special operations" were in the hands of a secret core organization known as the Military Committee, staffed by men who had undergone special training, had worked clandestinely, and were committed to violence. Obsessive where security was concerned, Abu Nidal was at pains to protect the identity of the committee's members, laying down strict rules to restrict their contacts, even with each other. They were not allowed to meet at each other's homes, and the committee as a whole was utterly closed to all members not actually working in it.

Throughout the Baghdad years, the Military Committee was the heart of the organization. It was headed from 1979 to 1982 by an explosives expert, Naji Abu al-Fawaris, who had lost a hand and an eye in an accident in 1973. His specialty was car bombs. It was he who had handled the operation to kill Heinz Nittal, Chancellor Bruno Kreisky's friend, in Vienna in May 1981—which, as we have seen, is difficult but not impossible to square with the notion that Israel had penetrated the organization.

When the organization moved from Iraq to Syria in 1982–83, the Military Committee changed its name and became known as the Committee for Special Missions, directed in the mid-1980s, as has been mentioned, by Dr. Ghassan al-Ali, who oversaw most of the murderous operations of those years. Despite the change of name, the basic cadres—those with training and field experience—remained in place.

A bigger change occurred in 1985, when the Intelligence Directorate was formed, with four subdivisions. These were:

- the Committee for Special Missions, which was now absorbed into the new directorate;
- the Foreign Intelligence Committee;
- the Counterespionage Committee;
- the Lebanon Committee

From the start, this directorate was by far the most important in the whole organization. Like the old Military Committee, it was concerned with planting undercover agents abroad, establishing secret arms caches, gathering intelligence about potential targets, carrying out assassinations, and monitoring and penetrating hostile services. Inside the host countries it was responsible for instructors, weapons, and stores at the organization's various training establishments. Any information of a security nature gleaned by other directorates or committees was immediately passed to it. It was the control center to which everything of importance was referred.

The Intelligence Directorate maintained thirty or forty "residents" in foreign countries, who were responsible for dozens of arms caches, the largest of which was probably in Turkey—from where arms could be conveyed overland to Europe and to the Arab world. In the organization's history, there have been two main phases of arms distribution: the Iraqi phase, in which arms dumps were primarily established in Greece, Turkey, and France; and then the Syrian phase, when Cyprus, Italy, and West Germany were added to the list.

To an outside observer, there seemed to be periods when the directorate was intensely active and others when it was dormant. But an inside source told me that even when no operations were being mounted or planned, the directorate was always vigilant. Security arrangements at airports and seaports had to be constantly reviewed, alterations to visa and immigration stamps monitored, and a host of other subjects kept up to date; the training of staff was a daily preoccupation. "It was work all the time," the source said. "There were no periods of rest at all. The directorate could not afford to pause for a single moment."

This directorate was the object of Abu Nidal's special attention, and whoever else he might appoint as its titular head at any one time, he was its real chief.

At the beginning, when the directorate was first founded, in 1985, Abd al-Rahman Isa was a natural choice for the job. The longest-serving member of the organization, he had for years been Abu Nidal's shadow (which was the reason I had been so anxious to interview him when he defected, though I had to make do with his taped debriefing). He had been close to Abu Nidal ever since they had first met in Jordan in the 1960s. Abu Nidal had taken Isa to the Sudan and then to Iraq as his assistant and private secretary, entrusting him with all sorts of personal and family matters.

When the organization planned to move to Syria in the early 1980s, Isa was sent ahead to run things until the arrival of Abu Nizar and other Central Committee members.

Although physically ugly, unshaven, and shabbily dressed, Isa had charm and was quick and shrewd. On one occasion he was stopped by a customs officer at the Geneva airport and asked if he had anything to declare. As it happened, he was carrying $5 million in notes, which Abu Nidal had asked him to deposit in one of the organization's numbered accounts. Without hesitation, he declared the full amount. Respectfully, the customs officer detailed one of his colleagues to escort Isa to the bank of his choice.

But Isa was restless. He had the instincts and reactions of an intelligence agent and saw the whole world in terms of plots and covert operations. Hailing from the village of Amin, near Jenin in the West Bank, he was consumed, like many Palestinians of similar background, with the bitterness of the refugee. He was an old-fashioned believer in armed struggle, in the conviction that violence alone would make Israel yield and return him to his home in Palestine.

If anyone deserved Abu Nidal's confidence, it was Abd al-Rahman Isa: They had been partners in crime for close on two decades. But in the mid-1980s, Isa made the fatal mistake of associating himself closely with such leading men as Mustafa Murad (Abu Nizar), then Abu Nidal's deputy, and Atif Abu Bakr, the reformist ideologue who was seduced by events in Lebanon and came to believe that the organization could emerge aboveground and take its place in the mainstream of the resistance movement.

Abd al-Rahman Isa was to pay for his mistake. Hardly had Abu Nidal settled in Libya in the summer of 1987 than he demoted Isa, excluded him from the center of affairs, and publicly humiliated him. Isa tried to resign, but Abu Nidal insisted that he stay on in the directorate in a junior capacity, to be ordered about by men whose boss he had been and whom he had himself protected in their time. Abu Nidal even gave instructions that Isa should be treated with particular contempt—thus encouraging the small fry to believe that their own promotion depended on deriding their former chief.

Although Isa had been one of the founders of the organization, by 1988 he found himself alone in a small office, forbidden to contact anyone in the directorate, and having to report daily to Abu Nidal on any telephone calls or visitors he might have received.

In Isa's place at the head of the Intelligence Directorate Abu Nidal appointed two men: Mustafa Awad (code name Alaa), who took charge of the Lebanon Committee and was based in that country; and his deputy, Ali al-Farra (code name Dr. Kamal), who was based in Libya and took charge of the directorate's three other committees: Special Missions, Foreign Intelligence, and Counterespionage. In theory, Alaa was the senior of the two, with the title head of the Intelligence Directorate, but as Dr. Kamal worked with Abu Nidal in Libya on a daily basis, he was the true intelligence supremo. From then until the present, Alaa and Dr. Kamal have been Abu Nidal's most malleable instruments.

Alaa was a sensual, violent, good-looking man in his forties (in 1991). Like Dr. Ghassan and Abu Nidal, he drank and probably used drugs. He was a West Banker from the village of Tal and had studied in Pakistan before joining Abu Nidal in the 1970s. But as with so many of his colleagues, Abu Nidal had acquired a special hold over him. In 1978, Alaa had been one of a group of Baghdad-based fighters whom Abu Nidal had sent to Sidon to help Abu Dawud harass the Israelis during their invasion of Lebanon that year. Arafat had interpreted the arrival of these fighters as a mass penetration of his ranks by Abu Nidal and had rounded them up and interned them.

Rather than face detention, Alaa had joined Fatah and had talked, revealing everything he knew—in effect betraying Abu Nidal, who promptly condemned him to death in absentia.

When Israel invaded Lebanon a second time, in 1982, and the PLO was expelled, Alaa switched allegiance yet again and rejoined Abu Nidal. Some members wanted to execute him for his earlier defection but others believed he should be given a second chance. Abu Nidal exploited the situation by making Alaa understand that if he made the slightest mistake, his past would be dredged up and he would be killed.

Thereafter, Alaa tried to satisfy Abu Nidal's every whim, displaying exemplary obedience and loyalty. He became one of the fiercest members of the organization, and was soon up to his ears in blood. His special talents were moving weapons about, hiding them, and planning and carrying out operations.

For whatever reason, Abu Nidal promoted Alaa rapidly, brought him into the Political Bureau in 1986 and, in personal matters, allowed him exceptional leeway. Abu Nidal was forever lecturing his members about the need for strict sexual morality—adultery was a crime in the organization, punishable by death—but Alaa was known to sleep with women prisoners, with many women outside the organization, and even with several of his comrades' wives. Abu Nidal ignored this.

There was, for example, the pathetic case of Bassam al-A'raj, an old cadre who had lost most fingers of both hands in an attack on the PLO office in Karachi in the 1970s. In due course he married a Lebanese girl from Sidon, Abir Qubrusli, only to discover that Alaa was involved with her. When he objected to this, he found himself accused of a security crime, imprisoned in the Balawi refugee camp, and then killed in North Lebanon in 1987, leaving Alaa free to continue his relationship with his wife.

There were several aspects of Alaa's career that struck me as odd. He had defected but been let back in; he was sexually promiscuous but got away with it. When I found out he had prevented a Mossad cell that had been uncovered in Lebanon from being "played back" (an incident we shall hear more of later), it dawned on me that he might be in on the Mossad deal, if there was one, with Dr. Ghassan. I put him on my short list of suspected penetration agents. As the Lebanon-based intelligence chief of the organization, he was admirably placed to manipulate events to Israel's advantage.

The Libya-based intelligence chief, Ali al-Farra (or Dr. Kamal, as he was more usually called), was also guilty of sexual peccadilloes, which Abu Nidal either indulgently excused or used as evidence against him. He had gotten hold of photographs of Dr. Kamal in diverse sexual positions, allegedly taken by the French police in a Paris brothel, and held them over his head, threatening to send them to his family and his village.

Dr. Kamal was a tall, bald, bespectacled man of about forty (in 1991) who came from Khan Yunis, in the Gaza Strip, and had dropped out of Alexandria University, in Egypt, after two years in its engineering department. He had joined Abu Nidal's Military Committee in Iraq, where he climbed the intelligence ladder. Once the organization moved to Tripoli, Dr. Kamal's special responsibility was the daily relationship with Libyan intelligence. But Abu Nidal also used him as a troubleshooter and special envoy to foreign countries or terrorist organizations with which the organization had intelligence dealings. He was the contact man with ASALA, the Armenian secret army, and with the New People's Army of the Philippines. He also handled Abu Nidal's delicate undercover relationship with French intelligence.

Dr. Kamal was married to Alia Hammuda, sister of Atif Hammuda, Abu Nidal's main colleague in the Finance Directorate. At one time he and his wife lived in rooms above Abu Nidal's office, and had to suffer his constant harassment. For example, Abu Nidal would summon Dr. Kamal's wife downstairs and scold her about her cooking—it smelled—or for being too fat or for allegedly stealing some trivial object that had arrived at the office or even for gossiping with other wives about him. He accused her of giving his telephone number to the CIA. Bullying was Abu Nidal's way of controlling everyone around him.

At meetings, Abu Nidal would spend the first half hour haranguing those present with sarcastic, slighting remarks, browbeating them so that when it came to discussing serious matters, they were at a psychological disadvantage. "You marry slim women," was one of his favorite themes, "but within a month they turn into elephants. It must be all that chocolate you feed them! If *I'm* given a piece of chocolate on a plane, I take it home to my son. But you take chocolate out of the mouths of your children and eat it yourselves!" His members listened meekly to such inanities.

THE ORGANIZATION DIRECTORATE

This directorate dealt with the recruitment of new members, their education in the rules and philosophy of the organization, and their preparation for a job within it. In theory, it should have served as a sort of mother directorate, except that it was always in a state of upheaval because Abu Nidal was convinced its leaders were spies in the employ of hostile powers. It had three main branches: the Committee for Foreign Countries; the Committee for Arab Countries; and the Palestine/Jordan Committee.

The first of these committees was the important one, because it dealt with Palestinian students at foreign colleges and universities, who from the very beginning were the bedrock of Abu Nidal's whole structure. In the first phase, in the mid-1970s, groups of students were enlisted and sent to Yugoslavia, Spain, Britain, Turkey, and Pakistan, the main centers at the time for his concentrated instruction. The students were instructed to spread the word, to recruit others, to gather useful data, to investigate potential targets—and to set up secret arms caches. But they would not usually be involved in military or paramilitary operations. When an operation was planned, a specially trained hit team would be sent in to do the job.

Some students joined Abu Nidal because they needed money; others were fanatics, attracted by his political views. The organization preferred to recruit very young men, whose minds had not yet been formed. Most were country boys from one of the six hundred or so villages of pre-1948 Palestine. Such students were usually recruited before they were sent abroad to study. The organization's technique, much like that of other Palestinian factions, was to approach young people who had just left school and did not know what to do next. "Here is a scholarship to Poland or East Germany!" The student would be hooked as long as the organization could afford to pay him.

Abu Nidal spent millions on students—he was the best payer among all the Palestinian factions. In Eastern Europe, Fatah used to give its students $50 a month; Abu Nidal gave his $500. No one could compete on this level. Of course, he gave his scholarships to young men he considered politically loyal. Many of them were good revolutionary material, good patriotic fighters. But instead of putting their idealism to work for Palestine, he implicated them in criminal acts. They came to see the world through the prism of his bitter philosophy and, in their isolation, he owned them.

In Western Europe, Abu Nidal was even more successful, because he could afford to meet all the expenses of his students—rent, board, fares, pocket money—which allowed them to settle down into big-city European life and to be ready for action when he needed them. In Spain, he built up a strong organization by taking over most of Fatah's students: He was able to pay them well; Fatah was not.

In the 1980s, there was a radical change of climate in several of the countries where Abu Nidal operated. His presence in Spain was virtually wiped out after his assassination of a defector had alerted the Spanish police to his activities; in Britain, after the crackdown that followed the attempted assassination of the Israeli ambassador, he found it difficult to maintain even a foothold; in Turkey, too, the organization was hit hard after it assassinated a Jordanian diplomat in Ankara in July 1985; and in Pakistan it suffered from harsh repression after the hijacking of the Pan Am jumbo jet at Karachi in 1986. Its presence in Yugoslavia, once a major center of its operations, was also much reduced, and in the late 1980s several of Abu Nidal's students were moved from there to Hungary.

As operations in Europe became more difficult to mount and counterterrorism became more effective, the organization shifted its emphasis to Southeast Asia, especially to Thailand and the Philippines; also to India; and in a sketchy way, to Latin America and a number of African countries. As Jorde's career illustrated, such faraway operations had nothing whatsoever to do with the Palestinian cause. By this time Abu Nidal was running a protection racket—raising funds by blackmail and extortion.

As its name suggests, the Organization Directorate's Committee for Arab Countries looked after members in those Arab countries where the organization had a presence, which was by no means all of them. After its departure from Iraq and Syria, the organization maintained a small underground presence in these two countries. In Algeria it was well represented, and in Libya it was, of course, present in strength. But in most other places it was a matter of a few individuals living a shadowy existence.

The Jordan/Palestine Committee was the weakest of all. The organization had been strong in Jordan in the 1970s, but when in the 1980s it started hitting Jordanian targets on Syria's behalf, it faced tough repression: Its leaders and prominent cadres were arrested and, in many cases, spent years in jail. As for Palestine, the real scandal was that in spite of its strident propaganda and exaggerated claims, Abu Nidal's organization was virtually absent from the occupied territories: For much of its existence, 1974 to 1990, its military activity there was nil. It did not throw a single stone during the *intifada,* let alone anything more lethal. This, more than anything else, I reflected, gave a clue to Abu Nidal's real priorities.

Until 1986, the head of the Organization Directorate had been Fu'ad al-Suffarini (code name Umar Hamdi), who had joined Abu Nidal when he was a young clerk in Abu Dhabi and had given himself over completely to the organization. He had served as the head of Abu Nidal's private office and knew all his secrets; he had overseen the attempt to murder Syria's foreign minister, Khaddam, in the United Arab Emirates; and he had interrogated and executed a number of people in the organization's prisons. As a result, Suffarini had been promoted to head of the Organization Directorate, a position very close to the center of power.

But in 1986, Suffarini could no longer cope psychologically with the terrible things he had witnessed. He fell into a depression and voluntarily asked to be passed over. Knowing Abu Nidal's methods, Suffarini must have feared he would be killed. He locked himself in his house, and whenever anyone from the organization knocked on his door, his wife would not open. There came a point when he would deal only with those members he felt would not betray him. Because his loyalty was not in doubt and he seemed genuinely in need of a rest, Abu Nidal sent him as his representative to Greece—and it was from there that Suffarini fled to Jordan in 1987.

Had Abu Nidal suspected that he was planning to defect, he

would have ordered Suffarini's execution there and then and denounced him as a spy for the "traitor king," his standard phrase for King Hussein. But clearly things had gone badly wrong in the organization if a man of Suffarini's seniority felt that his only way out was to escape to Jordan—a country that was his enemy, against which he had mounted lethal operations, but from which he now felt he could expect more mercy than from Abu Nidal.

Suffarini was replaced at the head of the Organization Directorate by Mustafa Murad (Abu Nizar), Abu Nidal's deputy, who had now fallen from grace. In his case, the move to the directorate was a substantial demotion, for Abu Nizar had occupied the number-two position in the whole organization for many years.

Abu Nizar's career had been typical of the contemporary Palestinian resistance experience. He was born on March 15, 1946, in the Palestinian village of Umm al-Fahm, which was overrun by the Israelis in 1948. His family first fled to Jenin, then to Tulkarm, in the West Bank, where he grew up and went to school in a refugee camp. He attended a teachers' training college at Irbid, in Jordan, worked briefly as a teacher, and then joined Fatah at the age of twenty, in 1966.

He was a brave, strong youth and soon distinguished himself in clashes with the Jordanian army. Captured during the battles of September 1970, he was badly beaten and suffered severe leg wounds, which later required an operation in Czechoslovakia. By this time he had moved with many other fighters to Iraq, where he joined Abu Nidal after the 1974 split and was put in charge of the newly formed Military Committee.

Abu Nizar was involved, it will be recalled, in Abu Nidal's botched attempt to kill Mahmud Abbas (Abu Mazin), of Fatah, in Damascus in 1974. This was the operation that earned Abu Nidal a death sentence, passed by the PLO in absentia, and that put Abu Nizar into a Fatah jail in Syria for eighteen months. On his release in 1976, he returned to Baghdad and again took charge of the Military Committee. In 1979, at the time of the Naji Allush crisis, he played a decisive role in bringing the whole organization back under Abu Nidal's control and was suitably rewarded. When the organization moved to Syria, he was elected Abu Nidal's deputy.

Abu Nizar was a large, energetic man, popular with the rank and file, many of whom he had trained, but politically something of a simpleton. He was ill prepared for the in-fighting that was to start in 1985–86, when, on his return to the Middle East from Poland, Abu Nidal started scheming to consolidate his control over the organization—and to destroy his deputy.

The battle over the deputy leadership started in Damascus in 1985, when Abu Nidal was still abroad, traveling between Poland and Libya. He sensed—and rightly so—that Abu Nizar, who had run the show in his long absence, had become a powerful figure in his own right, with a personal following swollen by the influx of new recruits in Lebanon. So Abu Nidal, as was his custom, started to attack Abu Nizar in sharply worded letters to the Central Committee and conspired to replace him with a young man in his mid-thirties, Isam Maraqa (code name Salim Ahmad).

Maraqa was generally considered mediocre, but he had two features that endeared him to Abu Nidal: He was the husband of his wife's niece, and therefore part of the family; and he was slavishly loyal to Abu Nidal. Born in the early 1950s, he was a blond, blue-eyed man from Khalil, in the West Bank, who had gone to Iraq in the early 1970s to study at the Basra Agricultural College, but he had dropped out to join Fatah before finishing his course. In 1974 he sided with Abu Nidal and went to work in the Military Committee. Abu Nidal took to him and pushed him up the ladder, securing his election to the Central Committee in 1986 and then, in the teeth of opposition from the rest of the leadership, to the Political Bureau itself. It was the first time a member had risen so high without a majority vote in his favor in the leadership.

Enraged at the opposition to his plans for Maraqa, Abu Nidal denounced Abu Nizar, who, puzzled and hurt, withdrew to his house for several months and refused to attend meetings. He was persuaded to resume his duties only by the need to mobilize for the War of the Camps—which, in Abu Nidal's mind, it turned out, was yet another reason to kill him.

By the time the organization left Syria in 1987, Abu Nidal had secured the appointment of Isam Maraqa as his deputy—based in Lebanon, with Dr. Ghassan, head of the Secretariat—while Abu Nizar, stripped of his powers, was shunted aside to the Organization Directorate and transferred to Libya, under Abu Nidal's direct control.

THE MEMBERSHIP COMMITTEE

This ultrasecret committee controls the files of every member of the organization, whoever and wherever he may be. Originally paper files, they are now being computerized. No one knows for certain how many members Abu Nidal has and who they are. PLO sources put the total at several hundred. In 1986, Israeli intelligence estimated the strength at five hundred to eight hundred active members and several hundred sympathizers. Western sources suggest the membership could be as large as two thousand men, since the organization has the allegiance of many Palestinian students at universities in different parts of the world.

Since 1987, the committee has been based in Sidon, Lebanon, and has been headed by Aziz Abd al-Khaliq (code name Awwad), a West Bank Palestinian, born in 1947, who joined the organization in Baghdad as a young man.

Abu Nidal made every effort to keep this committee hermetically sealed off from the rest of the organization. No one was allowed access to its offices, and no direct contacts—not by the leadership, still less by ordinary cadres—were allowed with its staff. The committee functions both as an information bank and as a security sieve, for it has the power to accept or reject recommendations for membership submitted by other committees and directorates.

Its personnel files contain whatever is known about each member of the organization: birth, family background, education, relatives, marriage, children, career history, political allegiances—and, of course, details of any intelligence or security agencies with which he might have been involved. Also included is the member's photograph, photographs of his wife, children, and relatives, and photocopies of his passport. A key entry is the long autobiographical statement that each member, and each candidate for membership, is obliged to write, spelling out the details of his life to date. Supplementary information may be called for if the committee sees fit. It might, for example, ask a member or would-be member if he knows the names of anyone in Jordanian intelligence or in the CIA or merely anyone rich. It might ask a member if he suspects his fiancée of having had relations with other men before him and, if so, with whom. Answers must be given in full, and the committee's decision is final.

Once accepted into the organization, a member may still have to face further questioning months or years later, and he might, as happened to Jorde, be asked to write out his autobiographical statement again, or face further probing if fresh material surfaces about him.

The committee will also pronounce on where in the organization the new member is to be placed, but clearly, members of the leadership also have a say in such matters. If a cadre is seen to have military qualities, for example, someone in the leadership can recommend his transfer to a suitable position. If he is thought to have political potential, he is assigned to political work. Abu Nidal intervenes when someone is spotted with a talent for intelligence or security work.

Most members join the organization on the recommendation of an existing member, but once in his job, a new member is forbidden to have any contact whatsoever with the cadre who first recommended him for membership. If a person recommends himself for membership, he will immediately be suspected of being a plant and will have to undergo a long, difficult examination. The investigation may be prolonged. If suspicions are thought to be well founded, the usual procedure is to accept the candidate for membership, transfer him to a "training camp," arrest and interrogate him, and, more often than not, kill him. To prepare for such eventualities, the organization takes the precaution of making would-be members sign a form, as Jorde did, saying that they agree to be put to death if treachery can be proved against them. When the organization was in Syria, any such suspect candidates for membership were usually transferred to Lebanon and dealt with there.

A good deal of poaching takes place from other Palestinian organizations—a task to which the Intelligence Directorate applies itself. In fact, each directorate and committee is involved in poaching and recruitment—from the street, from refugee camps, from villages, from other organizations. And constant efforts are made to infiltrate and plant members on other organizations.

THE POLITICAL DIRECTORATE

This directorate is in many ways the most overt part of the organization. It administers two committees, the Publications Committee and the Political Relations Committee; and like some of its sister institutions, its activities are divided between Lebanon and Libya, with the Libyan end known as the Bureau of the Political Directorate Abroad.

The main function of the Publications Committee is to publish *Filastin al-Thawra* (*Palestine the Revolution*), the organization's weekly journal and principal mouthpiece. (Its name is the same as the PLO's magazine, another example of Abu Nidal's wish to present himself as a rival and alternative to Yasser Arafat's movement.)

The magazine was first edited in Baghdad; it then moved to Damascus, from the early 1980s to June 1987; and then, after the organization's departure from Syria, it established its headquarters in Lebanon, in the southern Shuf, in territory controlled by the Druze leader Walid Jumblat. About twelve thousand copies a week are printed and distributed.

Because the organization is isolated and clandestine, and at war with a host of Palestinian and other enemies, the magazine is its voice and platform. It is Abu Nidal's main medium of information, of propaganda, of political expression, but also the means by which he communicates his current political line to his scattered members. Occasionally, it has been used to transmit coded instructions. When the organization was in Syria, an attempt was made to publish an English-language edition of the magazine, but only two issues appeared.

The Publications Committee also produces posters, postcards, and other publicity material, as well as a series of booklets, of which ten have so far appeared under the imprint Manshurat Filastin al-Thawra (Palestine the Revolution Publications). In the late 1980s, Abu Nidal was believed to be spending about $165,000 a month on the activities of the Publications Committee.

When based in Syria, the Publications Committee owned and operated a printing press and a news service under the cover of Dar Sabra (the Sabra Publishing House). Its editorial department was housed in two Damascus apartments, while the computers, electronic typesetting, and German press (which had been purchased in 1984 for 22 million Syrian lira) were housed in a works outside the city.

Dar Sabra was headed by a Palestinian journalist, Dr. Ahmad Abu Matar, an able man with a doctorate in Arabic literature, whose allegiance to the organization was not generally known. He had had a career in radical Palestinian politics, having been involved with Dr. Wadi Haddad's PFLP in the 1970s, before secretly joining Abu Nidal in 1983. He used to claim that the apartments and the printing press were jointly owned by himself and his wife's family, but they in fact belonged to the organization, and Dr. Matar was paid a salary of $1,300 a month, together with a house, car, and travel expenses. With his wide range of contacts in journalism, politics, and the world of intelligence, he made great play of being independent, even writing critical articles about Abu Nidal in the Beirut press. However, he also reported regularly to Abu Nidal on intelligence and security matters.

When the organization left Syria, much of Dar Sabra was closed down, except for the news service, which Dr. Matar continued to run as a private business (although it has been suspected of links with Syrian intelligence). Dr. Matar has left the organization but has not wholly escaped Abu Nidal's attentions: Since 1989, a number of attempts have been made to abduct him to Lebanon, presumably to kill him there.

In Lebanon, the organization controlled a news service called Manara Press, which bought material from free-lance writers and sold it to news agencies and newspapers. On the surface it was a straightforward journalistic outfit, but it too provided the organization with political intelligence, gleaned from its contacts. In Beirut, Manara Press was for several years managed by a Lebanese woman, called Ibtissam Abbud, on a contract basis. She knew that Abu Nidal controlled the company, but she was not a member of his organization. In 1987, rebelling against his dictatorial methods, she decided to resign and claim statutory compensation. The organization's answer was to try to kill her. On orders from Alaa (the Lebanon-based head of the Intelligence Directorate), a car in which she and her fiancé were driving came under fire. He was killed and she was seriously wounded. Reporting the incident, the Lebanese press spoke of "unknown assailants."

At one time, Manara Press also had a Damascus branch, run by one of Abu Nidal's nieces, Salwa al-Banna, a relatively independent-minded journalist who had specialized in Palestinian affairs and had built up a good range of contacts. But her family connection did not spare her Abu Nidal's harsh discipline. When she refused to marry within the organization and attempted to have a social life of her own—an aspiration he found wholly reprehensible—he had her imprisoned for a year in Iraq. Suitably chastened, she eventually agreed to marry Ibrahim al-Tamimi (code name Tariq Mahmud), a member of the Publications Committee, and in 1987 she returned to full-time work with the organization, joining the editorial board of *Filastin al-Thawra.*

But the editorial side of the magazine, like the rest of the organization, was subject to draconian controls. Abu Nidal laid down a whole dictionary of terms and expressions that had to be rigidly adhered to. The PLO was invariably referred to as "the so-called PLO"; Israel, as the "Zionist entity"; Jordan, as the "East Jordan regime"; Saudi Arabia, as "the regime of the Saudi family" or as the "Zionized family." Abusive sneerings constituted the entire political content of the articles.

Members of the committee trembled as they wrote, because any departure from the formula laid them open to security accusations. You could be a journalist one day and on trial the next. Failure to grasp the organization's political line, as laid down by the supreme "brain" and "architect," was a serious crime. Having to write to Abu Nidal's dictation, the editors were more like hostages than journalists. Copy arriving from Libya—it was reverently called "central material"—had to be used intact and without alteration. Even grammatical errors had to go uncorrected.

For a brief period, 1985 to 1987, the journal broke out of these shackles and became a genuinely Palestinian magazine able to compete with those of other groups. It was edited at that time by Atif Abu Bakr, the reformist ideologue, who tried to address Palestinian concerns: the War of the Camps; disunity in Palestinian ranks; the dangers facing the Palestinian people; and so forth. When Abu Nidal sent him an article that alleged that Arafat was suffering from AIDS, Abu Bakr refused to run it. Was it political AIDS, he inquired mockingly, or the real thing? If it was the illness, then it was simply untrue and slander was not the way to challenge policies with which one disagreed. But by 1987 Abu Nidal had regained control, and the magazine reverted to its old ways. Arafat was once more the "enemy within," the traitor who was steering the Palestinian ship onto the rocks.

There were, of course, other changes of tone in the magazine, depending on where it was based. When it was in Iraq in the 1970s, Syria was depicted as "the treacherous, Alawi, sectarian regime," while Iraq was the "nationalist regime," the "backbone of the Arab revolution." When the organization moved to Damascus, it was Syria's turn to be praised as the "champion of strategic balance." On Abu Nidal's orders, a photograph of President Assad appeared in every issue to illustrate flattering articles about Syria. Meanwhile, Iraq was abused as a "fascist dictatorship," Iran's victories in that Gulf war were extolled, and Iraq's foreign minister, Tariq Aziz, became the special butt of Abu Nidal's venom: His Christian origins and "Crusader mentality" were constantly attacked. He was the tool of "a Vatican conspiracy against the Arabs," it was claimed. Then, when the move to Libya took place, Assad's picture was dropped, together with all flattery of Syria, and Qaddafi and Libya were praised.

The Political Directorate's second committee was the Political Relations Committee, in charge of handling all the organization's political relationships—with Arab and foreign states, with political parties, with other Palestinian factions—except for those of an intelligence or security nature. Abu Nidal could not resist poaching from the committee those relationships that interested him—such as the relationship with France, for example—on the argument that they were really an intelligence matter. But he was clever enough to realize that some relationships were better handled by reasonably open-minded people on the committee, able to conduct sensible political discussions, rather than by the thugs of his Intelligence Directorate.

Atif Abu Bakr was head of the Political Directorate from 1985 to 1987. He was replaced by Mansur Hamdan, a mild, cultured man who, in return for a quiet life, was evidently prepared to do Abu Nidal's bidding. As for the Political Relations Committee, it was divided into two when the organization left Syria, one part going to Lebanon to supervise relations with Palestinian and Lebanese factions, and the other to Libya, where it reported directly to Abu Nidal. Since 1987, the head of this committee has been Rizk Sa'id Abd al-Majid (code name Walid Khalid), who came to the attention of the foreign press at the time of the *Silco* affair, for which he acted as the organization's spokesman. As we shall see later, *Silco* was a converted French fishing boat captured by the Libyans in 1986 somewhere between Malta and Libya. A year later, in November 1987, Abu Nidal claimed this was his operation, in order to get Qaddafi off the hook.

THE FINANCE DIRECTORATE

The headquarters of this directorate were situated wherever Abu Nidal happened to be—in Iraq, Poland, Syria, or Libya—and the men who ran it were never anything more than employees, with full allegiance to him. All money matters were kept firmly in his own hands. It was Abu Nidal himself who monitored the foreign bank accounts, who determined the size of the organization's budget, who approved the monthly transfers of funds and made all the investment decisions. The more I investigated Abu Nidal's organization, the clearer it became to me that what he cared most about was the millions tucked away in foreign banks—together with his personal security, which in turn dictated his political relations with his host countries. His preoccupation with money and with the broad political and diplomatic picture meant that he left the planning and conduct of operations largely to others, giving men like Dr. Ghassan al-Ali and Alaa great leeway.

The Finance Directorate was divided into two branches, one dealing with expenditure, the other with investments. The first dealt with the organization's spending on a day-to-day basis; the second managed funds, kept an eye on companies owned or partly owned by the organization, traded in arms and other commodities, collected commissions due on middleman activities. Although the directorate is at present based in Libya, where Abu Nidal can control it, a senior member of the leadership lives in Lebanon and supervises expenditure in that country.

The real head of this directorate is Abu Nidal. His deputy, Atif Hammuda (code-named Abu Siham), is an uninspired but useful technocrat who has been with the organization since its foundation. Although he has been a member of the Central Committee for years, he has never been known to utter a word at any of its meetings. As the custodian of the organization's financial secrets, he is not allowed to have social contacts with anyone and lives in great isolation. His sister is married to Ali al-Farra (Dr. Kamal), the Libyan-based intelligence supremo and Abu Nidal's right-hand man.

(Hammuda's predecessor as deputy head of the Finance Directorate was a certain Khalid al-Madi who, being less of a doormat, dared voice certain reservations about his work. To chastise him for not displaying the right slavish mentality, Abu Nidal removed him from his post and from the Central Committee and demoted him to being an ordinary cadre. In a further twist, characteristic of Abu Nidal, a pension paid to his old mother, who was then living with him, was stopped and the air conditioner from his house removed—a grueling enough punishment in Libya in mid-summer.)

In the 1980s, two men were largely responsible for the foreign investments of the group. One was Dirar Abd al-Fattah al-Silwani, a member of the command of the Finance Directorate, who, from offices in East Berlin, ran one of the organization's companies, called Zibado. But Dirar defected first to West Germany and then to the United States, spilling the beans to the CIA about Abu Nidal's investment and trading network.

A second important overseas manager was Samir Najm al-Din (code name Abu Nabil), who, from a base in Warsaw, ran the SAS Foreign Trade and Investment Company, a large corporation with several branches and interests, ranging from property development to arms trading. (SAS stood for the first letters of the names of three members of the Finance Directorate: Samir Najm al-Din himself; Adnan al-Kaylani; and Shakir Farhan—the last name an alias for Atif Hammuda.)

Samir Najm al-Din was a Palestinian from Iraq with a head for business who in the 1980s was already in his sixties. He made SAS a commercial success, which may have been the reason for his downfall. In 1987, Abu Nidal summoned him to Libya and demoted him. He forbade anyone to have dealings with Najm al-Din, and to break him further, he had his son-in-law, whose name was Dr. Sadiq, arrested, held captive for a year, and then murdered in September 1989. Abu Nidal then claimed that Sadiq had been killed by the Mossad.

When Abu Nidal first thought of branching out on his own in the early 1970s, he had very few assets. His first real acquisitions were Fatah's assets in Iraq, valued at some $4 million, which the Iraqis handed over to him. (This estimate excludes the $15 million worth of arms that they also gave him.) Then the Iraqis gave him another $5 million when Fatah condemned him to death. He was clever with money and managed, with these relatively small sums, to make sound high-return investments. No one in the organization knew the details of the banks or the brokers through whom he dealt. Such matters he kept very much to himself.

He made a lot of money from blackmail and extortion, adding substantially to his assets. Sources inside the organization told me that he had been shaking down the Saudis since the 1970s, using contacts he had made when he worked in Saudi Arabia. The go-between was a Saudi living in London. From blackmailing the Saudis and lesser Gulf rulers, he is estimated to have collected some $50 million in the twelve years from 1976 to 1988.

More money came from arms trading. Iraqi intelligence sources told me that Abu Nidal fronted for Iraq in buying weapons on the international market and shipping them to political factions and liberation movements that Iraq wished to support. By using Abu Nidal as an intermediary, the Iraqis were able to deny all knowledge of the traffic. "He made millions through his arms deals on our behalf," the Iraqis told me.

Those mid-1970s deals put Abu Nidal in touch with Polish and Bulgarian suppliers and with Syrian, Lebanese, and Iraqi dealers. In the late 1970s he made still more money selling Polish small arms and light machine guns to tribesmen on the borders of Saudi Arabia and the People's Democratic Republic of Yemen, a betrayal, incidentally, of the Saudis, who had been buying him off for years. He would buy a Kalashnikov in Poland for $120 and sell it in South Arabia for ten times that sum. He also bought cut-price copies of Western weapons from Bulgarian state corporations. He made money from these deals, but more importantly, he used these East-bloc countries as safe havens for his various operations.

Before the Iraq-Iran War, Abu Nidal had about $120 million, but by the end of the war in 1988, this sum, Western intelligence sources told me, had grown to $400 million. Like many other dealers, he made a fortune selling arms to both Iraq and Iran. The big money came in the 1980s, most of it from selling East-bloc weapons.

Most of his funds are salted away in nominee companies or deposited in banks in Switzerland, Austria, and Spain. Funds he deposited with the Bank of Credit and Commerce International (BCCI) in London were lost when it was found out in 1991 that the bank was run by bigger crooks than himself. Ghassan Ahmad Qasim, a former manager of BCCI's branch on Sloane Street, West London, said on the BBC's "Panorama" program on July 29, 1991, that an account containing about $50 million was opened at a BCCI branch in London in 1981 by Samir Najm al-Din, Abu

Nidal's commercial adviser, and was used to finance arms deals with British companies. Qasim said he had escorted Abu Nidal on shopping trips during three visits he made to London in the 1980s. He also said that he had been recruited by MI5, Britain's security service, in 1987 to pass on information about Abu Nidal's financial dealings with BCCI.

Much of Abu Nidal's money was deposited in foreign banks in the names of his wife; his son, Nidal; his daughter, Badia; her husband; and other members of his family. He was said to have placed $20 million in an account in the name of his wife's sister's son—when the boy was still underage. Large sums were also deposited in the names of leading members such as Abu Nizar, Samir Najm al-Din, Dr. Ghassan, and others, usually with two signatories per account. But in 1985, Abu Nidal regained control of these funds. According to Atif Abu Bakr, Abu Nidal said to Abu Nizar, "Your joint account with such-and-such a bank in Geneva has been identified. We now think it best that it be transferred to the name of so-and-so." So Abu Nizar would go to the bank and relinquish his signatory rights to the person whom Abu Nidal had named. This was usually Atif Hammuda, deputy head of the Finance Directorate, who in turn gave Abu Nidal power of attorney over all the funds held in his name. He was one of the more mobile members of the directorate, investigating the organization's companies abroad, withdrawing or depositing funds in Swiss banks, and monitoring the various accounts. He behaved, according to one inside source, like Abu Nidal's lap dog, and Abu Nidal often referred to him as "you damn dog!"

THE COMMITTEE FOR REVOLUTIONARY JUSTICE

This infamous committee runs the organization's prisons, interrogation centers, and places of execution. Its main base is in the village of Bqasta, in the southern Shuf Mountains of Lebanon, a location leased by Abu Nidal from the Druze leader Walid Jumblat. Two neighboring Druze villages, Karkha and Alma, are used by Abu Nidal as an arms depot and a military base. In exchange for the use of Druze territory, Abu Nidal supplies Jumblat with arms, expertise, funds, and security. It is a mutually convenient arrangement.

The committee is officially headed by Abdallah Hasan (code name Abu Nabil), a former schoolteacher now approaching sixty, who is not directly involved in interrogations or torture. But since he signs execution orders, he is nevertheless implicated in the committee's crimes.

Hasan was a senior and long-standing member of Fatah who left to join Colonel Abu Musa at the time of the 1983 Fatah mutiny. When that mutiny collapsed, he rallied to Abu Nidal in 1985. But he was not wholly trusted and, in fact, faced interrogation in 1987, which resulted in a heart attack. With his hands still manacled, he was rushed to the Ghassan Hammud hospital in Sidon, where he recovered. He was reinstated in his job on the committee but lives in the shadow of a sort of permanent blackmail.

The real boss of the committee is Mustafa Ibrahim Sanduqa (code name Khaldun), who is married to one of Abu Nidal's nieces. He is a member of the Central Committee and used to take the minutes at its meetings. He therefore knows many of Abu Nidal's secrets. In the following chapter, I shall describe the events of November 1989, when a Mossad agent was discovered. This episode led me to suspect that if there was an Israeli connection, Sanduqa, like Dr. Ghassan and Alaa, was probably part of it.

THE TECHNICAL COMMITTEE

This small unit, responsible for forging passports, visas, immigration stamps, and diverse documents, used to be an independent body but, since the move to Libya, has been attached to the Intelligence Directorate and, like the principal committees of that directorate, is based in Libya, close to Abu Nidal.

The need for passports is an enduring preoccupation and one to which Abu Nidal gives his personal attention. All members' passports are in his personal custody. When in Syria and Lebanon, the organization made use of Armenian expertise in the printing business, through its contacts with ASALA, the Armenian secret army. Forged passports printed in Italy and Japan were also acquired, while the Sudan proved a useful source of genuine passports, largely because the political upheavals of recent years opened its bureaucracy to corruption and bribery.

One member of the Technical Committee is Isma'il Abd al-

Latif Yusuf (code name Hamdi Abu Yusuf), a Palestinian from Gaza, who has concerned himself with forgeries over many years. Recently, he has been in charge of computer programming at the organization's Sidon offices. He also worked at one time as Abu Nidal's private secretary, is one of his protégés, and knows many of his secrets. The only shadow over his career is a spell in a Turkish jail in the 1970s when, under interrogation, he is believed to have told the Turks what he knew.

THE SCIENTIFIC COMMITTEE

This is another small committee, specializing in developing and manufacturing weapons and explosive devices—car bombs, suitcase bombs, guns concealed in briefcases (which fire when the handle is squeezed), lethal cigars, chemical poisons, methods of sedation, and the like. Its team of specialists attempts to follow developments in these fields and apply them to the organization's needs.

The present head of the committee is Mustafa Abu al-Fawaris (code name Naji), who headed the old Military Committee when the organization was in Baghdad and who lost a hand and an eye in one of his own experiments in 1973.

Fawaris has had no scientific training as such, but through long service with the organization he has acquired a good deal of practical experience. He was a military instructor at a Fatah camp in Iraq in 1968 and stayed on when Abu Nidal "inherited" Fatah's assets in that country.

The committee occupies several buildings in the Lebanese village of Wardaniyya, in the southern Shuf.

THE PEOPLE'S ARMY (SOMETIMES KNOWN AS THE MILITARY DIRECTORATE)

Wholly separate from the organization's other directorates and committees, the People's Army is a regular militia closely resembling those of other Palestinian factions. It is found only in Lebanon and concerns itself with Palestinian guerrilla fighters, their bases, training, weapons, and equipment.

It has no connection whatsoever with the secret agents and arms caches of the Intelligence Directorate or with special missions, foreign operations, assassinations, kidnappings, and so forth. Nor should it be confused with the former Military Committee that later grew into the Intelligence Directorate.

The People's Army was set up in 1985, when the organization came aboveground in Lebanon and started recruiting members en masse. As has been mentioned, it benefited from the 1983 mutiny in Fatah, when large numbers of fighters came over to Abu Nidal from Abu Salih. The role played by the People's Army in the War of the Camps increased its visibility and contributed to the organization's transformation from a purely secret network.

The head of the People's Army is Wasfi Hannun, a member of the Political Bureau and the only link with the organization as a whole. He used to be a sensitive, well-educated man. Originally from Anabta, in the West Bank, Hannun completed his studies at Mosul, in Iraq. He started with Fatah but joined Abu Nidal from the very start in 1974. However, his association with Abu Nidal has driven him to commit crimes that have broken and perverted him. Of these, the most terrible was the killing of his own mother-in-law and sister-in-law in 1986, on Abu Nidal's false charge that they were agents of Jordanian intelligence.

The story is worth recounting as an illustration of what happens to men caught up in Abu Nidal's organization. It involves not only Wasfi Hannun but also his brother-in-law, a cadre named Mahmud Tamim (code name Ali Abdallah), who now heads the Bureau of the Political Directorate Abroad—that is to say, the Libyan end of the Political Directorate. Tamim has also had a painful and checkered history, and the story begins with him.

Before being posted to Libya, Tamim was employed by the organization in Lebanon, where he was accused of working for Jordan. With his wife and children, he was jailed for over three months, and as a form of coercion, they were all forced to bark like dogs. On being let out, the children continued to bark when spoken to, because they had become used to it.

Tamim's wife was one of a family of four sisters, one of whom was married to Wasfi Hannun. When Tamim and his wife were arrested, his wife's mother, accompanied by her youngest daughter, came to Damascus from Jordan to see what had happened. On arrival, they were seized, taken to Lebanon, and executed on the grounds that they, too, were Jordanian agents. Abu Nidal even alleged that the young woman had been sent to seduce Hannun and recruit him for the Jordanians. In a sick flight of fantasy, he described the pink nightgown she was supposed to have worn and her stock of poisons. Abu Nidal condemned them to death but specified that Hannun himself was to execute them.

The experience of killing his mother-in-law and sister-in-law to save his own life evidently unhinged him. Inside sources say that Wasfi Hannun is now resigned to perishing before long. He knows that his role at the head of the People's Army is largely a decorative one.

From my investigations, I concluded that real power in Lebanon was in the hands of Sulaiman Samrin (Dr. Ghassan al-Ali), first secretary of the Central Committee and head of the Secretariat; Mustafa Awad (Alaa), head of the Intelligence Directorate; and Mustafa Ibrahim Sanduqa (Khaldun), boss of the Justice Committee.

chapter

10

INVISIBLE STRINGS

The case for suspecting a possible link between Israel and Abu Nidal rests on a body of evidence, much of it inferential and conjectural, some of it more substantial. In the previous chapters I discussed the possible involvement of Israeli agents, principally North Africans, in the murder of Palestinian moderates generally attributed to Abu Nidal. I then sought to identify the senior men inside the organization who might be directing these agents and otherwise manipulating operations in Israel's interest.

IMMUNITY FROM ATTACK

A curious aspect of Abu Nidal's activities, especially in Lebanon, also attracted my attention and fed my suspicions. Since the late 1960s, Israel has repeatedly bombed, shelled, raided, and overrun the positions of its Palestinian and Shi'ite oponents in Lebanon—whether they be Fatah, the PFLP, the DFLP, the PFLP–General Command, Hizballah, or others. Israel has had a largely free hand in Lebanon. It controls the skies over Lebanon, and even on the ground in the south, there is little to stop it. Hardly a month passes without the publication of an Israeli military communiqué announcing a raid against "terrorist positions," which usually ends with the ritual formula "Our planes returned safely to base."

Since the 1970s, Israel has also regularly sent ground forces on punitive missions north of its self-styled security zone, established in southern Lebanon in 1978. And as we have seen, it has also sent hit teams to many countries to seek out and kill prominent Palestinians. Most of these attacks are described as preemptive, intended to keep the enemy off balance. If the Palestinians do from time to time manage to slip a punch through Israel's defenses, massive retaliation always follows: It is Israel's official policy that attacks on it must never go unpunished—and with one curious exception, they never do go unpunished.

Abu Nidal has very largely been left alone. Despite his attacks on the El Al counters at airports in Rome and Vienna, his murderous assaults on synagogues in Istanbul and several European cities, and other anti-Jewish crimes, his organization in Lebanon and Libya has never seriously been hit by the Mossad's assassination squads or by the Israeli air force, which has so extensively bombed other Palestinian positions. That Abu Nidal should be left to kill Jews with impunity is an extraordinary—indeed outrageous—departure from Israeli policy. A German expert on counterterrorism told me in London in 1990, "Those that the Israelis want to destroy, they destroy, even if it means sending in assassins. But what have they ever done to Abu Nidal in fifteen years? He seems more like a protected species that the Mossad wants to keep alive!"

Abu Nidal's large establishment near the village of Bqasta, east of Sidon, in Lebanon, known as the Cadres School, is in fact a military camp, standing alone and exposed in the mountains. It presents an unmistakable target from the air. Only once, in the summer of 1988, has the Cadres School been attacked, when an Israeli precision bomb hit a single tent, killing eight female trainees but leaving intact dozens of other buildings housing Abu Nidal's troops and staff.

Before a split within Abu Nidal's ranks that would make them fear each other, the top men in his organization moved about southern Lebanon unprotected, as if they knew they were not at risk from Israel. They slept in unguarded houses and, in spite of their rhetoric about being threatened by "hostile services," lived perfectly normal lives. This complacency reigned even though everyone knew that the organization had hit Israel's ambassador in London in June 1982, to say nothing of the Istanbul synagogue and other Jewish targets.

There have been no victims of Israeli reprisals among Abu Nidal's top leadership.

OPERATIONS IN THE OCCUPIED TERRITORIES

Another aspect of Abu Nidal's activities puzzled me. Palestinian nationalists from the socialist left to the Islamic right regard the *intifada* in the occupied territories as the great national battle, a unique effort, after years of passivity, to liberate the territories. Abu Nidal has struck targets in nearly all parts of the world—Bangkok, Australia, Peru. Yet he has not thrown a stone in the occupied territories, either before or during the *intifada.* In all the years I have been talking to people from the territories, no one has ever heard of a single operation—no matter how trivial—attributed to Abu Nidal. Eight-year-old children throw stones at Israeli troops. Old women brave tear gas. Abu Nidal does nothing. Palestinians from the territories hardly know his name, because he has committed no men, donated not a penny, done nothing at all—absolutely nothing—to support their struggle against Israeli rule. When the United National Leadership of the Uprising (UNLU), the umbrella organization running the *intifada,* was set up in 1988, Abu Nidal's publications considered it an extension of Arafat's PLO and ignored it completely.

Abu Nidal's inattention to the Palestinian cause is reflected in the structure of his organization. The Intelligence Directorate's Committee for Special Missions—which mounts assassinations—employs dozens of cadres and has unlimited funds. The Organization Directorate's Palestine/Jordan Committee has almost no funds or facilities and was for a long time manned by only two persons—Samir Darwish, who was sent on a mission to Peru, where he was arrested, and Fadil al-Qaisi, who died in London after undergoing heart surgery. Throughout the entire *intifada,* Abu Nidal has given no additional resources to the Palestine/Jordan Committee and mounted no operations in southern Lebanon, like those by other Palestinian organizations, to harass the Israelis.

In 1988, Atif Abu Bakr called for a special session of the leadership to see what could be done to help the *intifada.* Abu Nidal sabotaged the meeting by discussing such trivia as whose wife had been seen at the hairdresser's? Who had lunched at a fancy restau-

to a number of rival parties and militias of widely differing composition and ideology—Shi'ite, Druze, Nasserist, communist, Ba'athist, pan-Syrian, as well as the various Palestinian factions—which often clash as they seek to defend their turf. Men from several of these groups have told me that whenever one Palestinian faction clashed with another, Abu Nidal's men would fire at both sides, provoking further conflict. Abu Nidal has also used similar tactics against the two Shi'ite factions, Amal and Hizballah.

Sidon is the major port of southern Lebanon. It is presided over by the "Nasserist" leader Mustafa Sa'd, whose city lives next to, and in reasonable amity with, the large PLO-dominated refugee camp of Ain al-Hilwa. Yet a defector from Abu Nidal's organization told me that Abu Nidal repeatedly sent masked men to infiltrate the refugee camp at night, to throw grenades and wreak havoc there, and at the same time plant bombs in Sidon, as if to incite hostilities between the PLO camp and Sa'd's militia. In the summer of 1990, these tactics were uncovered and several of Abu Nidal's members were expelled from both Sidon and Ain al-Hilwa.

Former officers of Abu Nidal's People's Army told me that Abu Nidal himself used to instruct his people in Lebanon to report to him on the strength, dispositions, and operations of other forces in Lebanon, and particularly the Syrian army. The Syrians once intercepted a messenger carrying reports back to Abu Nidal. Why and for whom, they wanted to know, was Abu Nidal collecting information about them?

A former member of Abu Nidal's Justice Committee told me that when Mossad agents were captured by the organization, they would usually be killed almost at once, often on the very day of their arrest. The standard practice is to keep such prisoners alive long enough to extract as much information as possible from them. If a prisoner is killed before he has talked, then the killing is usually to prevent him from talking. My informant suspected that someone had been planted in the Justice Committee to kill off captured Mossad agents before they could confess.

THE CASE OF ZIYAD ZAIDAN AND FATHI HARZALLAH

In July 1989, Abu Nidal's People's Army, his militia in Lebanon, learned that a two-man Mossad cell was operating in the big Pales-

rant in Switzerland instead of making do with a sand
who had thrown away a kilo of perfectly edible toma
training camp?

Far from supporting the *intifada,* Abu Nidal has c
interfered with it, as, for example in the case of the mys
Col. Ma'mun Mraish. Universally known in the Palestir
ground as Ma'mun al-Saghir, Mraish was one of Fatah's
most active officers. He was based at its clandestine nava
Greece, where, in association with Abu Jihad, he was
concerned with moving men and weapons into the occup
ries. The Mossad had every reason to want him dead.

But there was a further dimension to Mraish. I
sources say that he had excellent contacts with the Sovie
given them information, and even sensitive technical e
which he was well placed to acquire. The CIA must ther
been on his trail as well.

On August 20, 1983, a hot summer's day, in a coas
of Athens, a gunman riding pillion on a motorcycle car
Mraish's car and killed him outright with a burst of ma
fire. The PLO concluded that either the Mossad or the
responsible.

But the Russians did not let the matter rest. They c
Mraish their man and wanted his killer. They investigate
for several months and concluded that Mraish had beer
Abu Nidal. They presented their evidence to Atif Abu I
head of Abu Nidal's Political Directorate, and demanded
nation. Was Abu Nidal aware, they asked, of the risk
running by killing Soviet agents?

When I interviewed him in Tunis after he had defe
Abu Nidal, Atif Abu Bakr told me that he had confro
Nidal with the Soviet accusation and that to his great surp
Nidal had said they were right, he had killed Mraish to g
Fatah. But he made it clear, Abu Bakr added, that he did
his part in the affair to come out. Many Palestinians k
Mraish was one of the most effective links between the PL
West Bank, and Abu Nidal, therefore, did not want it to l
that he had killed him.

It was not only in the occupied territories that Ab
behavior seemed to me suspect. It is well known that
Lebanon, north of Israel's security zone, has for years be

tinian refugee camp of Ain al-Hilwa, near Sidon. One of these Mossad operatives, Ziyad Zaidan, voluntarily confessed his links with the Israelis to the head of security of the People's Army in South Lebanon, who was code-named Sufyan. He said he wanted to clear his conscience and wash away the stain on his past. He was prepared to die for the terrible wrongs he had done to the Palestinian cause.

He told Sufyan that he had been captured by the Israelis near Sidon during the 1982 war, taken to Israel, jailed, recruited, trained, and sent back to Lebanon as a spy.

Zaidan revealed that he and his colleague, Fathi Harzallah, a relative from the West Bank town of Tal, near Nablus, had worked for the Mossad in South Lebanon since 1982, interpreting aerial photographs taken by Israeli reconnaissance aircraft. They would be sent films (he had one with him at the time, which was several meters long) of the Ain al-Hilwa camp and other locations, on which individual buildings were numbered in red. His job was to identify the buildings and tell the Israelis who was living and working there and when they were most likely to be at home.

He told Sufyan that over the years, he had radioed to Israel, using a cipher he had been given, no fewer than seven thousand messages and that he had been responsible for scores of Israeli air raids on Lebanon and for hundreds of Palestinian casualties. He said he was making good money at it.

Zaidan had returned to Israel two or three times for debriefing and further training. He would be told by radio where to wait on the shore for a small boat with frogmen in it to pick him up, usually before dawn. In the case of trouble, Zaidan and his colleague Harzallah could raise a white flag on a certain rooftop and be whisked away by an Israeli helicopter or be rescued from the beach by an Israeli patrol boat.

Abu Nidal's cadre Sufyan was immensely excited by Zaidan's confession. His first thought was that the cell could be "turned" against the Mossad. At the very least, Zaidan and Harzallah could serve as bait to draw onto the shore an Israeli boat or aircraft, which could then be shot up or captured.

Immediately, he took Ziyad Zaidan to see Wasfi Hannun, head of Abu Nidal's People's Army Directorate, who referred the case to Mustafa Awad (Alaa), Abu Nidal's highest-ranking intelligence officer in Lebanon, who was in constant touch with Dr. Ghassan al-Ali and with Abu Nidal. Alaa seemed indifferent to Zaidan's story, even bored by it. He said Sufyan's suggestion of playing back the cell was foolish. It would never work. Puffing calmly on his pipe, he tried to give Sufyan the impression that uncovering a Mossad cell, complete with film and intercepted messages, was routine, unimportant. Alaa did suggest, however, that Zaidan's partner, Fathi Harzallah, be brought in and made to confess his role in the affair, on pain of imprisonment or death.

When Harzallah was confronted, he admitted he was frightened of Israeli reprisals against his two wives and children if he quit. But if he did agree to be turned, he wanted the organization to pay him the $1,500 a month he said he was getting from the Mossad. Harzallah's family and connections in the West Bank seem to have been more heavily involved as collaborators with Israeli intelligence than were Zaidan's. Some years earlier, Fathi had gone to the United Arab Emirates in search of work and had been recruited by Jordanian intelligence. Then, he said, a man from his hometown had come to see him and suggested that if he returned home, the Mossad, in view of his background in intelligence work, would give him an even better deal than Jordan had done. He complied and was recruited and was then sent to Lebanon to work with Zaidan.

Though Alaa discouraged the idea, Sufyan and Zaidan went to the trouble of convincing Fathi to let himself be played back against the Israelis. He finally agreed to cooperate.

Within a day or two of this decision, the Mossad sent Zaidan a radio message summoning him to Israel, only the third such message he had had in the seven years he had been working for the Mossad. Sufyan argued that this was a good opportunity to kill or capture whoever the Israelis sent to pick up Zaidan. He drew up a plan, which he submitted to Alaa, and proposed that if the organization did not have the military resources needed for the operation, another Palestinian group, such as Jibril's PFLP–General Command, would be glad to help.

A day later and without telling Sufyan, Alaa, on direct orders from Abu Nidal, suddenly arrested Fathi Harzallah and charged him with working for the Mossad. The local PLO, which as usual was watching Abu Nidal's operations, learned of Harzallah's arrest and what he was charged with. It immediately arrested Zaidan, the man it knew to be his colleague—even though it was Zaidan who had first confessed and had indicated his readiness to be turned.

Alerted by the arrest of their agents, the Israelis aborted their planned landing. The operation was blown. Within a month of Zaidan's original confession, any hope of exploiting the Mossad's intelligence failure had collapsed completely.

Palestinian sources with direct knowledge of the case pointed to several suspicious features:

> Alaa's skepticism and seeming lack of interest;
>
> the fact that, a year after Fathi Harzallah's arrest, Abu Nidal had still not released anything about his trial or punishment and had not shared with other Palestinian organizations information it may have gathered about Mossad methods, about other links Harzallah may have had, or about the estimated damage done to Palestinian security by the cell;
>
> when Zaidan first approached Sufyan, he remarked that he had hesitated a long time before turning himself in, because of his suspicions about Abu Nidal's organization: Its methods of work, its tradecraft, and its communications, he said, were uncomfortably similar to those of the Mossad, in which he and his fellow agent had been trained;
>
> finally, that Alaa, on orders from Abu Nidal, had aborted the operation suggested complicity with Israeli intelligence.

Sufyan was convinced by Abu Nidal's suspect handling of the case that it was time for him to leave the organization.

THE CASE OF MUSTAFA IBRAHIM SANDUQA

Sanduqa, as we have seen, was in charge of the Committee for Revolutionary Justice, the body responsible for prisons, interrogation, torture, and executions. He had previously served as the minute-taker at meetings of the Political Bureau and Central Committee and was married to one of Abu Nidal's nieces.

In October 1989, a certain Yusif Zaidan (no relation to Ziyad Zaidan) emerged as yet another link to the Mossad.

Yusif Zaidan was a German-trained scientist who, on graduation, had joined the PLO's Scientific Committee, first in Beirut, then in Baghdad. When Abu Nidal split from Arafat in 1974 and took over the PLO's Iraqi-based assets, Zaidan made the switch as well and was employed in Abu Nidal's Scientific Committee—a career that, until that point, was not unlike that of Dr. Ghassan al-Ali, the British-trained chemist who was head of the Secretariat and who is widely suspected by intelligence sources throughout Europe of being the high-level link to Mossad.

In November 1989, Yusif Zaidan disappeared in Lebanon. I was told by my sources that Abu Nidal immediately suspected that he had been kidnapped by his new principal rival, the breakaway Emergency Leadership, which Atif Abu Bakr had formed that month. A man was sent from Sanduqa's Justice Committee to attempt to penetrate the Emergency Leadership and locate Zaidan.

The attempted penetration was discovered, and Sanduqa's man was arrested and interrogated in June 1990—by none other than our old friend Sufyan, the defector from Abu Nidal's organization, who was now representing the Emergency Leadership. The interrogation was done conscientiously, without torture or undue force, according to Atif Abu Bakr, and was videotaped, so that it could be shown in Palestinian camps in South Lebanon (as part of the Emergency Leadership's campaign against Abu Nidal).

Sanduqa's man confessed 1) to working for Mossad; 2) that his case officer was none other than Mustafa Ibrahim Sanduqa; and 3) that his mission had been to find Yusif Zaidan, to help him escape, and if he couldn't, to kill him.

The Emergency Leadership concluded that it had stumbled on a Mossad cell inside Abu Nidal's organization, the members of which included not just Zaidan and Sanduqa but the biggest fish of all, Sulaiman Samrin, otherwise known as Dr. Ghassan al-Ali.

Yusif Zaidan and Dr. Ghassan had been friends since the early 1970s, in the days of Fatah's Scientific Committee. PLO intelligence sources confirm that there had been security worries about both of them, because it was feared that they might have been contacted by the Mossad during their student years. They had, in fact, been transferred by the PLO from Beirut to Baghdad, to remove them from the center of PLO operations. But when Abu Nidal took them over in 1974, he instead promoted them. Dr. Ghassan, in particular, rose rapidly.

The Emergency Leadership concluded that when Yusif Zaidan disappeared and was presumed kidnapped, both Dr. Ghassan and Mustafa Ibrahim Sanduqa must have feared that they would be exposed if Zaidan talked. So Sanduqa's man was sent to find Zaidan, to free him or kill him. Atif Abu Bakr's assumption, which he put to me, was that the Israelis had in Dr. Ghassan al-Ali and Mustafa Ibrahim Sanduqa agents at the highest level in Abu Nidal's organization, well placed to carry out, as we shall see, the mass executions by Abu Nidal of his own fighting men in 1987–88.

The Emergency Leadership issued a communiqué declaring that those torturing and killing the organization's members on spying charges were themselves Mossad spies.

THE UTHMAN BROTHERS

According to my sources Faruq Uthman was an actual link between the Mossad and Abu Nidal. His brother, Nabil Uthman, was for many years a member of Abu Nidal's Organization Directorate, at one time responsible for the Palestine/Jordan Committee. In the late 1980s, he became Abu Nidal's undercover representative in Kuwait. According to PLO intelligence sources, Nabil's brother, Faruq, has, since the early 1970s, been a Mossad agent, working in the occupied territories and abroad; he is said to have betrayed scores of Palestinian families to the Mossad.

Faruq Uthman's minder, according to Atif Abu Bakr, is a Mossad officer who is said to have helped plan the killing of Majid Abu Sharar, an important and influential Fatah official, in Rome in 1981; the raid on PLO headquarters in Tunisia at Hammam al-Shatt in 1985; and the killing of Abu Jihad, Arafat's deputy, in Tunis on April 16, 1988, by an Israeli assassination squad. In this last operation, the Mossad officer worked with Faruq Uthman.

According to Tunisian intelligence sources, Faruq was in Tunis between April 1 and April 17, 1988, traveling on a forged Egyptian passport. On April 17, the morning after the killing of Abu Jihad, he flew from Tunis to Malta, then from Malta to Libya (on a Jordanian passport, said to be the one he normally uses), to visit his brother, Nabil, Abu Nidal's man, and stay in one of Abu Nidal's safe houses in Tripoli.

Abu Nidal knew about Faruq Uthman's background from his cadres, but he did nothing. He said he did not want to embarrass Faruq's brother, Nabil, and told one of his members that offering hospitality to a Mossad agent might one day prove useful.*

*More than two years after Abu Jihad's murder, the London journal *Middle East International* reported, on October 12, 1990, that Muhammad Ali Mahjubi, the Tunisian police

THE CASE OF MUHAMMAD KHAIR

Muhammad Khair was a Palestinian from Gaza, born in 1961, who had been a student in Turkey. Abu Nidal trusted him, and in 1986, when the organization was based in Syria, he was put in charge of the archives of the Political Directorate.

But Atif Abu Bakr, then head of this directorate, told me that he disliked Khair's dry manner and his habit of trapping his comrades in unguarded talk so that he could write reports about them. Abu Bakr transferred Khair to Beirut.

A short while later, the organization arrested a Mossad agent in Beirut. Muhammad Khair was told to interrogate him, but instead he killed him immediately, so that he had no chance to tell what he knew about the Mossad. This aroused the suspicions of Khair's colleagues. He was arrested and interrogated in turn—and confessed that as a student in Turkey, he had committed some misdemeanor and been jailed. The Mossad heard about him and, upon his release, had recruited him.

Khair surprised his interrogators by admitting that one of his tasks had been to kill Atif Abu Bakr by poisoning his coffee. When Abu Bakr was told about this, he was intrigued. Why should the Mossad want to kill *him*? He was not a terrorist. He was against terrorism and, since 1985, had endeavored to distance the organization from criminal activities and focus it instead on political work. Spurred by the War of the Camps, he had engineered a political and military transformation in the nature of the organization, much to Abu Nidal's displeasure.

When Muhammad Khair was asked about this in Beirut, he replied: "That was just it. The organization had been a criminal gang before Atif tried to politicize it. From Israel's point of view, he had made it far more dangerous. That is why they wanted him dead."

---

commissioner at the time of the killing, had been arrested. Press reports recalled that the police patrol on permanent duty outside Abu Jihad's house was absent on the night of April 16. Mahjubi was said to have been in contact with a woman who owned a fashionable hairdressing salon, much patronized by the wives of senior Palestinian officials, who was also put under arrest at the same time as Mahjubi and for the same reason—as a suspected Mossad agent.

MASSACRES AND SENSELESS TERROR

Abu Nidal's massacres of the late 1980s, which I shall describe later, pose one of the greatest riddles of his career. How did an organization whose numbers rarely exceeded a few hundred decide to kill half its members? As we shall see, Abu Nidal in Libya gave the order for the mass liquidation and his faithful henchmen Dr. Ghassan al-Ali, of the secretariat, and Mustafa Ibrahim Sanduqa, of the Justice Committee, carried it out in Lebanon.

Some sources told me that Abu Nidal gave the order for these murders when he was drinking heavily. They said that it was then, usually late at night, that he suffered most acutely from paranoia and feared plots against himself—fears that may have been deliberately fed by men like Dr. Ghassan. Yet the internal tensions in his organization were in fact not so fierce that he would have *needed* to kill these men to save himself. On the contrary, it was *because* of these awful killings that Atif Abu Bakr finally rebelled against him and, with others, broke away in late 1989.

However, among former members of the organization, the explanation most frequently heard for Abu Nidal's murderous behavior is that he wanted to destroy the autonomous group that had emerged in Lebanon in 1985, regain full control, and go underground in Libya.

Whichever way one looks at it, to kill several hundred young men is still an extreme solution, not wholly explicable by Abu Nidal's circumstances at the time. When Atif Abu Bakr and I discussed the killings, he said that Israel had directed Abu Nidal, either directly or through Dr. Ghassan and a few others, to exterminate the organization's best men. "The men they killed were the cream of the organization," he told me, "the best officers and the bravest fighters." Atif Abu Bakr was also amazed to discover that some of the most able agents of the Intelligence Directorate had also been killed. "Undoubtedly, the greatest service Abu Nidal rendered the Israelis was to massacre more than six hundred Palestinian fighters," he concluded.

Then, after the start of the *intifada* in December 1987, Abu Nidal mounted a series of operations (which I shall describe in "Foreign Affairs") that had no other apparent purpose than to undermine the uprising and damage the Palestinians' interests in countries that had always been friendly to them. A car bomb in

Cyprus in 1988 killed and wounded fifteen people and alienated Cypriot opinion; bomb attacks in the Sudan eroded support for the Palestinians in a country that had long and fervently defended them; explosions in Athens and the attack on the *City of Poros* cruise ship dealt a heavy blow to Greek sympathy for the Palestinian cause; the killing of Saudi diplomats did nothing to win friends in Riyadh; and taking French children hostage on board the *Silco* did not endear the Palestinians to French opinion.

But before I examine these incidents, there is one other case that contributed to Abu Iyad's belief that Abu Nidal was working for the Israelis or being manipulated by them. This was the Argov affair, the attempted assassination of the Israeli ambassador in London, which provided the pretext for Israel's invasion of Lebanon in 1982.

THE ARGOV AFFAIR

All his life, Menachem Begin had wanted to absorb into the "land of Israel" the territories, conquered by Israel in 1967, that he liked to call Judea and Samaria but are are known as the West Bank. Contrary to Begin's wishes, the local Palestinian population did not want Israeli rule and looked for deliverance to Yasser Arafat's PLO, which was at that time encamped in Lebanon. Begin believed that for Israel to make the West Bank part of "greater Israel," the PLO in Lebanon had to be smashed.

Begin entrusted the destruction of the PLO to his violent defense minister, General Ariel Sharon, who had made a reputation for boldness, brutality, and even recklessness. In 1981, Sharon devised a plan whose main objectives were to invade Lebanon and destroy the PLO; boot out the Syrian expeditionary force that had been there since 1976; and put in power in Beirut the Christian militia leader Bashir Gemayel, who had been groomed as an Israeli vassal.

With Syria neutralized and Lebanon under Israeli control, Israel could integrate the West Bank into a "greater Israel" without internal or external challenge. That was Begin's vision and Sharon's plan.

The circumstances for the enterprise seemed favorable. Israel was overwhelmingly strong, its Arab neighbors weaker and more divided than usual. Egypt, the largest of the Arab states, had made peace with Israel; Syria was isolated and on bad terms with both Iraq and Jordan. Internationally, its name was mud as a result of the massacre at Hama in February 1982. After its five-year struggle against the fundamentalist Muslim Brotherhood, Syria was in no shape to fight. As for the PLO, the main focus of Begin's obsessive hatred of the Palestinians, its quarrelsome militias were badly led, poorly armed, and deeply penetrated by Israeli agents. The PLO was an ineffective military force. Another important factor for Israel was the sympathy and support it enjoyed in Washington from President Ronald Reagan and his secretary of state, Alexander Haig, an excitable soldier-politician who had presidential ambitions and was keenly aware of Israel's muscle in American politics.

But Israel lacked a pretext to invade its defenseless northern neighbor. Haig told Sharon Israel needed "a major, internationally recognized provocation" before it attacked Lebanon.

For months, Begin and Sharon tried to provoke the Palestinians into an armed action to justify a large-scale Israeli attack. Five times between July 1981 and June 1982, Israel massed troops on the frontier—and five times called them back because the Palestinians refused to fight: In those eleven months, not a single shot was fired by Palestinians across Israel's northern border. It was the same with the Syrians. On December 14, 1981, probably to goad Assad into action, Begin extended Israeli law to the Golan Heights, captured in 1967. Assad knew that if he made a military move, Israel would seize the pretext to hit him. So he did nothing.

What was Israel to do? Begin and Sharon were frustrated. It was at this moment—of keen apprehension by the Arabs and furious impatience by the Israelis—that Abu Nidal—deliberately, Abu Iyad believed—supplied the provocation Israel so badly needed. On June 3, 1982, one of his gunmen shot and seriously wounded Shlomo Argov, Israel's ambassador to Britain, outside the Dorchester Hotel in London. The gunman and two accomplices were arrested by the British police. They were Nawaf Rosan, an Iraqi passport holder, and Hussein Sa'id and Marwan al-Banna, who carried Jordanian passports. Banna turned out to be a distant cousin of Abu Nidal.

Certainly, Begin knew that Abu Nidal had nothing to do with the PLO, that he was Arafat's most bitter enemy. But Israel was not about to hesitate over such a detail. "Abu Nidal, Abu Shmidal," scoffed Israel's chief of staff, Rafael Eitan, in a famous phrase. "We have to strike at the PLO!" On June 4 and 5, Israeli aircraft bombed West Beirut, while long-range artillery and naval guns pounded Palestinian refugee camps, causing hundreds of casualties. On June 6, Israeli ground forces surged across the frontier. Begin's Lebanon war had begun. In the first seven weeks, according to UN figures, seventeen thousand Lebanese and Palestinians, mostly civilians, were killed.

Abu Nidal claimed to be a Palestinian patriot, yet how could his people possibly benefit from bringing Israeli bombs and shells raining down on their heads? It might be argued that he wanted Israel to destroy the PLO, so as to leave the Palestinian field open to him. But this theory hardly bears examination. It is true that Abu Nidal had moved his organization to Syria, intending to infiltrate from there into Lebanon, which for him was a prize because of its large Palestinian population, a constituency he hoped to capture from Arafat. But an Israeli invasion of that country, the expulsion of large numbers of Palestinians, and a Lebanon under Israeli or Maronite control certainly would not have furthered his Palestinian ambitions. At this volatile moment in Middle East affairs, it is unlikely that Abu Nidal would choose to kill Argov—and provoke an entirely predictable Israeli response—without strong outside encouragement. It seemed to me obvious that either he did the job for one of his sponsors—Iraq, Syria, possibly Israel—or that he was manipulated, wittingly or unwittingly, into doing it.

The Israeli writer and editor Uri Avnery, in his book *My Friend, the Enemy,* writes that Syria put him up to it to provoke the Israelis into destroying Arafat so that Syria could create a new PLO under its control. But from 1976 onward, and especially in the prelude to the war in 1981–82, Syria had done all it could to deny Israel a pretext for invading Lebanon. Syria's efforts to tame the Palestinians, including its controversial and widely condemned use of force against them, were intended to keep them from provoking Israel's attack. The cautious Assad, militarily weak and fearful of Begin's bellicose mood, would do anything to avoid a war with Israel. To suggest that Syria had orchestrated the attack on Argov ignores Syrian fears and policies at that time.

A somewhat more plausible case can be made that Iraq instigated the attack on Argov. The argument is that, ensnared in his war with Iran, Saddam Hussein was looking for an honorable excuse to declare a unilateral cease-fire. An Israeli invasion of Lebanon might provide such an excuse. In fact when Israel invaded, Saddam immediately called for a cease-fire in the Gulf. The Iranians ignored him and the war continued, but there are flaws in this argument, too. By June 1982, Abu Nidal was already on exceedingly bad terms with Saddam and would hardly have wanted to help him. He was busy moving his base out of Baghdad and trying to ingratiate himself with the Syrians—who also happened to be Iran's allies. Abu Nidal had a fine nose for the subtleties of Arab politics. He would not have done such an explosive job for Saddam and chance outraging Assad, his prospective patron, by putting at risk Syria's national security, which is what a war in Lebanon would do.

It is also possible that the Mossad manipulated Abu Nidal into providing the pretext for the invasion that Begin and Sharon so badly wanted. Isam Sartawi, who never missed a chance to declare that Abu Nidal was an Israeli agent, was certain that Sharon had directly ordered the attack. A flaw in this argument is that Abu Nidal would not have wanted to offend Syria on Israel's behalf any more than he would have wished to do so on Iraq's behalf. And would Israel have wished to kill or wound its own London ambassador as a pretext to invade Lebanon? Such crude cynicism is hardly attributable even to the right-wing extremists who were then in power. However, one of my best Western intelligence sources says that Israeli penetration agents might have received general instructions to mobilize Abu Nidal's organization into providing Israel with the pretext it needed. The attack on Argov may have been an individual initiative resulting from some such general instruction.

That the operation seems to have been thrown together in a hurry lends some support to this view. The attack showed no sign of Abu Nidal's usual careful planning. No provision appears to have been made for the hit team to escape. And against all the organization's rules, a resident "sleeper," Marwan al-Banna, Abu Nidal's distant cousin, who was a genuine student rather than a trained terrorist, was roped in to help—and is now, with his accomplices, two of Abu Nidal's student-members, serving a thirty-year prison sentence in Britain. The attempted assassination of his ambassador remains an unlikely expedient for Begin, but perhaps not so unlikely for someone like Dr. Ghassan al-Ali.

Although the Argov affair attracted world headlines, it was not the only such incident at the time. Basil, then one of Abu Nidal's field commanders in Lebanon, told me, when I interviewed him in a seaside hotel in Tunis in 1990, that on the eve of the Lebanon war, someone higher up in the organization had urgently ordered him to mount cross-border operations against Israel. To Basil at the time, it seemed crazy to provoke Israel, but he obeyed orders, even though ground operations against Israel were not what the organization was used to. He started training a raiding party, but the Argov affair and the Israeli invasion happened before he could act. He and his men scampered back to the Bekaa Valley, out of Israel's reach, in time to save their skins.

The Argov case was not the only occasion on which Abu Nidal, whether deliberately or not, served as agent provocateur in Israel's interest. On July 28, 1989, an Israeli helicopter-borne commando unit entered South Lebanon and kidnapped Sheikh Abd al-Karim Ubaid, a leading member of the Shi'ite organization Hizballah, greatly increasing tension in the region. Groups holding Western hostages threatened to kill them if Ubaid was not released—and indeed, on July 31, Colonel Robert Higgins, of the U.S. Marine Corps, who had been kidnapped in South Lebanon in February 1988 when attached to the United Nations truce-supervision organization, was hanged in retaliation.

Everyone in the Bekaa was on the alert, fearing Israeli military action. At this delicate moment, orders came from Abu Nidal to mount operations against the Israelis within forty-eight hours. Isam Awdah (code-named Zakariya Ibrahim), second-in-command of Abu Nidal's People's Army, came especially from Sidon to the Bekaa to convey these orders to Basil, then Abu Nidal's military commander in the Bekaa.

"I found the request amazing," Basil told me. "Somebody was obviously trying to start a war. Abu Nidal was trying to give Israel an excuse to strike.

"Aware how tense things were, I refused to obey the orders. I then learned that the organization had approached other military groups in the area, notably the militia of the Syrian Social Nationalist Party [a pan-Syrian movement active in Lebanon] with the same request for action, but that they too had refused."

One such episode, I reflected, could perhaps be explained away, but here were two occasions, one in 1982 and the other in 1989, when Abu Nidal's organization had been used to precipitate a conflict from which Israel alone stood to gain.

In 1982, Abu Nidal may not have been aware of the instructions given to Basil. He was in Poland when these events took place, while his organization was in a sort of halfway house between Baghdad and Damascus, making it perhaps more vulnerable to manipulation, perhaps by Dr. Ghassan, the man who many Palestinians believe serves the Mossad's purposes within Abu Nidal's organization.

When, in Algiers in 1987, Abu Iyad asked Abu Nidal about the Argov operation, he answered evasively and seemed unhappy to be reminded of it. Abu Iyad's impression was that Abu Nidal had not been fully in control at the time. Argov's wife, apparently no sympathiser of Begin's Likud coalition, later, in a newspaper article expressed dismay at the use Begin had made of the attempt on her husband's life.

In any case, the provocation that Haig said was necessary had occurred and the invasion went according to Sharon's plan. Palestinian forces were routed and the refugee camps overrun. There were many deaths; Syria's air force and its air defenses in the Bekaa Valley were shattered; Israeli troops linked up with Bashir Gemayel's militiamen, and Beirut was bombed and besieged. Arafat's fighters were forced to withdraw from Lebanon, and they dispersed throughout the Arab world. Bashir Gemayel was elected president as Israel's proconsul. Though it proved nothing about why Argov was shot, no one benefited more than Israel from the ambassador's unfortunate predicament—before, that is, things in Lebanon started to go wrong.

From the earliest days of the Israeli state, the techniques of intelligence, of both conventional and irregular warfare, have been used to consolidate the Zionist enterprise and frustrate its enemies. Ruse; deception; the penetration of the Arab environment; the disruption of Arab military programs; the diversion of Arab military force by abetting unrest among minorities such as the Kurds; the secret alliances with neighboring non-Arab powers such as Iran and Ethiopia; the massive use of reprisal and preemption as in South Lebanon; the ceaseless struggle to quash any and every manifestation of Palestinian nationalism—these have been the staples of Israeli policy for over forty years.

Against this background, I thought it not inconceivable that Abu Iyad was right, that Abu Nidal, the archterrorist, had been subtly manipulated in what might one day come to be seen as one of Israel's greatest intelligence coups.

chapter

11

OPERATION TERROR

Abu Nidal's reputation as a terrorist rests largely on the bonfire of violence he lit in the mid-1980s. The casual wickedness of his assaults was shocking—the grenade attack on tourists at the Café de Paris in Rome in September 1985; the hijack of an Egyptian airliner in November 1985, which ended in a massacre at Valletta; the attack on El Al ticket counters at the Rome and Vienna airports in December 1985; the slaughter of Pan Am passengers in Karachi and of worshipers in an Istanbul synagogue in September 1986.

Yet only a year earlier, skulking in Poland and virtually absent from the scene, he had seemed ready to retire from his terrorist career. In June 1984, *Newsweek* reported that he was on his deathbed, an exaggeration, but it reflected the view, held even by insiders at the time, that he was probably finished. He had broken irrevocably with Iraq, and his relations with Syria had soured. In Lebanon, he seemed in danger of losing control as new cadres, in revolt against his policies, tried to rejoin the mainstream Palestinians and give up terror. Having committed their forces to defending the Palestinian camps, these new cadres were building bridges to Fatah, the movement against which Abu Nidal had fought bitterly for a decade.

It was then that Abu Nidal, with Libyan backing, took a new lease on life with a series of eye-catching international atrocities aimed at Western rather than Arab targets. As if to lay to rest speculative reports of his demise, he gave three boastful and defiant press interviews in 1985 alone—to a Paris news sheet called *France–Pays Arabes,* to the German magazine *Der Spiegel,* and to *al-Qabas,* a leading Kuwaiti daily. In them, he railed as usual against "imperialism" and "Zionism," but he also declared with outrageous bluster that he would kill several world leaders, including Ronald Reagan, Margaret Thatcher, Hussein of Jordan, and Mubarak of Egypt. He claimed some of the world's most violent organizations as his allies—the Irish Republican Army, the Basque separatist movement ETA, Germany's Red Army Faction, and France's Action Directe, a signal perhaps that Abu Nidal was going on the offensive. No doubt his new haven in Tripoli, and the wide range of favors and facilities given him by Qaddafi, his new and generous sponsor, contributed to this change of mood.

Certainly, many of his operations at this time were carried out on Qaddafi's behalf, but as defectors were later to tell me, he also had more compelling objectives in mind: to embarrass the Syrians so that they would expel him and make his defection to Libya seem plausible; to reverse the "reformist" trend that had surfaced in Lebanon; and, above all, to regain control of his organization.

Abu Nidal knew that if he hit at Western targets while he was still in Damascus, Syria would come under intense Western pressure to expel him. It had barely managed to avoid the consequences of his terrorist attacks on Jordan and on the Gulf sheikhdoms, but it would be a different matter if he set off bombs in Europe. The point was that he did not want to be seen to run away from Syria: He wanted Syria to *evict* him. Thus he could pose as a Palestinian hero who had been punished for not taking Syria's side in the War of the Camps. Expelled from Syria, he could then regain control of a movement that, in Lebanon, had grown too big—and too overt—for his liking. These were among the reasons for his murderous spectaculars of the mid-1980s.

VARIETIES OF TERROR

There is hardly a player in the Middle East that has not at one time or another resorted to terror. Iraq's government under the Ba'ath was based on terror, as Samir al-Khalil detailed in *Republic of Fear*

(1989). Armenians used terror against Turks to wring from them an admission of guilt for the genocide of their people. Shi'ites in Lebanon used terror in support of Iran during its war with Iraq, and to frustrate Israeli attempts to dominate them. Shi'ite fighters harried the Israeli army, blew up the American embassy, slaughtered American marines, took Western hostages. Syria used terror against its own inhabitants at Hama when they challenged the regime in 1982; it encouraged its proxies to use terror to drive Israel out of Lebanon; and it used terror against Jordan to draw it back from the brink of making a separate deal with Israel.

Israel has also used terror. Even before the creation of the state, Zionist terrorists killed Lord Moyne, the British resident minister in Cairo, in 1944, and very nearly killed the high commissioner in Palestine, Sir Harold MacMichael. In the middle of the Palestine war, the extremist LHI (or the Stern Gang, as it was known, after its founder) murdered the UN mediator, Count Bernadotte, who had negotiated a truce and was attempting to make it permanent—which would have limited Israel's further expansion. In his book *Bernadotte in Palestine, 1948* (1989), Amitzur Ilan shows that LHI's leaders, Nathan Yelin-Mor, Dr. Israel Eldred, and Yitzhak Shamir, were directly responsible for the assassination. As we have seen, Israeli agents bombed Jewish targets in Baghdad in 1950 to terrorize Iraqi Jews into fleeing to Israel. In 1954, an Israeli undercover unit bombed the U.S. information center in Cairo in an attempt to damage U.S.-Arab relations. This was the notorious Lavon affair, named after Israel's defense minister at the time. From 1967 to 1972, Yitzhak Shamir and Geula Cohen, both former terrorists, actively encouraged Rabbi Meir Kahane's Jewish Defense League to harass, sabotage, and bomb Soviet and other targets in the United States and Europe, including the Jewish impresario Sol Hurok, who was promoting Soviet artists in America. Hurok's secretary died in one attack. As Robert I. Friedman has related in his biography of Kahane, *The False Prophet* (1990), the object was to put U.S.-Soviet relations under such strain that rather than risk damaging détente, Moscow would release hundreds of thousands of Jews, many of whom would have to settle in Israel—a strategy that was to bear fruit in due course.

For decades, Israel has armed the Kurds against Baghdad, the southern Sudanese against Khartoum, and the Maronites in Lebanon against the Palestinians, as Conor Gearty has suggested in

Terror (1991). And the same charge of state terrorism must be made against its long record of assassinating scientists engaged on Arab arms programs, beginning with its attacks on German scientists working for Nasser's Egypt in the 1960s. The latest such victim was Dr. Gerald Bull, the Canadian inventor of Iraq's "supergun," who was killed by Israeli agents in Brussels in March 1990 (as described by William Lowther in his book *Arms and the Man: Dr. Gerald Bull, Iraq and the Supergun* [1991]). Moreover, Israel has bombed, shelled, and dynamited Lebanese towns and villages, intercepted vessels in international waters and aircraft in international airspace, launched long-range raids against Baghdad and Tunis, and kidnapped, tortured, and imprisoned many suspected opponents.

But whereas Israel's terror always served long-term political goals, Abu Nidal's was usually fitful and purposeless, although several of his attacks were aimed at securing the release of some of his men held in European jails after earlier, and often botched, operations, and his attacks on European targets in the mid-1980s were, as I suggested, intended to embarrass Syria so as to explain his departure from that country. Israel's terror was coherent, professional, and largely successful in achieving its objectives; Abu Nidal's was incoherent, incompetent, and invariably counterproductive to Palestinian interests. Israel wanted to smash the PLO, quell the Lebanese resistance, maintain its military edge, preempt potential threats to its security, and destabilize its Arab environment. Abu Nidal's terror took the form of "services rendered" to his various Arab hosts or exercises in extortion inspired by no strategic vision.

His claim that he wanted to prevent a compromise between the PLO and Israel so as to recover Palestine was not a credible objective. The vast imbalance of strength between Israel and its opponents made such a pursuit suicidal. By degrading the Palestinian liberation struggle to mere criminal violence, Abu Nidal offered Israel the pretext for refusing to negotiate and for giving the Palestinians nothing but the sword.

TANGLED THREADS OF VIOLENCE

At this stage in my researches I decided to make another list—this time focusing on international acts of violence that were related to

Middle Eastern players—to see if I could discern a pattern as I had been able to do from the earlier list. I began with the attack on Argov in 1982 but looked more closely at the period 1984–86, when terror in the Middle East was at its height. I marked operations attributed to Abu Nidal with an asterisk so as to set his operations against the background of violence of others.

*June 3, 1982—Israel's ambassador to Britain, Shlomo Argov, is shot and seriously wounded in London by an Abu Nidal gunman.

June 6, 1982—Israel invades Lebanon, committing to battle 76,000 men; 1,250 tanks; and 1,500 armored personnel carriers, supported by the air force and navy.

June 9, 1982—Israel destroys Syria's entire SAM air defense network in the Bekaa Valley, the most prestigious symbol of Syria's presence in Lebanon.

June 13, 1982, to August 12, 1982—Israel bombs and shells Beirut from air, land, and sea.

September 1, 1982—Over ten thousand Palestinian fighters are forced to leave Beirut.

September 1, 1982—President Reagan announces his "Reagan Plan" for Middle East peace. He rules out permanent Israeli control of the occupied territories, calls for an immediate freeze on settlements, and pronounces in favor of Palestinian self-government "in association with Jordan." Israel's Prime Minister Begin says it is "the saddest day of his life."

September 14, 1982—President Bashir Gemayel, groomed by Israel to rule in Lebanon, is assassinated, almost certainly with the complicity of Syrian agents. He is succeeded by his brother Amin.

September 16–18, 1982—To avenge Bashir, Christian militiamen massacre over a thousand Palestinian men, women, and children in Sabra and Shatila camps, under the eyes of Israeli troops.

November 11, 1982—The Israeli army headquarters at Tyre is blown up, killing sixty-seven Israelis—part of a rising tide of hit-and-run attacks by the Lebanese resistance.

December 28, 1982—Israel-Lebanon talks open under American auspices, with a view to concluding a bilateral peace treaty.

April 18, 1983—The U.S. embassy in Beirut is blown up by a suicide bomber driving a truck packed with explosives.

May 17, 1983—An American-brokered accord between Israel and Lebanon is signed, giving Israel a wide measure of control over its northern neighbor. Syria and its allies in Lebanon declare war on the accord.

August 29, 1983—Demoralized by Israel's mounting casualties in Lebanon, Menachem Begin resigns as prime minister of Israel.

September 3–25, 1983—Israel pulls its forces out of Lebanon's Shuf Mountains, whereupon Syrian-backed Druze and Shi'ite forces expel Israel's Maronite allies from the area and lay siege to the presidential palace. Hundreds of civilians are massacred and tens of thousands displaced from their homes.

October 16, 1983—In a clash with a vast crowd of Shi'ites gathered in South Lebanon for the annual Ashura ceremonies, Israeli troops kill many civilians. Shi'ite anger is directed at Israel's ally America, as well as at Israel itself.

October 23, 1983—A car-bomb attack on the U.S. Marine barracks near Beirut airport kills 241 men.

*October 1983–November 1985—Syria uses Abu Nidal to wage a terrorist war on Jordan to deter King Hussein from entering into separate negotiations with Israel. (See chapter 6 for details.)

November 1983—U.S. secretary of state George Shultz revives a U.S.-Israel agreement on strategic cooperation (first concluded in 1981, suspended when Israel annexed the Golan Heights, but activated in 1982 by Alexander Haig), giving Israel wide opportunities to influence U.S. Middle East policy.

December–January 1983–84—American war planes and the battleship *New Jersey* attack Syrian-backed forces in the Lebanese mountains.

December 4, 1983—Eight more U.S. Marines are killed in Lebanon, and two U.S. planes are shot down by Syrian gunfire.

January 26, 1984—In his state of the union address, Ronald Reagan declares: "We must not be driven from our objectives for peace in Lebanon by state-sponsored terrorism."

February 29, 1984—The Israel-Lebanon accord of May

17, 1983, is abrogated. President Amin Gemayel travels to Damascus to pay homage to President Assad.

March 1984—William Buckley, CIA station chief in Beirut, is kidnapped and killed in June. Several other Westerners are taken hostage in Lebanon by Shi'ite militants between 1985 and 1988.

April 3, 1984—President Reagan signs a directive authorizing reprisals and preemptive strikes against "terrorists." Pinpointing Syria, Libya, and Iran, George Shultz declares that "state-sponsored terrorism is in fact a form of war," a view echoed by Vice President George Bush and CIA director William Casey.

April 17, 1984—A British policewoman, Yvonne Fletcher, is killed when a gunman inside the Libyan People's Bureau in London opens fire on anti-Qaddafi demonstrators. Britain breaks off diplomatic relations with Libya.

May 23, 1984—Israel's state attorney's office indicts twenty-five Israeli settlers for involvement in a Jewish terrorist underground. They include men who car-bombed and maimed Palestinian mayors on the West Bank in June 1980.

In the summer of 1984, Israel, which had for years labeled all Palestinian fighters "terrorists" so as to deny them legitimacy, greatly expanded its exploitation of this issue, aiming to shape American attitudes. By this time, both the United States and Israel had recognized the grave setback to their policy in Lebanon. The Israelis were being driven out, while the American embassy had been blown up and American marines slaughtered in their barracks. The collapse of American diplomacy was evident in the abrogation of the Israel-Lebanon accord, which George Shultz had brokered.

The new focus was on "state-sponsored terrorism," the phrase used by Ronald Reagan and George Shultz and echoed by Vice President George Bush and CIA director William Casey. America's policy in the Arab-Israeli dispute would thereafter be limited largely to counterterrorism rather than an attempt to trace the roots of violence to the dispossession of the Palestinians, to Israel's invasion of Lebanon, or to the Shi'ites' burning sense of injustice.

President Reagan was apparently greatly influenced, at this time, by the proceedings of a conference organized in Washington in June 1984 by Israel's Jonathan Institute. Edited by Israel's UN ambassador, Benjamin Netanyahu, these proceedings were later published in a book titled *Terrorism: How the West Can Win.* Like Claire Sterling's *The Terror Network* in the early Reagan years, the conference papers became the master text of America's obsession with terrorism in Reagan's second term. Part of an elaborate campaign of psychological warfare directed against the PLO, Syria, and Libya, the book helped persuade American opinion that Israel's enemies were also America's, that Arabs in dispute with Israel were terrorists, and that brute force against them was legitimate and desirable.

In a speech at the conference on June 26, 1984, Israel's defense minister, Moshe Arens, called for the closing of all PLO offices around the world because they are "nothing more than support centers for terrorist operations." He identified Syria as the key terrorist state whose "worldwide intelligence apparatus" made use of Palestinians, Armenians, Japanese, and even Thais!

I continued my list (once again marking Abu Nidal's operations with an asterisk):

June 29, 1984—The same month in which it mounts its new counter-terrorism propaganda campaign, Israel intercepts a ferry boat sailing in international waters from Cyprus to Beirut and detains nine passengers.

July 18, 1984—Israel intercepts a Lebanese merchant ship off the port of Tripoli, escorts it to Haifa, and interrogates the crew.

*March 24, 1984—A bomb explodes in the forecourt of the Intercontinental Hotel in Amman two days before a planned visit to Jordan by Queen Elizabeth of Britain. Abu Nidal claims responsibility.

*March 28, 1984—Ken Whitty, a cultural-affairs counselor at the British embassy in Athens, is killed when a gunman opens fire on his car. In Beirut, the Revolutionary Organization of Socialist Muslims (an Abu Nidal front) claims responsibility.

*November 27, 1984—Percy Norris, Britain's deputy high commissioner in Bombay, is shot dead. In a phone call to a London news agency, the Revolutionary Organization of Socialist Muslims claims responsibility.

*November 29, 1984—The British Airways office in Beirut is bombed. The Revolutionary Organization of Socialist Muslims again claims responsibility.

The killing of British diplomats in Athens and Bombay and the bombing of the British Airways office in Beirut, like the later kidnapping of a British journalist and the attack on British tourists at an Athens hotel, were crude attempts by Abu Nidal to put pressure on the British government to release four of his men held in British jails—three of them in connection with the Argov affair, the fourth, Ramzi Awad, sentenced for smuggling arms into Britain.

February 12, 1985—In London, three Israelis believed to be Mossad agents and a Nigerian are given prison sentences ranging from ten to fourteen years for kidnapping and drugging Umaro Dikko, Nigeria's former transport minister, in July 1984. Dikko had been sought by the Nigerian authorities for embezzling millions of dollars.

February 21, 1985—Israeli army units raid eleven Shi'ite villages east of Tyre, killing and wounding many civilians and using bulldozers to crush cars and buildings.

March 8, 1985—A massive car bomb kills eighty people near the Beirut apartment of Hizballah's "spiritual guide," Sheikh Muhammad Hussein Fadlallah. He escapes injury. Two years later *The Washington Post* reported that the explosion was the work of a CIA-trained team under a Reagan-authorized covert action program. In *Veil,* his book on the CIA, Bob Woodward wrote that CIA director Casey solicited $3 million from the Saudis for the operation.

March 10, 1985—A suicide car bomber kills at least twelve Israeli troops and wounds fourteen others in an attack on a convoy near the Lebanese border.

March 21, 1985—Israeli army units raid nine villages in South Lebanon, near Nabatiya and Sidon, killing and wounding scores of people and blowing up many houses.

March 24, 1985—*The Washington Post* reports that CIA-backed "counterterrorist" squads have been established in at least twelve countries, including Lebanon.

*March 28, 1985—Alec Collett, a British journalist working with the UN relief agency UNRWA is kidnapped by the Revolutionary Organization of Socialist Muslims, which demands the release of its members held in Britain.

*May 24, 1985—Egyptian police arrest an Abu Nidal agent who was planning to detonate a truckload of explosives outside the U.S. embassy in Cairo. He is said to have received his instructions from the head of Libyan intelligence in Rome.

June 14, 1985—A TWA airliner on a flight from Athens to Rome is hijacked by Shi'ite militants and flown back and forth across the Mediterranean between Algiers and Beirut. A U.S. navy diver on board is murdered. The hijackers demand the release of 766 detainees, mostly Lebanese Shi'ites, from Israel's Atlit detention camp.

*July 1, 1985—A bomb destroys the Madrid office of British Airways. In Beirut, the Revolutionary Organization of Socialist Moslems claims responsibility.

*August 7, 1985—A bomb attack on a hotel in the resort of Glyfada, near Athens, injures thirteen, including six British citizens. The attack was claimed by the Revolutionary Organization of Socialist Moslems, which alleged that the hotel had been used by British groups as a "spy center against the Arabs and Islam."

September 11, 1985—Israel intercepts a boat in international waters between Cyprus and Lebanon and kidnaps Faisal Abu Sharah, a senior commander in Force 17, a PLO security unit. He is taken to Israel for interrogation and imprisonment.

*September 18, 1985—A grenade attack on the Café de Paris on Rome's Via Veneto injures forty people. The Revolutionary Organization of Socialist Moslems claims responsibility, calling the café "a den of American-British intelligence services."

*September 18, 1985—Michel Nimri, a Jordanian journalist known for his support for PLO chairman Yasser Arafat, is killed in Athens by an Abu Nidal gunman.

September 25, 1985—To avenge the kidnapping by Israel of Faisal Abu Sharah, three Israeli civilians are murdered on a yacht in Cyprus by gunmen from the PLO's Force 17. Israel says the victims were tourists; the Palestinians say they were Mossad agents monitoring Palestinian naval traffic out of Cyprus.

October 1, 1985—To avenge the three Israelis murdered in Cyprus, Israeli F-16's raid PLO headquarters near Tunis, killing fifty-six Palestinians and fifteen Tunisians and wounding about one hundred others. Arafat narrowly escapes death.

October 9, 1985—In response to the Israeli raid on Tunis, an extremist Palestinian faction, Abu'l Abbas's Popular Liberation Front, hijacks an Italian cruise ship, the *Achille Lauro,* and murders Leon Klinghoffer, a crippled American Jew on board.

November 7, 1985—After a meeting with Egypt's President Mubarak, PLO chairman Yasser Arafat publishes the "Cairo Declaration," in which he condemns all forms of terrorism.

November 9, 1985—Israel shoots down two Syrian MiG-23's over Syrian territory as they make for home after approaching an Israeli surveillance aircraft flying over Lebanon.

November 21, 1985—Jonathan Jay Pollard, a U.S. Navy intelligence analyst, is arrested in Washington on charges of spying for Israel.

*November 23, 1985—An Egyptian airliner is hijacked by four Abu Nidal gunmen on a flight from Athens to Cairo and is forced to land in Malta. Six passengers are killed before Egyptian commandos storm the plane the following day. Of the ninety-seven passengers who embarked in Athens, sixty die in the ensuing fire and confusion.

December 1985–February 1987—Encouraged by Britain's prime minister, Margaret Thatcher, Israel's Shimon Peres tries to draw King Hussein into bilateral peace talks free from Syrian "interference."

*December 24, 1985—Abu Nidal gunmen open fire and hurl grenades at El Al ticket counters at Leonardo Da Vinci Airport in Rome and Schwechat Airport in Vienna. The seven gunmen, four in Rome and three in Vienna, kill eighteen persons and wound at least 110 others before four of their number are killed by security guards and the other three are wounded and captured.

January 7, 1986—President Ronald Reagan says there is "irrefutable evidence" of Colonel Qaddafi's support for Abu Nidal. He calls the Rome and Vienna attacks "only the latest in a series of brutal terrorist acts committed with Qaddafi's backing."

He signs an executive order declaring that the Libyan

government's actions "constitute a threat to the national security and foreign policy" of the United States. The order ends "virtually all economic activities" between the U.S. and Libya.

On January 8, a second executive order freezes all Libyan government assets in the U.S. and in branches of U.S. banks abroad. "If these steps do not end Qaddafi's terrorism, I promise you that further steps will be taken," the president declares.

January 11, 1986—Brig. Gen. Gideon Machanaimi, an adviser on counterterrorism to Israel's prime minister, Shimon Peres, says the best way to combat terrorism is to kill terrorist leaders. He declares that Abu Nidal is living in Libya. But Israel takes no action against him.

January 12, 1986—Italian prosecutors issue an international arrest warrant for Abu Nidal on charges of mass murder, and on February 12, 1988, he is sentenced in absentia to life imprisonment for the Rome airport attack.

January 12, 1986—PLO chairman Yasser Arafat again condemns all forms of terrorism directed at innocent people. He adds that some Arab secret services recruit Palestinians for terrorist operations.

January 5, 1986—Colonel Qaddafi denies that Abu Nidal is in Libya. He warns President Reagan against attacking his country and threatens to send suicide squads to attack targets inside the United States.

February 4, 1986—In Tripoli, Qaddafi chairs an urgently convened conference of the "National Command of Revolutionary Forces in the Arab World," which undertakes to strike at American interests if the U.S. attacks Libya.

February 4, 1986—In an attempt to capture Palestinian leaders, Israeli fighters intercept and divert to Israel a Libyan executive jet carrying home to Damascus a Syrian delegation led by Abdallah al-Ahmar, assistant secretary-general of the Ba'ath party. In the Security Council, the U.S. vetoes condemnation of Israel's "act of piracy."

March 13, 1986—A massive car-bomb explosion in central Damascus is variously blamed on Israeli agents, the CIA, Iraq, and the Muslim Brotherhood.

March 23, 1986—A U.S. Navy task force off Libya begins "freedom of navigation" exercises in the disputed waters of the Gulf of Sidra. When Libya fires missiles at American warplanes, the U.S. responds by attacking Libyan ships and missile installations on the Libyan mainland.

April 2, 1986—A bomb on board a TWA jet flying from Rome to Athens tears a hole in the fuselage. Four Americans are sucked out of the plane, which manages to land in Athens.

April 5, 1986—A bomb at La Belle discotheque in West Berlin, popular with U.S. troops, kills two people, including an American serviceman, and injures about two hundred others, including more than sixty Americans. U.S. officials say there is "strong circumstantial evidence" linking Libya to the bombing.

April 15, 1986—U.S. aircraft, some carrier-based, others flying from Britain, bomb Colonel Qaddafi's home compound in Tripoli and other Libyan targets. Qaddafi escapes unharmed but dozens of Libyan civilians, including his adopted baby daughter, are killed.

April 16, 1986—Bombs on trucks and trains in different parts of Syria kill 144 people and wound many more. Some observers blame the attacks on a dirty-tricks outfit set up by Colonel Oliver North of the National Security Council and Amiram Nir, Shimon Peres's counterterrorist expert, to strike back at the alleged sponsors of Middle East terrorism.

April 17, 1986—In response to the U.S. attack on Libya, two Britons and an American—Leigh Douglas, Philip Padfield, and Peter Kilburn—who had earlier been kidnapped in Lebanon are shot dead by their captors.

*April 17, 1986—An Israeli security guard at London's Heathrow Airport discovers Semtex explosives in the false bottom of a bag that Nizar Hindawi, a Jordanian recruited by Syrian intelligence, gave to his pregnant Irish girlfriend to take on board an El Al flight to Tel Aviv. Hindawi is arrested after implicating the Syrian embassy. As we shall see, Abu Nidal was involved.

*April 23, 1986—In retaliation for Britain's role in the U.S. attack on Libya, the Revolutionary Organization of Socialist Moslems releases a videotape in Lebanon purporting to show the "execution" of Alec Collett, the British journalist kidnapped in March 1985.

May 14, 1986—Colonel Qaddafi calls on Cyprus to close down British bases on the island which he says helped the U.S.

to launch "its vile, barbaric, vicious, Crusader aggression against us."

May 17, 1986—In an interview with *The Washington Post,* President Assad of Syria denies any connection between Syria and terrorism. In a speech in Athens on May 28, he calls for an "international forum" to distinguish between terrorism and legitimate acts of national resistance.

*August 3, 1986—Rocket and mortar shells are fired at a British military base at Akrotiri, Cyprus, injuring two British women and a Cypriot. In Lebanon, the "Nasserite Unified Organization—Cairo" (an Abu Nidal front) claims responsibility.

*September 5, 1986—Gunmen seize a Pan Am jumbo jet at Karachi airport with 358 passengers and crew on board. When Pakistani troops storm the plane, a score of passengers are killed. The hijackers surrender. On September 10, U.S. defense secretary Caspar Weinberger accuses the Abu Nidal organization of responsibility.

*September 6, 1986—Two Abu Nidal gunmen kill twenty-one Jewish worshipers in an attack on the Neve Shalom Synagogue in Istanbul during the morning Sabbath service. Though Abu Nidal claims responsibility, the Israelis do not retaliate.

September 30, 1986—Mordechai Vanunu, a Moroccan-born Israeli nuclear technician who sold secrets of Israel's Dimona bomb-making plant to the *Sunday Times* of London, is lured by a female Mossad agent from London to Rome, where he is kidnapped and taken to Israel. He is put on trial and given an eighteen-year prison sentence.

*October 12, 1986—The British Home Office confirms that six persons suspected of being members of Abu Nidal's organization have been asked to leave the country.

October 24, 1986—Nizar Hindawi, convicted of attempting to blow up an El Al airliner in April, is sentenced to forty-five years' imprisonment, the longest sentence in British criminal history. Within hours of the verdict, Britain breaks off relations with Syria.

November 3, 1986—A Beirut newspaper, *al-Shira,* publishes the first report of the covert U.S. arms-for-hostages trade with Iran. The subsequent Irangate scandal shows how Israel drew the U.S. into covert dealings with Iran in order to provide cover for its own secret arms sales to Iran, designed to keep the Gulf war going, tie down Iraq, and so prevent the emergence of an Iraqi-Syrian "eastern front."

The first conclusion to emerge from this list is that Abu Nidal was hardly the only or even the most dangerous terrorist at large in the mid-1980s. But what distinguished him from most of the others—the individual as well as the state terrorists—was that none of his attacks seemed to be in the Palestinian cause. His motives appeared to be either self-serving or mercenary, and to be so reckless as to guarantee a hostile backlash. Abu Nidal had come a long way from his early commitment to the Palestine cause. He had become a gun for hire, a nihilist.

The attempt to blow up a truckload of explosives outside the American embassy in Cairo in May 1985 and the hijacking of the Egypt Air Boeing to Malta that November were both anti-Egyptian mercenary operations carried out on Libya's behalf. They should be seen in the context of the quarrel raging at that time between Cairo and Tripoli: Egypt had accused Libya of sending saboteurs to kill its citizens as well as Libyan exiles, and destabilize its government, while Libya retorted by expelling Egyptian workers and denouncing Egypt's "treaty of submission" with Israel.

Defectors from Abu Nidal's organization later told me that Abu Nidal simply lent his services to Libya in the hijacking of the Egyptian plane. Using diplomatic passports to avoid controls, members of Libya's People's Bureau in Greece delivered the weapons to Abu Nidal's team in the transit lounge of Athens airport. The team then carried the weapons on board and took control of the plane when in flight.

The original plan was to fly the plane to Libya, but fearing adverse publicity, the Libyans decided at the last minute not to let it land and diverted it to Malta. An enraged Mubarak deployed troops on the Libyan frontier and sent commandos to Valletta to storm the plane, with great loss of life.

To divert attention from himself, Abu Nidal claimed responsibility in the name of the Organization of Egyptian Revolutionaries, saying that the aim of the operation had been to free the group's prisoners from Egyptian jails. In fact this radical Egyptian group, connected in the Arab mind with Khalid Abd al-Nasser, son of the late Egyptian president, had nothing to do with the hijacking. But

Abu Nidal wanted to cash in on the support it had gained for its attacks on Israeli and American officials in Cairo between 1984 and 1987, in which two Israelis were killed. (In 1991, an Egyptian court acquitted Khalid Abd al-Nasser of channeling funds to Egypt's Revolution, but sentenced the organization's leader, Mahmud Nur al-Din, to life imprisonment with hard labor.)

As for the rocket-and-mortar attack on Britain's Akrotiri, Cyprus, base in August 1986, this too was a mercenary operation on Libya's behalf, and followed closely on Qaddafi's speech calling on the Cypriots to close down the British bases. Sources inside Abu Nidal's organization told me that the weapons were brought into Cyprus by Libyan diplomatic bag and that the small boat used by the team to land on the island and then escape from it was also Libyan. Hani Sammur, a well-trained officer of Abu Nidal's organization, led the attack, which was directed from Lebanon by the then head of the Intelligence Directorate, Abd al-Rahman Isa, whose taped recollections were given to me by Abu Iyad. One member of the team, Hisham Sa'id, was arrested. Once again, Abu Nidal claimed responsibility in the name of a nationalist-sounding Egyptian group, the Nasserite Unified Organization—Cairo. But the Egyptian connection was wholly bogus.

ROME AND VIENNA

The most spectacular of Abu Nidal's operations at this time—and the most destructive to the Palestinian cause—were the attacks in late December 1985 on the El Al ticket counters at Rome and Vienna airports. Their random cruelty marked them as typical Abu Nidal operations.

Austria and Italy were the two European countries with which the PLO had had the closest relations, and with their encouragement, a European-Palestinian dialogue had been developing satisfactorily. Behind the scenes, leaders of these countries were attempting to bring together Palestinians and Israelis interested in reaching a peaceful understanding. The blow fell at precisely this moment, and it was inevitable that the PLO would assume that the object of the attack had been to force Italy and Austria, under pressure from their own public opinion, to sever their ties with the PLO.

The gunmen were Palestinian youngsters, the bitter products of refugee camps, who had been brainwashed into throwing away their lives in what they supposed to be a worthwhile cause. The only gunman to survive the Rome attack had lost his father, a taxi driver, in the Sabra and Shatila camp massacres. Another, who died in the attack, was a certain Muhammad Nazzal who, I was told, was actually in possession of a valid Lebanese passport and a visa for the United States, where he hoped to start a new life. Before setting out, he had asked the organization to give him some military training, which he thought might come in handy. It was during a brief course in the Bekaa Valley that he was persuaded to take part in the senseless operation that cost him his life.

Doped on amphetamines, the young killers had been instructed to throw their grenades and open fire blindly at the check-in counters. They had been told, I later learned, that the people they saw standing at the counters were Israeli pilots in civilian clothes, returning home from a training mission—the same pilots who had bombed their families in South Lebanon. This is what Abu Nidal later claimed to believe when his associates demanded an explanation for the operations. Fatah sent its own intelligence officers to Italy and Austria to investigate his claim but, of course, found that it did not stand up.

To this day, no one in the Palestinian movement knows why these operations were mounted, but a former close aide of Abu Nidal told me that the original plan was to hit not just Rome and Vienna but the Frankfurt airport as well—with the help of Ahmad Jibril, head of the PFLP–General Command and one of the most effective military officers in the whole guerrilla movement, who had a long record of anti-Israeli operations. The Frankfurt job had been assigned to Jibril, who at the time was competing with Abu Nidal for Qaddafi's favors, perhaps hoping to escape his dependence on Syria.

But shortly before the agreed date for the attack, Abu Nidal changed his mind. Jealous of Jibril, or perhaps fearing that Jibril's group had been penetrated and might expose him, Abu Nidal decided to go ahead on his own. Angrily, Jibril complained that Abu Nidal had gone back on their agreement and criticized the way the Rome and Vienna operations had been conducted: Since the weapons had been smuggled into the transit area at the airports, the strikes could have been made with greater precision and inflicted more damage on the Israelis.

When I discussed these operations with Abu Iyad in Tunis in the summer of 1990, he told me that after Rome and Vienna he had given perhaps twenty press interviews to explain that the PLO had nothing to do with these atrocities. But it was not easy. "When such horrible things take place, ordinary people are left thinking that all Palestinians are criminals," he said. The damage to the PLO was immense.

He told me that most people in the West, and even many Arabs, could hardly distinguish between Abu Nidal's Fatah and Arafat's. When Abu Nidal perpetrated a massacre, all anyone remembered was that Palestinians had done it—and that the PLO was a liar. Its claim to have renounced terror was obviously a fraud. "Abu Nidal, and all those who plot with him, want people to doubt our word—and I fear they have succeeded," Abu Iyad said.

"How can we convince Europeans of the justice of our cause?" he added. "How can we convince Gulf Arabs that the murder of Ghubash [the UAE minister of state killed by Abu Nidal in October 1977] had nothing to do with us? How can we convince the family of the UAE ambassador murdered in Paris that we don't have blood on our hands? I saw their faces when I went to pay my condolences. How do we convince Kuwaitis that the bombs in their cafés were not thrown by us? In their minds, all Palestinians are guilty."

Former members of Abu Nidal's organization told me that Libyan intelligence took part in the planning and supplied the weapons, which, in traditional fashion, were given to the gunmen by a contact man at the very last moment. The Tunisian passports used by the gunmen were passports that Libya had confiscated from Tunisian workers expelled from Libya in 1985. The Libyan news agency, JANA, hailed the attacks as "heroic operations carried out by the sons of the martyrs of Sabra and Shatila." Qaddafi himself was too crafty to discuss such operations with Abu Nidal, but his intelligence officers, according to my informants, certainly did—men who specialized in assassination and terror, like Sayyid Qaddaf al-Damm, Abdallah Hijazi, and Salih al-Druqi.

On Abu Nidal's side, the chief planner of both the Rome and Vienna operations was Dr. Ghassan al-Ali, head of the Intelligence Directorate's Committee for Special Missions. His colleague Alaa directed the operations on the ground and was in Vienna at the time, watching things from afar. These men were, of course, on my short list of possible Israeli penetration agents.

Abu Iyad was convinced that in the case of Rome and Vienna, Abu Nidal's organization had been manipulated by Israeli agents. Only Israel stood to gain from such outrages, he said. He didn't know whether Abu Nidal himself had been recruited by Mossad, but he believed that his criminal and embittered character made him exceptionally vulnerable to external manipulation.

When Abu Iyad told me this, I could not believe—and still cannot believe—that the Israelis would deliberately attack El Al ticket counters and kill their own people. Israel would not massacre Jews, whatever political or propaganda advantages could be derived from such an operation. Yet the puzzling and inexplicable fact was that although everyone knew Rome and Vienna were Abu Nidal's operations and that he had moved his headquarters to Libya, which was perfectly accessible to an Israeli strike, Israel did not retaliate—not against Libya or against Abu Nidal or against the men directly involved, Dr. Ghassan and Alaa. If, as Abu Iyad suspected, these men were the Mossad link, it was hard to explain why they had attacked Israeli targets. But they had, and Israel, uniquely in this case, had done nothing to punish them. But whoever ordered the attacks, the intended political effect was clear: to stop short the developing contacts between Italy and Austria and the PLO for an accommodation with Israel.

As the principal victims of Abu Nidal's terror, both in the number of men killed and in the loss of reputation, the PLO was particularly concerned to discover who had penetrated and manipulated Abu Nidal's organization. The Rome and Vienna operations had created violent anti-Arab feeling in the West; they had enabled Israel to make political capital out of the terrorist issue; and—together with the bomb at La Belle discotheque in Berlin, in which Abu Nidal had no part—they had prepared the ground for the American attack on Libya of April 1986.

Abu Iyad told me: "When I met Abu Nidal in 1987, I asked him about Rome and Vienna, but he couldn't tell the story straight. He floundered and kept contradicting himself. He couldn't justify the operations at all.

"I then told him the following story. On a visit to Austria in 1988, I attended a party given by the Friends of Palestine and was struck by a handsome woman who spoke with enthusiasm about the Palestine cause. A former foreign minister of Austria, who was present, turned to me and said that the lady had actually been one of the passengers at Vienna airport. A grenade had landed at her feet but had failed to explode. Yet she had remained a friend of the Palestinians! 'They do these things out of despair,' she cried. 'I now support them more than ever!' "

When Abu Iyad finished this story, Abu Nidal could say only, "If twenty more had been killed, it wouldn't have mattered. They're all Zionists!"

According to Abu Iyad, the American raid on Libya that hit Qaddafi's residence and other sensitive installations could have found the targets for their smart bombs only with the help of someone inside Libya. On April 17, 1986, *The Washington Post* reported that Israeli intelligence had provided continuous updates on Qaddafi's whereabouts, the last at 11:15 P.M. Libyan time, just two hours and forty-five minutes before the U.S. attack began. Abu Nidal's organization, working closely with Libyan intelligence, could easily have given this information to the Israelis.

In Abu Iyad's admittedly obsessive view, Libya and other sponsors of Abu Nidal put themselves at grave risk by allowing such a suspect organization to operate freely on their territory, to use their facilities and enjoy access to their intelligence services. The implication he drew—and in view of his hatred of Abu Nidal, it was a self-serving one—was that Abu Nidal's organization provided Israel with a means to penetrate not just the Palestinian movement but Arab society as a whole. Libya's involvement with Abu Nidal, he believed, had undermined its security and exposed it to physical attack.

THE HINDAWI AFFAIR

At London's Heathrow Airport on April 17, 1986, an Israeli security guard discovered 1.5 kilograms of Semtex, a powerful plastic explosive of Czechoslovak manufacture, in the false bottom of a bag that an Irishwoman, Ann Murphy, was about to carry onto an El Al flight to Tel Aviv. The bomb's detonator was disguised as a pocket calculator. Ann Murphy, a chambermaid at a London hotel, had been given the bag by her Jordanian boyfriend, Nizar Hindawi, by whom she was five months pregnant. He had promised to join her in Israel, where they were to be married. The thirty-two-year-old Hindawi had taken his fiancée to the airport in a taxi, priming the bomb on the way by inserting a battery in the calculator. It was timed to go off while the aircraft was in flight.

Leaving his fiancée at Heathrow at about 8 A.M. on April 17, Hindawi traveled back into London and later that morning boarded a Syrian Arab Airlines bus to return to the airport to catch a 2 P.M. flight to Damascus. But before the bus set off, news broke that a bomb had been discovered at Heathrow. Hindawi left the bus hurriedly and went to the Syrian embassy, where he asked the ambassador, Dr. Lutfallah Haidar, for assistance.

I had investigated this terrorist incident, which implicated the Syrians, when I was researching my biography of President Assad. Could Assad have known about it? Given his anxiousness to avoid war with Israel, I could hardly believe that he would sanction the Heathrow bomb. Had the destruction of an Israeli civilian aircraft been traced to Syria, Assad's country and regime would have been at immense and immediate risk.

What I did not know then, but what I learned in 1990 from a well-placed defector in Tunis, was that Abu Nidal's Technical Committee had manufactured the suitcase bomb and had delivered it to Syrian air force intelligence, the outfit that sponsored Abu Nidal in Syria. Air force intelligence then sent the bomb by Syrian diplomatic bag to London, where it was handed over to Hindawi. Apart from Hindawi, the only people thought to be in the know were two or three officers in Syrian air force intelligence, including its chief, General Muhammad al-Khuly, and two or three of Abu Nidal's members.

It was widely supposed that Khuly's motive was revenge for an incident two months earlier, when Israel, hoping to capture Palestinian guerrilla leaders, had intercepted and forced down in Israel the executive jet returning Syrian officials to Damascus. On this interpretation, the Heathrow affair seemed to be a bungled rogue operation by an uncontrolled branch of Syrian intelligence. However, Abu Nidal's involvement gave it another dimension.

Hindawi was known to Dr. Haidar, the Syrian ambassador in London. In 1985, some months before the Heathrow incident, Haidar had recommended Hindawi to Syrian intelligence as a London-based free-lance writer and opponent of the Jordanian regime who might come in useful in the campaign Syria was then waging against Jordan. (What Haidar did not know was that his radio message to Damascus about Hindawi was intercepted by British intelligence—

and most likely circulated to a number of countries, including Israel, cooperating with Britain on counterterrorism.) So when Hindawi showed up at the Syrian embassy asking for help, the ambassador, presuming him to be a Syrian agent in some sort of trouble, passed him on to his security men, who took him to their lodgings, where they attempted to alter his appearance by cutting and dyeing his hair.

But early the next morning, April 18, for reasons that are unclear, Hindawi fled the Syrians and, after contacting his brother, a clerk at the Qatar embassy in London, gave himself up to the British police.

He was interrogated intensively for a number of days, during which his sleep was interrupted. He then confessed that he had met General Khuly in Damascus in January 1986 and that a month later one of Khuly's officers, Colonel Haitham Sa'id, had given him a Syrian service passport in a false name and instructed him to place a bomb on an El Al aircraft in London. He was sent to Britain on a practice run. On his return to Damascus, Sa'id had shown him the suitcase bomb and told him how to prime it. On April 5 he was sent back to London and was given the bomb and detonator by a man he thought was an employee of Syrian Arab Airlines.

This confession was to be the basis of the prosecution's case at Hindawi's trial at the Old Bailey in October 1986. However, in court, Hindawi retracted his confession and claimed he was the victim of a conspiracy, probably by Israeli agents. He alleged that the British detective sergeant who had arrested him and taken part in his interrogation had threatened to turn him over to the Mossad and had told him that his father and mother, who lived in London, were also under arrest. He complained that the police had invented statements attributed to him and had forced him to sign them unread.

Unimpressed, a British jury found him guilty, and he was sent to jail for forty-five years, the longest sentence in British criminal history. Within hours of the verdict, Britain broke off relations with Syria, and urged its allies to do the same.

However, to Mrs. Thatcher's anger, the French prime minister, Jacques Chirac, said in an interview with the *Washington Times* on November 10, 1986, that West German chancellor Kohl and foreign minister Genscher both believed, as he said he tended to do himself, that "the Hindawi plot was a provocation designed to embarrass Syria and destabilize the Assad regime." Behind it were "probably people connected with the Israeli Mossad."

In interviews with senior Jordanian officials in Amman, I learned that the Hindawi family were originally Palestinians who had settled in the East Jordan village of Baqura and they had a history of involvement with the Mossad. The father had worked as a cook in the Jordanian embassy in London before being revealed as an Israeli agent. He was tried in Jordan and sentenced to death in absentia, but he escaped sentence by staying in Britain. It was in his father's apartment in a London suburb that Hindawi stored the suitcase bomb for ten days in April 1986. Hindawi himself had a record as a petty free-lance agent, courier, and contact man with no ideological commitment. A senior Jordanian official told me that he had worked in various small capacities for Syria against Jordan, for Jordan against the Palestinians, for the clandestine Jordanian Communist party—and for the Mossad, "and been paid for it."

For some years he had been a pawn in the shadowy middle ground between hostile Middle East intelligence services. Because of his background, Jordan had refused to renew his passport in 1985, and he had offered his services to Syria. In the Heathrow incident, there were several odd aspects to Hindawi's behavior: He had rushed to the Syrian embassy once the bomb was discovered to ask the ambassador for help (their conversation was monitored by British intelligence); he had then run away from the Syrian security men; and he had not attempted to go underground or flee the country. Instead he had given himself up. It was as if he had gone out of his way to implicate the Syrians.

There was, of course, no doubt about the involvement of Syrian air force intelligence in the Heathrow incident: It had recruited Hindawi, given him an official Syrian government passport in a false name, and sent him to London, where it supplied him with the suitcase bomb. But could Hindawi, who is said to have worked for several intelligence services, including the Mossad, have been a double agent, working for Syria but controlled by Israel? Could he have been deliberately planted on the Syrians or spotted as a potential double once Syria had recruited him? On this theory, he was the instrument for an Israeli penetration of Syrian intelligence, an agent provocateur whose mission was to smear Syria as a terrorist state. If this was true, then the Heathrow bomb was never intended to go off and its discovery by an Israeli security guard was a charade, rather than the result of exceptional vigilance. Hindawi himself may have been persuaded that he would get only a short sentence, since nobody had been hurt.

The political background to the affair lends some support to this interpretation. On March 13, 1986, there was a massive car-bomb explosion in central Damascus, the opening shot in a campaign apparently designed to destabilize Assad's regime. On April 15, the United States attacked Libya; on April 16, bombs on trucks and trains in different parts of Syria killed no fewer than 144 people and wounded many more; on April 17, Hindawi's bomb was discovered at Heathrow, bringing instant worldwide condemnation of Syria.

In the months preceding these events, Israel's prime minister, Shimon Peres, had launched a vast diplomatic offensive aimed at drawing King Hussein of Jordan into direct talks with Israel. Drumming up support in Europe and the United States, he had called on the king to come forward. He made plain that the PLO was unacceptable at any price, that the Soviet Union was ineligible, unless it restored diplomatic relations with Israel—and that Syria was the main obstacle. Blackening Syria as a "terrorist state" would be a way of elbowing it out of the way.

Peres was strongly supported by Maraget Thatcher, whose close relations with King Hussein made her well placed to promote the Israel-Jordan accord Perez wanted. She seemed unable to grasp why Syria objected to Jordan's doing a separate deal with Israel. She believed that Assad was against peace in general.

In the wake of the Hindawi verdict, condemnation of Syria reached its climax, while Israel redoubled its efforts to draw Jordan into separate talks, the high point being the so-called London Agreement of February 1987. It was reached at a secret meeting of Peres and Hussein at which they approved American terms for a bilateral negotiation. (To Peres's great disappointment, the London Agreement was not followed up, because Shamir's obstruction paralyzed the Israeli government.)

On hearing of the Heathrow incident, Assad believed it was the prelude to a physical attack on Syria, either by Israel alone or in conjunction with the United States. He suspected his enemies wanted to bring him down to allow the Israel-Jordan deal to go forward and give Israel regional supremacy. In an interview with *Time* magazine on October 20, 1986, he claimed that Israeli intelligence had planned the Hindawi operation. Senior Syrian officials told me, after conducting their own postmortem of the affair, that their intelligence had fallen into an Israeli trap. Some parts of their service had been penetrated and manipulated in order to smear Syria with terrorism and isolate it internationally. Colonel Mufid Akkur, an officer of air force intelligence whom Hindawi named in court, was arrested in Damascus on suspicion of working for Israel. His chief, Colonel Haitham Sa'id, disappeared from view for a while. The head of the service, General Khuly, Abu Nidal's former protector, lost his powerful job and was transferred to another air force post.

But if Syrian intelligence had been penetrated, what role had Abu Nidal played in it? He had supplied the suitcase bomb. But had he—or perhaps Dr. Ghassan al-Ali—also sold the Syrians the idea of an attack on El Al in the first place? Had his organization been the main channel for an Israeli penetration?

Senior Syrian officials told me they were convinced that their country's security had been compromised by Abu Nidal's relationship with General Khuly's air force intelligence, and they recalled an earlier incident of lesser importance, in which one of Abu Nidal's men, a certain Adnan al-Faris (code-named Sami Abu Haitham) had been arrested at the Damascus airport in 1985, carrying an intelligence report about various internal matters in Syria, the second time something like this had happened. Abu Nidal's organization had apparently been collecting information about the Syrian army, scandals involving leading Syrians, even the workings of the black market and the price of bread. The Syrians now suspected that Abu Nidal had been trading this information for facilities elsewhere, and some of their intelligence analysts believed that Israel was involved. In late 1986, the Syrians finally put the organization under surveillance and tightened their controls over it.

HIJACKING AT KARACHI

The Hindawi affair strained Syria's relations with Abu Nidal severely, but the incident that finally ended the relationship was the hijacking of a Pan Am jumbo jet, with 358 passengers on board, at the Karachi airport on September 5, 1986.

Technically, it was well done, at least in its opening stages. Four gunmen, dressed as Pakistani security personnel and riding in a passable imitation of a police van, managed to enter the airport and board the Boeing 747 when it stopped for refueling early in the morning, on its way from Bombay to New York. The passengers and crew were soon overpowered. But a few hours later things started to go wrong. The captain managed to leap from the cockpit and immobilize the plane. The hijackers lost their nerve and started firing. As Pakistani forces stormed the plane, someone opened an emergency exit and screaming passengers came tumbling out. Over twenty people were killed in the confusion before the hijackers surrendered.

From defectors, I learned that the strategist of the operation was one of Abu Nidal's most cunning men, Samih Muhammad Khudr, whose first important assignment, eight years earlier, had been to lead the team that assassinated a friend of President Sadat, Egyptian editor Yusuf a-Siba'i, in Nicosia in February 1978. By the mid-1980s Khudr was based in Lebanon, the proud holder of three genuine Lebanese passports and the husband of three foreign wives—a Swede, a Finn, and a Dane—whom he had married for cover and whom he visited in their respective countries whenever his work allowed. As the real dynamo behind Abu Nidal's foreign operations, he was in Karachi at the time of the hijack but escaped capture (although his assistant, Muhammad Harb al-Turk, also known as Salman Ali al-Turki, was arrested).

The team had been trained on a model of the plane at a camp in the Bekaa Valley run by Abu Nidal's Intelligence Directorate. To persuade them to volunteer, its members were told that the aircraft would be flown to Israel and blown up over an important military installation. The team was prepared to die. But the team leader, code-named Abbas, who was to carry the explosives in a belt around his waist, was secretly instructed to destroy the plane as soon as it was airborne. On completing their training, the men were taken to Syria and told to prepare for departure from the Damascus airport.

In Damascus, Abbas had second thoughts about his mission, which he confided to his maternal uncle, Fu'ad al-Suffarini, a high official in the organization. But Suffarini, who had served as the director of Abu Nidal's office in the 1970s and had planned several early operations, was himself contemplating defection (and later fled to Jordan). He persuaded his nephew not to throw his young life away on a senseless enterprise.

At a crucial moment in the hijackers' negotiations with the control tower, Abbas pushed one of the American stewardesses into the lavatory and began to fondle her—evidently, an attempt to abort the operation. With Abbas occupied with the stewardess, the plane's captain escaped. Other members of the team, who may also have had their doubts about suicide, lowered their guard. The plane was then stormed.

As with so many Abu Nidal operations, the Karachi hijack was a criminal act that served no conceivable Palestinian purpose and was probably meant to avenge the U.S. attack on Libya the previous April.

A spokesman for Abu Nidal's organization denied all involvement in the fiasco. But when photographs of the hijackers appeared in the press and were recognized by members of the organization, they realized that the operation had indeed been one of theirs.

Usually, if an operation failed or aroused great hostility or if Abu Nidal was uncertain of the approval of his sponsor, he would claim responsibility for it in the name of some fictitious organization. His anti-British operations, for example, were carried out in the name of the Revolutionary Organization of Socialist Moslems; the Rome and Vienna operations were claimed by the Cells of the Arab Fedayeen; the bomb attacks on Kuwaiti cafés were ostensibly the work of the Arab Revolutionary Brigades; and the hijack of the Egyptian airliner was the work of the Organization of Egyptian Revolutionaries. On each occasion, the communiqué was couched in language to fit the made-up name.

But Abu Nidal also took credit for operations in which he had played no part. When Zafir al-Masri, the Israeli-appointed mayor of the West Bank city of Nablus, was assassinated in March 1986, Abu Nidal issued a long communiqué claiming credit in the name of his organization, whereas everyone in the Palestinian movement knew that it was George Habash's PFLP that had been responsible.

Among Abu Nidal's more outrageous lies was his claim to have mounted the IRA attempt to kill Margaret Thatcher at Brighton in November 1984 and to have been behind the devastating fire at Bradford City's soccer ground in England in May 1985. When the American spaceship *Challenger* exploded in flight, he published a congratulatory note in his magazine and ordered sweets to be distributed to his members, leading the small fry to imagine that their organization was capable of such exploits. When Pan Am 103 was downed over Lockerbie, Scotland—an act of terrorism with which he had no connection—he said with an air of mystery, according to one of his associates, "We do have some involvement in this matter, but if anyone so much as mentions it, I will kill him with my own hands!" If an American soldier tripped in some corner of the globe, Abu Nidal would instantly claim it as his own work, his associate added.

EXPULSION FROM SYRIA

From the summer of 1986, Abu Nidal started quietly moving his organization out of Syria. Though he had engineered the situation so as to become *persona non grata* in Syria, he nevertheless wanted to leave on his own schedule, not be caught unawares by an expulsion. His first move, following the Karachi raid, was to instruct his intelligence chief, Abd al-Rahman Isa, to remove the organization's archives and other important documentary material to Libya. (Two copies of the archives were made: one for the organization, which Isa hand-carried to Tripoli, the other for Abu Nidal's personal use.) Gradually, whole directorates and their staffs were transferred to Lebanon and Libya. Cadres who were blindly faithful to him were sent to Lebanon; others, like the ideologue Atif Abu Bakr, the voice of the new, more liberal trend that Abu Nidal detested, were sent to Libya, where he could control them.

At the same time, a number of offices and apartments were disposed of. The Syrians had thought that he operated out of about a dozen buildings, but they were later surprised to discover that his organization had occupied more than two hundred locations. Not a single document or piece of paper was found in any of them.

But as efficiently as the move was planned, an arms cache was mistakenly left behind. Over the years, Abd al-Rahman Isa and others had, on Abu Nidal's instructions, smuggled arms into Syria. Suitcases full of pistols and submachine guns had been brought in on Libyan diplomatic passports. "If the Syrians find a single gun, we'll be in real trouble," Isa had warned. "Today's ally is tomorrow's enemy. We may need the guns inside Syria," Abu Nidal replied. In any event, a large cache of weapons, some seventy submachine guns, mainly Polish Scorpions and Israeli Uzis, had been walled in and plastered over in the basement of a house owned by the Intelligence Directorate. Abu Nidal must have forgotten they were there because, in the months when he was planning to leave Syria, he asked his financial people to sell the house, which was bought by a Syrian officer.

Some three years later, in 1989, someone dug the arms cache out of its hiding place in the basement wall and gave it to the Syrians as a gift. (When Assad heard about it, he is said to have exclaimed: "With such an arsenal, the opposition could have killed me and the whole government!") In the organization there was consternation when the news got out. Who had blundered? Who had betrayed them?

One of the few people who knew about the weapons was the man who had walled them in—Nidal Hamadi (code name Bajis Abu Atwan), known in the organization as the Executive. He was the minute-taker of the Intelligence Directorate, which meant that he kept the archives and the secret maps of overseas arms caches. Bajis had joined the organization in Iraq when he was very young and had worked in intelligence almost since childhood. He had a detailed knowledge of the organization's foreign operations and its clandestine relationships with foreign groups and states.

Now, at the very time when the weapons were dug out and handed over to the Syrians, Bajis decided to defect to Syria—with his father, brother (both also members of the organization), and no fewer than fifteen other members of his family. Some sources say it was Bajis who gave the guns to the Syrians. Others say that on hearing of the gift, he decided to run for his life because he knew that he would be in danger once Abu Nidal heard of the affair. In February 1990, he was reported to have left Syria for Jordan, where the authorities are believed to have offered him safe haven. Abu Nidal is said to have made several attempts to kill him there.

The Syrian authorities neither knew nor approved the Egypt Air hijacking of November 1985, the Rome and Vienna operations a month later, or the Karachi hijacking in September 1986, though the Pakistanis sent Syria a dossier showing that Abu Nidal's gunmen had made use of the Damascus airport and other Syrian facilities. Despite these embarrassments and repeated protests from the United States and other countries, the Syrian authorities had been slow to act against Abu Nidal.

But the Hindawi affair gave them a serious jolt: Syria was publicly implicated and its international reputation severely damaged. Perhaps more to the point, the internal power structure was shaken because the culprit appeared to be the powerful General Khuly. For several months, the Syrian government investigated the complicated affair, trying to establish responsibilities. Only then were the Syrians convinced that Abu Nidal was a dangerous associate and that it was time to be rid of him.

But the Syrian system works slowly, and matters did not come to a head until March 1987, when ex-President Jimmy Carter made a private visit to Damascus, having been briefed by the State Department to raise the Karachi incident with President Assad. Assad called for the dossier the Pakistanis had sent to Syria and privately read it for the first time. On June 1, 1987, all members of Abu Nidal's organization, together with their wives and children, were expelled from Syria and their offices closed.

But Abu Nidal did not wait for the expulsion order. Two months earlier, on March 28, 1987, Abu Nidal had left Syria for good. Accompanied by his intelligence chief, Abd al-Rahman Isa, he had first gone to Poland before flying on to Libya three days later, on March 31. Libya was to become his permanent place of residence. His wife, Hiyam, and their three children, Nidal, Badia, and Bissam, stayed on in Damascus until August to pack up the big house in Zabadani.

Whether or not Abu Nidal or his senior colleagues had worked for Israel, inside his organization Abu Nidal had achieved what he wanted: The dangerously reformist, aboveground trend in Lebanon had been contained; the organization would soon be purged, and split between Lebanon and Libya. So far as he was concerned the attacks at Rome, Vienna, Heathrow, and Karachi had served their purpose.

According to his testimony in the taped debriefing I listened to, March 31, 1987, was a memorable date in Abd al-Rahman Isa's diary.

"Why do you keep going on about that date?" Abu Nidal asked him more than once.

"Because it marks the end of our wretched life in Syria and the prelude to real joy in Libya!" Isa replied.

chapter 12

FOREIGN AFFAIRS

In Libya in the late 1980s, Abu Nidal's twisted soul seemed at last fulfilled. His wealth gave him a sense of omnipotence; he had found in Qaddafi a congenial sponsor who shared his own pleasure in violence. He was eliminating potential rivals, especially Atif Abu Bakr, and had regained absolute control over his organization by extricating it from Syria, splitting it between Libya and Lebanon, and making it clandestine once more.

AN UNEASY TYRANT

Abu Nidal's former colleagues told me that Libya brought out the worst in him. He had always been dictatorial; now he was a tyrant. He would not allow his members to socialize with each other, not even to make contact outside their official duties. This prohibition applied even to the most senior members, such as Abu Nizar, for many years his deputy, and Abd al-Rahman Isa, his former intelligence chief. If, occasionally, Abu Nizar broke the rules and called on Isa at home, he would take the precaution of telephoning Abu Nidal to say, "Look, I spent the evening with Abd al-Rahman Isa." And Isa would do the same. Abu Nidal's obsessive fear of plots was such that an unreported meeting could mean death.

Abu Nidal imposed his discipline in a thousand petty ways. He ordered that all passports, genuine or forged, be handed over to him. Even heads of directorates had to comply: No one could think of taking a trip without his personal approval. Ordinary cadres were not allowed a telephone. If one of them rented a house that had a telephone, Abu Nidal would have it removed. Members of the leadership were allowed telephones but for local calls only.

Cadres sent abroad on foreign missions were warned not to venture into duty-free shops. Even the purchase at an airport of a bar of chocolate or a carton of cigarettes could, if discovered, raise a storm. On Abu Nidal's part, this was less a way to save money than to humiliate and control his members. He had a genius for ferreting out his members' trivial lapses and using them to assert his authority. He insisted on personally approving any expenditure, however small, over and above the budgets of the directorates, which he reviewed monthly. On one occasion, Atif Abu Bakr challenged the system: In Tripoli, he bought a coffee table and two easy chairs for his living room and sent the receipt for reimbursement to Atif Hammuda, head of the Finance Directorate. The timid Hammuda asked whether Abu Nidal had approved the purchase. Abu Bakr complained to Abu Nidal, who, in a characteristic switch, gave Hammuda a scolding in front of Abu Bakr. "You donkey!" he cried. "Of course Atif Abu Bakr can sign chits."

All contacts between cadres in Libya and their colleagues in Lebanon went through Abu Nidal, and he was not above suppressing letters and rewriting minutes of meetings to ensure that one wing of the organization was kept in ignorance of the other. By splitting the leadership between Libya and Lebanon, he weakened it and made himself all-powerful. Half the Secretariat, half the Political Bureau, and much of the People's Army, the overt military wing of the organization, remained in Lebanon, but these bodies could do nothing without permission from Abu Nidal, in Tripoli. He personally ran the Intelligence Directorate, the Finance Directorate, and the Libyan end of the Political Relations Committee. He personally supervised the management of the desert camp, where, apart from fighters and trainee terrorists, he kept twenty-three families in air-conditioned isolation, away from their menfolk in Tripoli. He even took over the editorship of *al-Tariq,* the organization's in-house bulletin.

Abu Nidal sought to instill in his members a solemn approach to work. Jokes were forbidden. At meetings, any attempt to discuss matters unconnected with work would be met with astonishment, even alarm, by anxious members.

Yet for all this, there was something ambivalent about him. His colleagues noticed that although he was addicted to power, he seemed unable to exercise it with ease or confidence. He was nervous when forced to address more than half a dozen people at a time. In front of a larger audience, he became stilted and tongue-tied. He was unkempt and rarely slept two nights running in the same house. His wife and children were often abroad. (It was rumored that they often went to Austria to stay with the eldest daughter, Badia, whose husband, Khalid Abd al-Qadir, was Abu Nidal's secret representative in that country.) He lost weight because of the diet prescribed by his doctors for his heart complaint. His arms and legs grew thin, but his chest had an unnaturally robust look because of the bulletproof vest he wore under his jacket. He now wore a full wig of dark hair.

Because of his long years underground, he no longer seemed to know how to live normally. In Libya, he went to great pains to conceal the facts of his daily life, even from his own members. They knew nothing about where he lived, where he held his secret meetings, where his weapons were stored, and where his archives were kept. For security reasons, he never entertained in his own residence. If he had a visitor for the evening, he would commandeer the house of one of his aides, whose wife would be expected to cook and serve a meal at short notice.

On such occasions, he usually arrived after his guest, accompanied only by a male secretary. His bodyguards would remain outside. He tended to greet his visitors formally, waving to his secretary to take notes of the conversation. Yet he also managed to give the impression of being shy and self-conscious, speaking in a soft voice and looking down at the carpet. But he could move to the attack without warning, suddenly becoming verbally aggressive, as if to show who was in charge. And, though he seemed to live very much alone, Abu Nidal struck his visitors as clever and well informed. He read widely in Arabic and, for foreign books and articles, employed a small team of translators to produce digests for him.

CONSOLIDATION IN LIBYA

In the years 1987–1990, Abu Nidal concentrated his forces in Libya—in the camps, farms, and numerous offices and residences that Qaddafi had turned over to him. The organization operated two radio stations, one linking the Secretariat to the desert camp, the other linking the Secretariat to both Lebanon and Algeria.

Libya became the organization's nerve center for its foreign operations. As has been mentioned, Libyan intelligence provided facilities of all kinds—from training to travel documents to the transport of arms to the import of equipment and supplies. There was mutual benefit in it, and much exchange of intelligence. The Libyans introduced the organization to its contacts, and vice versa. In Libya, Abu Nidal's people met representatives of the Japanese Red Army and the New People's Army of the Philippines and were encouraged to invite to Libya any foreign armed group or political party with which they hoped to establish a working relationship.

Abu Nidal's relations with the Libyans were conducted through two channels: Libyan intelligence and Qaddafi himself. He had no relations with other Libyan government departments, most of which had never even seen him. No one in the organization was allowed to know the exact nature of his relationship with Libya: All communications with the Libyans passed through him.

The Libyan leader treated Abu Nidal more generously than he did other Palestinians, paying him a monthly stipend to cover his expenses in Libya and allowing him to bring in dollars and change them on the black market at something like three and a half times the official rate. Qaddafi also gave Abu Nidal lump sums to invest in Europe and elsewhere so as to generate income to meet his expenses in Lebanon, a form of support Abu Nidal preferred because it gave him independence and protection against sudden cuts.

Preoccupied with his personal security, Abu Nidal instinctively clung to the intelligence and security services of his host country. He did everything possible to ingratiate himself with Abdallah al-Sanussi, Qaddafi's key man in internal security, calling him sir, like a soldier addressing his superior officer. Qaddafi, he addressed as the Leader (privately taking his members to task if they dared call him Brother Muammar), describing him with cloying hyperbole as "a latter-day Saladin." No hint of criticism of Libya was allowed to appear in any of the organization's internal reports, for fear that these might fall into Libyan hands.

It would enrage Abu Nidal if anyone in the Political Bureau protested that the organization was becoming a creature of Libyan policy. He claimed that such loose talk risked destroying them all. "You keep your pride," he would say. "I have to protect you and the organization!" He would also boast that he had his hands gripped tight round the Libyans' throat and that he knew so much about them that they could never get rid of him. As if to demonstrate his sense of immunity, he would regale his colleagues with scurrilous stories about Qaddafi's love life.

Members of the Libyan end of the Political Bureau and Central Committee would occasionally live for a while in Algeria, which Abu Nidal saw as a possible alternative haven should Qaddafi turn hostile. He even thought at one time of moving his wife and children there and wanted to expand relations with Algerian intelligence, which had begun in 1986. The Algerians, in turn, liked to keep in touch with all Palestinian factions and, whenever possible, help patch up their quarrels.

UNDERMINING THE *INTIFADA*

A few months after the start of the *intifada* in December 1987, Abu Nidal mounted three operations that would gravely damage the Palestinian cause—consistent with the pattern of anti-Palestinian activity evident from the start of his career.

Cyprus, in the eastern Mediterranean just off the Syrian coast, had long been sympathetic to the Palestinians, having supported them during Israel's siege of Beirut in 1982 and given them a haven when Arab states expelled them. Cyprus sometimes seemed more committed to the Palestinian cause than many Arab countries—much to Israel's annoyance.

On May 11, 1988, Abu Nidal's organization detonated a car bomb in Nicosia, killing and wounding fifteen people, including a Cypriot woman who was in a car behind the booby-trapped vehicle and a retired Cypriot diplomat, Andreas Frangos, who was walking nearby. To his own people, Abu Nidal claimed that the plan had been to blow up the Israeli embassy, but the car exploded two hundred yards from the embassy building, which was undamaged. In the wake of this, Cypriot opinion turned against the Palestinians, the island authorities tightened their controls over Palestinians coming in and out, and several resident Palestinians were thrown out.

Four days after the Nicosia bomb, Abu Nidal's gunmen struck again, this time in the Sudan, a country even more consistently pro-Palestinian than Cyprus. In simultaneous attacks at 8 P.M. local time on May 15, 1988, a five-man hit team attacked two "soft" targets in Khartoum—the Sudan Club, reserved for British and Commonwealth citizens, which they machine-gunned, and the Akropole Hotel, an old Greek-run establishment, where they hurled a rucksack full of grenades into the restaurant, killing a Sudanese waiter, a Sudanese general, and five Britons: Sally Rockett, a thirty-two-year-old teacher, and a family of four, Christopher and Clare Rolfe, both in their mid-thirties, and their two children, aged three and one. One of the children was beheaded by the blast. The Rolfes were Quaker aid workers who had arrived in the Sudan two months earlier, after spending three years with Somali refugees. About seventeen other people were wounded, among them an American, a Swiss, a Pole, and a Frenchman.

Abu Nidal tried to justify the attacks to his colleagues by claiming they were directed at places from which Falasha Jews, escaping from Ethiopia, were taken to Israel. But anyone familiar with the area would know at once that this was absurd.

The operation, which was strongly condemned by both the Sudanese government and the opposition, embarrassed the Palestinians in the Sudan, robbed the *intifada* of Sudanese popular support, and caused considerable problems with the authorities for Palestinian fighters who had taken refuge in the Sudan after their expulsion from Lebanon in 1982. A couple of weeks after the attacks, Abu Nidal issued a communiqué in the name of the Cells of the Arab Fedayeen, yet another fictitious organization, in which he claimed that the targets had been "nests of foreign spies." But the communiqué, several pages long, went on to discuss political and economic conditions in the Sudan as if to imply that the Sudanese opposition had been involved in the attacks. In fact, the Sudanese opposition had no interest in seeing a foreign group that resorted to contemptible terrorist methods assume the mantle of Sudanese nationalism in its name and was incensed at Abu Nidal's attempt to exploit its struggle.

Five of Abu Nidal's young fanatics, aged twenty-two to thirty, were arrested and sentenced to death, but the sentences were not carried out. Sudanese public opinion, in spite of its revulsion at the outrage, could not tolerate the execution of men who called themselves Palestinian guerrillas. The Sudanese Lawyers' Association condemned the terrorists but, in lingering sympathy with the Palestinian cause, undertook their defense. On January 7, 1991, to the dismay of the British and American governments, all five Abu Nidal terrorists were released, after "blood money" was paid to the families of the Sudanese victims and a pardon allegedly secured from the families of the British victims. If, as some of Abu Nidal's former colleagues believe, the operation was inspired by the Mossad, it was a spectacular success, for it cast the Palestinians as heartless murderers and destabilized the Sudan—which may also have been one of Abu Nidal's aims in staging it.

Some of his former colleagues told me that he had "sold" the operation to Qaddafi as a means to embarrass, and perhaps even overthrow, the new government that Prime Minister Sadiq al-Mahdi had formed a few days earlier, on May 11, 1988. This "national unity" government brought together the main political forces in the country—al-Mahdi's own Ummah party, the Democratic Unionist Party (friendly to Egypt), and the National Islamic Front (the local branch of the Muslim Brotherhood, campaigning for the application of Islamic Sharia law). John Garang's southern rebels, who had for years been waging war against the Khartoum government and against the extension of Sharia law, were excluded. Qaddafi, in neighboring Libya, did not like these developments. Not only did he support John Garang, but he wished to increase his own influence in the Sudan at the expense of Egypt's and put pressure on Chad. He therefore welcomed Abu Nidal's bid to destabilize Khartoum.

Abu Nidal had scores of his own to settle with the Sudan. Two years earlier, in 1986, he had sent a secret representative to Khartoum, traveling on a Libyan passport in the name of Ibrahim Hussein al-Mughrabi and posing as a businessman. His real name was Abd al-Karim Muhammad and he was a member of Abu Nidal's Political Directorate. But the contacts he made in Khartoum attracted complaints from Egypt, the PLO, and the United States, and Sudan eventually expelled him (but not before he had taken delivery of and hidden some weapons that Abu Nidal had sent him, probably through the Libyan diplomatic bag, which, my sources believe, were later used in the attacks). In a series of memos to Prime Minister al-Mahdi, Abu Nidal tried to get his man reinstated, but he was not successful, and this left him with a grievance. He had started his career as Fatah representative in the Sudan, and he was particularly sensitive to snubs from countries where he had lived and pretended to have influence. No doubt revenge helped dictate his choice of targets in the Khartoum bombings.

So Abu Nidal and Qaddafi had reasons of their own to destabilize the Sudan, reasons that provided an alternative explanation for the attacks, whose main impact was to discredit the Palestinians at a time when they needed all the support they could get. At the very least, Abu Nidal had allowed other considerations to supersede his loyalty to Palestine, but it is more likely that his organization had once again been manipulated. The alternative explanation looked very much like a cover story.

There was a further twist to the story. Once his five terrorists were in jail, Abu Nidal sought to bribe the Sudanese government to release them. He approached the Sudanese embassy in Algiers with an offer of $250,000 for flood victims in Sudan and dispatched two of his members to Khartoum with the money, which was accepted by a government minister and mentioned in the media. But when the envoys tactlessly raised the question of the five prisoners, an indignant Sudanese government realized that Abu Nidal's gift had strings attached and expelled the envoys. From the Palestinian point of view, Abu Nidal had managed to worsen an already bad situation.

Another grave blow to the Palestinians was the grenade-and-machine-gun attack on July 11, 1988, on the *City of Poros,* a Greek cruise ship with hundreds of tourists on board. A five-man Abu Nidal hit team killed nine passengers and wounded another eighty. No conceivable Palestinian or Arab interest was served by such random savagery. Greece was the European country most sympathetic to the Palestinian cause, and its prime minister, Andreas Papandreou, was the European leader who had most effectively defended the Arabs against Israel's charge of terrorism. For example, at the height of the Hindawi affair in 1986, when Syria believed it had been victimized by an Israeli "dirty tricks" campaign, Papandreou welcomed Hafez al-Assad to Athens and gave him a platform from which to defend himself.

Now Abu Nidal had attacked Greece and predictably, the Greeks were furious that the Palestinians had damaged Greece's all-important tourist trade and hastened the fall of the Papandreou government. Several intelligence sources I consulted were convinced that the attack on the *City of Poros* was a typical Mossad-inspired operation.

The attack overshadowed another incident on the same day in Athens, in which a car blew up as it was heading for a ferry, killing its driver, the same Samih Muhammad Khudr who had worked in Abu Nidal's Intelligence Directorate. His fingerprints were found to match those of the terrorist who, ten years earlier in Cyprus, on February 18, 1978, had led the team that assassinated Egyptian editor Yusif al-Siba'i, and had had then tried to escape by plane after taking hostages, only to be forced back to Cyprus when no airport would allow them to land. This was the incident that ended in a gun battle between Egyptian commandos and the Cyprus National Guard.

At the time of his death in the Athens car bomb, Khudr was head of the Intelligence Directorate's Foreign Intelligence Committee and a veteran of several operations, including the Karachi hijacking and the bombing of cafés in Kuwait. He had also masterminded the *City of Poros* operation. Keys found in his car turned out to be those of his flat in Sweden, where one of his three foreign wives lived and where, according to sources in the organization, he was due to go to ground after the operation.

Several of his former colleagues did not think his death was accidental. Abd al-Rahman Isa, after his defection, told Abu Iyad (as I learned from the tape of his debriefing) that Samih Muhammad Khudr's death had been engineered by Abu Nidal. He explained that the attack on the *City of Poros* had been planned as a suicide mission: The hit team was to have been followed on board by a car laden with dynamite timed to explode within sixty minutes. The plan was for Khudr to drive the car to the ferry, ready for loading, and then hand it over to a member of the team. But Khudr did not know that Abu Nidal had given orders to one of his men, Hisham Harb, to prime the bomb to go off within fifteen minutes—thus ensuring it would explode when Khudr was at the wheel of the car rather than on board the ship as planned.

Some sources inside the organization say that Abu Nidal killed Khudr because he had become too powerful; others say that his death was a gesture to placate Western governments that were putting pressure on Libya to stop harboring terrorists; others still, such as Abd al-Rahman Isa, claimed that Khudr had had an argument with Abu Nidal over the *City of Poros* operation. Khudr could not see the point of it. "What good will it do?" he kept asking. And indeed the operation can have had no purpose except to disrupt relations between Greece and the Palestinians. Khudr, apparently unaware of Abu Nidal's possible Mossad connection, was beginning to ask awkward questions, which is probably the real reason for his murder.

THE *SILCO* COVER-UP

In the late summer of 1986, a Libyan patrol boat sailing between the Libyan coast and Malta stopped and searched a converted sardine-fishing boat, the *Silco.* Two couples and four children were found on board. Some of them spoke Flemish, which the Libyans mistook for Hebrew, and one of the adults had a passport with an Israeli stamp. The ship was towed into Tripoli and its crew taken prisoner. Having been attacked by the United States a few months earlier, and in constant fear of hostile penetration along their two thousand kilometers of exposed Mediterranean coastline, the Libyans were more than jumpy. The seizure of the *Silco* was a serious mistake.

So began one of the more extraordinary Middle East hostage sagas. Qaddafi, embarrassed and fearful of French opinion, did not dare announce the capture of the *Silco.* So he asked Abu Nidal to provide a cover story, and the latter was glad to oblige. On November 8, 1987, Abu Nidal's organization announced in Beirut that a Palestinian gunboat had captured the *Silco* off the coast of Gaza and that its crew of suspected Israeli spies was being held prisoner in southern Lebanon. Qaddafi didn't want the French to think ill of him, but Abu Nidal did not mind embarrassing Palestinians.

By this time, the two couples and their children had settled into reasonably comfortable captivity in a Libyan seaside villa that Qaddafi had put at their disposal. They were two Belgian brothers, Emmanuel and Fernand Houtekins; Emmanuel's wife, Godelieve, and their teenage children, Laurent and Valerie; and Fernand's French girlfriend, Jacqueline Valente, and her two young daughters by another man, Marie-Laure and Virginie, whom, it later emerged, she had abducted from her former husband, Pascal Bétille, just before going on the cruise. In the first year of their Libyan stay, Jacqueline Valente gave birth to a third daughter, Sophie-Liberté, this time by Fernand Houtekins.

This motley group of hostages was eventually freed—but only in installments. First to be released, on December 27, 1988, were Jacqueline's two older children, Marie-Laure and Virginie, thanks to the "intervention" of Colonel Qaddafi.

Then, on April 10, 1990, Fernand Houtekins, Jacqueline, and Sophie-Liberté were released in Beirut and allowed to fly to France after an "appeal" by Qaddafi to all Muslims to free hostages and political prisoners on the occasion of Ramadan. In an obvious trade-off, and in defiance of a European Community embargo, France returned to Libya three Mirage jets that had been impounded in 1986 and President Mitterrand sent Qaddafi a personal message of thanks. His foreign minister, Roland Dumas, went so far as to praise the colonel's "noble and humanitarian gesture"—a remark that caused some irritation in London and Washington, where it was known by this time that Qaddafi had been the kidnapper. Suppression of the truth about the *Silco* may have been part of the price Abu Nidal had extracted from the French in return for his cooperation.

It was not until January 8, 1991, that the last four hostages, Emmanuel Houtekins, his wife, and two daughters, were released in Beirut—having been flown from Libya to Syria and then driven to southern Lebanon, to sustain the fiction that they had been held not by Qaddafi but by Abu Nidal. In their case, too, a price was paid. President Mitterrand spoke warmly of "the major role" Qaddafi had played in securing their release, while the Belgian government agreed to free an Abu Nidal terrorist, Nasir al-Sa'id, who had served ten years of a life sentence for hurling grenades at Jewish youngsters on the Agudat Israel school bus in Antwerp in 1980. David Kohane, fifteen, had died in that attack and sixteen other young people had been wounded.

There was a curious postscript to the *Silco* affair. On January 15, some days after the Houtekins family had been exchanged for Nasir al-Sa'id, Abu Nidal's Beirut-based spokesman, Walid Khalid, was spotted in central Brussels by a passerby, who alerted the police. Desert Storm was only days away, and the Belgian police, like other European police forces, were on full alert for fear of Iraqi-sponsored terrorism. And here was a live terrorist in their midst. Khalid was arrested. But he was swiftly released when it was discovered that he had actually been given a visa by the authorities to come to Belgium for talks with Jan Hollants Van Loocke, director of political affairs at the foreign ministry. In the embarrassing furor that followed, Van Loocke and a senior colleague resigned, the foreign minister, Mark Eyskens, narrowly survived a confidence vote in parliament, and Prime Minister Wilfried Martens, anxious to avoid a government crisis, ordered Khalid to be deported.

Abu Nidal had sent Khalid to Brussels to see what more could be extracted from the Belgians, an incident typical of his dealings with foreign governments. He would mount an attack on their territory, use it to establish a relationship with their intelligence service, and then exploit the channel to press for concessions and facilities. Such blackmail, as we have seen, had made Abu Nidal rich.

Apart from the abduction of Belgian citizens aboard the *Silco,* he had "softened up" the Belgians with four other contemptible assaults: one in 1980 on Jewish children at Antwerp; the 1981 killing of Na'im Khudr, the PLO representative in Brussels; the May 1988 kidnapping of a Belgian doctor in the Palestinian refugee camp of Rashidiya in Lebanon; and the killing in 1989 of the imam of the Brussels mosque and his assistant. The Belgians were more than anxious to buy him off.

It later emerged that Abu Nidal had demanded from Belgian intelligence not only the release from jail of Nasir al-Sa'id but also a "bonus" of $30 million. It took weeks of bargaining to get this figure down to $6.6 million, paid over two years and disguised as aid for needy Palestinians, and for the package to include two scholarships for Abu Nidal's candidates. Abu Nidal was keen on student scholarships, the backbone of his foreign networks. Whether this deal has survived the political storm in Belgium over the Walid Khalid affair, I have not been able to discover.

The families on board the *Silco* were not Mossad agents; they were kidnapped far from the Israeli or Lebanese coast, and Abu Nidal's role in the affair was only as Qaddafi's front man. When he negotiated the release of the captives, he sought nothing for the Palestinians. He wanted only benefits for himself and his Libyan paymaster. Just when world sympathy was aroused for the Palestinian children of the *intifada,* he managed to fill the pages of the world's press with the ordeal of French, Belgian, and Jewish children at the hands of Palestinian terrorists.

Abu Nidal has had a long clandestine relationship with

France. After the killing of Izz al-Din Qalaq, the PLO representative in Paris in 1978, and the discovery of a number of arms caches, the DST, France's internal security service, decided that the best way to neutralize Abu Nidal was to strike a deal with him. Several meetings took place between Abu Nidal's members and DST officers in the early 1980s, first in countries bordering on France, then in France itself.

An agreement was reached in 1984 (though some sources say it was in 1985) for a secret representative of Abu Nidal to live in France to keep open a channel of communications with the DST. This representative was changed fairly often. The last one known to be there, in 1990, was Emile Saab, a Lebanese, who reported to Ali al-Farra (Dr. Kamal), Abu Nidal's Libya-based intelligence chief, who was a frequent visitor to France. In addition, the French authorities gave occasional visas to Abu Nidal's members; allowed him to set up commercial ventures; treated some of his patients in French hospitals; gave him a gift of ambulances and Peugeot cars in Lebanon; and awarded scholarships to three or four of his members for study in France.

In return, Abu Nidal pledged that he would not bring arms into France, mount attacks on targets in France, or use French territory as a springboard for operations elsewhere. Of course, the French knew the truth about the *Silco* and other Abu Nidal operations, but they went along with the lie. It was cheaper to pay him off than to fight him. Details of Abu Nidal's agreement with the French were reported to me by former senior members of his organization who had been party to the negotiations. No French official has been willing to confirm it.

Switzerland is important to Abu Nidal because much of his money is deposited there and he is anxious to protect it. He needs privileges in Switzerland: residence permits, visas, the freedom to move in and out for himself and for key members of his organization. He does his utmost to conciliate the Swiss authorities, frequently sending his representatives, Atif Hammuda, of the Finance Directorate, and Ali al-Farra, of the Intelligence Directorate, to negotiate with the Swiss. But when he feels the dialogue is flagging, he does not hesitate to use forceful measures. In 1988–89, when some of his international financial dealings were revealed (following the defection to the West of Dirar Abd al-Fattah al-Silwani, manager of his trading enterprise in East Berlin), he feared that Switzerland might be persuaded to freeze his accounts there. He immediately sent a message to Swiss intelligence threatening havoc at the Zurich airport and, in a characteristic preemptive strike, kidnapped two Swiss delegates of the International Red Cross at Sidon in October 1989. When the crisis passed, the delegates were released. His cynical tactic on such occasions is to offer to mediate with the "kidnappers," who are, of course, his own men.

Abu Nidal has tried to establish more of a presence in Western Europe, but with only partial success—and with many setbacks. For instance, after Swedish police discovered an arms cache near the Stockholm airport in 1988, they traced two Palestinian brothers, members of his organization, to the small town of Umeaa, 540 kilometers north of the capital, and expelled them in December 1990. The Italians have refused all contact with Abu Nidal and have passed harsh sentences on some of his members. He himself is under sentence of death in Italy for the attack on the El Al ticket counter at the Rome airport. Spain is still holding some of his men in jail. The French arranged a meeting in Paris between his representatives and Spanish intelligence, but the Spaniards ignored his crude efforts at blackmail. They decided that opening even the smallest window to him would merely whet his appetite for more.

In the late 1970s and early 1980s, Abu Nidal made Istanbul the main secret headquarters for several of his committees. He used Turkey as a place in which to store arms and move them into Western Europe. But his killing of a Jordanian diplomat in Ankara and his attack on the Istanbul synagogue roused the Turks against him. Turkey is today among his principal antagonists.

Another is Britain. Its intelligence and security services have been extremely hostile and confrontational ever since his attempt to assassinate Ambassador Argov in 1982. Sources close to Abu Nidal report that he made several attempts to force the British to deal with him—killing British diplomats in Athens and Bombay; kidnapping the British journalist Alec Collett in Lebanon; bombing British airline offices; and also offering to trade information that he had gleaned in Libya on the Irish Republican Army—but the British rejected his approaches. Abu Nidal is said to believe that Britain heads a concerted European intelligence effort against him. But my impression is that there is little pooling of information among European states about Abu Nidal. Each country keeps to itself what it knows about him, often reluctant or embarrassed to tell others of its contacts with him.

According to Abu Iyad, the PLO would dearly like to work

closely with all Western governments in defeating Abu Nidal and in clearing the Palestinians from the charge of terrorism. But despite the PLO's overtures, some European intelligence services (and particularly the British) continue to ignore it. Several killers of PLO representatives in Europe have been released after serving just a few years in jail. For example, Kayid Hussein and his accomplice, Husni Hatem, the killers of Izz al-Din Qalaq, were released by the French in February 1986, after serving only half of their fifteen-year sentence. In Portugal, Muhammad Hussein Rashid, a member of the hit team sent to kill Isam Sartawi in Portugal, guffawed in court when he heard that he had been sentenced to only three years. From the PLO's standpoint, Europe has either bowed to Abu Nidal's blackmail or has chosen to rid itself of prisoners whose presence in European jails might provoke Abu Nidal into further terrorist acts to secure their release.

ASALA AND OTHER TERRORISTS

Abu Nidal has repeatedly boasted of alliances with other international terrorist organizations, but there appears to be little substance to his claims. According to his former colleagues, Abu Nidal had no link whatsoever with the IRA, although Libya did. His alleged relationship with the Basque separatist movement ETA was pure fantasy, limited to a single meeting in Algeria with some of its representatives. Equally, his ties with the Japanese Red Army and the French Action Directe were minimal. In Belgrade, his members paid courtesy calls on Khalid Abd al-Nasser, son of the former Egyptian president and the figurehead of Egypt's Revolution, a terrorist group that attacked Israeli and American targets in Cairo. But in making such visits, they were merely paying homage to the son of an Arab national hero rather than forging an operational connection with the son. Abu Nidal was in touch with some of the Baader-Meinhof splinter groups, but there was no collaboration or structural link. With the Mafia, he had had some small dealings over arms and forged passports, but little else. Western media reports of a closely integrated terrorist underground are greatly exaggerated.

Abu Nidal did have a relationship with ASALA, the Armenian Secret Army for the Liberation of Armenia, a small extremist group, of anti-Western, third worldist, and anti-Zionist tendencies, founded in Lebanon in the mid-1970s and further radicalized by the revolutionary militancy of the Palestinian factions it encountered there. ASALA militants hoped that killing Turks would force the Ankara government to admit Turkey's earlier responsibility for the massacre of Armenians and could lead to the creation of an independent Armenia in eastern Anatolia.

Inspiration for the movement had come from an elderly Armenian, Gourgen Yanikian, who, taking belated revenge for Turkish brutalities against his family in 1915, murdered two Turkish diplomats in a hotel room in Santa Barbara in 1973. The crime stirred many diaspora Armenians into a sharper consciousness of the misfortunes that had befallen their nation. ASALA set itself up in opposition to the establishment party of the diaspora, the Armenian Revolutionary Federation, which it accused of ineffectiveness. Instead, it rallied young radicals to the cause of Armenian nationalism, giving them a reason, if often a violent one, for staying within the fold of the Armenian community. By the mid-1980s, at least twenty-eight Turkish diplomats or their dependents had been killed in over twenty countries.

Sharing a history of exile and dispersal, Armenians and Palestinians were natural allies. Between 1977 and 1982, ASALA and such radical Palestinian groups as the PFLP shared training facilities in South Lebanon. But the Israeli invasion of 1982 drove them out of the south, and most PLO fighters out of Lebanon altogether. Left stranded by the PFLP's departure, ASALA was then taken up by Abu Nidal's organization, with offers of financial aid and the use of its base camps in the Bekaa Valley.

The relationship can be illustrated by the short career of an ASALA hit man, code-named Hagop Hagopian (the Armenian equivalent of John Smith). To some he was a dedicated patriot, to others a professional terrorist committed, like Abu Nidal, to violence and blackmail. In Palestinian circles he was known as Mujahid. He was an Armenian from Iraq who could pass as an Arab. Many Palestinians did not know he was an Armenian.

Before the foundation of ASALA, Hagopian had been a member of Wadi Haddad's militant wing of the PFLP and had in fact been shot and very nearly killed in Beirut in 1976 by another PFLP member, whom he had denounced as a KGB agent. In 1982–83, Abu Nidal's top men, Abu Nizar and Abd al-Rahman Isa, introduced Hagopian to officers of Syrian air force intelligence, notably to Colonel Haitham Sa'id (who was later to be involved in the Hindawi affair), with whom they ingratiated themselves. As a result, Hagopian was given facilities in Syria and was allowed to set up a secret center for forging passports and other documents, using the well-known printing skills of Lebanese Armenians.

ASALA's partnership with Abu Nidal encouraged it to undertake large-scale terrorist operations that attracted much hostile attention, not least from Armenians, and that were eventually to destroy it. In September 1982, two Armenian terrorists attacked the Ankara international airport, killing ten people and wounding eighty. One of the terrorists was captured and sentenced to death. He revealed that Hagop Hagopian had told him that Abu Nidal had supplied the weapons used in the attack. The following year, in July 1983, a time bomb exploded at Orly Airport, outside Paris, killing eight people and wounding over sixty others, most of them Turks checking in for a Turkish airlines flight to Ankara, an operation for which Abu Nidal may again have supplied the logistics. In the manhunt that followed, the French arrested Varoujan Garbidjan, the leader of the ASALA hit team, and sentenced him to long-term imprisonment.

To strike back at France, a gunman believed to be Hagopian killed Colonel Christian Goutierre, a French military attaché, in East Beirut in September 1986. Hagopian was rash enough to boast about the killing in an interview with an Arabic-language magazine. Some months later, in 1988, Hagop Hagopian was shot dead in Athens (which he had made his headquarters after the Syrians expelled him in 1987, at the same time that they expelled Abu Nidal). He was on his way to the airport to fly to Belgrade for a meeting with members of Abu Nidal's organization. According to the terrorist underground, Abu Nidal, anxious to demonstrate his usefulness to the French, betrayed Hagopian to them. It is said that he put the French in touch with a rival group in ASALA, which they then encouraged to finish off Hagopian.

By this time ASALA had suffered a number of severe blows: the loss of its South Lebanon training facilities; splits and defections inside the organization caused by widespread revulsion at the Orly massacre; the arrest of many of its members in France; rivalry with other Armenian groups, such as the Justice Commandos of the Armenian Genocide, very probably an unavowed offshoot of the

Armenian Revolutionary Federation; the expulsion from Syria; the death of Hagopian; and finally, the diversion of Armenian attention to the struggle for Nagorni Karabakh, the beleaguered Armenian enclave in Azerbaijan.

In the late 1980s, Abu Nidal and Fatah fought over the remnants of ASALA, for what could be salvaged. Hagopian's widow still lives in Greece and is said to be the only person who knows where his funds are located.

THE EASTERN EUROPEAN HAVEN

The familiar charge that communist Eastern Europe helped Abu Nidal and other Palestinian terrorists mount attacks in the West is overstated. The evidence from Palestinian and Western intelligence sources suggests a more ambivalent relationship, though Abu Nidal made Poland his home for several years in the early 1980s and professed great admiration for Erich Honecker's East Germany. He often went on holiday to Hungary and appears to have had three main reasons for cultivating the Eastern Europeans:

First, needing secure places of residence for himself and some key members, he was anxious to conclude security agreements with Eastern European intelligence services. The argument he habitually used was that a relationship with him would give a state immunity from his operations, a form of blackmail he used against Western European states as well.

Second, trading in East-bloc arms was an important source of revenue for him.

Third, he wanted to undermine the close relations that the PLO had established with most Eastern European countries.

Several Eastern European states concluded agreements with Abu Nidal in order to neutralize him, but there is no evidence that they cooperated with him in joint terrorist operations. Much like their opposite numbers in the West, they had state interests to defend. A committee of Czechs, Hungarians, and East Germans met monthly to pool information on terrorism, and a larger committee, on which all Warsaw Pact members were represented, also met at intervals to review the security situation throughout the bloc. To intelligence and security officers from the East, like their Western counterparts, Abu Nidal was a terrorist who had to be contained.

There was hardly any ideological content in Abu Nidal's relations with Eastern Europe, or indeed much coherence in his political stance. He liked to portray himself as a Palestinian nationalist who had been influenced by the theories of Marx, but he detested the Soviet Union and frequently attacked it in his publications. He declared himself a Maoist and expressed admiration for the Chinese experiment, but he never returned to China after his brief visit there in 1972 (when he was still in Fatah) and never developed any sort of relationship with the Chinese. He sometimes used to say that Albanians were the only true Marxists left in the world, but he had no relations with them either.

Abu Nidal tended to take on the political coloring of whichever group he happened to be with. With Marxists, he was one of them; with Arab nationalists, he claimed to be a nationalist; with Islamic fundamentalists, he would profess himself a strict Muslim; with Shi'ites, he swore by the Imam Ali and in South Lebanon even went so far as to alter the code names of his cadres so as to make them sound more attractive to the local Shi'ite population. When in Libya, he would endeavor to work into his communiqués the name of Umar al-Mukhtar, the hero of Libya's struggle against the Italians in the 1920s. But in Eastern Europe, he found the best way to make friends was less by professing Marxism than by distributing "gifts"—an expensive watch here, a present for someone's wife there, or simply quantities of cash all around (in dollar bills). In Poland, in particular, he found it easy to bribe his way into the centers of power.

Abu Nidal's oldest relationship in Eastern Europe was with Yugoslavia, where Palestinians had been going to study in large numbers since the 1960s. When Abu Nidal broke from Fatah in 1974, he managed to poach some of Fatah's students in Yugoslavia and used them to start recruiting in earnest, causing violent clashes between his supporters and Fatah's. In April 1980, his men in Belgrade threw a bomb at a car in which Abu Iyad was thought to be traveling. Not wanting further headaches of this sort, Yugoslav intelligence decided to open a line to Abu Nidal.

The Yugoslavs considered Abu Nidal a terrorist and did not approve of him. But they ignored his activities in the hope of persuading him not to forge links with separatist movements inside

Yugoslavia and not to conduct his bloody feud with Fatah on their territory. He, of course, exploited such tolerance for all it was worth. From 1980 onward, he kept a secret representative in Belgrade: first Ali al-Farra (Dr. Kamal), then Iyad Muhammad (the husband of one of his nieces), then Ali Afifi, followed by others. As a result, from 1980 to 1985, Yugoslavia became the organizational center for Abu Nidal's European operations. Weapons were stored there; his teams of assassins coming in from Libya or Lebanon used Yugoslavia as a staging post on their way to other destinations; and weapons were moved from there into the rest of Europe. Inside the organization, Yugoslavia was considered "semisecure" in the sense that if its members got into trouble, the organization could usually strike an under-the-table deal with the Yugoslavs to get them out of it.

Abu Nidal's relationship with East Germany began almost by accident when one of his cadres, Adnan Faris, an official in the Political Relations Committee, was spotted at the Berlin airport in 1984 and stopped for questioning. Boldly, he suggested some form of cooperation, a proposal he reported to his superiors on his return to Syria. Members of the Intelligence Directorate then visited East Germany, and the relationship commenced.

At least four major contacts were made in the second half of the 1980s:

> In 1985, Abu Nidal paid a visit to Berlin and had a long talk with Erich Mielke, the veteran head of East Germany's all-powerful state security service, the Stasi.
>
> Not long afterward, a twenty-six-man delegation from the organization, led by Isam Maraqa (who was shortly to become Abu Nidal's deputy), attended a three-month training course in East Germany at the invitation of the Stasi.
>
> Later in 1985, another political delegation, headed this time by Fu'ad al-Suffarini, of the Organization Directorate (who was to defect to Jordan), visited East Germany.
>
> In early 1986, a twenty-man military delegation, headed by a cadre code-named Jamil, attended a weapons-and-explosives course at the 12,000-acre Stasi training camp at Mossow, south of Berlin. One of the men at the course recalled that Abu Nidal paid them a visit at that time and, addressing their hosts,

spoke in fulsome terms of the East Germans as "the bravest socialists in the world."

The Stasi, however, did not help Abu Nidal in any of his foreign operations, nor did East Germany ever publicly acknowledge its links with Abu Nidal. In fact it made him promise not to store weapons in East Germany or transport them across its territory or mount operations in West Berlin. It did, however, allow him to set up his East Berlin trading company, Zibado, a sort of joint venture. But when its manager, Dirar Abd al-Fattah al-Silwani, defected, information about its activities was leaked to the press and the company was closed down.

To his chagrin, East Germany did not allow Abu Nidal to disrupt its close relations with Arafat's PLO. When in 1983 Arafat was besieged in the North Lebanon port of Tripoli by Fatah rebels backed by Syria, Erich Honecker sent him boatloads of arms, medicines, clothes, and foodstuffs—all free of charge. Not only did the PLO have its own extensive contacts with the Stasi, but it also dealt directly with the East German Foreign Ministry through its embassies abroad and it had a channel to institutions of the Communist party, which supplied the PLO with some three hundred medical grants a year and one hundred scholarships. The collapse of the communist regime was therefore a blow both to the PLO and to its archenemy, Abu Nidal.

In Poland, Abu Nidal had a residence and was given a score of scholarships for his students. But his relations with the Poles were ambivalent. He claimed to have high-level political contacts with them, but this was a fabrication. His only real contacts were with the intelligence and security services. Political leaders would not meet him, and half the time even the security people did not know he was there. His practice was to conceal his true identity and travel incognito. Like other Eastern Europeans, the Poles gave him safe haven in order to earn hard currency by exporting their weapons, and to prevent him from mounting operations against them or from their territory.

The Hungarians became interested in Abu Nidal when one of the terrorists who took part in the Vienna airport attack of December 1985 revealed that he had flown to Budapest and then driven to Vienna by car. To prevent future trouble, the Hungarians concluded a security agreement with Abu Nidal, which was negotiated by Atif Abu Bakr, who, before defecting to Abu Nidal's organization, had been the PLO "ambassador" in Budapest, in 1983–84. As others had done, the Hungarians submitted to blackmail by allowing a dozen of Abu Nidal's students to take courses in their country and by ignoring movements of his men in and out of the country. By 1986, Budapest had replaced Belgrade as a key center for Abu Nidal's European operations.

The Czechs considered Abu Nidal a terrorist and had no relations with him, although they were on good terms with Atif Abu Bakr, who had been PLO "ambassador" in Prague.

Bulgaria, which Abu Nidal visited often and where he liked to hold meetings, allowed him to establish a small student presence, sold him some weapons, let his men use Sofia as a staging post, and gave him a villa near the Hotel Vitusha, where he sometimes spent part of the summer. But they were not happy when they discovered that he was smuggling weapons from Turkey through their country to European destinations. Some consignments were seized and some of his men landed in jail.

The Romanians were the most hostile of all Eastern Europeans to Abu Nidal and had been ever since the killing of a Jordanian diplomat, Azmi al-Mufti, and the wounding of another in Bucharest in December 1984. Abu Nidal tried blackmailing the Romanians in every way he could, including placing bombs in their embassy in Beirut, but they refused to be cowed and arrested his members whenever possible.

Abu Nidal never went to the Soviet Union in an official capacity or met with any Soviet leaders (although for added safety, or so he thought, he sometimes chose to transit through Moscow on his way, say, from Geneva to Damascus). Members of his organization used to call at Soviet embassies in Baghdad and Damascus, but these contacts ceased when the organization moved to Libya. Stung by Western accusations that Moscow supported international terrorists, Soviet diplomats were distant and cautious in their contacts with Abu Nidal, and on Palestinian issues, they made it clear that they supported Arafat's moderate line and opposed terrorism.

BETWEEN IRAQ AND IRAN

On March 29, 1989, a Saudi cleric, Sheikh Abdallah al-Ahbal, spiritual head of the Muslim community in Belgium, the Netherlands, and Luxembourg, was shot dead at his mosque in Brussels, together with his Tunisian librarian. The killing was immediately associated in the public mind with the death sentence passed six weeks earlier, on February 14, 1989, by Iran's leader, Ayatollah Khomeini, on the British writer Salman Rushdie for his irreverent treatment of the Prophet Muhammad in his novel *The Satanic Verses.* The Brussels imam, a moderate, had apparently not endorsed the Ayatollah's death sentence and it was supposed that this had cost him his life, presumably at the hands of Muslim fanatics. Responsibility for the murder was claimed by the Organization of the Soldiers of Justice, in a communiqué couched in language such as that used by Hizballah, Islamic Jihad, and other pro-Iranian Islamic groups.

These were false trails: It was Abu Nidal who had ordered the killing. The assassination was part of the campaign of blackmail and extortion he was waging against Saudi Arabia, which was to earn him some millions of dollars in "protection money." He also wanted to sell Iran his services.

From the moment he was evicted from Iraq in 1983, Abu Nidal wanted a link with Iran. He offered Tehran intelligence about Iraq's military dispositions; he tried to lure it with arms deals worth hundreds of millions of dollars; his men in Damascus paid regular visits to the Iranian embassy, then headed by the hard-liner Ali Akbar Mohtashemi (later to become Iran's minister of interior and later still a leader of the radical camp opposed to President Hashemi Rafsanjani), in the hope of a relationship with Iran's Revolutionary Guards; he was lavish in his praise for Iran's war effort and denounced Saddam Hussein's "fascist regime." And whenever the press reported that Iran was secretly buying arms from Israel, Abu Nidal's magazine rushed to refute the charge, as if he himself had stood accused.

But the Iranians would not swallow the bait, and the invitation to Tehran Abu Nidal kept hoping for never came. Despite his efforts to court them, the Iranians believed that he was still tied to Iraqi intelligence, which had helped set him up in the first place. They did not need his help in mounting foreign operations; they did not wish to burden themselves with someone of his reputation; and they preferred to deal with groups that shared their Islamic ideology, which he did not.

However, on the ground in South Lebanon, Abu Nidal's men did make some limited contact with Hizballah, and he himself claimed to be on good terms with Sheikh Muhammad Hussein Fadlallah, Hizballah's spiritual guide. But contrary to reports in the press, this did not lead to significant operational cooperation.

There is no evidence that Abu Nidal played any part in Hizballah's numerous operations against Israel's self-styled "security zone" in southern Lebanon. Nor did Hizballah play any part in Abu Nidal's attack on the Greek cruise ship *City of Poros* as is sometimes alleged. Because that attack, on July 11, 1988, took place in the final stages of the Iraq-Iran war, only a few days after the USS *Vincennes* shot down an Iranian civilian airliner over the Gulf with the loss of 290 lives, many jumped to the conclusion it was an act of revenge in which Hizballah and Abu Nidal had joined forces. But this was another false trail. Iran and its friends had no hand in the *City of Poros* affair, and indeed Tehran was one of the first capitals to denounce the operation.

By the time Iraq invaded Kuwait in 1990, Abu Nidal had given up wooing Iran and was seeking to benefit from the crisis by ingratiating himself with members of the anti-Iraq coalition. But Desert Storm came and went without his entering the fray or drawing attention to himself—save to kill Abu Iyad in Tunis on the eve of battle, a murder that many in the intelligence world believed was inspired by the Mossad, though Abu Nidal had, as usual, his own reasons for murdering his former patron.

chapter

13

THE GREAT PURGE

Abu Nidal started to kill early in his career in Baghdad—first in his struggle with Fatah, a parent he rejected and for whom he developed a lifelong hatred.

Fatah's sentence of death on him, passed in absentia in 1974, and its murder that same year of his friend Ahmad Abd al-Ghaffur, unleashed a torrent of violence in him. If Fatah could behave like this, so could he. It was Fatah that had taught him to kill, he said, and it was fear of Fatah, of its revenge, of its penetration of his organization, of its enveloping powers, that would become his obsessive preoccupation. If one of his members so much as telephoned a Fatah office, Abu Nidal considered it treachery.

EARLY BRUTALITIES

From the early 1970s, Abu Nidal built his organization on brutality and fear. Scores of his members disappeared on his orders during the Baghdad years, ending up in pits at the Hit training camp or buried in cement at Center 85 in Baghdad. When the intended victim was too prominent to be murdered in Iraq, Abu Nidal would arrange to send him "traveling" on a foreign mission and have him killed abroad. Abd al-Rahman Isa, his intelligence chief at the time, recalled that Abu Nidal asked him about the location of a certain arms cache in Europe. Isa had replied that the man who knew about it was so-and-so. Pensively, Abu Nidal looked into the distance. "Wasn't he one of the members we sent traveling?" he asked. The man who had buried the weapons had himself been buried. In such cases it was usual for the organization to claim the missing man as a "martyr" and mourn his passing with an obituary notice in its magazine.

No doubt Abu Nidal was influenced by the ferocious system Saddam Hussein was then putting in place in Iraq. But his casual resort to murder owed much to his own brutal paranoia. It was also a deliberate strategy: Ruthlessness, he believed, would make his enemies fear and respect him. That the victims were often innocent did not concern him. Their deaths would keep others in line. Once he began prowling in the darkness beyond the campfire of society, legal and moral restraints had no further hold on him, nor did a sense of common humanity.

In the late 1970s, a well-known Palestinian engineer, Ahmad Jum'a, and his bride of a month, shopping in a Baghdad supermarket with one of Abu Nidal's cadres, were kidnapped on the street, bundled into a car, and taken to Center 85, where they were tortured and killed. Jum'a had been a founder member of Fatah's Iraqi branch but had left it in 1974 to join Abu Nidal's organization, where he had risen to some prominence. His kidnapping and death seemed motiveless: No evidence was produced against him or his wife. But the cadre with whom they had been rash enough to go shopping had recently been to Beirut, where he had met some Fatah people—enough to arouse Abu Nidal's suspicions. For this, all three had to die. In an obscene twist, the men who kidnapped them in Baghdad took home to their own children the groceries Jum'a and his bride had bought at the supermarket.

Another notorious case was that of Nabil Abd al-Fattah, whom Abu Nidal had entrusted with the key job of running his counterespionage unit in Iraq, a position from which he had sent many men to their death. Abu Nidal told his members that Abd al-Fattah hailed from Nablus, a major West Bank city, but in fact little was known about him as he had had no background in Fatah or in any other Palestinian organization. Eventually, Abd al-Fattah fell out with his chief and fled to Jordan, whereupon Abu Nidal screamed that he was not a Palestinian at all but a Jordanian, that he was in the pay of Jordanian intelligence, and that he had been planted on him. But no one dared ask Abu Nidal where he had found this man and why he had promoted him.

In the early eighties, when the organization moved to Syria, Abu Nidal managed to lure Abd al-Fattah to Damascus on the pretext of renewing contact with him. He and his wife were then taken to Lebanon and killed. (His wife was Nuha al-Turk, sister of Muhammad Harb al-Turk, now serving a prison sentence in Pakistan for his part in the hijacking of the Pan Am airplane in Karachi of September 1986.)

Was Abd al-Fattah innocent or was he a plant? Somewhere between the two "identities" Abu Nidal had given him, the truth was lost. And what of the dozens of people who had passed through his hands to be tortured and executed? One of Abu Nidal's more disturbing habits was to get people to do his dirty work for him and then kill *them* once they had served his purpose.

In 1983, when the organization was expelled from Iraq, it was still holding in its prisons some twenty members who had fallen under suspicion but whose interrogation was not yet complete. What was to be done with them? If the Iraqis attempted to release them, Abu Nidal gave orders that grenades were to be thrown at once into the prison cells. Eventually, Abu Nidal moved the prisoners to Syria and then to Lebanon, where he murdered many of them.

Basil, the bluff, straightforward soldier with fair hair and pink cheeks, who would not have been out of place in a British officers' mess, was a Palestinian born in 1950. He had joined Abu Nidal in the early 1970s but had refused to have anything to do with his foreign operations. Instead, he had spearheaded the organization's entry into Lebanon and, in the mid-1980s, had risen to be chief of military operations for Abu Nidal's militia, the People's Army. However, sickened by the brutalities he had witnessed, he defected to the breakaway Emergency Leadership, which we will soon learn about, that Atif Abu Bakr established in November 1989, and agreed to be interviewed by me in Tunis in 1990. We met furtively a number of times in small seaside hotels.

Basil told me he had spent sixteen years with the organization, but only when he left did he grasp its real nature. Inside the organization it was considered treachery even to ask a question. Each member lived in isolation and was subject to Abu Nidal's total control. But an incident in 1985 had made Basil uneasy. Fatah had captured five of Abu Nidal's men in the Bekaa Valley and killed them. To avenge them, a Fatah office was raided and two of its men were captured and shot at once. It turned out, however, that one of them was not a member of Fatah at all but a student whose brother worked in the Fatah office and whom he had come to visit. Finding him absent from his desk, the student had sat down to wait for his brother—only to be kidnapped and killed. "They didn't even ask the poor fellow his name before shooting him!" Basil told me.

Another case of which Basil had firsthand knowledge was that of a Palestinian student from the occupied West Bank who had come to study at Damascus University. On the way, he stopped off in Jordan to see his aunt, who gave him a bag of food for her son, Faruq, who worked for Abu Nidal in Syria. The student came to the organization's office at the Yarmuk refugee camp, in Damascus, and asked to see his cousin.

"He's in Lebanon," they told him. "We've got a car going there and can give you a lift."

The student was arrested on arrival, given a severe beating, and accused of being a Jordanian agent. For eighteen months he was held in prison in appalling conditions. By the time they released him, his passport had expired and the Jordanians would not renew it. The Israeli stamp allowing him to reenter the occupied territories had also expired, so he could not return home. He had become a refugee.

Basil was told to speak to him. "I had to explain to him that the harsh treatment he had received was only to be expected, as the organization was itself under constant threat. Forced to mouth clichés about Zionism and imperialism, I suddenly realized how little I actually believed in them!

"I tried to buy him some clothes and make sure he had something decent to eat. But he was a broken man. In the end, I was left speechless at the spectacle of such needless suffering." It was cases such as this that led Basil to defect.

THE JUSTICE COMMITTEE

Based in the village of Bqasta in the hills above Sidon in South Lebanon, some twenty miles north of the Israeli border, the Committee for Revolutionary Justice oversees the cruel charade of interrogation, torture, and execution that in the organization passes for due process of law. This is the committee headed by Mustafa Ibrahim Sanduqa (code name Salim Ahmad), who is married to one of Abu Nidal's nieces and, as such, is a member of his extended family. It will be recalled that I had put him on my list of suspected Mossad agents, together with Dr. Ghassan al-Ali and Alaa.

Several prisoners held by the committee in 1990 were guilty of nothing more serious than minor offenses against the organization. But in an outfit gripped by permanent spy mania, the most common accusation is that of treachery—of working for a hostile service. Under torture, most prisoners confess their crime. Often, they beg to be killed, to bring their ordeal to an end. Some of Abu Nidal's stronger victims have survived imprisonment and torture, though, and have later been found innocent of the charges against them. They are usually executed anyway, to make sure word of such methods doesn't leak—but enough has leaked for a sordid picture to emerge.

In his taped debriefing, Abd al-Rahman Isa said, "Abu Nidal would summon me to his office and say very sternly, 'Information has reached me that so-and-so in our organization is a suspect!' He would then place a file on the table in front of him—but he would neither open it nor read out anything from it. Nor would I. I would take his word for it. I believed him!"

When he defected from the organization in 1989, Abd al Rahman Isa published a statement in which he declared that he had been lied to for seventeen years. He had been made to kill on the basis of an empty file on a table. However, by acquiescing in such methods, men like Isa were also signing their own death warrant. As we shall see, Isa himself would soon become a target.

Methods of torture used by the committee were exceptionally barbarous, even in a region known for its disregard for human rights. They included hanging a man naked for hours and whipping him until he lost consciousness; reviving him with cold water; and rubbing salt or chili powder into his wounds. Or forcing a naked prisoner into an automobile tire with his legs and butt in the air; then whipping, wounding, salting, and reviving him with cold water; then repeating the process. On occasion, plastic melted under a flame was allowed to drip onto a prisoner's bare skin. Another method was to heat oil in a frying pan and then, while holding the prisoner steady, fry his male member.

In the committee's prisons, each man was confined alone in a tiny cell, built on two levels like a step. Bound hand and foot, the prisoner could move his hands only enough to take and eat food thrown in to him from an opening in the cell wall. He could urinate and defecate only with great difficulty.

(Such prisons are not unique in the area. On June 26, 1990, Israel's human rights organization, B'tselem, reported on detention centers for underage Palestinians in Jerusalem. "Almost every minor we interviewed testified that he had been beaten, usually severely—slaps, punches, kicks, hair pulling, blows with clubs and iron bars . . ." the report said. Others reported that their manacled hands were bound behind them to a pipe in an open courtyard, where they were left in awkward positions for hours in the sun and rain, and during the night. Other young prisoners reported being held for days in a dark and smelly isolation cell measuring 1.5 square meters, and containing a toilet seat. Some said they were held for hours in what they called "the closet," a very narrow cell one meter long in which the inmate can stand but cannot move. Other testimony described the "grave," a sunken boxlike cell covered by an iron door in which handcuffed inmates must sit bent over. The cell is soiled, since prisoners are not allowed out to the bathroom and excrement accumulates under them. The iron door keeps in the noisome smells.)

If Abu Nidal's prisons happened to be full, and while the committee waited for its leader in Libya to confirm a death sentence, a prisoner might be placed in a freshly dug grave and have earth shoveled over him. A steel pipe in his mouth sticking out of the ground would allow him to breathe. Water would be poured in from time to time to keep him alive. When word came from Libya, a bullet would be shot through the tube, which was then removed and the hole filled up.

INTERNAL MASSACRES

With the passage of years, the blood shed by Abu Nidal swelled into a torrent. Dozens of men were murdered in the 1970s, when the organization was based in Iraq. Twoscore and more, including women and university students, were kidnapped in Syria in the 1980s, smuggled out to Lebanon, and butchered in the Badawi refugee camp, in the north of the country. Another forty-seven prisoners being held in a jail at Aita, in the Bekaa Valley, could not be transported when the organization moved from there to South Lebanon, so they were killed en masse in 1987, without even having been interrogated. By 1986–87, beatings and torture in the organization's prisons had become routine. According to eyewitnesses, interrogators seemed hardly concerned to discover the truth about detainees or to investigate their background. Sentences were passed on the basis of confessions, and condemned men would be shot at night and buried in the woods.

These killings were merely the prelude to the orgy of murder in both Lebanon and Libya that started in November 1987 and continued more or less unabated until the end of 1988, when Abu Nidal, encountering opposition from his colleagues, found it prudent to pause. In a little over a year, it is estimated that Abu Nidal murdered some six hundred of his own people, between a third and a half of his total membership, mostly young men in their early twenties—almost as many Palestinians as Israel killed in the first three years of the *intifada.*

These mass killings were mainly the work of the four-man team in charge of Abu Nidal's operations in Lebanon: Mustafa Ibrahim Sanduqa, of the Justice Committee, with its prisons and interrogation centers, torturers, and executioners; Isam Maraqa, Abu Nidal's thirty-five-year-old deputy, who was married to Umm Nidal's niece; Sulaiman Samrin, the powerful first secretary, better known as Dr. Ghassan al-Ali; and Mustafa Awad, known as Alaa, the violent and unscrupulous head of the Intelligence Directorate.

Over three hundred men were killed in South Lebanon by these four, 171 of them on a single night in November 1987—on the fabricated charge of being Jordanian agents. According to a defector, a bulldozer was brought in to dig a deep trench. Blindfolded, roped together, and with their hands tied behind their backs, the men were then lined up, sprayed with machine-gun fire, and immediately pushed in for burial, some of them struggling and still alive.

About 120 men then fled the People's Army and sought refuge in the Bekaa Valley with Abu Ahmad Fu'ad, the military commander of George Habash's PFLP. In an angry communiqué, Abu Nidal accused Fu'ad of being a Jordanian agent as well—and, for good measure, of being in league with Yasser Arafat and the Americans.

Those Abu Nidal was unable to liquidate in Lebanon he transferred to Libya and exterminated there. In the mass killings at the desert camp where Jorde was held, 165 men died in 1987–88 and were buried in communal graves. Most of these were Palestinian youngsters who had been sent from Lebanon on the pretext that they were on their way to Chad to fight alongside Libyan forces in the struggle for the contested Aouzou strip. Abu Nidal's was one of several Palestinian and Lebanese factions, friendly to Qaddafi or funded by him, that had contributed men to Libya's war effort. But Abu Nidal believed these youngsters were conspiring against him, and they never got further than the Libyan camp. According to a friend of Jorde who had also been at the camp and who later escaped, one of their executioners was driven to suicide by what he had done.

Al-Hajj Abu Musa was a veteran instructor in his late fifties who had been with Abu Nidal since the Iraq days and was now with him in Libya. Over the years, Abu Musa had trained many of his recruits. He was a soldier, a killer, but in the circumstances more benign than most, and his personal following among the fighters appears to have aroused Abu Nidal's jealousy. "You know, Abu Musa," he would say to him at meetings, "there are many traitors to be found among the Palestinians—but the highest percentage is among the over-fifties!"

Abu Nidal sent Abu Musa to Libya and put him in charge of the training camp, where he had him arrested and killed—on grounds of sexual perversion. In a sadistic afterthought, he told the Hajji's anxious wife, Umm Musa, an old peasant woman who dressed in traditional embroidered Palestinian clothes like the rural women of her generation, that her husband had been posted to Libya to prevent him from taking another wife. Abu Nidal then arrested Umm Musa, who had been like a mother to many of his young recruits, and had her thrown into jail and killed on a charge of lesbianism. Husam Yusif, the Hajji's successor as commander of the Libyan camp—the man in charge there when Jorde passed through—was also purged.

"What people don't understand," Abu Dawud once said to me, "is that Abu Nidal takes his decisions to kill in the middle of the night, after he has knocked back a whole bottle of whiskey." But this was not an adequate explanation. For Isa, who had worked closely with Abu Nidal for twenty years, there could be no question that Abu Nidal was now insane. Abu Iyad and Atif Abu Bakr believed, as we have seen, that Abu Nidal was acting in Israel's interest—destroying one of the best Palestinian fighting forces in South Lebanon. But whether the source of his behavior was alcoholism, madness, or the Mossad, or all three, Abu Nidal so terrorized his organization that no one could stop him.

THE KILLING OF MILITARY OFFICERS

In Lebanon, among the first to die in November 1987 were the organization's two best officers, Jasir al-Disi (known as Abu Ma'-mun) and Ayish Badran (Abu Umar), both seasoned soldiers who had begun with Fatah, attended military courses in India and the Soviet Union, and joined the organization after the Fatah mutiny of 1983. Disi had been elected a member of Abu Nidal's Central Committee, while Badran, who had commanded the organization's forces during the War of the Camps, was appointed deputy head of the People's Army Directorate. Their death destroyed the military effectiveness of the People's Army.

Basil had been Jasir al-Disi's deputy. In Tunis in the summer of 1990, at one of our meetings by the sea, he told me what had happened, his broad pink face sweating. First Disi and then Badran had disappeared, suddenly and without warning, leaving him in charge. He supposed they had been sent abroad on short notice. Then Wasfi Hannun, the head of the People's Army Directorate, came one day to his headquarters to take him to an important meeting with Isam Maraqa, Abu Nidal's deputy, and Dr. Ghassan.

Hannun drove Basil into the hills above Sidon to a building that belonged to the Intelligence Directorate. As they approached, Basil saw a large contingent of guards outside, men he recognized as the personal bodyguards of Isam Maraqa and Dr. Ghassan. He greeted them warmly, but they seemed puzzled by his presence.

"It was only when I got inside," Basil told me, "that I saw that I was in an interrogation center. There were electric cables for torture and a cement block for the accused to sit on, facing his interrogators. Five men, who looked as if they had been there for days, sat behind a table laden with files, thermos flasks of coffee, dirty cups, and overflowing ashtrays. The atmosphere was dense and smoky.

"Isam Maraqa said they wanted to ask me some questions

about Disi and Badran. What did I think of them? I answered that they were capable and experienced officers who had had good careers with Fatah before joining us and had played a full part in the War of the Camps.

"Maraqa then said bluntly that they had confessed to plotting and were both in detention. They had named *me* as someone on whose help they hoped to count. Had they approached me about their plot?"

Basil replied angrily that he considered himself one of the builders of the organization and that he was not proposing to tear down his own work. Did they imagine that he would keep quiet if he had heard even a whisper of sedition? After about half an hour's questioning they let him go.

Many men then started disappearing from the units. At first Basil thought they had been transferred to Libya or sent to fight in Chad, but he was amazed to discover they were held prisoner in Sidon and brutally interrogated in the name of a supposed conspiracy. It was soon learned that Disi and Badran had been executed—as Jordanian spies—and that dozens of others had been shot and were buried in a mass grave near Bqasta.

Badran left a widow and nine children in the village of Dummar, on the outskirts of Damascus.

ASSORTED VICTIMS

In my interviews with ex-members of the organization whom I was able to track down in Tunis, Malta, Cyprus, and Marseilles, I learned of several other cases of sudden and violent death.

• Ibrahim al-Abd, an able cadre of the Finance Directorate who had headed the organization's Zurich-based trading company, was arrested in 1987, accused of being a spy for the Mossad and the CIA, and executed. At the time, Abu Nidal was reorganizing his Swiss bank accounts to bring them more tightly under his family's control. Abd may have known too much about these funds, as did another cadre from the Finance Directorate, killed at about the same time, named Musa Rashid, who had run a finance company in Kuwait belonging to the organization. He was summoned to Libya and shot as a Jordanian spy.

• Muhammad Khair (code name Nur Muharib), a member of

the Political Directorate's Political Relations Committee, was another victim of Abu Nidal's paranoia. Before joining the organization in the late 1970s, he had spent a year or two studying in Turkey, which convinced Abu Nidal that he had been enlisted by Turkish intelligence. From there, it was only a step to suppose that the Turks had introduced him to the Mossad, which encouraged him to offer his services to Jordanian and Syrian intelligence. So Nur Muharib was charged with being an agent of four intelligence services.

In 1987, Muharib had met and married Fatima Skaf, a young Syrian schoolteacher from a Shi'ite family, who taught in a primary school in Damascus. Four months after their marriage, they were both arrested and, in 1988, executed. That she was a new bride, who had not known her husband for long and knew nothing of the organization and no one in it, did not spare her. When her parents made inquiries, they were told that she had been sent abroad on a mission with her husband. To this day, they are uncertain of her fate.

Nur Muharib had an uncle called Mustafa Umran, a Palestinian writer and poet from Gaza, with an M.A. in Arabic literature from Cairo University. He had been a follower of the Fatah rebel Abu Musa, but in 1987 joined Abu Nidal's organization and, because of his writing skills, was given a job in the Political Directorate's Publications Committee. It was while he was working there that he came across his nephew, Nur Muharib, whom he had not seen for twenty years.

When Nur was arrested, his uncle was taken as well and tortured terribly until he confessed that he was the head of a Mossad network whose special role was to indoctrinate Arabs in the subversive view that normal relations with Israel were possible.

These two men, respectively in the Political Relations Committee and the Publications Committee, had climbed to well-placed jobs. They were considered comrades and revolutionaries. But from one day to the next they were accused of being spies and traitors and were exterminated. As usual, no evidence against them was ever produced. They were nonpersons. No one could say a word in their favor. Colleagues of such dead men would learn of their fate from the organization's magazine or from an internal memorandum.

• Mujahid al-Bayyari (code name Zuhair Khalid), another

victim, was one of the terrorist stars of the Intelligence Directorate, a prominent cadre in foreign operations who had spent two years in a Spanish jail for traveling on a forged Moroccan passport. He had been involved, among other outrages, in the bombing of the open-air cafés in Kuwait in 1985.

One day in 1986, when the organization was still in Syria, Syrian air force intelligence asked its contact man in the organization, Abd al-Karim al-Banna (Abu Nidal's nephew), if he knew of a member called Mujahid al-Bayyari; they wished to interview him. When Abu Nidal heard of these inquiries, he seemed deeply disturbed. He blustered that the Syrians probably wanted to hand Bayyari over to the Kuwaitis—because of the bombings of the cafés—and get paid handsomely for it. He refused to allow Bayyari to be interviewed.

The fact was that in July 1979, at Nice, on the French Riviera, Bayyari had been part of an Abu Nidal hit team that, on Iraq's instigation, had assassinated Zuhair Muhsin, the head of Syria's own Palestinian faction, al-Sa'iqa. When the Syrians asked to interview Bayyari, Abu Nidal immediately suspected that they had learned of his role and were bent on revenge. He instructed Bayyari to set off a car bomb (one of his specialties) in Israel's security zone in southern Lebanon but, by chance or premeditation, the bomb went off prematurely in Sidon and Bayyari was killed.

Abu Nidal then sent the Syrians a message: Would they like him to kill the leader of the Arab Liberation Front, Iraq's Palestinian faction? As one of Abu Nidal's ex-members explained to me: "Abu Nidal was telling the Syrians, 'Look, I killed Zuhair Muhsin at Iraq's behest; I'm ready to kill their man at your behest.' " The Syrians refused the trade.

REASONS FOR THE PURGE

How was the great butchery of 1987–88 to be explained? If Abu Iyad and others are correct, the Mossad may have instigated the purge. But as usual with such riddles, there was also an explanation to be found within Abu Nidal's own organization. For, as we have seen, Abu Nidal sensed that the organization was slipping out of his control. The one explanation, however, does not necessarily exclude the other.

For years, Abu Nidal, Abu Nizar, and Abd al-Rahman Isa had been inseparable and had together built up the organization. But by 1981, Abu Nidal had gone to Poland and had spent the next few years in Europe, between Warsaw and Vienna, Zurich and Berlin, trading arms, setting up finance companies, accumulating assets, and keeping out of the Middle East. He tried to run his organization from afar with his weekly stream of peremptory memos, chiding his hard-pressed associates, criticizing them, setting them against one another. But his absence and his dictatorial methods were resented by his colleagues, who shouldered the daily burden.

These early years of the 1980s were the time when, from its Syrian base, the organization developed rapidly, expanding almost tenfold into Lebanon. The men who actually ran the organization were proud of this expansion, but as we have seen, Abu Nidal was alarmed by it. For him, the new recruits were an indigestible body of men who were subverting his organization and who might even pose a serious threat to him personally. Drifting from one master to another in search of security and political direction, rough and untutored, politically inexperienced, prone to mutiny, they had had a checkered history. They had not been drilled in the organization's ten principles. They had none of the tortured loyalty to the organization of Abu Nidal's older cadres.

To judge these developments for himself, Abu Nidal came secretly to Syria for a week in October 1984, and then for two weeks in January 1985, during which he held long meetings with his command. Then, on October 22, 1985, he came to Syria again and stayed there on and off for a year and five months, until his final departure for Libya on March 28, 1987.

It was in this period that the internal dispute came to a head and that Abu Nidal made the brutal moves with which he eventually defeated his colleagues and regained full control.

These steps included:

- in 1985, replacing Abu Nizar and Abd al-Rahman Isa by members of his own family as signatories of the organization's bank accounts in Switzerland and elsewhere;
- in August 1986, ousting Abu Nizar from his position as deputy chief and replacing him with the young, slavishly loyal Isam Maraqa (Abu Nizar, as we have seen, was given

the much less powerful job of head of the Organization Directorate);

- engineering the organization's expulsion from Syria in June 1987 by mounting terrorist attacks in Rome, Vienna, Karachi, and Istanbul without the Syrians' knowledge or approval;
- splitting the organization between Lebanon and Libya, the better to control it;
- demoting Abd al-Rahman Isa in 1987 from head of the Intelligence Directorate to junior cadre and replacing him by Mustafa Awad (Alaa) in Lebanon and Ali al-Farra (Dr. Kamal) in Libya;
- then, beginning in November 1987 and as a climax to these moves, ordering the large-scale massacre of officers and men of the People's Army.

Slow to grasp the cumulative significance of these moves, his colleagues, with few exceptions, fell victim to Abu Nidal's superior strategy.

Was there any truth to Abu Nidal's charge that his once loyal colleagues were plotting to overthrow him in the autumn of 1987? What is certain is that from 1985 onward, he met more resistance from them. Men who had run the show during his long absence in Poland, who had established the organization in Syria, taken it into Lebanon, expanded it, fought in the War of the Camps and found their nationalist bearings, now resented his attempts to reverse the current and return the organization to its old molelike existence.

These colleagues did not like being forced out of Syria, nor did they appreciate the split between Libya and Lebanon, which weakened their position. They also felt the time had come to distance themselves from terrorism and demanded more of a say in policy making. Like Habash's PFLP or Jibril's PFLP–General Command or the myriad Lebanese resistance groups, they wanted to join the struggle against Israel, which, apart from its repression of Palestinians in the occupied territories, still occupied a substantial slice of South Lebanon, from which it regularly mounted raids northward.

Abu Nidal blamed the problems he was facing on the new men who had entered his high command from Fatah in 1985—and chief among them Atif Abu Bakr, the ideologue of the new "nationalist" trend. Strikingly cadaverous in face and body, with a stern, inward-looking expression, at times didactic and at times cutting, Abu Bakr was brighter than the others, a formidable opponent, as Abu Nidal recognized. Men of his caliber wanted the Political Bureau and the Central Committee to engage in real debate, and they had an altogether different vision of the organization's future than did Abu Nidal.

So the dispute smoldering in 1985–87 touched on power, money, operations, ideological orientation, relations with other groups, and decision making. The challenge never surfaced, but it was probably enough to make Abu Nidal fear that his colleagues might one day use their troops to oust him and, perhaps with Syrian help, take over the organization. Abu Nizar and Abd al-Rahman Isa had lived and worked in Syria and were on close terms with General Muhammad al-Khuly, of air force intelligence. For the paranoid Abu Nidal, this was reason enough to strike first. He was determined to "have his enemies for lunch before they had him for dinner."

This could have been why he placed in key posts men who shared his vision of a wholly clandestine outfit, living by its own savage laws, and then, with their help, massacred the officers and men who alone could have given his opponents the muscle they needed to mount a serious challenge.

THE FALL OF ABU NIZAR

The mass killings Abu Nidal ordered in Lebanon and Libya brought these tensions into the open. Abu Nidal was clearly capable of condemning to death anyone he chose and was strong enough to ensure that the sentence was carried out. Atif Abu Bakr was determined to expose the whole macabre setup. It was imperative, he felt, to tell all the members what was going on. To remain silent was to be an accomplice to Abu Nidal's crimes.

In May and June 1988, Atif Abu Bakr began addressing memoranda to members of the Political Bureau and Central Committee demanding the appointment of a committee of inquiry into the killings, an open challenge to Abu Nidal, which he was bound to resist. Abu Bakr did more than write memos: He tried to win over Abu Nizar, a founding member of the organization, a former deputy leader who was still powerful and popular enough to change the direction of the movement.

Abu Nidal responded by setting a masterly trap. When they left Syria in 1987, Abu Nizar's wife and children had moved to Algeria, where Abu Nizar was posted, but they were lonely there. Abu Nizar was often away on missions. The family debated whether to move to Cyprus or even to Czechoslovakia. With feigned innocence, Abu Nidal quietly suggested to Abu Nizar that his family might be better off if they returned to Damascus, where they had lived happily for several years. Abu Nizar accepted the suggestion in good faith, managed to get Libyan passports for his family, and at the end of August 1988, sent them back to Syria. Abu Nidal then accused Abu Nizar of being a Syrian agent. For his family to return to Syria after the organization had been expelled from there meant that Abu Nizar had contacted Syrian intelligence, which approved the move.

Abu Nizar and Atif Abu Bakr then made another tactical error, this time a fatal one. Not only did they have long private talks—a seditious breach of the organization's rules—but far worse, Atif arranged for Abu Nizar to meet secretly with Abu Iyad, the PLO's intelligence chief, in Algiers in early October 1988.

In Tunis in 1990, Abu Iyad gave me an account of this meeting with Abu Nizar. It was, he said, a long, sometimes stormy, sometimes extraordinarily candid talk that began at nine o'clock one evening and continued until three the next morning. For the first two hours, Abu Nizar had sounded like Abu Nidal's official mouthpiece. Listening to him, Abu Iyad reflected that this was the man who had been Abu Nidal's closest colleague for fifteen years, his partner in terrorism and crime.

"Then suddenly, as if his conscience had been aroused, his tune changed. He started telling me stories I could hardly believe. How Abu Nidal humiliated and insulted them. How he tried to dictate what their wives wore. How he meddled in absolutely everything. It was worse, he said, than living in a Chinese commune. And now, he went on, Abu Nidal had become a psychopath!

"What was he to do now? How could he escape? Would I guarantee his safety? Should he defect and take as many men as he could with him? I replied that this was exactly what Abu Nidal no doubt wanted him to do. Every dictator in history liked to get rid of the strong men around him—and then weep crocodile tears over them!

"I told him he should stay on and fight. He should do something drastic to break Abu Nidal's hold. Perhaps even take him prisoner. I didn't want to say bluntly that they should kill him, but we both knew very well that so long as Abu Nidal remained alive, he would be dangerous."

Somehow or other, perhaps by monitoring telephone calls, Abu Nidal heard about Abu Nizar's meeting with Abu Iyad: Direct evidence of the conspiracy he most feared and which could be punishable only by death.

A few weeks after the meeting, on the morning of October 18, 1988, Abu Nidal murdered his old comrade Abu Nizar on the outskirts of Tripoli, in a spacious house in the Suq al-Jum'a district, one of three villas in a large compound that Qaddafi had put at Abu Nidal's disposal. The main bedroom, the size of a whole apartment, had its own private bathroom and kitchen. This was a room Abu Nidal sometimes slept in, and it was here, according to several inside sources, that Abu Nizar was tortured and killed.

Abd al-Rahman Isa had been on a mission to the Sudan. According to what he said in his taped debriefing, he had flown back to Libya on the evening of October 17.

"It was my habit when I returned from a mission abroad to go straight to Abu Nidal's office to report to him before going home, especially if I had something sensitive to communicate.

"This time something strange occurred. I headed for my office and, still breathless, lifted the receiver to speak to Abu Nidal, believing he would want to see me immediately. My office was only a few minutes away from his by car.

" 'Hello! We're back!' I cried.

" 'Welcome back,' he replied in a deadly calm manner. 'We'll meet tomorrow evening.' "

So Isa made for home, where his wife told him that Abu Nizar had tried repeatedly to get hold of him. This openness on Abu Nizar's part surprised Isa, because members of the organization were not allowed to contact each other—and when he and Abu Nizar met, as they usually did when Nizar was in Libya, it was done quietly.

Abd al-Rahman Isa and Atif Abu Bakr later tried to reconstruct the events of October 17–18. On the afternoon of October 17, Abu Nidal had taken Abu Nizar and Atif Abu Bakr to call on Qaddafi at home. Then they had driven out to the house of Ahmad Jibril, head of the PFLP–General Command, in a village near Tripoli.

After these social calls, Abu Nidal had dropped off Abu Nizar at his hotel—he stayed at a hotel on his visits to Libya from Algeria—and then drove Atif to his home. They had all agreed that Amjad Ata, deputy head of the Secretariat, would come for Abu Nizar at eight-thirty in the morning to take him to a meeting and that Atif would be collected a little later, at around 10 A.M. But the next morning, no one came to take Atif Abu Bakr to the meeting. He telephoned Abu Nidal, who said he was busy and asked to postpone their meeting until the following day.

All that day, October 18, Atif expected Abu Nizar to ring or drop by, as he usually did on his visits to Libya, but there was no sign or word from him. And the next morning, when Atif went to a meeting with Abu Nidal, Abu Nizar was not present. When Atif asked about him, Abu Nidal said he had returned to Algeria.

At lunchtime that day, Atif telephoned Abu Nizar's house in Algeria and learned that he had not arrived there. That afternoon, he asked Abu Nidal about this, only to be told that Abu Nizar was on his way to Lebanon.

"I sensed that something was up," Atif Abu Bakr told me in Tunis in 1990, "and I grew even more anxious when I discovered that Abu Nizar's things were still in his hotel room—he had been staying on the eighth floor of the Bab al-Bahr Hotel. They remained there until Atif Hammuda of the Finance Directorate collected them on October 25, eight days after his disappearance.

"A few days later, a telegram arrived from Lebanon to say that Abu Nizar had arrived there. Abu Nidal sent me a copy, which was in itself unusual, since he was not in the habit of sending me copies of telegrams he received. This convinced me that something was amiss."

Atif Abu Bakr had to go to Aden at this time and returned to Libya only some two months later, in early 1989. Abu Nizar had still not reappeared. Abu Nidal was evading questions about him, but he was beginning to make gross accusations against his former deputy, telling everyone that Abu Nizar had embezzled the organization's funds to buy property for himself and his family and that $40,000 was missing from his accounts.

As there was still no proof that Abu Nizar was dead, his friends hoped he was being held in one of Abu Nidal's prisons. In April 1989, Atif Abu Bakr confronted Abu Nidal. It was now six months since Abu Nizar's disappearance, and he wanted to know if there was still some way of rescuing him.

The meeting took place at night in the Andalus quarter of

Tripoli, in one of the safe houses Abu Nidal sometimes used. Another villa across the road housed his bodyguards, and as they talked in the large, well-furnished reception room, four of his armed men hovered between the kitchen and the hall, occasionally looking in to see if they were needed.

"I was alone," Atif told me, "and felt I had walked into a trap. There was no way out. Even supposing I managed to reach the street alive, I would not be able to get very far.

"I asked Abu Nidal how he could justify the detention, perhaps even the execution, of a senior member of the organization without the knowledge or consent of the leadership. A member of the command was missing, and none of his comrades knew whether he was alive or dead!

" 'Are you accusing your own deputy of being an agent?' I asked. 'How will you explain that to the organization? If Abu Nizar is guilty of treachery, then so is my nine-year-old daughter!' "

Atif told me he had made an effort to talk in the calm yet forthright manner he knew Abu Nidal would expect of him. Abu Nidal seemed nervous. He kept getting up and then sitting down. Atif thought he was planning to kill him. He started to argue that Abu Nizar was a Syrian agent. "But he was your deputy," Atif cried. "In charge of everything in your absence—the weapons, the buildings, the cadres. Why should he betray you now? How could he possibly have become a Syrian agent suddenly in Algeria? It just doesn't make sense."

Finally, Abu Nidal asked him point-blank if he thought Abu Nizar and Abd al-Rahman Isa were conspiring against him. Atif replied that he believed them to be as innocent as his own daughter. Abu Nidal glowered at him as if he wanted to have him killed there and then, but could not quite bring himself to do it.

"At last, he let me go at midnight," Atif told me. "To placate him, I agreed to see him the next day, but I came away absolutely convinced that he had murdered Abu Nizar."

A short while later, in May 1989, Atif Abu Bakr learned that Umm Nizar had written a long letter to the organization about her husband. Atif demanded to know its contents. So Abu Nidal and other members of the Central Committee came to his house and Amjad Ata agreed to read the letter aloud to the assembled company.

Atif described the scene to me. "Abu Nidal sat down opposite me and watched my face throughout the reading. 'You will see that this is not Umm Nizar's language,' he said. 'It must have been written for her by an intelligence agency!'

"In fact the letter was brave and to the point and was written in Umm Nizar's own hand. At one point she described how, in the search for her husband, she had gone to see Dr. Ghassan and Isam Maraqa in Sidon and how badly they had treated her and how humiliated she had felt."

Atif told me: "I became very upset and tears streamed down my face. Abu Nidal got Amjad Ata to stop reading and asked me what was the matter. I said it was nothing and asked them to read on. But I was not really listening any longer. I was thinking, Is this the right moment, or should I wait a little longer? I decided it was now or never.

"When Ata had finished, Abu Nidal asked me for my opinion. I then spoke clearly and simply:

" 'The fate of Umm Nizar is what is in store for every one of our wives! This is where we part company. You are a bunch of criminals!'

"After I had had my say, Abu Nidal tried to patch things up. He said he would get in touch with me when I was less upset. But his looks were murderous."

chapter

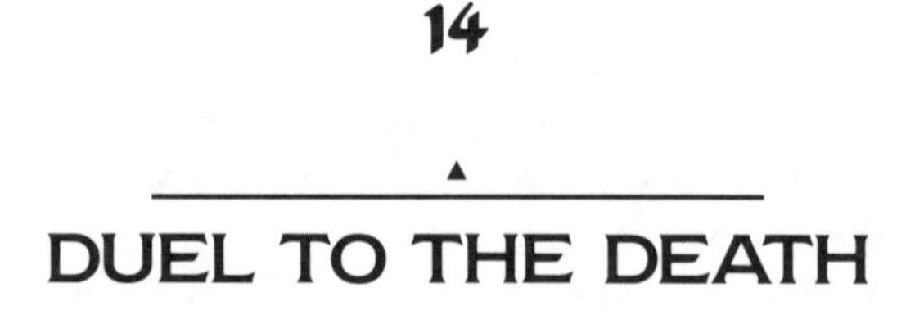

14

DUEL TO THE DEATH

In April 1987, Abu Iyad and Abu Nidal, two men who had tried to kill each other for a decade, met face-to-face in Algiers. Both were veterans of the world of intelligence, the former as the PLO's intelligence chief, the latter running his own large and well-funded service, with secret assets in many countries and an international network of hit men. They had fought many battles, but neither had scored a decisive win. They had once been friends, but their love turned to hate was a paradigm for the destructive quarrels that have plagued the Palestinian resistance movement from the beginning.

The protection Abu Nidal enjoyed at different times from various Arab states made it difficult for Abu Iyad to get at him. These were countries in which the PLO had vested interests: It could not simply hit and run without offending the local powers. Abu Iyad, too, was not an easy target. He was popular in the Palestinian movement and inspired loyalty. He was also well protected. It was difficult for Abu Nidal to find an assassin to gun him down. So each sought to neutralize the other by complicated diplomacy with Arab and European states and by penetration and manipulation, the traditional crafts of intelligence.

Abu Nidal's terrorism was Abu Iyad's greatest problem. His operations were so damaging to the Palestinian cause that Abu Iyad was forced to devote much time and energy to trying to stop them. He told me that since 1980, out of Abu Nidal's total of two hundred or so operations, the PLO had managed to foil about 120. "I feel we have spared the world a lot of horror. I don't particularly like mentioning these things because we don't want to be seen in the role of policing Europe!"

However, events in Lebanon in 1985–86 imposed a de facto truce on the two adversaries. As we have seen, during the War of the Camps, Abu Nidal's men sided with Fatah against Amal, the Syrian-backed Shi'ite militia. It was a healing experience. With Palestinian fighters joining forces on the ground, it made no sense for their leaders to go on trying to kill each other.

DIALOGUE IN ALGIERS

What had made the Algiers meeting possible was the eighteenth session of the Palestine National Council, the Palestinians' "parliament-in-exile," which met from April 20–26, 1987, at the Residence des Pins, a conference center some fifteen kilometers west of Algiers. This PNC session was billed as the "Session of Unity," and the mood among the Palestinian factions was conciliatory. Arafat was now under less pressure and therefore more inclined to be flexible: The Palestinian National Salvation Front, set up by his Syrian-backed opponents, was in decline. Abu Nidal had fallen out with the Syrians. His new friends Libya and, to a lesser extent, Algeria, the conference host, were both active behind the scenes trying to patch up intra-Palestinian quarrels.

Could the historic split in Fatah be mended? Could Abu Nidal and Fatah put an end to the war that had raged between them since 1974? The mediators worked hard. But each adversary feared the other's hidden agenda: Abu Nidal suspected that Abu Iyad was scheming to split his organization; Abu Iyad was convinced that Abu Nidal was plotting, with encouragement from Israel, to penetrate the PLO, brand it as a terrorist organization, and destroy it.

In Tripoli before the PNC session, Arafat and Abu Iyad were due to see Abu Nidal together, but at the last moment word came that Abu Nidal would not agree to meet with Abu Iyad. He was said to be enraged by an article in the French weekly *Le Nouvel Observateur* in which Abu Iyad was quoted as saying (erroneously, he later told me) that Abu Nidal's mother had been an Alawi servant girl. So Arafat went to the meeting alone, returning at 2 A.M. to the villa he was sharing with Abu Iyad.

"He knocked on my door," Abu Iyad later told me, "and seemed upset. 'I wish I'd not gone,' he said." It seemed that Abu Nidal had demanded to appoint representatives to the PLO's two key bodies, the Executive Committee and the Palestine National Council. When Arafat demurred, Abu Nidal had used coarse language and had raised his voice, in ways Arafat found unacceptable.

It took some deft mediation by the then head of Algerian intelligence, Lakhal Ayyat, and a senior Algerian diplomat, Lakhdar Brahimi (now Algeria's foreign minister), for a meeting to be arranged between Abu Iyad and Abu Nidal in a villa close to the Residence des Pins. Tactfully, the Algerians suggested that the two adversaries be accompanied only by Algerian bodyguards, to avoid the danger of a clash between their men.

Abu Iyad took up the story:

"I entered and saw him there—for the first time in fourteen years. He looked pale and ill and had a mustache. Although we were both tense and cold, we shook hands and embraced. We were alone. He was modest, humble, and overly polite. We couldn't decide how to start on the painful subjects we had come to discuss."

Abu Iyad said that he wanted to ask Abu Nidal about many things—about their attacks on each other, about why he had mounted certain operations, about his hopes for the future—and about why he had behaved so badly with Arafat.

Abu Nidal replied that he had been offended by a huge guard Arafat had brought with him, who had remained in the room during their entire meeting. The man made him uncomfortable, but Arafat had not dismissed him. His main complaint was, of course, that Arafat had refused to let him join the PLO.

They sparred for a long while, reviewing the history of their mutual assassination attempts. "You taught me how to kill!" Abu Nidal exclaimed. "You killed my friend Ahmad Abd al-Ghafur. I'm only following your example." Abu Iyad took him through the list of PLO representatives shot in cold blood—Hammami, Yassin, Qalaq, Khudr, Sartawi. Abu Nidal would admit only to having killed Hammami—because of his secret contacts with Israelis. He deserved to die, Abu Nidal declared, as an example to others. "What about the others?" Abu Iyad inquired, and when he taxed him with being penetrated and manipulated by Israel, Abu Nidal calmly admitted it. Yes, he said, Israeli agents were present in his organization. They sometimes fed him information, but he was trying to liquidate them one by one.

His conversation, Abu Iyad told me, was full of wild and empty boasts. He claimed to have captured four hundred Jordanian intelligence agents and said he was going to kill them all in a single day. He had told the Algerians that he would kill five thousand Europeans if any harm befell the delegates to the Palestine National Council meeting in Algiers. He had men awaiting his orders in over thirty countries, including agents in the White House and at the Saudi royal court. He needed his vast wealth, which he put at hundreds of millions of dollars, to buy such well-placed agents. Grandly, he offered to share these assets if Fatah chose to cooperate.

Bravado soon gave way to bathos. "You are the only one who really understands me," he confided. And he unbuttoned his shirt to show Abu Iyad the scars from his heart surgery. "I'm a sick man," he said. "Months pass without my being able to leave the house. I will probably die within the year. But before I die, I want to be recognized. I want to tell the world that I've abandoned the secret life in order to enter politics." He said he considered his organization second only to Fatah in the Palestinian movement. It should therefore be represented on all Palestinian bodies, like other factions. "*You* have to help me achieve this," he pleaded.

Now, Abu Iyad thought, the strategy was clear. Abu Nidal wanted to be let into the core institutions so as to be able to discredit the whole PLO and ensure that it never escaped the terrorist label.

"But you've hated the PLO all your life," Abu Iyad countered. "You know very well that we can't have you represented inside the PLO as Fatah: The Revolutionary Council. We're not in the business of selling varieties of watermelons! We can't have dozens of Fatahs on display—Arafat's and yours and Abu Musa's and so on. It's absurd!"

Abu Nidal became angry. When he calmed down, he asked whether there was to be any concession to him at all. Abu Iyad suggested a six-month truce, during which Abu Nidal's intentions and behavior would be put to the test.

" 'What sort of an agreement do you want?' Abu Nidal asked me. 'Here, write it down.' He was reluctant to write himself, because he was conscious of having a very childish hand, so I took pen and paper and wrote the following:

"1. a halt to all propaganda wars between us;
"2. cooperation on all matters to do with the occupied territories;
"3. a complete ban on all terrorist operations—against Arabs, Westerners, and Israelis."

Abu Nidal said he had to consult his members before agreeing. They set up a time to meet again. At the second meeting, at a seaside villa closely guarded by Algerian intelligence, Abu Nidal put on a great show of anger: "What sort of an agreement is this?" he asked querulously. "You want me to stop killing and mounting operations. You want me to shut up and not meddle in anything. If I agreed to all this, what would I have left to do?

"Look," he argued with Abu Iyad. "You're an overt organization and I'm an underground one. Why don't we work together and complement each other?"

"Fine," Abu Iyad replied, "but on condition that we give the orders."

Abu Nidal seemed to consider the suggestion seriously. He proposed one last discussion session, at which his senior colleagues would join them. But no sooner had they all gathered than Abu Iyad realized he had been wasting his time. With his men in the room, Abu Nidal became abusive, mocking, and aggressive.

"Let me tell you a little story about Abu Iyad," he told the meeting. "On the day of Karameh [the battle in 1968 when Israel attacked a Fatah camp in Jordan] people were frantically looking for Abu Iyad, worried that he'd been killed. 'Don't you worry,' I said to them. 'He's safe, all right! In fact, he's at my house, shivering with fear!' "

Abu Iyad could hardly believe his ears. "You liar!" he cried. "You shameless liar! It was you whom no one could find." It was the last time they ever saw each other.

ATIF ABU BAKR'S DEFECTION

The Algiers negotiations of April 1987 proved no more than another round in the duel between Abu Nidal and Abu Iyad. Convinced more than ever that the Mossad was directing Abu Nidal's moves, Abu Iyad sought to penetrate his organization and encourage defections. He knew that an unstable internal situation would worry Abu Nidal, force him to switch his energies from foreign operations and protect himself.

Some Palestinians later came to believe that Abu Iyad had planted Atif Abu Bakr, an old and crafty Fatah loyalist, on Abu Nidal as an agent provocateur as early as 1985, to provoke an internal explosion in his ranks. Abu Nidal certainly thought so when Abu Bakr broke away. I have talked at length to both Abu Iyad and Atif Abu Bakr, and I doubt this theory. Abu Bakr seemed too principled and prominent a revolutionary to lend himself to such a scheme.

Abu Nidal carried out few terrorist operations in the remaining months of 1987, the period in which he destroyed his own forces in Lebanon, killings that may have been inspired in part by fear that Abu Iyad was stirring up his comrades against him. These internal massacres reached their bloody culmination in October 1988 with the murder of Abu Nizar, by which time Abu Nidal had resumed his terrorist career with the attacks in Cyprus, the Sudan, and Greece.

By 1989, the brief moment of intra-Palestinian reconciliation had passed, and Abu Nidal's organization, more vicious and dangerous than ever, had returned underground. By May of that year, Atif Abu Bakr had had enough. The murder of Abu Nizar, the massacre of hundreds of fighters, and Abu Nidal's persistent resort to senseless terrorism, which greatly damaged the Palestinian cause, drove him into open rebellion.

News of the mass killings could not be hidden for long, and when the men in Libya learned of the horrific happenings in South Lebanon and the Lebanon group heard of the torture and killings in Libya, Abu Nidal's members scrambled to save their skins. Dozens of fighters sought refuge with other Palestinian factions in Lebanon; dozens more fled to Syria. Some cadres escaped to Jordan, others to the Gulf, to Europe, and to Canada. From Libya, where the organization trembled under Abu Nidal's iron command, some men managed to flee to Tunisia. Among those who remained, morale was low.

Abu Bakr remained for a while in Tripoli, but after hearing the letter from Abu Nizar's wife and having called Abu Nidal and his men a bunch of criminals, he broke from the organization. Like Abu Iyad, he was now convinced that Abu Nidal was an instrument of Israeli policy. He doubled the locks on his doors; recruited friends in Ahmad Jibril's organization to serve as his bodyguards; and warned Abu Nidal not to try to kill him. He let it be known that he was thinking of leaving for Moscow, Aden, or Budapest, only to learn that Abu Nidal had said he hoped it would be Budapest, because there he could kill him easily.

Abu Bakr's main anxiety was for his wife and nine-year-old daughter. He feared that if he were kidnapped and his house keys taken from him, Abu Nidal's thugs might abduct his family. Whenever he left the house, he hid his keys under a stone in a garden across the road. One day, watching him from an upstairs window, his wife saw him hide the keys. She went down to recover them and that evening asked him for an explanation.

"You're obviously in some danger," she said. "It would be better if you told me." Her first question was about Abu Nizar. She wanted to know what had happened to him. When Atif told her that Abu Nidal had killed him the previous October, she said she had guessed as much when she heard him talking on the telephone to Abu Nizar's wife in Damascus.

Atif Abu Bakr told his wife about the secret trials, the torture and the killings, the children who had disappeared or been given to strangers to bring up. Although she had had some knowledge of her husband's work, she was profoundly shocked by what she heard. Horror at the details, or panic for her own child, affected her eyesight: She could hardly see. An eye doctor found that her pupils had become unusually enlarged.

On August 28, 1989, Atif Abu Bakr managed to escape by air to Algeria and immediately made arrangements for his wife and daughter to join him there. He had procured two joint diplomatic passports for his wife and daughter, one Algerian, the other Yemeni. Speaking to her in Czech on the telephone—a language they had learned in Prague when he was the PLO representative there—he instructed her to take the next day's plane to Algiers, using her Algerian passport. For safety's sake, she was to arrange to be accompanied to the airport by their Libyan neighbors and by Ahmad Jibril's local representative.

But a disappointment awaited her. Airport officials, probably in Abu Nidal's pay, kept her waiting for five hours as they examined her papers, until the plane finally left without her. She knew she was trapped. Defiantly, she ripped up her air tickets in front of Abu Nidal's man at the airport. "Tell Abu Nidal," she said, "that if he's spoiling for a fight, he should go fight Israel and not a woman!" Not daring to return home, she asked Ahmad Jibril's representative to take her and her daughter in for the night.

Meanwhile, in Algiers, Atif Abu Bakr decided not to meet the plane from Libya for fear Abu Nidal would attempt to kill him there. So he sent someone else, who reported to him that his wife was not on the plane. He rang Ahmad Jibril's representative in Tripoli and learned to his relief that his wife and child were with him.

"Speaking in Czech, I said to her, 'Follow my instructions carefully. I'm going to ring Abu Nidal's people and ask why there was a problem at the airport. I'll seem very normal. I'll tell them you are planning to leave on Sunday and ask them to make the necessary arrangements.

" 'In the meantime, you must leave tonight by road for Tunisia. Travel on your Yemeni passport and ask our Libyan neighbors to go with you.' "

So Abu Bakr's wife left by car with her daughter and their Libyan friends, arriving safely in Tunis after a twelve-hour journey. It was only then that her eyesight returned to normal. Abu Bakr flew in from Algiers, and they were reunited there.

THE EMERGENCY LEADERSHIP

Abu Bakr was a commanding figure in Palestinian circles, and his defection was a serious blow to Abu Nidal. Anxious to limit the damage, he sent a delegation to Algiers in October 1989 to offer Abu Bakr Swiss visas for himself and his family, full expenses, and a cash bonus of half a million dollars if he would agree to end their quarrel. Led by a member of the Political Bureau, Shawki Muhammad Yusif (code-named Munir Ahmad), the delegation included the demoted intelligence chief Abd al-Rahman Isa. But Abu Bakr refused. Instead, he met Isa secretly and, with the agreement of Algerian intelligence, talked him into defecting as well, which Isa did in late October 1989, joining Abu Bakr in Algiers.

On October 27, Abd al-Rahman Isa issued a lengthy communiqué devoted almost entirely to denouncing the "blind executions" of members of the organization, and especially the assassination of Abu Nizar. He called for the facts to be put before an international tribunal.

On November 1, 1989, Abd al-Rahman Isa and Atif Abu Bakr issued a joint communiqué, which was in effect a declaration of war—a war that at the time of writing is still raging. They announced the formation of an Emergency Leadership, with the declared aim of taking control of the organization and punishing the criminal Abu Nidal. "Our martyrs fell in the wrong wars," they declared. "The operations of Rome, Vienna, Sudan, Athens, Paris, and Karachi were senseless and did us immense harm. Our martyrs should have fought in Palestine, but Abu Nidal turned his back on the just struggle. We will never compromise with a butcher whose hands are stained with the blood of our brothers." Their agenda stated: no to intra-Palestinian killings; no to the language of blood and to futile foreign operations; yes to the PLO, the sole legitimate representative of the Palestinians; yes to full support for the *intifada.*

Disgusted by Abu Nidal's methods, Abu Bakr, poet, thinker, and sharp-tongued radical, returned with relief to Fatah, the movement to which he had made a lifelong commitment. Abd al-Rahman Isa was a practical man, not a theoretician. He was reluctant to renounce terror unconditionally, because for twenty years he had been Abu Nidal's closest associate, the planner of many of his operations. Isa knew the real identity of the cadres; the location of the secret arms caches and bank accounts; the contents of letters Abu Nidal had exchanged with foreign governments and intelligence services. Unlike Abu Bakr, he had no nostalgia for Fatah and, as an old-style rejectionist, he could not easily rid himself of the notion that Fatah was a treacherous organization.

If there was a Mossad link with Abu Nidal, Abd al-Rahman Isa apparently knew nothing about it. He was not close to Dr. Ghassan or to his own replacement, Alaa, and he may have lost his job because he was beginning to ask awkward questions. In any case, he was a loser in the internal power struggle. After Abu

Nizar's murder, Isa had begun to think about his own safety. Abu Nidal had killed his right-hand man. Might he not soon turn against his left hand? Fearing Abu Nidal's vengeance, he fled to Algiers.

As he had done with Abu Bakr, Abu Nidal sent several emissaries to urge Isa to return to Libya for talks. These included a prominent Egyptian soldier, General Sa'd al-Din Shazli, who had been President Sadat's chief of staff during the 1973 October War but, having fallen out with him, had taken refuge in Algeria. Isa knew enough to say no. "Let them send me Abu Nizar as an emissary," he told the general. "They claim he is still alive. If so, let me shake his hand. If I see that he is well, I'll go back!" He knew, of course, that Abu Nizar was by then long since in his grave, buried in cement under Abu Nidal's Libyan villa.

On the morning of April 25, 1990, when Isa was standing alone outside his seafront villa on the outskirts of Algiers, he was attacked by three men wearing stocking masks, who tried to bundle him into a car. He put up some resistance, but they attacked him with an ax, shot him twice, and made their escape, leaving him for dead. He was severely wounded, but he lived. Surgeons at the Algiers military hospital managed to save his sight, but they had to remove one of his kidneys. He identified his assailants: Hamdan Abu Asba, Abu Nidal's chief representative in Algiers, and his deputy, Hisham Muhammad Saqr; the third man was believed to be one of Abu Nidal's radio operators.

Once Atif Abu Bakr and Abd al-Rahman Isa had published their communiqué setting up the Emergency Leadership, messages of support flowed in from other disgruntled members in Lebanon, Syria, and Algeria. An early recruit was Basil (or, by his real name, Ziad Sahmud), commander of the People's Army in the Bekaa region of Lebanon, who had become sickened by the mass killings of his own men. He brought other cadres with him. These were men who had escaped the purges by the skin of their teeth. They had seen their comrades slaughtered and were desperate to avoid the same fate.

Armed and financed by Fatah, protected by Abu Iyad, the Emergency Leadership was soon battling it out with Abu Nidal in the refugee camps of southern Lebanon. In mid-June 1990, tit-for-tat assassinations in Rashidiyeh, a camp near Tyre housing some fifteen thousand Palestinian refugees, escalated into a gun battle in which Abu Nidal's men were routed. A fiercer engagement followed in September further up the coast, near Sidon, at Ain al-Hilweh, the biggest of Lebanon's camps, which housed 150,000 refugees. In a three-day battle, eighty guerrillas were killed and another 250 wounded as Abu Nidal's fortified headquarters were overrun.

However, Abu Nidal still retained a number of strongholds, notably in the hill villages of Bqasta and Karkha, near Sidon, where some of his most sensitive committees are housed in territory controlled by the Druze leader Walid Jumblat; and in Sidon itself, where his computer center is located and several of his top cadres live under the protection of Sidon's "strongman," the Nasserist leader Mustafa Sa'd. Abu Nidal pays his "hosts" tens of thousands of dollars a month.

In the summer of 1991, as this book went to press, the two sides were still skirmishing in and around Lebanon's camps, but by this time Abu Nidal had won an important round—perhaps the biggest coup of his career—with the murder of his old adversary Abu Iyad, in Tunis on January 14, 1991.

WHO ORDERED THE KILLING?

There is no doubt that Abu Nidal killed Abu Iyad, using Hamza Abu Zaid as his instrument. So much is agreed by everyone I interviewed in connection with the case. This view rests in the first place on Hamza's own confession: He told his interrogators that he had been ordered to kill Abu Iyad by a man in Abu Nidal's organization. Moreover, the terms in which he denounced his victim—traitor, corrupter of the Palestinian revolution, "enemy within"—are those that Abu Nidal has used to denounce Fatah over the years. At the very moment of gunning down Abu Iyad, Hamza cried out: "Let Atif Abu Bakr help you now!"—a clear indication that Abu Nidal wanted vengeance on the man he believed Abu Iyad had planted on him to destroy his organization. During the siege in the villa, Hamza, as we have seen, repeatedly demanded that Atif Abu Bakr be brought to him, presumably so that he could kill him, too.

Abu Iyad often said to me with a wry smile that Abu Nidal hated him not only because of their many attempts to kill each other, not just because Abu Iyad had kept him out of the PLO and had engineered splits and defections in his organization, but because Abu Nidal could not bear to acknowledge his debt to Abu Iyad for the help and protection he had given him in his early years. The murder of Abu Iyad must therefore be seen as a final settlement of old scores.

Abu Nidal had plenty of reasons to kill Abu Iyad, but Western and Arab intelligence officers I talked to speculated about a possible "hidden hand" behind the killing—with Libya, Iraq, and Israel among the suspects.

PLO sources concede that Abu Iyad had been on poor terms with Qaddafi for several years. It was partly a matter of personal dislike, they said, and partly Qaddafi's knowledge that Abu Iyad was friendly with Abd al-Mun'im al-Huni, a former head of Libyan intelligence who had escaped to Cairo and who Qaddafi suspected was conspiring to topple him. Qaddafi had also been angered by Abu Iyad's efforts to destabilize Abu Nidal's organization, which was under his protection and which he considered an arm of his own intelligence.

According to these sources, the Libyan leader would probably have given Abu Nidal his permission to kill Abu Iyad if Abu Nidal had asked for it, but they doubted that he had initiated the suggestion. Qaddafi would have feared PLO reprisals, or rousing the hostility of the Palestinian community at large. Just as Shi'ites had not forgiven Qaddafi for the disappearance in Libya, and presumed murder, of the charismatic Lebanese Shi'ite cleric Imam Musa al-Sadr in 1978, so Palestinians would not easily forgive him the death of so prestigious a Palestinian leader as Abu Iyad. While Qaddafi might not have intervened to stop the murder, his own motives would probably not have been strong enough to order it.

Some press comment has suggested that Saddam Hussein, rather than Qaddafi, was behind the killing of Abu Iyad. The argument states that Abu Iyad, unlike Arafat, was not happy with the PLO's alliance with Baghdad and, for the alliance to survive, had to be eliminated. Furthermore, there have also been allegations that Abu Nidal left Libya for Iraq just before the outbreak of the 1991 Gulf war, transferring his allegiance back to his first sponsor.

It is true that Arafat was much more vocal in support of Iraq during the crisis than was Abu Iyad. But there was no divergence between them on the fundamental PLO position: to uphold the principle of an Iraqi withdrawal from Kuwait; at the same time to reject American intervention and avoid war; to find a settlement within an Arab framework; to demand "linkage" between Kuwait and Palestine as the basis for a peaceful solution—that is, to put Iraq's occupation of Kuwait and Israel's occupation of Arab territories on the same footing.

This was the formula Saddam Hussein had proposed for a negotiated settlement of the crisis. He, too, had demanded linkage. He wanted Palestinian support, indeed whatever Arab support he could muster. In order to give his quarrel with Kuwait a pan-Arab dimension, he had posed as the Palestinians' champion from the early days of the crisis. It therefore makes little sense to suppose that he would have chosen that critical moment, with war only hours away, to kill Arafat's closest colleague.

I found no confirmation of the rumor that Abu Nidal had moved back to Baghdad. According to my best informants, he spent the war in Libya, where Qaddafi, afraid of allied retaliation, kept him under tight control. According to Western intelligence sources, Qaddafi would not even allow Abu Nidal to use his radio station during the conflict, for fear that Libya would be accused of sponsoring international terrorism. Not a single act of terrorism attributable to Abu Nidal was reported throughout the 1990–1991 Gulf crisis anywhere in the world—except for the killing of Abu Iyad. If Saddam had controlled Abu Nidal, as some have alleged, he would undoubtedly have used him against Iraq's many enemies.

Of the four founding fathers of Fatah, only Arafat remains. Muhammad Yusif al-Najjar was killed by an Israeli assassination squad in Beirut in 1973; Khalil al-Wazir (Abu Jihad) was killed by Israeli commandos in Tunis in 1988. It is not inconceivable that Abu Iyad's murder, too, and that of his colleague Abu al-Hol, might be part of this pattern.

Abu Iyad's killing took place in January 1991, on the eve of the allied attack on Iraq. Ever since Iraq invaded Kuwait in August 1990, Israel had urged the use of force against Saddam Hussein. In public statements and private advocacy, in contacts with the U.S. and other governments, in comments and reports and urgings by its friends in the media, Israel pressed resolutely for war. It opposed any concession to Saddam and any negotiation with him. It secured two crucial undertakings from President Bush: that the U.S. would accept no linkage between Iraq's occupation of Kuwait and Israel's occupation of the West Bank, Gaza, East Jerusalem, the Golan

Heights, and South Lebanon; and that the U.S. would destroy Iraq's nuclear, chemical, and biological weapons—otherwise Israel would do the job itself.

In 1967, Nasser's mistake of closing the Tiran straits gave Israel the occasion to smash him. In 1990, Saddam Hussein in turn presented the world with a *casus belli,* and Israel was determined in this case to make the most of it. During Iraq's eight-year war with Iran, Iraq had acquired and developed ballistic missiles, chemical weapons, and other systems that challenged Israel's military advantage, a development Israel viewed with alarm. Hence its eagerness for war against Iraq over Kuwait. Israel knew that the destruction of Iraq as a military power would transform its own strategic environment as radically as had the defeat of Egypt in 1967—and this time, if the allies did the job, at no cost to itself. Israel would retain its regional monopoly of weapons of mass destruction. It would be without challenge.

The United States had its own reason for going to war, to do with overcoming the Vietnam syndrome; preserving the status quo in the Arabian peninsula, which Saddam threatened to upset; controlling Middle East oil resources; and affirming American supremacy in the "new world order" emerging after the collapse of communism and the disintegration of the Soviet Union. Nevertheless, Israel strongly urged American intervention, and influenced America's decision to fight.

Of course Iraq's Arab opponents—Saudi Arabia, Syria, Egypt, and the others—also wanted Saddam weakened, removed from Kuwait, and contained behind his frontiers. They would have been happy to see him overthrown. But only helpless Kuwait wanted Iraq destroyed. Even Saddam's old enemy Assad, of Syria, knew that the destruction of Iraq would enfeeble the whole Arab world, and until the last minute he pleaded with Saddam to pull back and avoid war. Israel, however, wanted Iraq destroyed.

Beyond wanting Iraq's military challenge removed, Israel wanted to resolve the Palestine problem on its own terms once the Gulf crisis was over. Israel knew that after the war, the Bush administration was likely to address the Arab-Israeli conflict more vigorously than before, and Israel would insist that the PLO would have no part in it.

But in the prelude to Desert Storm, the PLO's activities posed a considerable threat to this Israeli agenda. In Baghdad, Arafat was straining to pull Saddam back from war. If he could persuade him to start withdrawing from Kuwait, or even to say he would do so, it would be far more difficult for the coalition to attack Iraq. Moreover, if Arafat could claim credit for defusing the crisis, the PLO's greatly enhanced prestige might guarantee it a place at the Arab-Israeli negotiating table. From Israel's point of view, the PLO was a problem.

On January 14, 1991, as the UN ultimatum was about to expire and the world held its breath, Abu Nidal's agent Hamza Abu Zaid killed Abu Iyad and Abu al-Hol, the heads of PLO intelligence and security. A grieving Arafat abandoned his diplomatic efforts in Baghdad and immediately flew back to Tunis to mourn his murdered colleagues. The Palestinian movement was thrown into disarray. As Desert Storm broke over Iraq, the PLO experienced yet another defeat.

But what of Abu Nidal's motives? His main business was now either Mafia-style extortion and protection rackets or anti-Palestinian terrorist operations that seemed in Israel's interest. I was still unsure whether there was a Mossad connection, but if there was one, he was part of it. How could a Palestinian who had called himself a patriot cause such tremendous damage to Palestinian interests, damage that fit so neatly with Israeli interests? If Abu Iyad was right that Abu Nidal was an Israeli agent, the evidence was still circumstantial and would remain so until the Israelis themselves tell their side of the story, if they ever do. In the meantime, there were still loose ends to Abu Iyad's theory, notably Abu Nidal's operations against Israeli and Jewish targets, which Israel could not possibly condone, however much they may have lent Abu Nidal credibility in Arab eyes as a cover for his real activities. Perhaps, if Abu Iyad's suspicions were correct, these were the work of wild cards in his organization who were not in on the Mossad connection or whom he did not fully control. What complicated the puzzle further was Israel's odd behavior in not pursuing and punishing Abu Nidal as it had every other Palestinian faction.

Pondering the puzzle of Abu Nidal, I remembered what so many of my sources had told me—that for him, self was all-important, his personal security paramount. His deals with Iraq, Syria, and Libya had all been in return for protection. Protection was what he craved. He could not survive without it. In the terrorist underground he inhabited, one country could protect him better than any other: Israel was the most powerful state in the Middle East, the only one whose planes, commandos, hit teams, and intelligence agents, indifferent to national boundaries, could reach any part of the region. Israel had a long record of seeking out and destroying its enemies. Israel could easily end Abu Nidal's career if it chose to do so. But it had not done so. Why? Was he still useful? Abu Nidal needed immunity. Israel needed his services. Here, I reflected, was yet another source of Abu Iyad's conviction.

EPILOGUE

After Abu Iyad's murder in January 1991, I tried to trace Jorde to the Mediterranean haunts where we had first met the previous summer. He had disappeared. Some of his mates said he was afraid Abu Nidal would kill him and he had gone into hiding. Others believed he had made his way back to Spain, to the tourist bars and discos of Barcelona. He was resourceful, and I had no doubt that he would survive somehow, perhaps even cross my path again one day.

But Jorde was not the only one to hide. The murder of Abu Iyad robbed many people of their protector. In Tunis, where the PLO had gone after being thrown out of Beirut in 1982, it was as if someone had overturned an ant heap, sending its inhabitants in all directions. The PLO had not recovered its nerve since the Israelis had killed its military supremo, Abu Jihad, in Tunis in 1988. The murder of Abu Iyad made matters even worse. By killing Abu Iyad, Abu Nidal had shown that he could hit the very top of the PLO's intelligence and security apparatus. No one was safe. Arafat's organization was shown up yet again as lax, chaotic, and infiltrated. No one trusted anyone else and PLO morale was terrible.

Atif Abu Bakr and his colleagues in the Emergency Leadership were also in trouble. They had vowed to wrest Abu Nidal's organization from him. But having lost Abu Iyad, they too dispersed, terrified of being killed. Some went underground. Others, like Abu Bakr, who was now penniless, scraped up what they could and left Tunis in search of safer haven abroad. These men could scarcely count how many times they had been forced to pack their bags.

The disaster suffered by the PLO and by the Emergency Leadership was soon made vastly worse by the ignominious defeat of Saddam Hussein, whom Arafat had supported. Arafat, who had wanted to be recognized by the West, now found himself condemned by much of it, and by most Arabs too—by Saudi Arabia, Egypt, Kuwait, and their allies in the wartime coalition, who had now stopped sending money to the PLO. Many Palestinians were now sick of Arafat, although most could not say so out loud. The structure of Palestinian resistance outside the occupied territories was collapsing. Years of diplomatic effort had been thrown away. By the summer of 1991, the PLO seemed weak and more isolated than ever.

Arafat's misfortune was Abu Nidal's good fortune, although this was not always understood by outsiders at the time. During the 1990–1991 Gulf conflict, the Western press had speculated that Abu Nidal would place his terrorist network at the disposal of Saddam Hussein, his first sponsor. But this was to misread Abu Nidal, who was too shrewd to back a loser; nor would he choose the same side the PLO chose. Far from supporting Iraq, he had immediately exploited the conflict to ingratiate himself with members of the anti-Saddam coalition.

In the early summer of 1991, as if suddenly oblivious of his terrorist record, Egypt, incredibly, let Abu Nidal open offices in Cairo—apparently, to punish Arafat for choosing the wrong side. With this move, Abu Nidal had been given a second chance in an Arab world more deeply divided than ever by the Gulf war.

Abu Nidal is a professional killer who has sold his deadly services certainly to the Arabs and perhaps to the Israelis as well. His genius has been to understand that states will commit any crime in the name of national interest. A criminal like Abu Nidal can flourish doing their dirty work. He could not have survived if his "clients" had not found him useful. They are responsible for his actions. Iraq set him up; Syria took him over; Libya inherited him; whether or not Israel manipulated and exploited him—and at the very least the evidence suggests there is a case to answer—it has certainly benefited from his attacks on the moderate PLO and has done nothing to stop him despite his attacks on Jewish and Israeli targets. And now Egypt has resuscitated him in opposition to Arafat, whom it despises for supporting Saddam.

Abu Nidal has served many masters with many interests. His shrewd grasp of regional politics, his lack of moral restraint, and his talent for survival have made him the king of the Middle East underworld, a world-class gangster.

Throughout Abu Nidal's career, the thread has been his hostility to Yasser Arafat and the PLO, a hostility shared by each of his sponsors, including most recently Egypt. This provides the clue to his success. Israel has for years wanted to destroy the PLO. Abu Nidal's Arab sponsors have also found the PLO threatening, and though they have been willing to buy it off, they have also felt it necessary to contain and enfeeble it, so as to frustrate Arafat's ambition of independent policy making. For years Abu Nidal has kept the Palestinian national movement down and both Arabs and Israelis have benefited.

Arab leaders have publicly supported the Palestinian cause, but they have, almost without exception, distrusted the PLO, which has often challenged their authority in their own countries, attracted Israeli reprisals, and even threatened to drag them into war. The PLO must share part of the blame for this Arab hostility. Under Arafat's leadership, it allowed itself to get involved in Arab squabbles; it clashed at various times with the state interests of Jordan, Lebanon, Syria, Tunisia and, most recently, Kuwait; its bureaucracy is incompetent and often corrupt; it clung too long to hollow warlike slogans and was fatally slow in defining realistic political objectives; it was hopeless at presenting its case to the West; it has been a babel of conflicting and self-serving voices rather than a disciplined liberation movement.

Yet Arafat is still owed the credit for renouncing terrorism and attempting to seek a negotiated settlement with Israel since 1974—a position that so alarmed both Israeli and Arab rejectionists that the most committed PLO doves were murdered by Israeli and Arab killers, the latter, Abu Iyad believed, acting on Israel's behalf. The truth is that the PLO has for years been the main victim of terrorism rather than its perpetrator, the antithesis of the popular perception encouraged by Israeli propaganda.

Today, although battered and stumbling from Israeli and Arab assaults, the PLO remains, for lack of an alternative, the champion of Palestinian aspirations for a homeland. Arafat will sooner or later pass from the scene, the *intifada* may be crushed or die from exhaustion, but Palestinian nationalism will not go away—and will perhaps become more violent—so long as there are five million people alive who call themselves Palestinian. The next Abu Nidal who emerges may not so easily be turned against his own people.

Until the Palestinians' legitimate grievances are met, Palestinians, and perhaps all Arabs, will never live in peace with Israel. The Arab leaders' betrayal of the Palestinians makes a joke of Arab nationalism, while Palestinian suffering at Israel's hands is the blackest stain on Israel's national record.

The Arab states have dealt harshly with the Palestinians out of weakness, probably because they could not defend them against a far more powerful Israel. One reason Arab leaders hate the PLO is that it is an unwelcome reminder of Arab impotence. Israel, meanwhile, has dealt harshly with the Palestinians from strength, because there was no one around to restrain it. No countervailing Arab power, no force in the region, and, apparently, no international pressure has sought to make Israel desist from the brutalities, listed by Amnesty International and others, that it inflicts on its captive Palestinian population.

Many of these problems—Israeli occupation, guerrilla resistance, civilian suffering, terror—stem from Israel's victory in 1967 over Egypt, Syria, and Jordan, when it seized great tracts of territory and emerged as an imperial power immeasurably stronger than all its neighbors put together. Isaac Deutscher, a historian of the Russian revolution, was one of the first to observe that colonizing a million or more Arabs would hurt Israel. He quoted the bitter German phrase *Man kann sich totsiegen:* "You can drive yourself victoriously into your grave."

Just a few days after the Six-Day War, Deutscher, a Jew and a distinguished anti-Stalinist, told an interviewer (*New Left Review,* June 23, 1967): "It was only with disgust that I could watch on television the scenes from Israel in those days; the displays of the conquerors' pride and brutality; the outbursts of chauvinism; and the wild celebrations of the inglorious triumph, all contrasting sharply with the pictures of Arab suffering and desolation, the treks of Jordanian refugees and the bodies of Egyptian soldiers killed by thirst in the desert. I looked at the medieval figures of the rabbis and *hassidim* jumping with joy at the Wailing Wall; and I felt how the ghosts of Talmudic obscurantism—and I know these only too well—crowded in on the country, and how the reactionary atmosphere in Israel had grown dense and stifling. Then came the many interviews with General Dayan, the hero and saviour, with the political mind of a regimental sergeant-major, ranting about annexations and venting a raucous callousness about the fate of the Arabs in the conquered areas. ('What do they matter to me?' 'As far as I am concerned, they may stay or they may go.')"

What would Deutscher have thought, I wonder, of Shamir and Rabin, of Arens, Sharon, Geula Cohen, and the rest of them, of the bone-breaking beatings and the tortures, of the grisly detention camps and the pitiless curfews, of the death squads, of the children murdered by the score, of the Palestinian girl of nineteen I read about the other day who was forced to give birth while handcuffed to the bars of her Israeli hospital bed?

How can Jews, who have known far greater suffering themselves, do such things? For the miserable career of Abu Nidal might never have happened had Israel been willing to talk with the PLO in 1974, when Arafat sent his four messages to Henry Kissinger saying that he was ready to sit down.

The Israeli writer Amos Oz says that Israelis and Palestinians have gone mad and, for their own protection, need to be separated until they can recover their sanity. This book describes a case of dementia. I have written it to show what bloodstained lunacy goes on behind the scenes. Palestinians and Israelis have been killing one another over a pocket handkerchief of territory—the West Bank—captured by Israel in 1967. Palestinian hopes of identity and self-respect rest on this sliver of land: For them, anything less than self-government there means a continued diaspora or bitter servitude. They kill and die to get it back. But many Israelis, claiming that the West Bank is an integral part of the "land of Israel," will kill and die rather than give it up. Without peace, the prospect ahead is of more terror and counterterror of the cruel, remorseless sort I have described in this book.

Over the years, I have come to believe that Israel's long-term security lies not in crushing Palestinian nationalism and the PLO but in coming to terms with them. Far from threatening Israel, a Palestinian statelet on its borders would strengthen Israel, by gaining it full acceptance into the Middle Eastern family.

Israelis tend to express their situation in existential terms as if under constant threat of extinction. But Israel faces no existential threat. The last time it faced such a threat was in the brief truce during the 1948 war, as Ezer Weizman, an Israeli war hero and former air force chief, has publicly acknowledged. The debate today is not about Israel's existence—that question was settled over forty years ago—but about the terms and nature of the peace that it must make with its Arab hinterland. It is a peace that I, for one, involved in studying the area for the past three decades, ardently hope for.

Although the Arabs want peace, there are in my estimation two things that they will not accept and that, if Israel insists on them, are bound to breed further terrorist violence such as Abu Nidal's, and in due course further wars. The first is the permanent oppression and dispersal of the Palestinian people: If Israel wants real peace, it must make room for a Palestinian homeland, as a partner not an adversary, within the boundaries of historic Palestine.

The second thing the region will not tolerate is permanent Israeli domination. Accepting Israel as a major player in the Middle East system, competing and interacting with Egypt, Syria, Saudi Arabia, and the others, is something the Arab players are reconciled to, indeed expect and look to. But they are not ready to live indefinitely in the shadow of Israeli power, in fear of attack by its far superior military force. Vulnerability and humiliation inevitably drive them to acquire the means to hold Israel in check. Such deterrent means may not yet be available to Israel's weak and divided neighbors, but the quest for them will go on—and, most likely, cause Israel to preempt, setting off a new cycle of violence.

Yet a stable and long-lasting peace between Israel and its neighbors can only rest on mutual deterrence, on an Arab-Israeli balance of power, and eventually on good neighborliness. Israel's security cannot forever be maintained at the cost of the insecurity of its neighbors—the formula of successive Israeli and American governments over the decades.

Readers must reach their own conclusions about Abu Nidal, bearing in mind that Abu Iyad and his Fatah allies had every reason to make a case against Abu Nidal and Israel, their two greatest enemies. If, despite his crimes, he is judged to be a Palestinian "patriot," then he proves how the conflict has reduced to gangsterism the Palestinians' yearning for a homeland. If Abu Iyad and others are right that he is an Israeli instrument, then he is proof of the political and moral depravity to which Israel and its Arab collaborators have sunk.

The cost of Israel's possession of the West Bank is incalculable. It has been paid by Palestinians in deaths and in shattered lives, but also by Israel, in the brutalizing of its society and its army; in the glaring absence, as it shapes its policies, of anything worthy of Jewish ethics; in the loss of its good name and the corruption of its diplomacy as it manipulates international opinion and ducks and weaves to avoid negotiations that might entail the return of the territories to their owners.

When Eduard Shevardnadze, Gorbachev's foreign minister, was accused by hard-line Soviet critics of having "lost" Eastern Europe and "allowed" Germany to unite, he thoughtfully replied, "It was the price we had to pay in order to become a civilized country." It is an answer that Israel might ponder as it considers the fate of the occupied territories, suffering and seething under its rule.

APPENDIX
Abu Nidal's Closest Associates

In 1990–91, membership of Abu Nidal's three principal institutions—the Political Bureau, the Central Committee, and the Revolutionary Council—was believed to be as follows:

Political Bureau

SABRI AL-BANNA (Abu Nidal), leader, known by his Arabic title of Amin al-Sirr

ISAM MARAQA (Salim Ahmad), deputy chief since 1987, when he took over from Mustafa Murad (Abu Nizar). However, in 1991, Maraqa lost the job to Mansur Hamdan, although retaining his membership in the Political Bureau

MANSUR HAMDAN, appointed deputy chief in 1991, formerly head of the Political Directorate and official spokesman

SULAIMAN SAMRIN (Dr. Ghassan al-Ali), first secretary of the Central Committee and head of the Secretariat

MUHAMMAD WASFI HANNUN (Wasfi Hannun), head of the People's Army

ISAM AWDAH (Zakariya Ibrahim)

ABDALLAH HASSAN (Abu Nabil), head of the Committee for Revolutionary Justice

SHAWQI MUHAMMAD YUSIF (Munir Ahmad)

Central Committee

The Central Committee consisted of members of the Political Bureau, plus the following:

THABIT ABD AL-KARIM MAHMUD (Zaidan), deputy head of the Organization Directorate

ALI AL-FARRA (Dr. Kamal), Libya-based intelligence chief

ATIF HAMMUDA (Abu Siham), head of the Financial Directorate

ALI AL-BATMA (Samir Darwish)

ISMA'IL ABD AL-LATIF YUSIF (Hamdi Abu Yusif)

ADNAN KHALIFA (Abu Hazim)

RISQ SA'ID ABD AL-MAJID (Walid Khalid), the organization's Beirut spokesman, who rose to prominence during the *Silco* affair

NABIL MUHAMMAD ABDALLAH SALIM (Sari Abdallah)

MUHAMMAD AL-TAHIR (Fu'ad Abu al-Tahir)

MUSTAFA IBRAHIM SANDUQA (Hussein bin Ali), the real boss of the Committee for Revolutionary Justice

HASAN AZIZ ABD AL-KHALIQ (Awwad), head of the Membership Committee

ISA JARADAT (Sulaiman), member of command of the Intelligence Directorate

ABD AL-KARIM AL-BANNA (Husam Mustafa)

GHANIM SALIH

Revolutionary Council

Membership of the Revolutionary Council consisted of members of the Political Bureau and the Central Committee, plus the following:

HAMDI ABU ASBA (Azmi Hussein), representative in Libya, 1985–87, transferred to Algeria in 1989

IBRAHIM AL-TAMIMI (Tariq Mahmud), member of the Committee for Revolutionary Justice

ALI ZAIDAN (Haitham), member of the Intelligence Directorate

ADNAN AL-FARIS (Sami Abu al-Haitham)

MAJID AL-AKKAWI, deputy head of People's Army in northern Lebanon

ABD AL-KARIM MUHAMMAD (Awni Jabr), sometime representative in Sudan, Aden, and Libya

KHALIL KHUDR SALAHAT (Ma'n Adham)

HISHAM HARB, a key man in foreign operations

SAMI ABU ALI (Mazen al-Khalili), People's Army Directorate

MUHAMMAD HABIB (Salim Abd al-Rahman)

MUHAMMAD AHMAD ABU ASAL (Abu Marwan)

MAHIR AL-RUSAN (Walid), brother of Nawwaf al-Rusan (Uthman), currently in jail in Britain for the attempt on the life of Ambassador Argov

SAMI AL-SHAYIB (Isam)

WALID ISA

SAMIH ABU ALI

Defections and Casualties from the Central Committee

AL-HAJJ ABU MUSA, chief military instructor, killed in Libya in late 1987

MUSTAFA MURAD (Abu Nizar), Abu Nidal's deputy, killed in Libya on October 17, 1988

ABD AL-RAHMAN ISA, defected in October 1989, survived an attempt on his life in Algeria

JASIR AL-DISI (Abu Ma'mun), prominent People's Army commander, killed November 1987

AYISH BADRAN (Abu Umar), prominent People's Army commander, killed late 1987

ATIF ABU BAKR (Abu Farah), defected November 1989 and formed Emergency Leadership

KHALID AL-MADI, of the Finance Directorate, downgraded to cadre

FAISAL AL-KAFRI (Kamal Mansur), defected

FU'AD AL-SUFFARINI (Umar Hamdun), defected to Jordan in 1987

Defections and Casualties from the Revolutionary Council

WAJIH MUSTAFA (Abu Mustafa), defected

BAHIJ YUNIS, in prison in Austria

UTHMAN AL-RUSAN, in prison in Britain for attack on Ambassador Argov

MUHAMMAD DAW MURTAH (Yunis Umran), Tunisian, rallied to the Emergency Leadership

ZIAD SAHMUD (Basil), a People's Army commander, rallied to the Emergency Leadership

NIDAL TAWFIQ MUSA HAMADA (Bajis Abu Atwan), key figure in Intelligence Directorate, defected to Syria, then to Jordan

AHMAD ABU MATAR, director of Al Sabra press, left the organization after it moved from Syria

ABD AL-SAMAD ABD AL-HAFIZ, former deputy head of the Revolutionary Council

MUSA AL-HUSSEINI (sometimes known as Musa al-Haidari or Abu Mazin)

MUHAMMAD ABU JABIR

MUJAHID AL-BAYYARI (Zuhair Khalid), killed by Sidon car bomb

SAMIH MUHAMMAD KHUDR (Zuheir al-Rabbah), key figure in Intelligence Directorate, killed in Athens by car bomb in 1988

ABD AL-FATTAH GHAZAL (Kifah Khalid), killed by a car bomb

UMAR HUMAIDI (Wahid Hasanain), killed in Rashidiyyah camp in Lebanon in 1990

FARID HIJAB (Kayid Abu Arisha), killed by a car bomb in June 1990

INDEX

ABOUT THE AUTHOR

PATRICK SEALE is one of Britain's best-known and most distinguished Middle East specialists. As an author and a former correspondent for the London *Observer,* he has spent thirty years studying the politics of the region and interviewing its leaders. He is the author of the standard biography of Hafez al Assad, *Asad of Syria: The Struggle for the Middle East,* and the classic history of Syria, *The Struggle for Syria.* Other books by Seale include *Philby: The Long Road to Moscow; The Hilton Assignment;* and *Red Flag, Black Flag.*